Making Our Research Useful

Making Our Research Useful

Case Studies in the Utilization of Anthropological Knowledge

EDITED BY
**John van Willigen,
Barbara Rylko-Bauer,
and Ann McElroy**

Westview Press
BOULDER, SAN FRANCISCO, & LONDON

Westview Special Studies in Applied Anthropology

Published in 1989 in the United States of America by Westview Press, Inc., 5500 Central Avenue, Boulder, Colorado 80301, and in the United Kingdom by Westview Press, Inc., 13 Brunswick Centre, London WC1N 1AF, England

Library of Congress Cataloging-in-Publication Data
Making our research useful.
  (Westview special studies in applied anthropology)
  Bibliography: p.
  Includes index.
  1. Applied anthropology—Case studies. I. Van
Willigen, John. II. Rylko-Bauer, Barbara. III. McElroy,
Ann. IV. Series.
GN397.5.M35 1989   306   88-27804
ISBN 0-8133-7718-8

Printed and bound in the United States of America

The paper used in this publication meets the requirements of the American National Standard for Permanence of Paper for Printed Library Materials Z39.48-1984.

10   9   8   7   6   5   4   3   2   1

Contents

Figures and Tables

Figures

Tables

Acknowledgments

The editors wish to thank a number of individuals who assisted this project. Richard W. Stoffle of the Institute of Social Research (ISR) of the University of Michigan provided useful advice and support. Donald C. Pelz of the ISR provided guidance concerning the work of the Center for Research on the Utilization of Scientific Knowledge at ISR. Jean J. Schensul, Robert Wulff, Shirley Fiske, and William Partridge provided pre-publication copies of materials useful in preparing the first chapter. Melanie Sovine and Ruth Landman provided valuable comments on an early version of the first chapter that was presented at the 1986 annual meeting of the American Anthropological Association.

The staff of the University of Kentucky Computing Center provided facilities and advice in the initial production process. Teresa Epperson and Helen Crawford contributed to production by typing manuscript. Charlotte Zerof of the Department of Behavioral Science of the University of Kentucky Medical Center assisted in conversion of computer files.

The services and support of staff of the Department of Anthropology of SUNY Buffalo were also essential in this project. Special thanks go to Ezra Zubrow and to Warren Barbour for advice and guidance in use of computers during initial stages of the project. The Faculty of Social Sciences Microcomputing Lab of the State University of New York at Buffalo provided facilities for the major and final portion of production. We wish especially to acknowledge and thank Joseph E. Pittari, systems analyst for the FSS Microcomputing Lab, for his excellent services in compositional design and production. Without Joe Pittari's patience, persistence, and extraordinary knowledge of computers, this project could not have been completed.

The editors and staff at Westview Press have been most responsive and supportive throughout the production process. We owe a special note of thanks to Kellie Masterson, Editor, whose enthusiasm and keen understanding of anthropology have made our association most pleasant and productive.

We also wish to thank our families for their patience, support, and interest in this project: Jacqueline, Anne, and Juliana van Willigen; Daniel and John Michael Bauer and Jadwiga Rylko; and Roger, Andrew, and Catherine Glasgow.

Last, and certainly most important, are the authors, who were prompt, receptive to suggestions for changes, and enthusiastic about this project. The editors developed great respect for their work, skill, and commitment to making their research useful.

John van Willigen
Barbara Rylko-Bauer
Ann McElroy

Preface

The underutilization of social science research in public policy is a frequently noted problem (Lynn 1978; Weiss 1977), and one that has also been recognized in anthropology (Weaver 1985a). Given the expertise of anthropologists in studying and explaining community organization and human dynamics, it is a paradox that our research findings and recommendations have relatively little impact on public and international policy. The increasing involvement of anthropologists in various aspects of the policy process points to the importance of looking at this issue of knowledge utilization in a systematic manner. We need to understand the means by which knowledge is converted into action.

This set of case studies addresses the question of how to improve the use of applied or policy research done by anthropologists. However, these studies, which depict concrete methods for getting research used, should also have cross-disciplinary relevance, since the issue of knowledge utilization crosscuts all social science disciplines.

This book is an activity of the Applied Anthropology Documentation Project at the University of Kentucky. Sponsored by the Society for Applied Anthropology, The Washington Association of Professional Anthropologists, and the Society for Applied Anthropology in Canada/Societe d'Anthropologie Appliquée du Canada, the Project is organized to document the applications of anthropology and in so doing, to improve practice. This has resulted in the establishment of an archive collection of technical reports and other limited distribution materials produced by applied and practicing anthropologists in the course of their work.

The contributing authors were asked to write case studies based on their recent work which had knowledge utilization as a goal. To ensure some degree of comparability, as well as uniformity in form and focus, the authors were given an outline that served as a flexible guide in writing the case studies. The elements of this outline are described below.

- **Introduction**

  This provides an overview of the case study and may include a discussion of the historical context and development of the issue on which the study was focused.

- **Research Methods and Context**

  This section provides enough information about the research process so that the reader can understand what actually went on during the project. This includes information about data collection techniques, sampling or informant selection, and the theoretical orientation of the research. Most cases also discuss beneficiaries (those who were to benefit from the research), as well as the client group, which might include policy and decision makers, program managers, a community group or other "consumers" of research. The fact that there may be more than one client was often clearly drawn.

- **Utilization Methods and Process**

  This is the most important component of the case studies and addresses the question of what the practitioner did to increase the potential for having the research findings used. The authors were encouraged to provide a detailed description of this utilization process.

- **Project Impacts**

  This section looks at the outcome of this effort. To what extent were the utilization strategies successful? Why or why not? What were some of the impacts of the study?

- **Concluding Summary**

The first chapter of this book provides an introduction to the topic of knowledge utilization. More specifically, it presents a framework for thinking about methods and strategies for "making our research useful," based on our understanding of work in applied anthropology and a selective review of the literature on this topic from a variety of disciplines. The goal of this chapter (and of the book as well) is to outline principles for an effective knowledge utilization approach, which should take us one step closer toward developing a theory of practice.

There are many different ways of being effective, as the case studies demonstrate. While each of the cases reflects unique experiences, and it may be difficult to devise a single, unified set of principles which will solve the problem of underutilization, the authors document strategies which can be applied to many research and policy-making settings. In other words, underlying the diversity are some common principles that, when applied, increase the likelihood of success.

This is especially evident from Figure 1, which summarizes the major utilization strategies presented in each of these case studies. This figure is meant to serve as a specialized index to help the reader identify studies which demonstrate the principles presented in Chapter 1. It also underscores the complexity of knowledge utilization methods, how they need to vary, and how basic ideas appear again and again.

The case studies presented in Chapters 2 through 15 treat the problem of knowledge use from a variety of perspectives. Most focus on specific projects, while a few deal with a range of thematically related activities expressed throughout a portion of the author's career. As Glaser et al. (1983) point out, successful case studies serve an important role in demonstrating the different configurations of strategies that apply to each individual situation, which in turn allows further refinement of such principles into a framework and theory of practice. Each chapter starts with a quote from the chapter itself that emphasizes a key strategy of the study to follow. The concluding chapter by Lucy M. Cohen extracts themes common to all the papers and discusses the importance of our role in the achievement of social purposes.

With the tremendous increase in the number of practicing anthropologists, the discipline needs to prepare itself for the future in various aspects of practice. Very high in priority is the need to improve utilization methods so as to increase the likelihood of impact on public policy. Other areas of practice that need attention include public education, public participation in social impact assessment, and social action. Collections of cases and literature reviews would be useful in all these areas, and we encourage practicing anthropologists to publish, speak about, and otherwise share their experiences in knowledge utilization and other relevant areas. This set of case studies is offered as a means of sharing useful experiences and ideas amongst colleagues.

J. van W.
B. R.-B.
A. M.

Figure 1   Summary of the Knowledge Utilization Strategies Presented in the Case Studies

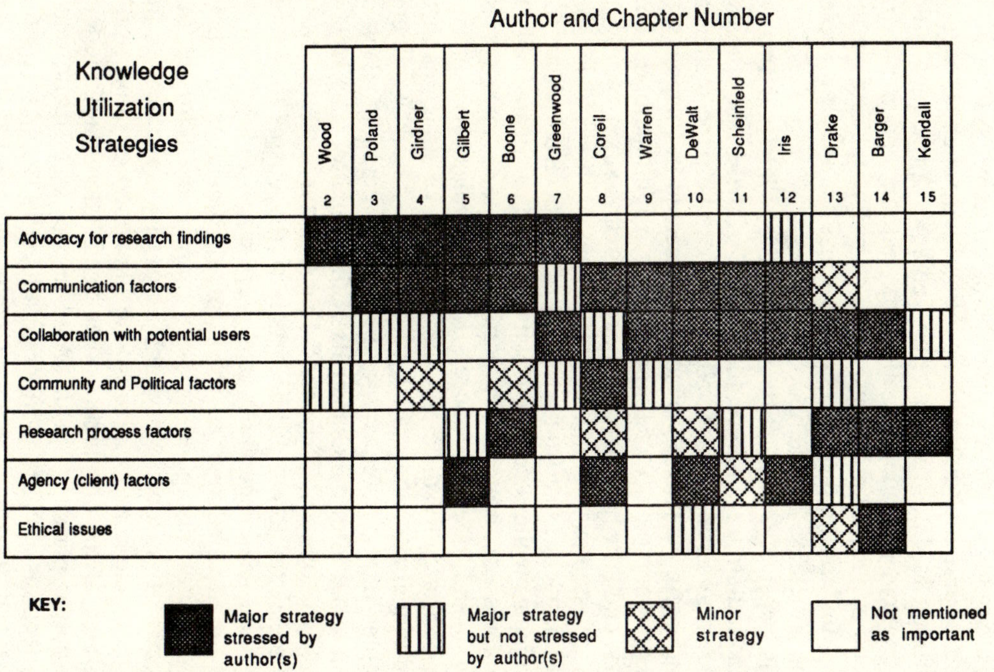

Author and Chapter Number

Knowledge
Utilization
Strategies

Knowledge Utilization Strategies	Wood 2	Poland 3	Girdner 4	Gilbert 5	Boone 6	Greenwood 7	Corell 8	Warren 9	DeWalt 10	Scheinfeld 11	Iris 12	Drake 13	Barger 14	Kendall 15
Advocacy for research findings														
Communication factors														
Collaboration with potential users														
Community and Political factors														
Research process factors														
Agency (client) factors														
Ethical issues														

KEY:

- ■ Major strategy stressed by author(s)
- (cross-hatched) Major strategy but not stressed by author(s)
- (horizontal lines) Minor strategy
- ☐ Not mentioned as important

An explanation of this figure is provided in the Preface. The knowledge utilization strategies listed here are discussed in chapter 1.

1

Strategies for Increasing the Use of Anthropological Research in the Policy Process: A Cross-Disciplinary Analysis

Barbara Rylko-Bauer, John van Willigen, and Ann McElroy

We need to direct our attention to the variable under the greatest control, our own performance, and develop a practical, comprehensive approach to doing utilization-focused policy research.

As anthropologists become increasingly involved in the policy process, working to solve practical problems, there is a greater need to understand the means by which knowledge is converted into action. The goal of this chapter, and the book in general, is to suggest improvements in research and practice which will enhance the use of anthropology. In doing so, we hope to contribute to a theory of practice. Applied anthropologists have noted the need to focus on such efforts, so as to advance the discipline toward new knowledge, more effective action, and the further development of anthropology as a policy science (Partridge 1987; Weaver 1985b).

In this chapter, we present a framework for thinking about methods and strategies for knowledge utilization. We begin by discussing the role of anthropology in policy and the various meanings of the concept of *knowledge utilization*. We then go on to outline and examine principles for an effective method, based on our understanding of work in applied anthropology and a selective review of studies on knowledge utilization from other disciplines. As Figure 1 (see Preface) indicates, the case studies presented in the following chapters demonstrate many of these principles at work.

What Is Policy Research?

If we define policies as guides for consistent action, then policy research is the process by which objective, representative information is collected, analyzed, and communicated to help decision makers set guidelines for the goals and activities of various kinds of groups such as agencies, firms, and governments. While policy research is often thought of in general terms (e.g., research that informs a public policy issue such as housing for the homeless), we also consider under this rubric research that contributes specifically to more effective program operations.

There are many specific types of policy research, including needs assessment (to define possible policy goals), social impact assessment, (to examine the effects or feasibility of certain types of policy decisions), social soundness analysis (to determine the cultural feasibility of a policy), technology assessment (to evaluate the social effects of technology), and evaluation (to assess program effectiveness or outcomes). In addition, there is a large category of *policy relevant research*, which may not be commissioned by policymakers directly but is focused on aspects of life which are part of policymakers' concerns or of general political concern.

Policy research is often referred to as separate from or opposed to basic research. In reality, this contrast is not very clear cut. The usual criteria of whether the research idea comes from an agency or from an individual researcher, and whether it is done to solve a problem or to contribute to knowledge, often do not hold up in actual research situations.

Anthropology as a Policy Science

The relationship between anthropology and policy research is longstanding (Goldschmidt 1979; Stull and Moos 1981; Wallace 1976; Weaver 1985a). The first professional positions for anthropologists in the United States were not in academic departments but in policy research organizations. The Bureau of American Ethnology, established in 1879 to "produce results that would be of practical value in the administration of Indian affairs" (Powell 1881), antedates the first Department of Anthropology established in 1888 at Clark University.

Many early research publications in anthropology were done for reasons of policy. Most noteworthy is James Mooney's *The Ghost Dance Religion and the Sioux Outbreak of 1890* (Mooney 1896), which is described by Wallace (1976) as an early occurrence of policy research in anthropology. Mooney was hired as a trouble-shooter to provide an assessment of the Sioux religious movements that concerned the Indian administrators.

It was World War II that stimulated many anthropologists to participate in policy research. Noteworthy was the work of the Committee on Food Habits which was concerned with wartime nutritional problems and included Margaret Mead, Ruth Benedict, and Rhoda Metraux, among others (Montgomery and Bennett 1979). The committee collected scientific information on nutritional levels of the American population, and its efforts led to improvements in the study of food habits. This illustrates a common pattern: Policy needs lead to funding for research, which results in expansion of anthropological research subject matter and methodological improvement. In addition to this project on the home front, there was much policy research done in conjunction with the war effort (Mead 1979), in particular, work with the War Relocation Authority concerning the internment of Japanese Americans during the war (Spicer 1979) and the work in the Micronesian Trust Territory (Barnett 1956).

It was after the Second World War that the idea of policy science was conceptualized by the political scientist Harold Lasswell (1968). Lasswell, collaborating with anthropologist Allan Holmberg, researched values, human rights, and development (Lasswell and Holmberg 1966). These ideas were then expressed by Holmberg in the action strategy of Research and Development Anthropology (Dobyns, Doughty, and Lasswell 1971; Holmberg 1958).

In the post-war period, anthropologists carried out a variety of policy-relevant projects. Some of these areas concerned relocation (Mason 1958), water resources development (Padfield and Smith 1968), health care delivery (Kimball and Pearsall 1954), disaster (Spillius 1957), and Native American administration (Stewart 1961). An important development was the emergence, under the leadership of George Foster, of a policy-oriented medical anthropology (Foster 1953). However, the development of policy research in anthropology during this time was curtailed by the very rapid growth of academic employment starting with the end of World War II and going until the late 1960s, as well as by the general distrust of government-related policy research that grew out of the controversy surrounding Project Camelot (which was concerned with the causes of revolution and insurgency) and the opposition to U.S. involvement in Vietnam (Stull and Moos 1981).

During the 1970s there was an increase, on a wide front, in anthropologists doing policy research stimulated by opportunities created by new federal legislation, such as the National Environmental Policy Act of 1969, and many others. The breadth and richness of this work is substantial and reasonably well documented by articles in *Practicing Anthropology* (a career-oriented publication of the Society for Applied Anthropology), by the collections of the Applied Anthropology Documentation Project at the University of Kentucky, in *Anthropology in Use: A Bibliographic Chronology of the Development of Applied Anthropology* (van Willigen 1980), and the impressive number of new case books in applied anthropology (Davis et al. 1987; Eddy and Partridge 1987; Green 1986; Messerschmidt 1981; Skar 1985; Stull and Schensul 1987; Wulff and Fiske 1987). The contemporary breadth of anthropological involvement in policy work is also indicated by the large memberships of practitioner organizations such as the Society for Applied Anthropology (SfAA), National Association for the Practice of Anthropology (NAPA), and Washington Association of Professional Anthropologists (WAPA).

In spite of this history and recent growth, Weaver (1985a, 1985b) has pointed out that anthropology has had limited success as a policy science. All of the social science disciplines have a policy research component, and they share some common problems concerning utilization. However, each discipline has unique conceptual and theoretical foundations, methodologies, and foci of interest that may either limit or advance its effectiveness as a policy science. Some of the features that may increase the potential of anthropologists as policy researchers are:

- *The effects of participatory field work* that tend to improve understanding of the realities of implementation or recommendation. There is empirical evidence that qualitative data may be preferred by some policymakers for this reason. That is, the collection methods lead to contact and rapport between the researcher and study participants, and this forms the foundation for subsequent utilization efforts. Also, such data incorporate recognizable, unique features of the setting, often lost in quantification, that the potential user may feel are relevant, based on his or her experience (Beyer and Trice 1982).

- *A holistic perspective* that considers multiple variables in research on human problems. The holistic, inductive approach so characteristic of traditional ethnography (Pelto 1970: 6,17) increases the researcher's chances of understanding problems in their full historical, cultural, and economic context. The holistic approach works especially well in applied medical anthropology studies, giving comprehensive coverage of behavioral, social, and environmental components of health (McElroy and Townsend 1989).

• *The development of regional expertise.* Even with the increased emphasis on theoretical specialization, anthropological training continues to focus in part on the time-honored "culture area" speciality. Thus many anthropologists function as an "Africanist" or a "Mesoamericanist," and so on, returning to the site of original work or to other communities in the same region to do comparative studies. This long-term continuity and regional expertise is of value to policymakers, who otherwise may lack historical depth and geographic coverage in their sources of information.

• *A problem-discovering, grounded research technique.* At least one study has found that client oriented research projects using grounded concepts were more likely to have an impact on policy decisions than similar projects that used a formal theoretical approach (van de Vall and Bolas 1980).

• *A strong tradition of going into the field* to collect data instead of staying in the office. This reflects a commitment to an "observer-near" rather than "observer-far" perspective that taps human experience through direct observation and interaction.

Despite these positive characteristics, there are a number of features of anthropology that may limit its effectiveness as a policy science. Many of these have also been noted by Weaver (1985a). They include:

• *The relative lack of time effectiveness* in research, including lack of familiarity with problem-focused, short term research techniques. Anthropologists are used to long-term research, whereas policy decisions are often made within a short time span, based on currently available information. Long-term studies, on the other hand, may be useful for monitoring the effects of these decisions.

• *A lack of experience in cross-disciplinary communication skills.* Anthropological methods, concepts and jargon need to be translated into the language of policymakers.

• *Relative lack of sophistication in use of quantitative analysis techniques.* Anthropologists do not always present their findings in a manner understood or preferred by policymakers, who may apply criteria of reliability and generalizability in assessing the usefulness of such findings to their policy decision making (Weiss and Weiss 1981).

• *The "underdog bias"* derived from field relationships. While some policy studies may require advocacy, Weaver (1985a) points out that they also require a willingness to compromise and balance loyalties between administrators and beneficiaries of the policies.

• *The small scale of the discipline* which precludes extensive lobbying for work-creating legislation.

• *The relative lack of a tradition of multi-disciplinary collaboration.*

While it is not certain how anthropologists are viewed by policy-makers, one study suggests that anthropological research is reasonably well respected. In the mid-1970s, the Institute of Social Research (ISR) at the University of Michigan carried out a study of the validity and reliability of research methods within the context of knowledge use. The ISR researchers interviewed 204 mid-level federal policymakers to determine their view of different aspects of the use of social science. Anthropology was rated by the research panel as most "valid" and "reliable" of the social sciences other than economics. Further, the most highly rated data gathering technique was "observation in a real-life situation by trained observers"; such techniques, of course, form the traditional core of anthropological data collection. Unfortunately, this study also showed that anthropology was the least used of the behavioral sciences (Caplan, Morrison, and Stambaugh 1975).

Much of the discussion of underutilization has centered around analyses of why anthropology has not been more successful as a policy science, or critiques of how and why policymakers are not ready for the contributions of anthropology. While such discussion may serve a limited purpose, focus on failure will not move us ahead (Glaser et al.

1983: 48,49,435). Given that we want to increase the use of our research and have an impact in the policy arena, a more constructive approach is to develop concrete strategies for making our research more useful and more used. As a step in this direction, we present such a set of strategies.

Defining Knowledge Utilization

Knowledge utilization is difficult to define and has been the focus of much discussion, debate, and empirical study within the social sciences in recent years. A number of researchers have pointed out that the overall negative assessment of social science contributions to public policy may be partly the result of an overly narrow definition of use that emphasizes immediate, direct, and concrete impact on decision making.

> When people discuss the use of social research for policy-making, the usual meaning involves a direct and instrumental application. Research will provide empirical evidence and/or conclusions that will help solve a policy problem. The model is a linear one. A problem exists; information or understanding is lacking either to generate a solution to the problem or to select among alternative solutions; research provides the missing knowledge; a solution is reached (Weiss 1977: 11-12).

Weiss goes on to note (and others have agreed with her) that such a narrow definition not only overlooks the complexity of public policy-making, but also fails to recognize that clarifying issues, justifying actions, and providing new understanding of program operation or future directions are also real impacts (Beyer and Trice 1982; Caplan 1977; Patton 1986; Weiss 1977, 1981).

For example, Patton et al. (1977) interviewed key people in 20 health evaluation studies to examine how they defined use and to identify factors that affected the degree to which it occurred. They confirmed the view that direct impact of evaluation research on policy and program development was minimal. However, they also found that federal decision makers used the research to reduce uncertainty, to fill in knowledge gaps, and to speed up decisions: The decision makers considered these to be real and important impacts.

This corresponds to what Pelz (1978, as cited in Glaser et al. 1983:18) has termed *conceptual* knowledge, which serves to enlighten policymakers and influence action in less specific ways, in contrast to *instrumental* knowledge (used directly to affect specific action or make a decision) and *symbolic* knowledge (used to legitimate and sustain predetermined actions or positions). Others have refined this framework (Dunn 1983; Leviton and Boruch 1983; Leviton and Hughes 1981). For example, Whiteman (1985) talks of *strategic use*, based on his analysis of congressional decision making. Weiss (1981), in turn, suggests that the use of research is better understood as a continuum, rather than as discrete categories.

It is evident from the growing number of empirical studies on utilization that diffuse, conceptual use may be more common than direct, instrumental use (Caplan et al. 1975; Rich 1977; Weiss and Weiss 1981), and perhaps more significant, since it may "gradually bring about major shifts in awareness and reorientation of basic perspectives" (Weiss 1981:23). In addition, decision makers and policymakers use multiple sources of information, of which social science is only one (Caplan 1976; Majchrzak 1986; Mitchell 1980; Patton et al. 1977). The key question, then, is what can we do to ensure that anthropological research is among the relevant sources of information? What can we do to make our research more useful and to increase the likelihood of having an impact on the policy process?

Developing a Comprehensive Utilization Plan

The first step is to recognize that utilization methods have to be designed, from the very beginning, into all the phases of a particular applied or policy research project (Glaser et al. 1983; Patton 1986). This, in turn, suggests the need to develop a comprehensive approach that would include a series of widely applicable action principles and methods for shaping practice to increase use of anthropological knowledge.

Analysis of current literature on knowledge utilization (derived mainly from other social science disciplines), supplemented with anthropological case studies that either focus on use of research findings or more generally on issues of application, could provide the basis for such an approach. This is the strategy that we have taken in this book.

Propositions need to be systematically compiled similarly to the way Rothman (1974) compiled "action principles" for community organization practitioners, Rogers (1983) examined factors relating to the diffusion of innovations, and Dillman (1978) identified a "total design method" for improving response rates in survey research. There are a number of scholars who have begun to develop such comprehensive approaches (Alkin 1985; Beyer and Trice 1982; Burry 1984; Davis and

Salasin 1975; Glaser et al. 1983; Patton 1986; Rothman 1980; Weiss 1977).

Perhaps most familiar to anthropologists is the work of Michael Quinn Patton and his approach to "utilization focused evaluation." He presents a systematic flowchart that provides guidelines for decisions and actions at various points in the research process, from start to finish, so as to enhance the potential for the use of evaluation study findings (Patton 1986: 331).

Several other approaches are worth noting. On the basis of a review of empirical studies concerning use of organizational research, Beyer and Trice (1982) develop a conceptual framework of the utilization process within an organizational context and provide a set of recommendations. Jack Rothman's *Using Research in Organizations: A Guide to Successful Application* (1980) is especially helpful because it contains a comprehensive checklist of factors that influence utilization, based largely on his study of social service agencies in greater London.

Empirical studies that measure or analyze the extent of use or nonuse of social science research have also contributed to the list of relevant factors and strategies that enhance the potential for utilization. For example, Weiss and Weiss (1981) interviewed 155 decision makers and 100 social scientists in the mental health fields to find out characteristics of research that make studies useful for decision making concerning mental health policy and programs. In comparing these two groups, they found that social scientists underestimated the impact of methodological factors and overestimated the importance of political factors on the judgments made by decision makers as to the usefulness of research.

Another example is the work of van de Vall and Bolas (1980), who sampled 120 projects of client-oriented social policy research in the Netherlands. They compared theoretical and methodological characteristics of the project reports to the projects' impacts upon organizational decision making, as measured through interviews with both the project researchers and policymakers responsible for translating the results into policy measures.

We direct the reader to other examples of such empirical studies that are discussed throughout this chapter: Alkin et al. (1979); Caplan and associates (1975, 1976, 1977); Glaser and Taylor (1973); Leviton and Boruch (1983); Patton et al. (1977); Rich (1975, 1977); Rothman (1980); Weiss and Bucuvalas (1980). Similar analyses of anthropological research could provide more specific insights into factors that may be particularly relevant to the methods and focus of research commonly conducted by applied and practicing anthropologists. However, this requires that we refine our current ways of documenting applied or policy work, so that such research is accessible for empirical analysis.

Elements of a Utilization Framework

Outlined below are some elements that need to be considered in creating a comprehensive utilization framework with anthropological practice and knowledge in mind. These reflect our experience and understanding of work in applied anthropology, as well as a selective review of knowledge utilization literature from other disciplines.

It is important to note that while these elements or factors are discussed here separately, in reality they intersect. In most successful projects it is the integration of several key strategies that leads to use of anthropological knowledge, as demonstrated by the case studies presented in the following chapters (and summarized in Figure 1).

The Personal Factor: Collaboration

Much of the current literature on knowledge utilization suggests that perhaps the single most significant factor in getting research findings used is the interest and involvement of the client in part or all of the stages of the research process (Alkin 1985; Burry 1984; Glaser and Taylor 1973; Glaser et al. 1983; Leviton and Hughes 1981; Rich 1975; Rothman 1980). Others have noted the need to involve *stakeholders*, a term referring to individuals or groups with a vested interest, or a stake, in the research process and findings (see volume edited by Bryk 1983). This is a more inclusive concept, since it includes not only clients and direct beneficiaries, but also other persons or groups who may be affected negatively or positively by the research process or ultimate decision outcomes.

Patton and his colleagues (1977) were among the first to empirically demonstrate the importance of this *personal factor* in their study of the use of health evaluation studies mentioned earlier. The presence of an identifiable individual or group of people who personally cared about the evaluation and the information it generated emerged as the consistently important factor. Where it was present, the evaluations were used; where it was absent there was much less impact. Therefore, Patton suggests that the first step in a utilization-focused approach is to identify who the relevant people are; not only those in formal positions of authority, but also those at lower levels. The second step is to discover the relevant questions, issues, and needs of these potential information users.

In fact, relevance seems to be one of the most commonly noted factors in discussions of how to improve the use of research findings (Glaser et al. 1983; Leviton and Hughes 1981; Rich 1975; Scheinfeld 1987; J. Schensul 1987; Whiteford 1987). For example, Caplan (1977) notes the importance of an explicit link between the problem or issue, the proposed research, and the intended use of this research toward addressing the problem. In a similar vein, Patton (1986) states that this *personal factor* is important throughout the research process, from the very beginning, through the design and data collection stages, to the final report and dissemination of results.

There are a number of ways in which involving potential users can increase the likelihood that research findings will be used (Glaser et al. 1983; Leviton and Hughes 1981; Scheinfeld 1987; S. Schensul 1987):

• Participation "demystifies" the research process. Clients and other users gain understanding of the methods and the opportunity to influence data collection.

• Understanding the research process also equips users to be advocates of change.

• The feedback that occurs because of client participation improves the researcher's understanding of the client's situation which, in turn, improves appropriateness of the data collected and quality of the recommendations.

• Participation leads to clearer identification of the ways that the research can be used.

• Participation increases the stake that users have in the success of the project. Their increased understanding, trust in the data, and investment of time increases their sense of "ownership" of the project.

There are some recent examples of case studies from other disciplines that have incorporated user-participation in the research process (Bryk 1983; Dawson and D'Amico 1985). Ballard and James (1983) present an approach to technology assessment which they call "participatory research." They have identified a number of strategies for involving potential users, such as the establishment of a research advisory committee, ongoing communication of findings through widespread distribution of draft reports and issue papers, and personal interaction with the participants in the system under study (which, of course, is a major approach to anthropological research).

Ballard and James acknowledge that participatory research is not a new idea, with theoretical and empirical roots in studies of innovation, decision making, organizational and planned social change. Anthropologists have been involved in all of these areas of study. These kinds of strategies have been at the base of many intervention techniques under rubrics such as "Research and Development Anthropology" (Dobyns, Doughty, and Lasswell 1971) and "Action Anthropology" (Gearing 1970). Perhaps most notable in this literature is Holmberg's idea of *participant intervention* (1955). Kurt Lewin's conception of action research anticipates the development of user participation research strategies in anthropology (Thompson 1950, 1951).

Of relevance to the concept of collaborative research is the tradition within anthropology of advocacy on behalf of the interest of a particular community, group, or cause. In discussing this point, Weaver notes as examples John Collier, who advocated for Indian rights and later became Commissioner of the Bureau of Indian Affairs in the 1930s. Another example is Franz Boas, whose anti-racist advocacy was related to his work documenting morphological changes in the U.S. immigrant population. "Anthropologists can contribute to policymaking in many ways, including championing causes for disadvantaged groups in order to influence decision makers" (Weaver 1985b:202).

More recent approaches place the anthropologist as an auxiliary to community leaders who advocate change, such as the community advocacy approach developed by Stephen Schensul within the context of a community mental health program in Chicago (Schensul 1973,1974), and later applied to other settings (Weber and McCall 1978).

In discussing collaborative research, Stephen Schensul (1987:214-217) has noted three basic (but not mutually exclusive) approaches used by anthropologists:

- Collaboration with the target community or population for the purpose of using research as a tool of self-development, to advocate on their own behalf with external agencies, and to develop their own research infrastructure

- Collaboration with institutions and agencies that are external to the target community

- Collaboration with community groups and leaders, as well as with external agencies, with the goal of establishing relationships and communication between these two entities. In some cases this may involve the anthropologist in the role of mediator (e.g., Parker and King 1987).

Examples of all three approaches can be found in the recently published casebooks, *Anthropological Praxis* (Wulff and Fiske 1987) and *Collaborative Research and Social Change* (Stull and Schensul 1987).

The idea of participatory or collaborative research seems to have developed in other social science disciplines as a result of concerns with improving knowledge utilization and impact on policymaking. In anthropology, however, it has arisen at least partly out of a value orientation that recognizes the validity of self determination as a major force in the process of sociocultural change.

> . . . social problems cannot be effectively addressed without political intervention . . . including policy changes, redistribution of economic or other scarce resources, and new legislation. Solutions to social problems involve factors beyond the scope of research and thus call for intersectoral and nonresearch collaboration. Anthropologists . . . are not usually primary actors in these situations and need to work with people who are (Schensul and Stull 1987:2).

It has been only recently that the idea of user participation has been explicitly developed in anthropology in relation to the issue of how to increase knowledge utilization in policy (Davidson 1987; J. Schensul 1987a; Stern 1985; Whiteford 1987).

For example, based on research in a state mental hospital, Scheinfeld (1987) proposes a set of principles for collaborative research that he considers minimal conditions for knowledge utilization to occur. These include the idea that the anthropologist act as facilitator of change rather than simply as observer and documenter, the need to develop ongoing working relationships with people of power and influence at various levels of the organization, and the need to work collaboratively with an established body for planning and problem solving.

While the advantages of user participation may seem fairly obvious, there are also potential technical problems and ethical dilemmas, especially when the collaboration is with the client agency. Most frequently noted is the opportunity for cooptation of the researcher, since participating clients may have a chance to shape the research so as to provide results that support or legitimate preferred or already existent policies and actions (Ballard and James 1983; Beyer and Trice 1982;

Dawson and D'Amico 1985). Mark and Shotland (1985) point out that selecting stakeholders for participation involves a value judgement; i.e., *whose questions* will guide the research? In addition, it provides the potential for a different sort of cooptation--the preempting of criticism of the project by stakeholders. Finally, unless efforts are made to provide stakeholders with necessary information so that they can be effective and knowledgeable collaborators, user participation may actually be a form of "pseudo empowerment."

Collaborative research, whether done with client agencies, community groups, or both, suggests two other elements that are important to the successful transformation of knowledge into action: an understanding of the structure and organization of the agency, and understanding of the community or group that may be client and/or beneficiary. These two factors are discussed in the following sections.

Agency Factors

An early step in increasing use is to research the nature of the policy makers' organization. Part of the research effort should focus on the following types of questions.

• Who are the relevant decision makers and potential users of the information that will result from the research (Patton 1986)? What are their roles in the organization, and what types of data sources do they use most often? (Majchrzak 1986)?

• How are decisions usually made within the organization?

• What are the values, philosophy, or perspective of the decision makers and administrators within the agency?

• What are the usual channels of communication? As noted earlier, the organizational complexity of bureaucracies can impede effective utilization (Leviton and Hughes 1981). In fact, Rothman (1980) suggests that researchers make sure they have structural access to planning activities and to key decision-makers and directors, so as to communicate research findings directly.

• What are the political and organizational constraints in the agency concerning use of the data?

• When are the decisions which are related to the research going to be made? Are there both immediate and long term potential uses for the research findings?

A number of models have been constructed to account for knowledge use or technology transfer, and they can serve as guides for developing additional questions (see Glaser et al. 1983:36-37 for a summarizing table). Perhaps the most parsimonious is the one proposed by Davis and Salasin (1975), made up of eight factors (Ability, Values, Information, Circumstances, Timing, Obligation, Resistance, Yield), forming the acronym A VICTORY, which the authors feel are necessary and sufficient to account for organizational behavior related to utilization.

One example of a successful project that included a "studying up" approach is the effort by a network of applied anthropologists in Memphis, Tennessee, to redesign the delivery of a housing weatherization program to meet effectively the needs of low and moderate income customers (Hyland et al. 1987). Their concurrent study of both the public utility agency and the target community led to the development of a communication network and a series of relevant programs that met the needs of both the agency and community residents.

Community and Political Factors

Most policy research, although undertaken at the request of a client group or agency, will result in findings and recommendations that have potential for impact on some group or community of individuals--this may be intentional or unintentional, and it may be positive or negative impact. The relationship between the client requesting the research and the community or group that may be affected by the findings also needs to be considered in examining knowledge utilization.

In many cases the client may be in a position of relative power vis-à-vis the community. It may also be the case that while the agency serves the community, it does not truly represent it; the agency's values, agenda, and bureaucratic needs may be in conflict with those of community members (van Willigen 1986). Under such circumstances, recommendations may never be converted to action because they are perceived as threatening and the community is able to mobilize public support to defeat such action. The flip side of the coin is nonaction on recommendations that the agency perceives as going against its best interests, even if they are beneficial to the community it serves. The role that the anthropologist may play in the dynamic of these relationships is variable; in fact, this example raises a number of ethical issues that will be covered in a later section.

An important, and perhaps obvious, step that the researcher can take is to become informed about the ways in which various communities and groups may become affected by both the research process and the outcomes. This, combined with the knowledge gained by studying the client group and its decision-making process (as suggested earlier), should provide the researcher with some understanding of the relationships between these two groups, the potential areas of conflict, the key people who make decisions or who represent each group, and potential ways and forums for resolving some of these areas of conflict. Brokering knowledge and action is something that anthropologists are ideally suited to do, since the ethnographic approach and research techniques produce relationships and understanding to accomplish this goal.

A recently published collection of case studies (Wulff and Fiske 1987) provides several examples of how this can be done. Perhaps the most relevant to our point here is a case study presented by Preister (1987). In conducting an environmental impact statement concerning the proposed establishment of a ski resort in a relatively undeveloped part of Colorado, Preister and his associates focused on the public issues surrounding the project. In this way they were able to identify the perceptions and concerns of various community members and groups, as well as those of other stakeholders, such as the developer and government officials. By communicating results, using both formal means (e.g., community meetings) and informal means (e.g., conversations) throughout the research process, they were able to diffuse tensions, improve communication among the various competing interest groups, help in getting some of the issues addressed, and help create a broad-based citizen involvement.

These suggestions also have relevance in situations where the anthropologist is working on behalf of a community. First of all, communities are made up of individuals who will invariably have different points of view concerning an issue or problem, its importance, how to address it, and when to take action. There may even be formal factions that exist within the community.

J. Schensul (1987a) also points out the need for a publicly recognized power base. Research results may not have much impact if the client group or community that is trying to effect change has little actual or perceived power. One strategy she suggests is to base the research in an established community institution, which can bring together and maintain coalitions that can speak effectively to bring about desired policy changes. In the example she cites, the Hispanic Health Council served such a role in helping to bring about various social and institutional changes that benefited the Puerto Rican community in Hartford, Connecticut.

Political factors at the regional or national level may also affect the extent to which knowledge gets used, how, by whom, and to what purposes. While such macro level factors may be difficult to predict and impossible to control, awareness of political realities can influence the design of research or program implementation, so as to increase the likelihood of success. An example of this is the Agroforestry Outreach Project ("wood as a cash crop") in Haiti. Recognizing that donor monies were often diverted for personal or political gain within the Duvalier government, Murray (1987) suggested an alternative channel for the flow of funds using private voluntary organizations. This proved to be a key factor in the success of this project.

Research Process Factors

There are four aspects of the research process related to utilization that we wish to address here: flexibility, credibility, quality, and applicability. The first of these, *flexibility*, relates specifically to methods, especially the qualitative techniques that form a major part of the anthropological research tradition.

Weaver (1985a:102, 1985b:200-201) has noted that anthropologists working in the policy arena have been criticized for their lack of sophistication in the use of quantitative techniques. However, there is a growing awareness among anthropologists that qualitative description, which is after all a kind of measurement within the scientific research tradition, does not preclude quantification (Bernard 1988:23-24). In fact, the creative combination of qualitative and quantitative data and analysis can provide an insightful, valid, and convincing representation of social reality, while at the same time meeting criteria of reliability and generalizability that policymakers often expect.

In addition, we need to find innovative ways of applying ethnographic techniques to policy research and analysis. For example, in discussing the potential for anthropological input into development policy and planning, Hoben (1982: 369-370, as cited in Weaver 1985b: 201) suggests that anthropological data from small, stratified samples can be used to design meaningful questions for large scale surveys, or to assess the plausibility of findings collected by census or survey techniques, especially for sensitive topics such as income, access to land, and community power relations.

The point of this discussion is the importance of maintaining flexibility and choosing a mix of research methods that are relevant to the time constraints, client needs and expectations, the unique features of the research setting, and the problem under study (J. Schensul 1987a; van Willigen and DeWalt 1985).

A number of scholars have suggested that use is directly related to the *credibility* of the research process and findings (Caplan 1977; O'Reilly and Dalmat 1987; Weiss and Bucuvalas 1980; Whiteford 1987). According to Patton (1986), this includes perceived accuracy, fairness, and understandability, as well as believability. Especially important is the face validity of the research design and methods. Do they make sense to decision makers and other potential users of the information? Surveys of policymakers also indicate that use is related to the extent to which results conform to users' expectations, intuition, or already existing knowledge (Caplan 1977; Leviton and Hughes 1981; Patton et al. 1977).

Credibility, of course, is related to *quality*; one is more likely to believe in findings of a study if one feels that the research is of high quality. Interestingly, there are conflicting reports as to the relationship between quality (usually defined in terms of methodological rigor) and utilization (Beyer and Trice 1982). Just because data are good does not mean that they will be used. Some studies report that methodological issues are less important than other factors (such as relevance and personal interest) in predicting or explaining research use (Dunn 1980; Patton et al. 1977).

On the other hand, a study by Weiss and Bucuvalas (1980) of 155 decision makers in mental health fields suggests that quality of the research may take on a more important role in situations of political debate, where the data have to be convincing and the policymaker cannot afford to have the research be discounted due to uncertain methodology. Weiss and Bucuvalas found that these decision makers applied two tests in assessing the usefulness of social science research. The first of these was a "truth test," based on the degree to which results met scientific standards and the degree to which findings conformed to user expectations. Research quality was rated as especially important in situations where findings were used to mobilize support for a position or point of view, and where studies would be used to change ways of thinking about an issue.

These same mental health decision makers also applied a two-dimensional "utility test." The first dimension was whether the research challenged existing policy, thereby providing new direction; the second was the extent to which a study was oriented to action, providing data on matters that they could do something about (Weiss and Bucuvalas 1980). This is what we mean by the *applicability* of the research. Others have also suggested that the potential for use is increased if research focuses on variables that can be acted upon, and if policy actions implied by findings are feasible (Caplan 1977; Patton et al. 1977). This requires a clear understanding of the political and organizational context, and the constraints that agencies and other clients operate under.

A note of caution: There are some potential dangers in focusing primarily on problems and variables that are perceived as manipulable. Such research may have little explanatory value and may avoid raising issues or offering recommendations that are controversial but provide a more accurate picture of the problem under study. It may also result in a form of cooptation, since it is reasonable to expect that decision makers will perceive as changeable those factors which do not challenge their own political power or their role within the organization (Beyer and Trice 1982).

Finally, at the risk of being redundant, we wish to stress the importance of involving potential users in as many phases of the research process as possible or appropriate. The "personal factor" (discussed earlier) can play a role from the start of the study, through research design, data collection, analysis, interpretation, as well as dissemination of results (Patton 1986).

Communication Factors

Presentation of research findings is often limited to the writing of a final report. However, policy research needs to be communicated in many other ways if we wish to increase the chances of it being used. "What happens *before* the final report is written will usually determine use" (Patton 1986:273).

Perhaps most important is to communicate preliminary findings throughout the research process and, if possible, to maintain an ongoing dialogue with feedback between the researcher and the information users (Glaser et al. 1983; Rich 1975). The potential for this is enhanced, of course, if decision makers and other practitioners are involved to some degree in the research process (Dawson and D'Amico 1985; Patton 1986).

A number of other things can be done to increase the potential for utilization:

• Use multiple and varied media and formats for communicating the information to a large and overlapping audience (J. Schensul 1987a). There are many innovative ways in which research can be presented; for example, through participation in workshops (O'Reilly and Dalmat 1987), conferences (Glaser et al. 1983), publications of findings in magazines read by users (Beyer and Trice 1982), and widespread distribution of short draft reports and issue papers to interested parties (Ballard and James 1983).

• Present findings in the language and style of the user. More specific recommendations on reports and other formats for dissemination can be found in De Loria and Brookins (1982), Glaser et al. (1983), Patton (1986), and Rothman (1980).

• Identifying relevant decision makers and communicating findings directly to them may be especially important in complex organizations. The nature of bureaucracies is such that information may be distorted as it is passed through the hierarchy or may never even reach the potential users (Leviton and Hughes 1981).

• Recommendations should be posed in action terms. They need to be concrete and specific as to what is to be done, who is to do it, and when it is to occur (Patton 1986:268-9). Feasibility of implementation is also important. In addition, recommendations should address both immediate applications of the research findings and long term planning (Whiteford 1987).

Time Factors

Time-effectiveness is another factor to be considered, especially in situations of short-term instrumental use. As Weaver (1985a:102) points out, "facts, that is, known, available empirical data are very important to policy matters; what is of limited value is research undertaken at a time when political decisions must be made immediately." Recognition of this has led to a number of developments by anthropologists doing policy research (van Willigen and DeWalt 1985):

• Use of large research teams

• Use of smaller samples than may be customary in standard research situations

• Less documentation of research results

• Development and use of problem-focused, short-term research techniques

• Substantial use of secondary data, or refocus of research done for other purposes

Three examples come to mind in this context. First is the "guerrilla research tactics" developed by Stephen Schensul (1974) in his work as an advocacy anthropologist in Chicago. This involved research efforts carefully planned and then executed in a day or so.

Another example is the so-called *sondeos* or rapid rural reconnaissance done in farming systems research (see van Willigen and DeWalt 1985: 27-35), where there is a heavy reliance on key informant interviewing, reading of documents, and on-site observation. The innovative aspect is that the work is done within strict time constraints, and each day may be a stage in the process. The product of such research would be a description of the farming systems of the region or community, probably referenced to a specific commodity.

Finally, there are the "rapid assessment procedures" (RAP) developed for the evaluation and improvement of primary health care services, and described by Scrimshaw and Hurtado (1987) in a manual of the same title. They present specific instructions for the use of anthropological methods in the rapid assessment of health and health care seeking behavior at the household level and interactions with traditional and modern health care providers.

Advocacy for Research Findings

Another way of improving the prospects for utilization is for researchers to take on the role of advocates for their research findings and recommendations (Jones 1976; Rothman 1980; Siegel and Tuckel 1985). The ability to do this will be enhanced if one has identified relevant decision makers and information users and if one has studied the client agency, so as to understand the decision-making process and the constraints that may limit the ability to use research findings. Taking on advisory or policymaking roles is another way in which anthropologists can influence the use of anthropological knowledge in the policy process (e.g., Reeves, DeWalt, and DeWalt 1987).

Ethical Issues

In our discussion of knowledge utilization, we make the assumptions that (1) anthropologists feel they can make a worthwhile contribution to policy decision making, and (2) anthropologists who undertake applied and policy research wish to have an impact and see their findings and recommendations used.   Otherwise, we may reasonably ask, why do it? Given these assumptions, we need to ask the following questions.

• What are the costs (social, political, and ethical, as well as economic) associated with policy research and knowledge utilization?

• Costs to whom or what--to ourselves, to our discipline, to research quality, to the client(s), to the intended beneficiaries, to other individuals or groups, to the "public in general," and to some abstract principles?

• Are we willing to accrue such costs?

• What can we do to minimize the undesirable costs associated with our involvement in the policy process while increasing the positive impact of our research on public policy?

In examining the factors and strategies for increasing knowledge utilization, it is evident that there are a number of ethical issues and questions that arise because of the unique nature of policy research. These relate to the fact that it is usually "client-commissioned," and it is "value-laden" because of its association with policy decision making, which is never value-free (Chambers and Trend 1981; Patton 1986; Weaver 1985b).

In this section, we wish to raise some points of ethics that come to mind when considering knowledge utilization within the context of anthropological research and tradition. First of all, to whom are we accountable when we do applied and policy research: the client(s) who commissioned the project and are paying for it, the intended beneficiaries, the community that may be affected (intentionally or not), other stakeholders, the discipline, our own personal values? The answer is probably a mix of all of these. The recommendations we make may conflict with the values and needs of intended beneficiaries and other community members, or with the interests of the client group. As noted in the previous section, one way of ameliorating this problem is to do our ethnographic homework and be well informed about the client(s), the community, and other interested parties.

In a related point, Ballard and James (1983:422-23) assert that those who conduct applied and policy research, especially in projects that may intervene in the local community, have a responsibility to the "immediate clients," the people who are most likely to feel the impact of the researcher's recommendations. This sense of responsibility is based on the principle of reciprocity, providing something in return for the confidence, time, and materials that members of the community offer during the research process.

One can also talk of accountability in another sense--the obligation to do research that is potentially useable (Patton 1986), and the obligation to take action based on our findings. Partridge (1987:230-31) talks of an "ethics of action":

> . . . that evolves from and in concert with practical activity . . . it is an ethics of responsibility within an organizational context . . . an ethics based in commitment to socially responsible science. This commitment requires that the practitioner employ the best professional tools available that are appropriate to the task. It requires a pragmatic strategy based in practical knowledge so that there is a *good chance of being ethically and politically effective.* It demands a commitment to human rights . . . It requires a *commitment beyond narrow professionalism to take action once analysis indicates a course of action* . . . Finally, it demands a willingness to accept moral responsibility for the consequences of one's actions. (Emphasis in the original).

Several ethical points have already been raised in the earlier discussion of client participation in the research process as one strategy for increasing commitment to use research findings. Briefly, these concern the potential for cooptation of the researcher, as well as cooptation of the client or other stakeholders who might otherwise have taken a critical view of the project.

There is also the concern that by focusing exclusively on ways of making our research more useable to the client, we may overlook the manner in which the research will, or can, be used. The concern with unintended use is, of course, relevant to both applied and basic research. However, the potential for policy research to be misused is greater since it is client-commissioned and focuses on issues and questions of specific relevance to the client. Patton (1986) has noted that evaluation research (as well as other types of policy research) is political in nature, since it provides information that leads to knowledge, which in turn reduces uncertainty and facilitates action, thus allowing accumulation of power. It is not enough to learn about the organization, values, and needs of the clients, and of those potentially affected by research outcomes; we need also to gain insights into the power relationships among these various parties-at-interest, especially in cases where the client is an agency with a target population.

We have only covered a few of the ethical issues concerning knowledge utilization, as well as the conduct of applied and policy research. This is an area that requires more discussion, as well as presentation of case examples such as those collected by Rynkiewich and Spradley (1976). The existence of these and other potential ethical dilemmas should not discourage those who wish to pursue *praxis*, but rather should increase sensitivity and challenge us to find new and better ways of making our research useful while "being ethically and politically effective" (Partridge 1987:231).

Conclusion and Summary

The problem of underutilization of policy research results is widespread and something to which all social science disciplines are subject. In dealing with this problem, we must remember to act on how we do policy research, rather than lament the defects of the potential users of our work. We need to direct our attention to the variable under the greatest control, our own performance.

As a discipline we need to identify factors which relate to high use of our findings and develop a practical, comprehensive approach to doing utilization-focused policy research. This would include:

   • *A collaborative relationship between researcher and relevant stakeholders*, or what Patton (1986) has called the *personal factor*. This means involving decision makers and other potential users of information (such as community members) in the research process, so as to identify their information needs, develop relevant research design and methods that have face validity for the clients, identify ways in which the clients can use the research, and increase their interest and commitment to doing so.

• *Agency factors*, such as identifying agency constraints and incentives, communication channels, as well as cultural, political, and organizational structures.

• *Community and political factors*, by which we mean being aware of the potential impact of our research findings and recommendations on the community or on specific groups, being aware of the relationship between these stakeholders and client agencies, and being aware of the political structures at the micro and macro levels.

• *Research process factors*, such as maintaining a methodological flexibility, and being sensitive to the credibility, quality, and applicability of our research data and recommendations, in light of client needs, expectations, and constraints on use.

• *Communicating* to increase utilization; for example, using language and style familiar to the client, providing information throughout the research process, eliciting feedback from clients, and framing recommendations in terms of action. A goal we can aspire to is that the final report be redundant and serve only as a means of documenting the project (Schein 1969).

• Developing *time-effective* research methods.

• Acting as *advocates* on behalf of our research findings and recommendations.

• *Ethical issues* which result from the fact that policy research is usually "client commissioned" and is never "value free."

In addition, we need to recognize that the single most important factor associated with high utilization is personal commitment, on our part as well as that of policymakers, to having it occur.

2

Political Action and the Use of Anthropological Research: Land and Religion at Big Mountain

John J. Wood

I recommend that we spend at least as much time studying the political and economic processes we are trying to influence as the client communities impacted by those processes. We have to become advocates for our research to ensure its use.

Big Mountain is a rural, isolated locale on Black Mesa in northeastern Arizona. Many of the traditional Navajos who live there are resisting relocation from ancestral lands partitioned to the Hopi Tribe in the legislative settlement (Public Law 93-531) of Navajo and Hopi interests in a several million acre reservation created by executive order in 1882. In addition to relocation, legislation and Federal Court decisions mandated livestock reduction, range restoration and management, and a freeze on new construction (Wood, Vannette, and Andrews 1982).

The Navajo and Hopi Indian Relocation Commission, the Federal body charged with managing relocation, estimates that around 400 families, about 1,700 people, remain on Hopi-partitioned lands, including the Big Mountain community. Navajos residing on Hopi-partitioned lands have not been able to add new improvements for about 15 years, and livestock numbers have been reduced about 90 percent since 1977. The stresses of livestock reduction, the building freeze, and relocation have seriously impacted their health and well-being (Wood, Vannette, and Andrews 1982; Wood and Stemmler 1981; Joe 1985).

In this group of about 400 families, there are some who are awaiting relocation benefits, some who are just waiting, and some who have said they will not move. A significant number of the people in the Big Mountain community say they will not move, even if they are threatened with force. This group is made up of some very traditional Navajo elders, who are concerned that relocation will end their lives as well as their traditions. Members of the Big Mountain community and spokespersons from the outside, such as the "Big Mountain (J.U.A.) Legal Defense/Offense Committee" in Flagstaff, Arizona, have actively sought to end relocation.

In late 1978, staff members of the Navajo and Hopi Indian Relocation Commission visited the Big Mountain area to inventory and describe sacred sites that members of the community identified as highly significant and as a major reason for their desire not to move. In late 1978 and early 1979, the Commission also contracted with Walter M. Vannette and myself to evaluate the significance of these sacred sites (Wood and Vannette 1979). At that time there was a possibility that there would be an adjustment of the boundaries of the partition of the 1882 Executive Order Reservation, and the Commission's intent was to help make a case for excluding the Big Mountain community from relocation by readjusting the boundaries.

In January of 1981, I was asked by the then Director of the Navajo-Hopi Land Dispute Commission for the Navajo Tribe, who has close kinship ties within the community, to return to the community to further assess the relationship between occupancy and religion. I was also asked to present the "human side" of the issue of relocation from Big Mountain in a report and in testimony before the Senate Select Committee on Indian Affairs which was meeting that May in Washington, D.C., to consider the Navajo and Hopi Indian Relocation Commission's "Report and Plan" (United States Senate 1983a).

Our findings, along with an analysis of their implications for the American Indian Religious Freedom Act, were included in the hearings of the Senate Select Committee on Indian Affairs on PL 93-531, "Report and Plan of the Navajo-Hopi Relocation Commission" (United States Senate 1983a), delivered to selected Congressmen and Senators, and discussed in person with Senators Goldwater and DeConcini of Arizona and with an administrative official in the Bureau of Indian Affairs.

It is impossible to say unequivocally that this research had anything to do with the future course of events, but the attempt to "make our research useful" is, hopefully, an instructive example of contemporary anthropological practice. I will emphasize research in the service of the Big Mountain community (Wood and Stemmler 1981), with the recognition that it was a continuation of earlier research sponsored by the Navajo and Hopi Indian Relocation Commission (Wood and Vannette 1979).

Research Methods and Context

Research began in 1978 with a thorough review of the literature on Navajo religion and sacred places, with the benefit of some preliminary research by staff of the Navajo and Hopi Indian Relocation Commission on specific sites at Big Mountain. We were also interested in finding parallel cases in the literature as well as specific issues raised in the then recent American Indian Religious Freedom Act (Public Law 95-341). This review was essential for placing everything in a broader context, and for helping design the fieldwork phase of the research.

In this earlier work for the Relocation Commission, our fieldwork was not as productive as it might have been because our guide-interpreter was an employee of the Relocation Commission, and we were identified with the Commission. We made some on-site visits, and conducted some interviews, primarily with persons who happened to be home. The results were suggestive when put together with earlier information from the Commission and from the literature, but we presented them as necessarily preliminary.

The research for the community in 1981 was more in the genre of participant observation and conducted over a much longer period of time. I spent almost every weekend in the community from mid-January through mid-March. My interpreters were members of the community, and I carefully explained the nature and purpose of the research in community meetings before and during the fieldwork. My chief interpreter was a leader in the Big Mountain Committee.

Most of the data were gathered in personal, taped interviews with twenty-five persons, representing most of the families in the community. The interviews were taken in Navajo with the assistance of interpreters and were relatively unstructured, although a guide was used that consisted of several questions about use and location of sacred sites. While there were a few ceremonial specialists in the sample, the majority of the interviewees had limited knowledge of the details of specific ceremonies. Because of the nature of the research, I was more interested in popular views of sacred space rather than in more esoteric knowledge.

At the conclusion of the project, the manuscript was read and edited by the three interpreters from Big Mountain. They checked the manuscript for accuracy and for information that, in their opinion, members of the community would not want mentioned in the report.

Client Groups

There were two principal client groups in the study: the Navajo and Hopi Indian Relocation Commission and the Big Mountain community. The target group for the study was to be the Senate Select Committee on Indian Affairs.

The Navajo and Hopi Indian Relocation Commission wanted a professional opinion concerning the significance of sacred sites at Big Mountain and independent confirmation of their findings. I suspect that the Commission may have been motivated in part by Senator Barry Goldwater's promise to help the Big Mountain people, made at Big Mountain in 1977. Political considerations notwithstanding, the staff of the Commission was receptive to the report.

Research for the second client group, the Big Mountain community, was a continuation of the earlier project. I was requested by members of the community to write a report explaining the "human side" of the impacts of relocation to "Washington." I chose to focus on the relationships among land use and religion, because I thought that side of the issue had not been fully addressed.

There was a hearing on the Navajo and Hopi Indian Relocation Commission's Report and Plan before the Senate Select Committee on Indian Affairs planned for later in the year, and that was the principal target group for the report. Arizona Senators DeConcini and Goldwater were both on the Committee and basically on opposite sides of the issue of relocation, although both sympathized with the Big Mountain community's request to be exempt from relocation. Other members of the Senate Committee were less committal. The report was also to be distributed to the relevant House Committees and to individual Congressmen.

Beneficiaries

The Big Mountain community was the intended beneficiary of the research. The goal of the research findings was to exempt members of the community from relocation and its attendant hardships, and allow continuation of their traditional way of life, as they saw fit. As noted above, the community was also a client group.

The Big Mountain "community" is made up of several localized clan groups related by marriage and descent. The elders in the community are represented by a Big Mountain Committee made up of persons from the community, who tend to be moderate in their brokering relationships with the "Anglo" world. There are others in the community who represent a hard-line approach, and who are supported by members of the American Indian Movement and others from outside of the community. Although there are differences in approach to the issue of relocation, there is considerable unity of purpose in the community, and there are several persons, including some elders, who actively participate in both networks.

Utilization Methods

In our reports and testimony we concluded that there are many religious sites of local, regional, and tribal significance at Big Mountain. More important, we found that location and use of sacred sites are intimately related to land use, definitions of occupancy, and social organization, which is our analytic way of translating the Navajo view of religion as life itself (Wood and Vannette 1979; Wood and Stemmler 1981).

We had no utilization plan for the product of our research for the Navajo and Hopi Indian Relocation Commission. The Commission planned to use the research in making a case for excluding the Big Mountain area from relocation, through land exchanges, but we were not privy to the details of that plan. Late in 1979, after it became clear that the boundary adjustments would not be made, I sent a copy of the report to the Task Force that was preparing a report to Congress as required by the American Indian Religious Freedom Act (Public Law 95-341) along with a cover letter suggesting that the Task Force look into the possibility that relocation was a violation of civil rights. I received a letter acknowledging receipt of the report, and my response, along with others, was acknowledged in their report to Congress, but nothing further was done by the Task Force.

As mentioned above, my charge from the representative of the Navajo Tribe who asked me to conduct the research for the Big Mountain community in 1981 was to present the "human side" of relocation in a report to "Washington." The details were left for me to work out and present in a community meeting. My previous experience at Big Mountain and a growing familiarity with the impacts of relocation convinced me that the "human side" of relocation that needed telling was the relationship between occupancy and religion. I presented my plan in a public meeting at Big Mountain. It was not elaborate. Basically the research would clarify the relationships among land use and religion, and the report would be submitted for the record at a Senate hearing on the

Relocation Commission's Report and Plan. This was interpreted as proposing to ask people questions about their sacred places and ceremonies and their reasons for not wanting to move. It was further proposed that their answers would be written down in a report to Washington.

The plan was an attempt to work within "channels," and, by 1981, that was clearly a proposal that appealed to the moderates in the community. With one exception, those present at the meeting supported the plan. However, there were several persons with less moderate views who did not support the project. At least one person spread rumors that were designed to raise questions about my credibility. And near the end of my research, when presenting my findings in a public meeting at Big Mountain, I was challenged by some young persons in the less moderate network. The elders responded to the challenge on my behalf and encouraged me to continue the research and present the results.

In traditional Navajo fashion, the execution of the plan was left up to me. There were no suggestions from members of the community regarding utilization. People either cooperated with the research or were uncooperative in ways I mentioned previously.

As the project evolved, the plan gradually took on more specific form. The stress and anxiety that I observed in interviews, and the hope expressed by members of the community that the research would help, convinced me that I must do everything I could to see that the research was used. I resolved to take the report to Washington myself to present it in the hearing and to deliver it in person to Senators Goldwater and DeConcini.

Contacts with Senator DeConcini's staff in Arizona helped place me on the agenda to testify at the hearing. Senator DeConcini has steadfastly opposed relocation, which undoubtedly accounts for his willingness to allow me to testify.

I took the report to Washington, to the hearings, and was prepared to testify on behalf of the Big Mountain community. One of the younger members of the community was also in attendance. The hearing was adjourned before we were able to testify, so I asked a staff member of the Senate Committee to enter the report in the record (United States Senate 1983a). The report, which was printed at the expense of the Navajo Tribe, was distributed by tribal representatives to selected Congressmen as well (Wood and Stemmler 1981).

Later that week, my wife and I delivered the report to Senator Goldwater in his office and discussed the Big Mountain community request for a brief time with him. We also talked to Senator DeConcini during a brief recess from the Senate floor about the issue. It is relatively easy to get an appointment with members of Congress if you are in Washington, and if you are part of their constituency, although you may have to schedule the appointment some time in advance. In my case, the timeliness of the issue I wanted to discuss and the fact that it was a local issue helped. I found both Senators attentive and cordial; however, there were no surprises from either of them.

My wife, the representative from Big Mountain, and I also got an appointment with an official in the Bureau of Indian Affairs and gave her a copy of the report and discussed some of the problems faced by the Big Mountain community. It was relatively easy to get an appointment in the Bureau, too, and we found the person with whom we talked sympathetic and understanding, but noncommittal.

Finally, through political connections, my wife and I lunched with a lobbyist and asked her how we might proceed. She suggested follow-up letters to key individuals on the Senate Committee, in addition to Senators Goldwater and DeConcini. To increase the likelihood of the Senators reading the letters, she further suggested that I include some praise of the Senators' staffs. I followed her suggestions. Senator Goldwater's response was: "As for Big Mountain, I hope something will be worked out between the Navajo and Hopi Tribes for a land exchange" (Goldwater 1981).

Utilization methods, then, evolved within the genre of political action. Based on earlier experience, and spurred on by a developing sense of commitment, I felt that producing information in the form of a report, however well-argued, was no guarantee that it would be used for the benefit of my clients, the Big Mountain community. It was necessary to get the report into the hands of the decision makers.

Project Impacts

The staff of the Navajo and Hopi Relocation Commission was receptive to the report we prepared for them in 1979 (Wood and Vannette 1979). But the anticipated boundary adjustment did not occur. The Commission subsequently supported legislation introduced by Senator Goldwater for a land exchange to mitigate relocation of Big Mountain Navajos, stating: "These families have a unique cultural attachment to their homesites that has been well documented in professional studies" (United States Senate 1983b:7). It is likely that our 1979 report provided some of the documentation referenced in this statement. However, the limited evident use of the report was part of the reason for taking a stronger position on political action in the 1981 project.

The Report and Plan of the Navajo and Hopi Indian Relocation Commission was accepted by the Senate Select Committee on Indian Affairs in May, 1981, and the inclusion of our 1981 report on Big Mountain in the record of the hearing had no discernible impact on its acceptance.[1] Of course, no one thought that it would. Rather, it was hoped that the report would stimulate a negotiated or legislated land exchange between the Hopi and Navajo.

In the summer of 1981, the Big Mountain Committee held a meeting and an appreciation meal for persons who had helped them. We were recognized for our assistance and given gifts. At that meeting, I gave all of the persons I interviewed a copy of our report. People seemed to be pleased with the results. And, perhaps it raised their consciousness as it did their hopes.

A little over one year following the hearing, Senator Goldwater introduced a bill for a land exchange that would exempt portions of the Big Mountain community from relocation (United States Senate 1983b). In the interim, the Navajo and Hopi Indian Relocation Commission had provided discretionary funds to the Big Mountain Committee for the purpose of drawing up a specific proposal for the exchange. This proposal was included in the record of the hearing. The President of the Big Mountain Committee, who was my principal interpreter, was the coordinator and a writer of the report. The legislation did not get past the hearing stage.

In 1986, I wrote Senator Goldwater and asked him, in so many words, to evaluate the impact of our research report. He did not directly answer the question, so I cannot say if it influenced him or not. This was his reply:

> The primary reason I introduced the land exchange legislation to which you refer is that I felt and still feel that the Navajos who live on Big Mountain should be able to stay there. It is the oldest and most traditional area for the Navajos and they have lived there peaceably with the Hopis. The legislation did not go past the hearing stage because there was a disagreement among the Big Mountain people as to acreage and also the two Tribal Chairmen agreed to try to meet and try to work out something between themselves (Goldwater 1986).

There was a bill introduced in March, 1986 from the House, drafted by a former staunch supporter of relocation, Arizona Congressman

Morris Udall, and Arizona Congressman McCain, a relative newcomer to the issue, which would have, among other things, exempted the Big Mountain area from relocation. The bill was subsequently withdrawn for unstated reasons.

The deadline for relocation, July 7, 1986, was marked at Big Mountain by a four day Sun Dance, introduced by the Lakota four years ago, and a demonstration march and fence cutting, but no one was moved. On July 8, the first Hopi home site was marked on Hopi Partitioned Lands.

The Bureau of Indian Affairs has been given the responsibility of moving Navajos to the new lands acquired near Sanders and Chambers, Arizona. They are proceeding, cautiously, with a needs assessment, some planning, and preparations for the first voluntary moves. Arizona Senator DeConcini introduced a bill in the summer months of 1986, in another attempt to mitigate relocation. It served to keep the issue before Congress, but, as far as I know, it did not make it out of committee. I have no idea if our work had any influence on the Senator's proposed legislation. The Hopi Tribal Chairman then announced a plan to move several hundred Hopis to homesites on Hopi partitioned lands. There have been two recent incidents involving Navajos, Hopis, and Bureau of Indian Affairs law enforcement officers; however, no one was seriously injured. At the time of this writing, then, the future is still uncertain and unsettled. Things are relatively quiet now, perhaps in anticipation of the possibilities of favorable legislation in 1987 with the retirement of Senator Goldwater and a new Congress in place.

A movement to file a First Amendment lawsuit to challenge the constitutionality of forced relocation, called "In Defense of Sacred Lands," is headquartered in Flagstaff, Arizona, and it appears to be gaining momentum. Our research at Big Mountain provides a rationale for the suit, and I have submitted an affidavit explaining the role of land and religion in traditional Navajo culture.

Relocation is an emotionally charged and highly politicized issue, and because so much goes on behind the scenes, it is difficult to sort out if and how the research findings were used. For example, relocation is basically seen as an Arizona issue in Congress, and the politics of which members of Congress side with which members of the Arizona delegation to effect legislation and what influences them to do so is difficult to fathom for an outsider. The only influence most of us have is in seeing that valid and reliable information gets to the right persons.

Members of the Big Mountain community have been instrumental in keeping the issues of relocation before the public and in putting pressure on the Relocation Commission and the Federal Government.

Community members have traveled to Washington on many occasions, to California, and to Europe to explain their position on relocation. They regularly attend the monthly meetings of the Navajo and Hopi Relocation Commission in Flagstaff. And they have attracted supporters from all over the United States and from as far away as Japan.

I am convinced that the tenacity and skill of members of the community and their supporters, and their local, national, and international visibility, are the principal reasons for the political interest in exempting them from relocation. There is no substitute for organized opposition in the political arena. However, the research and advocacy described here helped provide an "expert" rationale for the opposition. I can point to some successes in getting the research used: The research was delivered to the most influential persons in the decision making process; it may have been influential in support of legislation; it helped keep the issue alive in the legislative process; and it is essential background for a proposed First Amendment lawsuit. Nevertheless, the intended beneficiaries are still scheduled to be relocated as of this writing; in this sense, the larger goals of the research were not met.

Summary

There is an intimate relationship among land use, occupancy, and religion in Navajo culture that ties some traditional Navajos to the land so strongly that they would rather die than move. Navajos at Big Mountain, Arizona, faced with the likelihood of forced relocation, asked to have these ties made known to persons in Washington in hopes of having a legislated relocation decision reversed. This paper relates my involvement in the research to document the peoples' beliefs and practices, and my attempt to see that the research was used as they desired. The research was used, but it did not have the intended effect--the beneficiaries are still going to be relocated.

An issue of this complexity, with so much at stake politically and economically, presents a difficult challenge to those interested in improving the use of anthropological research. Based on my experience in this and other similar cases, I recommend that we spend at least as much time studying the political and economic processes we are trying to influence as the client communities impacted by those political and economic processes. Specifically, we need to understand the political arena we are addressing, its processes and personnel. I would like to see us develop a solid body of anthropological literature on political arenas in large scale societies, with applications in the forefront of interest.

Short of that, personal contact with key political figures, and participant observation, will help identify the right persons to get the research results, and the right time and the right way to present the results. We have to become advocates for our research to ensure its use.

Notes

1. As an example of the razor's edge that we sometimes walk in applied anthropology, it should be brought to the reader's attention that I wrote the section on population characteristics in the Report and Plan under an earlier contract with the Navajo and Hopi Indian Relocation Commission. The representative of the Navajo Tribe that contacted me to work at Big Mountain did not see that as a conflict of interest; I am not sure how the Relocation Commission viewed the situation.

3

Prenatal Care and Pregnancy Outcome: Applications of Research Findings to the Reduction of Infant Mortality in Detroit

Marilyn L. Poland and Paul T. Giblin

Be sensitive to the informational needs of those who support your research. Be willing and ready to reanalyze data to meet these needs.

In this chapter the roles of social scientists, clients, and beneficiaries will be explored in an ongoing program of research and program evaluation addressing high infant mortality in Detroit. The participants in these programs included local and state agencies as clients (Detroit/Wayne County Infant Health Promotion Coalition, Michigan Department of Public Health), pregnant women and high risk infants in the City of Detroit as beneficiaries, and the authors, an applied anthropologist in the Department of Obstetrics and Gynecology and a developmental psychologist in the Department of Pediatrics of Wayne State University's School of Medicine. We will describe conditions which lead to our involvement as social scientists, studies we performed to further identify factors associated with high infant mortality, and methods we employed to maximize the applications of this information.

Studies performed included an interview of women receiving varying amounts of prenatal care with over 40% receiving no prenatal care, and a retrospective chart review identifying maternal and family characteristics contributing to infant health and parenting behaviors for infants admitted to a Neonatal Intensive Care Unit. Methods to maximize the application of this information included active participation with the Infant Health Promotion Coalition and the Michigan Department of Public Health in defining research questions and applying results to outreach programs and health policy. In addition, we fostered the application of our results by maintaining direct access to the press, legislators and departmental policy makers, and by assuming responsibility for program development and implementation.

Infant Mortality as a Problem

In 1982, Michigan was experiencing the effects of a recent economic recession. There was continued high unemployment and many people were uninsured for health services. Limited public resources for health programs had been further depleted to support unemployment benefits and welfare payments. Michigan's high infant mortality statistics were reported in newspapers and magazines across the country. For example, in 1981, the United States had an infant mortality rate of 11.8 infant deaths per 1000 live births while Michigan's rate was 13.2 and Detroit had one of the nation's highest rates at 21.4. Local pressure to address the high infant mortality statistics came primarily from the press, through a series of prominently placed articles and editorials. These articles pointed to poverty, lack of health providers for the poor, and problems attaining health insurance as major contributing factors to inadequate prenatal care and high infant mortality. National publicity resulted from a report by a State Health Department official who stated that in one area of Detroit, "the death rate has hit . . . the level reported for Honduras, the poorest country in Central America" (see Table 3.1, April, 1982).

This growing awareness and concern for infant mortality in the state and in Detroit may be understood as an interplay of research findings, public awareness, policy and program development. Table 3.1, at the end of this chapter, summarizes this process by providing a time-line of key events addressing infant mortality in Michigan. For the purposes of this chapter, we have emphasized our participation in this process and will reference events in this table throughout this chapter.

Research Methods and Context

Following a year of newspaper articles and public reports comparing 1980 to 1982 infant death rates and identifying contributing factors (see Table 3.1), the first programmatic response to infant mortality was the establishment of the Detroit/Wayne County Infant Health Promotion Coalition in March 1983 to coordinate the concerns and activities of 47 local public and private organizations and institutions responsible for the health care of pregnant women and infants in the City of Detroit and Wayne County, Michigan. The Coalition was started by health officials from the City of Detroit and Wayne County and announced to the public during a press conference by the Directors of the Detroit and Wayne County Health Departments.

The charge to the Coalition was to identify causes of high infant mortality and to suggest policy and program changes to address this problem. Funding was provided from the existing budgets of the two health departments to pay the salaries of a coordinator, assistant, and one secretary. Representatives of the cooperating local agencies and institutions served on one of three committees: Problem Identification and Description, Service and Access Problems, and Communications and Media Approaches.

One of this chapter's authors (MLP), who represented Hutzel Hospital on this Coalition, the largest maternity hospital in Detroit, volunteered for the Problem Identification and Description Committee. While MLP was selected as Hutzel's representative due to her history of service and policy involvement, she had the additional distinction of being the only researcher on the Coalition. In addition, she had participated in earlier State reports on infant mortality (see Table 3.1, January 1983) which had led to her ongoing research program assessing patient access to prenatal services. As the maternity expert, she proposed (and the Coalition accepted) that a study be done to assess barriers to prenatal care by interviews with new mothers. The overall goal of the Coalition expressed by its support of this research was not only to provide information, but also to legitimize its function as an action task force proposing changes in health services. Specific objectives included a better understanding of: (a) why 9% of pregnant women in Detroit do not receive adequate prenatal health care, (b) associations between not receiving prenatal care, poverty, insurance, and teenage pregnancy, and (c) nature and effectiveness of outreach programs to bring pregnant women and infants to health programs.

The Coalition's utilization goal was to develop effective outreach programs to monitor conditions contributing to inadequate prenatal health care and to recruit women and infants to appropriate health care. Some women and infants had already been identified by the Coalition as being "at-risk," including those receiving inadequate prenatal care in previous pregnancies, having no medical insurance, having had a prior infant death, or being young teenagers. As reported in Table 3.1, MLP initiated a study of women not receiving prenatal care and presented a preliminary report to the Coalition in January 1984.

The second programmatic response to infant mortality occurred when the Michigan Department of Public Health (MDPH) requested proposals to evaluate the need for and feasibility of outreach programs to increase access to prenatal and infant services. The goals of this State initiative were similar to those of the Coalition including identification of barriers to prenatal and infant health care and development of a program to reduce these barriers. This grant allowed an expanded interviewing of new mothers who had received varying degrees of prenatal care (MLP) and studies of mothers and their infants admitted to Children's Hospital of Michigan Neonatal Intensive Care Unit (PTG).

The utilization goal of the research team regarding these two programmatic actions was to develop a sociobehavioral risk index predicting poor prenatal care and poor pregnancy outcome. Questions posed as we developed the risk index included: How do health beliefs influence seeking prenatal care? What are the effects of social isolation on pregnant women and how does it contribute to inadequate health care? What conditions predict parents' inadequate participation in their infant's health care?

Infant Mortality Studies

Two studies were conducted in response to these local and state initiatives: (a) an analysis of why women failed to receive adequate prenatal care, and (b) factors affecting maternal behavior toward her hospitalized infant. The design of these studies reflected the research team's view that infant mortality and morbidity was a complex phenomenon involving associated factors which did not fall within the domain of a single discipline. Variables were selected to identify underlying relationships between values and attitudes toward health care seeking and contributing factors such as poverty and poor access to health care. Finally, we were also concerned with the continued influence of these variables across the prenatal and postpartum periods.

Prenatal Study: One hundred and eleven women who delivered at Hutzel Hospital in Detroit were interviewed two to five days postpartum and their medical records were examined for sociodemographic and medical factors (Poland, Ager, and Olson 1987). Fifty-seven of these women were listed in hospital records as "walk-ins," or patients who did not receive prenatal care by a physician or nurse midwife associated with the hospital, and 54 were women who attended the hospital's prenatal clinic. The interview consisted of questions which were both open-ended and fixed-choice to assess the experience of pregnancy and prenatal care over the current and previous pregnancies. Responses were analyzed by content analysis and subjected to several statistical analyses.

NICU Studies: Two additional studies assessed maternal characteristics associated with seeking prenatal care, infant health at birth, and parenting. Giblin et al. (1988a) report a seven-year retrospective review of a computerized clinical data base (n = 3818) of infants admitted to a NICU assessing factors including mothers' characteristics of age, number of children, and socioeconomic status; maternal health factors such as complications of pregnancy and drug use during pregnancy; whether or not the mother obtained prenatal care; and infant birth weight.

The second (Giblin et al. 1988b) was a case comparison study which selected all infants of mothers reporting no prenatal care (n = 128) from the above data base and compared them to preceding and subsequent admissions to this NICU of infants whose mothers had received prenatal care. Medical records were reviewed to assess frequency of visits to the NICU (frequent, irregular, problem contacting parents); observed parenting behavior (favorable, neutral, unfavorable); and social work referrals.

Utilization Methods

Results of Prenatal and NICU Studies

The 111 women we interviewed in the prenatal study were all poor, and most were Black. They varied considerably in age, number of children, amount of prenatal care they received, and in pregnancy outcomes. Three levels of prenatal care were derived (adequate, intermediate, and inadequate) from a formula which accounts for expected number of visits and length of pregnancy. The women were compared across groups for sociodemographic and medical factors, maternal attitudes, values and beliefs about pregnancy and prenatal care, and social support. We found that women receiving inadequate prenatal care were older, had more children, were at higher risk of complications of pregnancy, had shorter pregnancies, and produced smaller babies. Other differences were noted. First, women in the inadequate care group suspected they were pregnant significantly later than women in the other two groups, and most were very unhappy about their pregnancies. Second, many did not have health insurance, although most were eligible. Those who were eligible but did not apply stated they they did not want to seek prenatal care, or that they did not want to bother with the difficulties of applying for insurance (including completing a 21-page application for Medicaid). Third, women seeking less prenatal care had fewer friends and relatives and perceived health professionals as being unhelpful. Finally, all women complained about transportation problems, long waiting times to see the doctor, confusing and often contradictory infomation, and unpleasant staff.

The retrospective review of the NICU clinical database identified many factors significantly associated with infant health as measured by birth weight, Apgar scores at 1 and 5 minutes, and gestational age. Poor infant health was associated with the mother being unmarried, having no private insurance, prenatal drug use, and receiving no prenatal care. Not seeking prenatal care was associated with maternal characteristics of being less than 17 or older than 34, high parity, having prenatal health problems, and prenatal drug use.

The case comparison medical records review of parenting behaviors observed while infants were in the NICU identified the no prenatal care group as visiting their infants less frequently, being more likely to display unfavorable parent-child interactions, and being less attentive to discharge teaching for the care of their infants. In addition to seeking no prenatal care, poor parenting was also associated with prenatal drug use and the lack of an involved father.

These studies addressed three issues: (1) conditions affecting maternal access to health care, (2) risk factors associated with poor infant health, and (3) links between prenatal and postpartum maternal behavior, i.e., lack of prenatal care seeking and poor parent-child interactions. We identified "high-risk" women with more negative attitudes toward their pregnancies, who were isolated from close network ties and the health care system, who were at greater risk of complications, and who had shorter pregnancies and smaller infants. Our results also pointed to a general dissatisfaction with the prenatal health delivery system and urged an outreach approach that would begin in pregnancy and continue through the infant's first year of life.

Means we employed to maximize the use of our studies' results may best be summarized in three areas: (1) aphorisms characterizing strategies to maximize the influence of one's information, (2) phases of a social scientist's involvement in public issues, and (3) unforeseen conditions relevant to the utilization of our research findings.

Strategies to Maximize the Influence of Presented Information

1. *Quickly establish a core set of research findings which are simple to understand and bear repeating.* When MLP was asked to provide the clinical perspective to rising rates of infant deaths, she completed her initial interviews (see Table 3.1, August 1982) in one working day and reported her findings to

the state official who was preparing his report. In turn, she requested summaries of his comparisons of state infant mortality rates for 1980 and 1982. She placed information from the local and state reports onto 3 x 5 cards pinned to the bulletin board next to her phone to be included in statements to the press. As new data were available, these cards were revised. Summary statements derived from these cards were shared with the press repeatedly.

2. *Never give a final report.* Rather, report findings of ongoing research. Over the last four years we have never presented a final report. Final reports are seldom read. We favored presenting preliminary findings of ongoing studies which emphasized the continuing nature of these problems and urged further review and action. To date, we have presented 12 preliminary reports.

3. *Be sensitive to the informational needs of those who support your research. Be willing and ready to reanalyze data to meet these informational needs.* We frequently reanalyzed our data to assess conditions which may influence infant mortality. For example, Dr. Jeff Taylor (Chief of the Division of Maternal and Child Health, MDPH 1982-1985) felt that demonstrating an association between infant mortality and teen pregnancy would obtain broad policy influence. Our analyses by age of mother did not demonstrate this association but did indicate that women of high parity who were towards the end of their childbearing years were at greater risk of poor prenatal care and infant health at birth.

4. *Keep your clients and others informed and encourage their active participation in your research.* For example, the interview guide used to assess prenatal care seeking patterns was developed as a collaborative effort with the Coalition and others. In addition, women who did not receive prenatal care identified specific problems or agencies that discouraged them from seeking health care. Coalition members were approached for clarification about agency policies and services. This process maintained the active involvement of the Coalition in all phases of data collection and analysis and encouraged examination of some obvious problems as data were collected.

5. *Maintain control of your data.* It is best to avoid contracts in which you complete work directed by others. Maintain the stance of an independent researcher who shares the concerns and interests of your client through joint participation in local groups. Independence is best facilitated when funding for work is obtained from a grant of your own design.

6. *Attain and maintain high personal visibility in the press through active participation in local associations and through a readiness to supply succinct and meaningful information.* (See Strategies 1 and 5.) High personal visibility in the press is a commodity which has value to state policy makers and public officials. This fosters their need to include you on task forces with access to policy making and resource allocation.

Social Scientist as Researcher, Policy Advisor and Program Director

Table 3.1 reports changing roles and responsibilities of MLP over the course of her involvement with infant mortality. Initially, she was approached to provide a clinician's view of infant mortality. When responding to this request, she suggested additional information to better understand infant mortality (i.e., chart review of "walk-in"--see Table 3.1, September 1982) and was subsequently cited as a contributor in a report given in hearings in Washington, D.C. (January 1983). Further, she established herself as a resource for information and clarification of issues by providing research findings and maintaining control of her own data. She disseminated her findings through a network of personal communication with state officials and local press, as well as through professional publications and presentations to local and national organizations (Poland 1986a; Poland and Giblin 1986; Giblin, Poland, and Waller 1986; Waller et al. 1986). For example, by presenting the 21-page application form for Medicaid to an audience of health professionals and policy makers (Poland 1986b) and requesting that they take a few minutes to "fill it out," the difficulties in completing this application became readily apparent. Eighteen months later, as a result of this demonstration, the Medicaid application was reduced to two pages. In March 1983, MLP became a member of the Coalition which allowed her to broaden her research and to participate directly in recommendations for policy changes to local participating agencies. Further, her findings became an integral part of annual press releases by the Coalition, thereby increasing her professional stature at state and national levels.

MLP had now progressed through two phases as an applied social scientist: researcher and policy maker. A third stage occurred when she joined with colleagues in Pediatrics (PTG) and Community Medicine (John B. Waller, Jr., Dr.PH.) to develop and implement an outreach program aimed at enhancing women's and infants' access to health care services. Concurrently, MLP and JBW were named to the Infant Mortality Task Force of the MDPH, thereby broadening their influence as policy advisors as well as increasing their proximity to appropriations. Finally, the activities of these three researchers were formalized in their University by the establishment of the Institute of Maternal and Child Health of the Wayne State University School of Medicine.

This review of the changing roles of the above social scientists illustrates that to advance the utilization of their research findings they assumed responsibilities as policy advisors and program directors. These opportunities were afforded them due to their high public visibility, their adaptability to the various perspectives and needs of individuals and organizations, and their maintenance of independence of both information and action. Their institutional placement in clinical departments also facilitated access to data and, from the university's perspective, their efforts were seen as an appropriate use of an academic resource.

Unforeseen Conditions Favoring Utilization of Our Research Findings

Concurrent events and conditions, to which we responded quickly, enhanced the utilization of our results and our assumption of policy and programmatic responsibilities. First, a sustained and insightful series of newspaper articles appeared in the local press over the last four years focusing on infant mortality and attendant conditions. Continued public pressure was thereby applied urging research and programmatic response. Second, a regionalization of maternal and child health services by MDPH reduced the direct advocacy role of this state department and shifted increased attention to independent efforts. Third, a lobbyist for maternal and child health was appointed and supported by a group of local agencies. This lobbyist was instrumental in promoting ties among individuals and agencies and fostered collaborative advocacy. Finally, Michigan has a long history of program response to the public health needs of the poor. Therefore, there was great sympathy to the rising rate of infant mortality and barriers to prenatal care.

Project Impacts

Five areas characterize project impacts.   First, our continued participation in documenting the nature and extent of infant mortality and morbidity was shared with press and other media, maintaining a growing public awareness of these issues. As noted in Table 3.1, two key newspaper articles, by Steven Franklin (May 1982) and Jane Daugherty (June 1986), summarized these concerns and led to immediate policy and programmatic response. Second, by our personal contacts and participation in local and state agencies, we were able to contribute to the development of policies insuring financial support for prenatal services to women in Michigan. Third, we designed and implemented a model for training and employing paraprofessionals to facilitate access to prenatal and infant services. This model was derived from our previous research findings in which identified barriers to health care seeking included lack of social support and lack of financial resources. Fourth, by our continued participation with these concerns, we established a collaborative network of agencies concerned with maternal and child health. We institutionalized these concerns within our University (i.e., The Institute of Maternal and Child Health) to continue our development of programs training professionals and paraprofessionals to address maternal and child health problems. Finally, a model of collaboration has evolved between University-based professionals and local and state agencies with shared concerns. This model has facilitated the careful development of service provision based on systematic evaluation of both process and outcome.

The above project impacts are most clearly demonstrated by the paraprofessional outreach program entitled "Maternal and Child Health Advocates for Improved Pregnancy and Infant Health Outcomes," funded jointly by the Michigan Department of Public Health, VISTA, and the Ford Foundation (see Table 3.1). In this program, we have employed information derived from our prior studies to (a) develop a sociobehavioral risk index for inadequate prenatal health care seeking, (b) establish a needs assessment protocol for low income pregnant women, and (c) develop guidelines for case management of these clients. Interventions in these programs address both continuing adjustments in service provision as well as patient education and counseling to foster health care. Information from this program will be shared with the local, state, and national agencies. Our reports will address: (a) the process of implementing this program with particular emphasis on the role of paraprofessionals and our efforts to recruit women to prenatal services, and (b) the attainment of our program goals of reducing infant mortality and morbidity, earlier and more frequent use of prenatal care services, and more adequate health care seeking for one's infant.

Summary

In order for research to be implemented, applied social scientists may be required to assume roles which are outside of their usual domains. These roles may include: (a) contributing directly to policy, program development, and program implementation; (b) sustaining a sense of excitement and importance in one's activities in presentations to the press, state and local agencies, and external sources of funding; and (c) maintaining an independence within one's self between the goal of a program director that his or her program succeed and the goal of a scientist that evalutions of program activities and outcomes are guided by objective empiricism. By these activities, applied social scientists may be obligated to revise their roles from that of a participant observer to a participant activist. In this latter role, the social scientist participates in identifying problems, developing research strategies, implementing and disseminating research findings, advising policy response, and developing and directing subsequent programmatic activities.

In this chapter, these changing responsibilities of a social scientist are described as she became an active participant in local and state coalitions to define and address high infant mortality rates in Detroit. Also described are subsequent research studies, means employed to disseminate findings of these studies so as to enhance their likelihood of affecting policies and programs, and specific projects undertaken to reduce barriers to prenatal and infant health care.

Table 3.1   **Infant Mortality Initiatives in Michigan and Detroit: 1982-1986**

April 1982
"Infant Deaths in Michigan: Analysis and Recommendation" (Jeff Taylor, Ph.D., Director of Maternal and Child Health, Michigan Department of Public Health).

: This report compared 1980 and 1981 infant mortality rates, demonstrating increases in Michigan and Detroit. "Detroit is suffering death rates which are nearly twice the state average. Neighborhoods within Detroit are experiencing an epidemic of infant deaths. In census area A, for example, the death rate has hit 33 deaths/1,000 live births, the level reported for Honduras, the poorest country in Central America".

May 1982
"Poverty and pregnancy: Lack of care takes its toll on infant lives" (Stephen Franklin, *Detroit Free Press*).

: This newspaper article established relationships between infant mortality rates, poverty, being black and being a teenager. "Detroit's black infant mortality rate is higher than that of an undeveloped country like Costa Rica, where the average income is $1,431 a year; in some neighborhoods, Detroit's black infant mortality rate soars to a level equal to Third World nations like Sri Lanka where average income is $200 a year."

August 1982
Request for data on clinical perspective of infant mortality by Jeff Taylor to Marilyn Poland. (Marilyn Poland, Ph.D., R.N., Hutzel Hospital and Department of Obstetrics and Gynecology, Wayne State University).

: Short report generated based upon interviews of clinicians at Hutzel Hospital and Children's Hospital of Michigan regarding women receiving no prenatal care ("walk-ins"), women with no insurance being sent to Hutzel for delivery ("dumps"), and parent abandonment of sick newborns.

September 1982
Chart review comparison of "walk-ins" at Hutzel Hospital: 1980 to 1982 (Marilyn Poland).

: Preliminary report of incidence, contributing conditions and characteristics of women with no prenatal care delivering at Hutzel.

January 1983
"The impact of unemployment on the health of mothers and children in Michigan: Recommendations for the Nation." *Report to Committee on Energy and Commerce*, Washington, D.C. (Bailus Walker, Dr.PH., Director, Michigan Department of Public Health).

: Presentation of findings of 1980-1982 comparison of infant death rates (J. Taylor) and "walk-ins," "dumps," and abandonment (M. Poland).

March 1983
Establishment of Detroit/Wayne County Infant Health Promotion Coalition (47 local agencies, M. Poland, representative of Hutzel Hospital).

: Coordinated efforts to assess and develop recommendations to alleviate high infant mortality rates.

June 1983
Meeting of Coalition Problem Identification and Description Subcommittee (M. Poland, member).

: Presentation of chart review study of "walk-ins" and proposal for prospective interview study at Hutzel Hospital (volunteer support for interviews provided by Coalition).

January 1984
"How women feel about prenatal care: Summary of a study conducted at Hutzel Hospital--1983" (M. Poland).

: Preliminary report to Coalition on interviews of "walk-ins" establishing relationships between no prenatal care and health system problems, insurance coverage, age and parity, illicit drug use, etc.

March 1984
"Prenatal care: A healthy beginning for Michigan's children" (Report of the Director's Special Task Force, Gloria Smith, Ph.D., Director, Michigan Department of Public Health).

: Proposal for establishment of prenatal and postpartum care as a basic health right. "Recent medical studies have shown that infant mortality rates in Michigan are among the highest in the nation. This critical situation can be traced directly to the lack of adequate prenatal and postpartum care for significant groups of women in this State" (Governor James J. Blanchard, January 23, 1984).

March 1984
"Infant Mortality: Analysis and Recommendations for Action." *Report to Committee on Energy and Commerce*, Washington, D.C. (J. Taylor).

: Review of infant mortality rates in Michigan and proposals for addressing high rates of black infant deaths, developing maternal and child preventive health services, and a national review of current infant mortality rates.

April 1984 to September 1985
Reorganization of Michigan Department of Public Health in which Division of Maternal and Child Health was regionalized.
Institution of Prenatal Postpartum Care program establishing these services as a basic right.

Continued newspaper articles on infant mortality.

September 1985
"Improved pregnancy outcomes through a focused program of surveillance and intervention." Funded one-year proposal from the Michigan Department of Public Health. (John Waller, Jr., Dr.PH., Director, Detroit Health Department and Chairman, Department of

Community Medicine, Wayne State University; Paul Giblin, Ph.D., Department of Pediatrics, Children's Hospital of Michigan and Wayne State University; Marilyn Poland, Ph.D., R.N., Department of Obstetrics and Gynecology, Hutzel Hospital and Wayne State University).

: Project to assess correlates of infant mortality and to develop an outreach program to enhance health care seeking.

December 1985
Establishment of Maternal and Child Health Advisory Committee, Michigan Department of Public Health (M. Poland, member).

: Comprehensive reviews of maternal and child health programs.

June 1986
"Maternal child advocates for improved pregnancy and infant health outcomes." (Funded three-year proposal from Michigan Department of Public Health to J. Waller, P. Giblin, M. Poland).

: Outreach program to foster prenatal and infant health seeking employing paraprofessional staff.

June 1986
"Babies born to die: State fails to get prenatal care to mothers" (Jane Daugherty, *Detroit Free Press*).

: Review of continuing high rates of infant mortality charging the Michigan Department of Public Health with delayed implementation of Prenatal Postpartum Care Program.

July 1986
Establishment of Infant Mortality Task Force, Gloria Smith, Ph.D., Director, Michigan Department of Public Health (M. Poland, Chair, Subcommittee on Access to Prenatal Care, J. Waller, member).

: Development of proposals to reduce Michigan's infant mortality rates.

October 1986
"Increasing access to prenatal care through problem identification and program evaluation." (Funded three-year proposal from Ford Foundation to P. Giblin, M. Poland, J. Waller).

: Expanded services and evaluation of state funded maternal advocate program.

4

Custody Mediation: Taking the Knowledge Act on the Policy Road

Linda Girdner

Working within the local community to disseminate knowledge and have it utilized is a grass-roots approach which involves direct contact with those who will be utilizing that knowledge on a daily basis.

Renato Rosaldo (1986) explains that the stories Ilongot hunters tell themselves about hunting reflect the nature of the hunting experience better than either a composite descriptive ethnographic account of the hunting process or an ethnoscientific classification of hunting. In the same way, my story about knowledge utilization in the area of child custody disputes will convey that experience and have greater utility than fitting that experience into a set of normative statements about or cognitive categories of applied anthropology.

My story focuses on my activities over the last decade in the area of child custody policies and practices. These activities relate to the acquisition, dissemination, and utilization of knowledge, and have been carried out in different contexts and in varying roles.

Research Methods and Context

My ongoing program of research has focused on policies and practices relating to child custody disputes between divorcing and divorced parents in the United States. My roles as researcher and practitioner have evolved and become intertwined over the years, and, thus, need to be understood in that context.

"Traditional" Fieldwork

My involvement began with research for my doctoral dissertation in anthropology. I was interested in examining the relationship between the legal criteria and the norms and symbols about gender and family which appeared in child custody hearings and how this interrelationship expressed an ideology of the family and formulated a code for conduct for parents. I received a Doctoral Dissertation Grant from The American University and a National Research Service Award from the National Institutes of Mental Health to conduct the research in 1978. That year NIMH considered "legal-mental health interactions" as an important funding priority. In my proposal I had said that I was interested in the possibility of becoming a "custody counselor" to help parents make these decisions.

The fieldwork took place in the circuit and family courts of a largely affluent, suburban county in the eastern United States. Fieldwork involved immersing myself in the "legal culture" of the courts for 18 months in 1978-79. I carried out the traditional ethnographic tasks of gaining entrée, establishing rapport, talking with informants, observing and recording behavior, and examining records. The primary methods of data collection were the direct observation and recording of contested child custody hearings, interviews with judges, commissioners, and attorneys, and the examination of legal documents and court records. Additional data came from informal talks with parents, witnesses, and attorneys while they waited in the courthouse prior to the hearing and during recesses, observations of their interactions during these times, and a concurrent year of participant observation at weekly meetings of a fathers' advocacy group (Girdner 1983).

In my dissertation I identified the legal rules and procedures which structured the discourse in these cases; the symbols of motherhood, fatherhood, and family which were manipulated; and the normative code for conduct about how to be a fit parent and how to raise children which was expressed. The cases were intellectually fascinating as data. As events happening to real people, I found them tragic and unnecessarily destructive. I was convinced that there had to be a better way to address this problem.

"Applied" Fieldwork

After my fieldwork I joined the first group to be trained by O.J. Coogler of the Family Mediation Association, known as the father of divorce mediation. Divorce mediation is a process in which a skilled neutral third party assists divorcing parents in managing their conflict and developing a settlement agreement on the property, support and custody issues of divorce. Custody mediation focuses on the parenting rights and responsibilities with the dual goals of helping the family restructure itself and develop a written parenting agreement. Custody mediation includes educating the parents about the effect of divorce on children and the various custody arrangements possible, then assisting them in making choices which are workable for their family.

After my training I worked for two years at the Divorce and Marital Stress Clinic in Arlington, Virginia, as the Coordinator of Mediation Services. I worked as a mediator in divorce settlements, spoke to lay and professional groups in promoting mediation as an alternative to the destructive conflict of adversarial litigation, became a mediation trainer and supervisor for the Family Mediation Association, and was active in the newly developing local and national organizations of mediators.

My activities during this time seemed that of the quintessential applied anthropologist. I was involved in a process that was to empower people to take control over their own lives, to help them make decisions on the basis of their values rather than having decisions imposed upon them. My understanding of American kinship, gender roles, law, and disputing processes gained from my anthropological study and my fieldwork in the courts were put into practice in this setting.

During this time I continued to think critically about this new practice of mediation. Critical thinking included double consciousness (Bruner 1986), being able to participate while remaining as an observer, and observing myself in the context of the ongoing action. Critical thinking also meant that I distinguished between ideological statements and practical realities. This type of critical thinking and reflexivity are so much a part of me that I sometimes forget that it is my training as an anthropologist which honed these already present tendencies. However, I was dismayed at the lack of these abilities among many of the professionals within the mediation movement. It seemed to me that this kind of thinking was necessary, not as an intellectual exercise, but as a means of examining one's own behavior and ideology which directs the way in which one practices--the way in which one intervenes with families.

I consider this phase as part of my fieldwork in mediation, and this experience affected my previous research in that I included a section in my dissertation on policy alternatives, briefly examining the benefits and pitfalls of mediation and joint custody. The knowledge I gained during my two years working as a mediator were to provide the foundation for the work I was to do in Illinois. In addition, the skills and experience I gained as a staff member of a mental health clinic were invaluable in effectively promoting the utilization of that knowledge.[1]

In 1981 I decided that I needed to remove myself as an active participant in the field in order to develop my thoughts of what the practice of mediation involved and what was happening in the mediation movement. My motivations included taking a break from the emotional intensity of working as a divorce mediator, making a contribution to the field through research and teaching which were possible in an academic environment, and utilizing my knowledge to promote mediation in a different part of the country. After receiving my Ph.D., I accepted a joint appointment at the Institute for Child Behavior and Development and the Department of Human Development and Family Ecology at the University of Illinois at Urbana-Champaign.

The Knowledge Base

At the University of Illinois I continued with the analysis of my doctoral research and followed through on several ideas which arose out of my experience as a divorce mediator. My work was presented at professional meetings (1982) and published in edited volumes and professional journals (1985a, 1985b, 1986a, 1986b, 1987, 1988). Here I will highlight the most significant aspects of the knowledge base derived from my analysis of the mediation field. In most cases mediation is more appropriate than litigation as a process for determining the custody of children. Parents who are empowered to make their own decisions are more likely to adhere to them than decisions imposed upon them by a judge. Mediation involves a delicate balance between empowerment and social control, which is endangered by many mediators having a bias toward joint custody, since that can restrict the degree of empowerment the parties have in making their decisions. Power imbalances in mediation can potentially lead to agreements reflecting relationships of dominance and acquiescence, which could lead to "blaming the victim." Lawyer-mediators and therapist-mediators operate with different theoretical orientations which affect the emphasis they place on various characteristics in mediation. I had begun my research examining child custody litigation, which led me to mediation as a policy alternative. My experiences in the mediation field, in turn, gave me a better and more complex understanding of mediation as a policy and a practice.

Knowledge is socially constructed. Knowledge relating to a social problem reflects notions of causality and interconnection. Social problems are dialectical and paradoxical in nature, and the tendency to use convergent reasoning leads often to two opposing solutions (Rappaport 1981). Policy debates often hinge upon these different solutions, each based on one side of the paradox. Thus, knowledge in relation to policy is not "objective information." I was interested in utilizing knowledge and having others utilize knowledge which recognized the dialectical nature of the social problem and was based more on convergent reasoning. This is reflected in my concern over the balance between empowerment and social control in mediation. First, the general body of knowledge about mediation in divorce and custody disputes already includes a redefinition of the custody problem, based on one side of the paradox. Divorce is seen as a normative family transition, parents as more appropriate decision-makers than the courts, and traditional gender roles are de-emphasized. Thus, the most objective level of information about mediation is a cultural reconstruction, which potentially redistributes power and responsibility. Secondly, my work involves the analysis of policies and practices involving the development and implementation of mediation services; thus, I interpret, criticize, and recommend based on my perception of how these policies and practices conform to the values and principles which they are meant to reflect, such as empowering families to make their own decisions, preventing the divorce process from creating victims, and providing checks and balances so professionals do not overstep their roles in helping families.

My decision to publish in the *Journal of Divorce*, *Mediation Quarterly*, and in edited volumes assured me greater access to mediators and other practitioners in the divorce field. I chose these outlets because they have greater potential for knowledge utilization.

Utilization Methods and Impacts

During the time that I was conducting research and writing on mediation policies and practices, I also was involved in utilizing that knowledge with the goal of developing mediation within the community and the state. Divorce and custody mediation essentially did not exist in Illinois when I came in 1981. Since then it has developed more or less independently in three counties: Cook, McLean, and Champaign. My activities have been aimed at knowledge utilization in the Champaign-Urbana community and to professionals on a statewide basis.

Looking back I can see that the success of my efforts has been based largely on three factors: my personal commitment and enthusiasm, the cumulative effect of various activities over an extended period which led to a dense network of active people, and other external factors which led to the readiness of divergent groups to utilize this knowledge. Three phases of knowledge utilization are evident in this case. The educational phase was primarily from 1981 through 1983. It was followed by the developmental phase from 1984 through 1986. Finally, 1987 brought the beginning of the implementation phase.

The Educational Phase

There are three types of activities which have been important to the educational phase of knowledge utilization. These are classroom teaching, presentations and workshops to professionals, and presentations to the lay public.

I taught divorce and custody mediation since 1982 in the Department of Human Development and Family Ecology at the University of Illinois and had developed a graduate specialization in that field. Most of the students were enrolled in masters' programs in family studies and social work, as well as some from the College of Law. In addition, several practicing mental health professionals from the community had enrolled in my courses as nondegree students. Several of the degree and nondegree students remaining in the area were to become active in the development of mediation in Champaign County.

One set of activities directed to the lay public were talks aimed at specific populations. These included a talk for parents on the effect of divorce on children, sponsored by the East Central Illinois Association for the Education of Young Children; one on co-parenting and custody to the local chapter of Parents without Partners, one on divorce mediation to the YWCA-sponsored UI Women's Forum, and later to the local chapter of the National Organization of Women. In addition I spoke on negotiation skills for women at the meeting of the Champaign-Urbana Women's Network and the Twin Cities Business and Professional Women's Organization. Although many of these talks did not focus on mediation in divorce and custody disputes per se, they covered related issues, which provided exposure for myself and mediation. Most of these talks were during 1982, when my aim was to "spread the word" locally about divorce and custody mediation, since most people had never heard of it before.

Another set of activities directed at the general public concerned media coverage, developed through a combination of assertive efforts and network ties. New developments and particularly human interest stories relating to a social problem are desirable commodities to those in the media industry. Many have policies of not promoting a particular individual's business, so I needed to assure them that I was not selling anything, but rather wanted to shed light on a new way of helping families, or a new controversial profession or policy. I first contacted the local free weekly newspaper, which ran a story on mediation. Then I met a psychiatrist who hosts a late night call-in television show, so I suggested that he have me as a guest along with an attorney. Later I was an invited guest on daytime call-in radio shows operated by the local public broadcasting station. A local television station news reporter interviewed me on child-snatching and custody in 1982. The University of Illinois News Bureau interviewed me for an article which was published in the local newspaper as well as a few others in the region. They followed the article with a telephone interview which was converted to a short radio spot sent to several stations in the midwest.

The difficulty with the media as a channel for knowledge dissemination is that you do not know how people will misinterpret, change, or distort the knowledge. With reporters, I have asked that they call me and read the article over the phone before it is printed. Although some are willing to do this, most state that their paper's "policy" prohibits it. I think that media coverage facilitates a particular issue being seen as legitimate and worthwhile. Local newspapers, radio, and television have provided important exposure for mediation and my activities in this field. Those who know me or have heard me speak before have that knowledge and the network tie reinforced by subsequent media events.

My educational activities geared to the professional audiences have included the academic, mental health, and legal communities. I was invited as a colloquia speaker by several university units, including the School of Social Work, the Department of Psychology, the Psychological Clinic, and the College of Law. I also instituted the Family Mediation Forum, a series of educational seminars relating to divorce and mediation. I presented several topics on mediation and invited other speakers, drawing on professors and practitioners, to discuss related topics, such as budget counseling in divorce, legal aspects of divorce, and gender issues in marital therapy. The attendance at the meetings averaged about 25, including students, faculty, mental health professionals, and attorneys. Some of the people who attended these early meetings were to become leading figures in the community effort to promote mediation.

The invitation to speak at the School of Social Work had been extended by Shirley Wattenberg, a professor in the School who had heard of me through a mutual colleague. After the colloquium, Shirley and I met regularly to discuss our common interests. She was knowledgeable in the area of children's experience and adjustment in divorce. We decided to take our knowledge on the road by offering one-day workshops to introduce custody mediation to legal and mental health professionals. With the help of the University of Illinois Division of Continuing Education we presented a one-day workshop in Decatur, Illinois, in November 1982 and Rockford, Illinois, in March 1983. The workshops were well-attended, but due to our other commitments we decided not to plan any further ones.

In February 1982 I presented a talk on divorce mediation as part of a program on displaced homemakers for Cooperative Extension workers through TeleNet. TeleNet is a state-wide communications system used for the continuing education of cooperative extension workers, originating in the College of Agriculture at the University of Illinois. Many of these workers specialize in the area of family life and child development and are important sources of information, especially in rural communities.

In 1983 I was invited to speak on divorce and custody mediation to two professional organizations. The first was at the annual conference of the Illinois Association of Community Mental Health Agencies. This occasion arose when the organizer heard about me through the woman who had organized my TeleNet talk. Later that year I spoke at the annual meeting of the Illinois State Bar Association (ISBA) Family Law Section.[2] This second opportunity arose out of several network contacts and activities. I was recommended as a speaker by a judge who had participated in one of my workshops.

The Illinois State Bar Association Family Law Section meeting was a watershed in many ways. I was flattered to be asked to be the speaker at their annual meeting. I had some doubts about the genuine interest of some of the attorneys when I learned that the meeting was scheduled in Champaign-Urbana every year on the same day as an important football game. I was delighted to find that they were a knowledgeable, thoughtful, and challenging audience. In the audience were Roberta Johnson, Robert Finch, Holly Jordan, and the Honorable Judge Harry Clem, all who were to become instrumental actors in the development of court-referred mediation in Champaign County.

I consider 1983 to be the end of the educational phase, since my activities after that point were geared more to having a direct impact on policy development and implementation. These activities could not have taken place without the groundwork that was laid, both in terms of the network which I had established and the knowledge which had been disseminated.

The Developmental Phase

Subsequent to my presentation to the ISBA Family Law Section, I was asked to consult with members of the Family Law Section Council on the development of standards for practice for family mediators in the state of Illinois. One member, a local judge with whom I later worked closely in the creation of the Champaign County program, described my contribution to the task as follows:

> Dr. Girdner graciously agreed to consult with the Council, provided us access to her extensive research in alternative dispute resolution techniques and gave us invaluable advice in regard to the standards which the Council ultimately formulated. The Council's proposal, denominated "Standards and Principals (sic) for Family Dispute Mediation," was adopted by the Board of Governors of the Illinois State Bar Association on July 13, 1984. The standards have been implemented in a number of courts in Illinois that have ongoing divorce mediation programs (Clem 1987).

One of the important aspects of knowledge utilization that I learned in this experience is that if the conditions are right one can have an impact with very little time investment. My task involved reading their initial draft of the standards and suggesting revisions. The draft was a well-prepared document; they had talked with others in preparing it, including the attorney responsible for drafting the standards recommended by a committee of the American Bar Association. In a few hours, I could apply the knowledge I had to this particular task, write my suggestions, and explain them so that the Council members could understand the reasoning behind them.

In 1984 and 1985 my energies turned from the local level to greater participation in the dispute resolution field on the national level. I became a member of the Editorial Board of a new journal, the *Mediation Quarterly*, and a member of the Education and Training Committee of the Academy of Family Mediators. I also was a member of the steering committee of the National Conference on Peacemaking and Conflict Resolution. These activities enhanced my reputation in the field and, thus, lent more credibility to my expertise in the community and state.

In 1985 circumstances in Champaign County changed, making conditions ripe for the development of mediation. The ISBA Family Law Section Council encouraged county family law committees to become more active in policy development and implementation. In Champaign County the former committee members resigned and new members took their places. These included Holly Jordan, chair of the committee, the Honorable Judge Clem, and Robert Finch. All three had heard me speak at the ISBA meeting in 1983 and were interested in promoting mediation in the county. Judge Clem also was an active member of the ISBA Family Law Section Council. The committee decided to make the development of custody mediation their top priority.

In the fall of 1985 Robert Finch asked me if I would be willing to mediate a difficult post-divorce custody dispute. He was representing the father, Holly Jordan was representing the mother, and Judge Clem was the judge involved in the case. They felt that this case would be a good "test case" for mediation. I agreed to take the case under certain conditions, but explained that it was unwise to set it up as a test case, since it was very likely that a protracted post-divorce case like this one would not be successful in mediation. In that eventuality, I did not want them to think then that mediation was not worthwhile. I did mediate the case and the custody issue was satisfactorily resolved.

As I began teaching my family mediation course in the fall of 1985, I encouraged my students to make contact with the Family Law Committee and to develop a project which would be useful for them and appropriate for the course. Roberta Johnson, a third year law student, chose to pursue this. She had also heard me speak on mediation in 1983 and had planned since that time to take my course in her last year. The Family Law Committee suggested that she examine possible models for developing mediation in the county. I suggested some people she could contact, who suggested others, and she was able to gather relevant information. Her final paper focused on a comparison between the court-connected mediation program in Cook County and a recently instituted court-referred program in McLean County. She recommended that Champaign develop a program more similar to that in McClean County.

Roberta Johnson continued her activities with the Family Law Committee after my class was over and became an official member of the committee after completing law school in 1986. The committee decided to create a mediation task force to spearhead the development and implementation of a court-referred mediation program. Invitations to the first meeting were sent out to attorneys, therapists, social service agencies, county board members, and many other community members. The first meeting consisted of a panel presentation by Judge Knecht, Dr. Lynelle Hale, Judge Clem, and me. My talk provided an explanation of mediation, Judge Knecht and Dr. Hale explained how their newly instituted program was working in McLean County, and Judge Clem explained how we would like to develop it in Champaign. Those present had the opportunity to ask questions and sign up for committees of the task force, including the standards committee, community education committee, and the training course arrangement committee. Policies were made and activities were coordinated by the steering committee of the task force, which consisted of two attorneys (Robert Finch and Roberta Johnson), two psychologists (Louisa Zink and Betty Scott), and two social workers (Paulette Johnson and Dana Strandberg). One of each category was a former student of mine. I was also a member of the steering committee and acted primarily as a consultant during the developmental phase.

The standards committee, headed by Judge Clem and Roberta Johnson, had the task of developing the standards and procedures for the county court-referred mediation program. I was asked to review the standards and many of my suggestions were reflected in the final version. First, the mediator's report to the court does not need to include any descriptions of the sessions, thus protecting the integrity of the mediation process. Second, Roberta Johnson and I both were aware of the growing concerns of feminist groups about women being referred or ordered into mediation with their battering husbands. Thus, we included in the standards that cases should not be referred to mediation where there has been child or spousal abuse or if one or both parents is chemically dependent to the extent that it interferes with mediation. Third, a high standard of professional entry was established for court-approved mediators.

I consulted with the training arrangement committee about various mediators who might be brought in to train local professionals in custody mediation. On my recommendation, the decision was made to invite Dr. Isolina Ricci, a national recognized custody mediator and author of *Mom's House/Dad's House* (1980). It was the last training she was to give as a private trainer, since she soon became Coordinator of Family Court Services for the State of California.

The training was scheduled for two 20-hour weekend sessions in October and November of 1986. I conducted a segment of the training and worked with Dr. Ricci in small group exercises and discussions. The trainees were primarily local professionals, including social workers, psychologists, and attorneys. Several were former students of mine.

The plan for the court-referred mediation program was that any custody dispute filed after a certain date would be referred to mediation. The parties would be able to choose their mediator from the list of court-approved mediators. They would be required to attend an orientation session, during which mediation would be explained to them and after which they could decide whether or not they chose to mediate. This system promotes mediation as an alternative to litigation, but still allows each party to decide, after being exposed to mediation, whether or not to pursue it.

We decided to develop a packet of materials, including an explanation of the court-referred program, the standards and procedures, the list of mediators, and an information form provided by each mediator. I developed the information form, which provided data on the fees, education, and experience of each mediator as well as a statement of his or her aims and goals in mediation. This form provided a better basis for comparison across mediators by prospective clients and avoided the extraneous materials and bulkiness of resumés and vitas. The focus was on how we can systematize the process in a way which meets the needs of the clients.

The steering committee also developed a tentative list of new committees which would enhance the success of mediation in the community. I became chair of the continuing education committee, responsible for the ongoing professional development of the mediators.

The developmental phase put into place the necessary infrastructure for the Champaign County court-referred program. During this phase, I worked primarily as the consulting expert. Much of the time-consuming work was done by the members of the committees, some of whom put in hundreds of hours of unpaid labor. The next step was the implementation of the program.

The Implementation Phase

The implementation phase involved several tasks. Mediators submitted their information forms by January 15, 1987. Packets were made up and disseminated to court offices, attorneys, social service agencies, therapists in private practice, churches, hospitals, police departments, and other community organizations in the county. The court-referred program was officially implemented on February 2, 1987, which means that any custody case filed in the court after that date will be referred to mediation, if appropriate.

The transition from the development to the implementation phase for the mediation program was a time of conflict for the steering committee. The goals of the development phase were shared and clear-cut. Now that these goals had been met, the task force was involved in identifying the priorities and goals for the coming year. This led to the emergence of differences in perceptions and interests, which made these meetings more difficult. At the same time, the strain of long hours of volunteer work and not enough recognition was beginning to take its toll.

As goals and priorities were clarified and agreed upon, the committee was able to move forward in a more unified manner.

We had another general meeting of the task force, inviting community members to join the task force committees. At that meeting, I provided an overview about mediation and Judge Clem described the court-referred program. Our goal was not only to explain how the court-referred program worked, but also to educate the community about mediation and promote its use by divorcing and divorced parents before they get to the point of filing a suit. The next meeting involved the election of new members to the task force.

I then worked with the research and evaluation committee of the Mediation Task Force to design an evaluation research project to assess the mediation program. This particular study focused more on quantitative variables, which was information needed by the court and the Task Force to assess the program. I left Illinois before the evaluation project was completed.

Success and Circumstance

I consider my efforts to have made a significant impact. This view is shared by others, such as Judge Clem (1987), who stated that: "In significant part, through Dr. Girdner's efforts, the task force's work was successful and a child custody/visitation divorce mediation program was implemented in our county on February 2, 1987." In addition, I was asked to be the keynote speaker at a conference on court-ordered mediation in Illinois, the purpose of which was to interest judges across the state in utilizing the knowledge we had about developing and implementing court-referred and court-connected mediation programs.

This was not a short-term project, nor did I do it alone. There are several factors which contributed to the success of the project. First of all, I was in a position as a faculty member to engage in public service activities without needing to depend on consulting fees or honorarium for my economic survival. I had other responsibilities, so I was not able to engage in these activities full-time. This coordinated well with the pace of change in the midwest, which often is slower than on the coasts. Considering my experiences with relatively rapid change (almost "fadism") in the Washington, D.C., area, I had found this difficult at first. However, I later realized that this allowed for more reasoned examination of the consequences of custody mediation policies and practices instituted elsewhere and, therefore, the capacity to utilize that knowledge in circumventing problems here.

Secondly, Champaign-Urbana is a university town with a population of about 100,000. The professionals within the community in academic, legal, and mental health fields form a dense network of relationships, including neighborhood, organizational, and kinship affiliations. Teaching my classes, speaking at academic colloquia, practitioner meetings, and local community organizations, and taking advantage of media opportunities created for me a network of people who became interested and knowledgeable about mediation. Some of these people committed themselves to going beyond just acquiring this knowledge to utilizing it for the purpose of helping divorcing parents and their children. A few of these people were in positions of power and responsibility. Without the interest and commitment of Judge Harry Clem, Associate Judge of the Circuit Court of Champaign County, the court-referred program would never have developed. The members of the Family Law Committee took an active role to promote the development of the task force and the mediation program. In many communities, lawyers have worked against mediation rather than for it. Primarily members of the mental health community made the commitment in time and money to train as mediators and to take on a new professional role. The task force steering committee involved the combined efforts of lawyers and therapists. The institutionalization of a new human service in a community is a monumental task and necessitates the coordination of many segments of the community.

Conclusions and Recommendations

In *Applied Anthropology*, John van Willigen (1986:144) discusses policy as a complex process "carried out in the political arena in which there is much competition for resources." The policy process can also be carried out through the judicial arena, which has been relatively neglected as an important policy-making body by those interested in the utilization of research. The policy process also takes place within the social arena of human services, as professionals redefine their policies and practices to address the needs of particular populations. Working within the local community to disseminate knowledge and have it utilized is a grass-roots approach which involves direct contact with those who will be utilizing that knowledge on a daily basis. The evaluation of local projects can then be added to the knowledge base to affect policy on the statewide level. My impression is that the policy process in the legislative arena is more polarized and ideologically loaded, which has an impact on the way in which knowledge is utilized.

The Champaign County Court-referred Program was possible because successful efforts were made to educate the practitioners, develop a cadre of new professional mediators, and gain the acceptance and approval of the court. I chose to focus on the local judiciary rather than the legislative branch in promoting child custody mediation. The judiciary often responds more quickly, is more directly responsible for the actual implementation, and is not stymied by lobbying groups. Recent changes in Illinois statutes will facilitate the court-referred mediation program but were not indispensable to its existence. As of January 1987 the new custody law states that it is assumed to be in the best interests of the child to maintain a continuing relationship with both parents, that the parents should develop a joint parenting agreement which details their responsibilities, and that if they cannot do that on their own the court has the power to order them into mediation. Although the court had the power to order mediation before, according to judicial procedure, this statute makes it explicit and thus reaffirms the idea. Although the Champaign County Court-referred Program would have existed anyway, the new law provided the impetus for other courts to learn about mediation and to consider instituting similar programs in their counties.

My involvement in the policy process can be explained in terms of the six stages proposed by van Willigen (1986:144). I began with an *awareness of need*, based on my dissertation research on child custody litigation, that there needed to be a better way for divorcing parents to resolve conflicts over the custody of their children. I became aware of *alternative solutions*, such as custody mediation, which would address that need. I trained as a mediator, worked in that capacity, and became knowledgeable of the various ways in which mediation was being practiced by different professionals and in different parts of the country, which involved *the evaluation of alternative solutions*. My credibility in the mediation field is not as an anthropologist, but as an expert on mediation. I recommend that other anthropologists pursue the appropriate training or certification for the fields in which they are working.

The next stage for me, which van Willigen does not include separately, was *knowledge dissemination*. In Illinois, I engaged in activities which were to raise the consciousness of professionals and the public about the need for mediation as a more humane way of addressing the problem of contested custody disputes. My teaching and public service activities were geared toward the dissemination of knowledge. My research activities focused on the evaluation of these policies and practices. The knowledge was disseminated to people in the community through teaching, speaking engagements, and media events. I suggest that anthropologists interested in the policy process consider the importance of knowledge dissemination through other means than written reports and articles. My written work did not have the impact that the above activities did.

The next step was the *formulation of policy* by those who were committed to utilizing that knowledge. The judiciary, the Family Law Committee, and the Mediation Task Force came together to develop a court-referred program, to institute standards and procedures, and to organize the training of qualified mediators. I served primarily as a consultant during that phase. Without the network-building over the years there would not have been the wide-spread community interest nor credibility for my role. Anthropologists have a good understanding of social networks and need to use that knowledge and develop skills in network building as a means of achieving their goals in the policy process.

The *implementation of the policy* incorporated many of the recommendations I arrived at after evaluating custody policies and practices in other parts of the country. My national network of contacts in the mediation field helped in this endeavor, especially since publications lag behind the latest information. And again, my credibility and expertise in the field and in the community lent weight to my recommendations. The last step in the policy process is the *evaluation of the implementations*, which I helped develop and was carried on by others.

Notes

1. I would like to thank the staff at the Divorce and Marital Stress Clinic for their support and guidance in socializing me to the nonacademic world of human services, especially Emily Brown, Director, Marge DePriest, and Florence Millstein.

2. The Illinois State Bar Association Family Law Section Council is a committee of lawyers and judges chosen to represent the interests of the 3,000 members of the Family Law Section of the state bar. The Council reviews proposed family law legislation, publishes a bi-monthly newsletter, and undertakes special projects at the request of the Board of Governors of the Illinois State Bar Association. In 1983, the Board asked the Council to examine mediation in family disputes. Therefore, they chose that topic for their annual meeting.

5

Policymaking Roles for Applied Anthropologists: Personally Ensuring That Your Research Is Used

M. Jean Gilbert

The most basic rule for getting my research used: make specific kinds of data available as directly as possible to those who can apply it in the course of work they do.

In the fall of 1986, the President-elect of the American Anthropological Association, Roy Rappaport, articulated to the Association as a whole a need to "undertake a broad program to increase both public awareness of anthropology and anthropology's influence on public affairs" (Rappaport 1986:1). In proposing this undertaking, Rappaport was expressing for the entire field of anthropology a need to ensure that the theories and findings of anthropological research have impact on human affairs, most particularly on the amelioration of social problems. This is an issue with which applied anthropologists have been wrestling for some time, and perhaps it is indicative of the growing influence of this segment of the discipline that the need for a stronger anthropological voice in the public ear is being felt. In addition, there is an increasing and well-founded conviction that the perspectives and data of anthropology have a great deal to contribute to the resolution of many social problems. How then do we better make ourselves heard?

Rappaport called for a discipline-wide programmatic approach to educating the public about anthropology's potential contribution to "matters of public significance and enlarging anthropology's role in public affairs." While heartily endorsing this call for a collective initiative, I believe efforts in these directions must also go forward at the individual level. If the utility of anthropological theory, methods, and findings is to receive practical consideration from those who make decisions on how human problems are resolved, we will have to carry our message to them personally and consistently. This can't be done by remaining on the periphery of the policymaking process and feeding in written data.   This paper argues for the individual anthropologist's responsibility to seek and accept the role of part-time policymaker as a major strategy in improving the use of anthropological research in the making of policy decisions.   Anthropology will have a wider role in public affairs only when anthropologists enact roles in public affairs. The question is: How do we go about doing this? What public roles are available to us? On what basis will we be sought after as policymakers?

My own experience over the past fifteen years suggests that opportunities to increase use of anthropological research through participation in the policymaking process is a natural outgrowth of doing problem-oriented research. The following discussion, therefore, is not a case study focused on a single piece of research; rather it is grounded in my experience of an ongoing process through which related applied research projects opened up opportunities for me to bring data and anthropological perspectives into several policymaking arenas in the public health field.   While in no way minimizing the importance of strategies undertaken to maximize use of specific research findings in the design of particular problem solving programs, I wish to illustrate how the researcher can use his or her *cumulative* research findings, experiences and skills in a wide array of policy-affecting situations.

Methods and Context:
Progressive Research in Human Service Arenas

Several characteristics of the research I conducted facilitated entry into policy-shaping roles. First, all of my research was focused on one ethnic group, Mexican Americans, either alone or in comparison with other groups. All projects took place in California and all were in one way or another public service-related. Mexican Americans comprise a significant proportion of the California population, and the group is rapidly increasing in size and in its need for services. Policymakers and service providers are under some pressure to devise effective and efficient means of delivering services to this population. Yet many who are in a position to plan and implement services have little knowledge or understanding of Mexican American culture and its variations. Thus the need for information on which to base culturally appropriate services is great.

Each of the succeeding research projects built on the findings of the previous research and allowed me to deepen and widen my cumulative information base with respect to Mexican Americans. All except one project were researcher initiated--that is, I conceived, designed, and proposed the projects based on what I perceived were research needs in discrete public service arenas.

My first study, in 1974 (Gilbert 1978, 1980), funded by the National Institute on Education, looked at family exchange and interaction among 120 second-generation Mexican American rural and urban families. A segment of this research examined how these families articulated with the school systems in whose districts they lived. Both qualitative and quantitative data gathering strategies were used: a structured survey interview and participant observation in family activities. Key informant interviewing was also undertaken with educators, clergymen, civic leaders, and naturally occurring information brokers.

The second piece of research, again funded by a federal agency, the Office of Child Development in 1978, was an examination of child-related service utilization patterns of Mexican American families, focusing on persons or agencies serving a gatekeeper function (Gilbert and Carlos 1979). Structured interviewing of parents and key informant interviews with human service providers and gatekeepers comprised the major data-gathering techniques.

A third research project, a 1976 study of Latino alcohol use patterns, was funded by the California Office of Alcohol and Drug Programs (Alcocer and Gilbert 1979). For this three-community study the state required an ethnographic component prior to the fielding of a household survey. Designing and implementing this component for a research and development firm was my first experience in rapid research design and in training and fielding several multidisciplinary research teams to do structured and systematic observations in natural settings. As a result of this research, I made my initial contacts with policymakers at the state level as I learned that California state contracts were very much more closely monitored than federal research grants and that there was a great deal of interaction with monitoring persons.

The next two research projects, a study of support networks utilized by Anglo and Mexican American couples at the birth of their first child, funded by the National Institute of Mental Health from 1979 to 1981, and a study of alcohol use patterns among Anglo and Mexican American couples, supported in 1982 to 1984 by the National Institute on Alcohol Abuse and Alcoholism (Gilbert 1980, 1985), continued my focus on such issues as the use of formal and informal support systems, parenting, family relations, and alcohol use. Participant observation, case studies, structured interviews, respondent diaries, family histories, and key informant interviewing were the data-gathering techniques used in these studies.

During 1987-1988, working in residential treatment centers for Mexican American men and women suffering alcohol-related problems, I used structured diagnostic instruments, acculturation scales, and cognitive assessment instruments in addition to observational methods. Support for this project came from University of California intramural sources.

When this type of research progression occurs, the result is not unlike that of restudies of a cultural group. However, each separate research effort requires focusing very intensely on one set of behaviors, such as child care practices or drinking behavior, and looking at this specific set of behaviors as it is integrated into the culture *and* as it relates to the service-providing instrumentalities of the larger society. As research progresses in this fashion, it also becomes easier to identify the policy-related applications of one's findings for those who can translate the data into programs.

Utilization Strategies and Impact

Research as a Point of Entry into the Policymaking Process: Laying the Groundwork

The process of conducting applied research over a long period of time allows the researcher to acquire an in-depth understanding of how human services function and are staffed and organized. These understandings are essential to assuming policy-affecting roles. As one's research focus shifts from one arena to another as mine has, one is brought into close contact with policymakers and providers associated with different facets of the human services community. Thus my first research project allowed me to work with educators, parent/school advisory groups, and school boards. My next research afforded interaction with many child-related public services: e.g., child care centers, recreational programs, rehabilitation agencies, and juvenile justice facilities. My first-baby study further intensified that interaction with a concentration on services and personnel associated with childbirth: obstetricians, pediatricians, midwives, childbirth educators, breastfeeding advocacy groups, parenting groups, hospitals, and clinics. Finally, alcohol-related research has acquainted me with the services associated with the substance abuse field: detox centers, recovery homes, outpatient clinics, referral centers, self-help groups, and the like. And, of course, one learns about the work of "umbrella" agencies such as family and community service centers.

As one moves slowly from sector to sector, one becomes familiar with the different philosophies and perspectives which shape services in each service area. It becomes apparent, too, that each service sector is organized differently and faces different service delivery problems. One learns about the kinds of resources which support the different services and the mechanisms through which that support is mediated. One observes the communication channels (or lack thereof) across public service sectors and about divisions, informal or formal, across these sectors. For example, I often, through knowledge of referral patterns, became familiar with coalitions and competitions among service providers and was able to identify barriers to service utilization.

Also important is learning the jargon of service provision, e.g., intervention, casefinding, prevention (primary, secondary, tertiary), intake, case review, risk factors. Overall, one becomes conversant in the language of policymakers and familiar with their culture, making it much easier to make the transition from the researcher role to the policymaker role when the opportunity presents itself.

Having these various types of information is very important in communicating research findings as one assumes non-research roles. It became clear to me, for example, that different types of data are more useful, and therefore received more readily, at different levels of the service providing structure. Local level providers are interested in the specific mechanisms of information brokering in their locale. Clinicians are eager to know how local variation in extended family structure affects use of mental health services and how variations in kinds of kin available can affect the course of therapy. County or state level administrators are more concerned with epidemiological generalizations and the overall patterning of service usage. I learned what, for me, has been the most basic rule for getting my research used: make specific kinds of data available as *directly* as possible to those who can apply it in the course of work they do. This almost certainly involves personal contact between the anthropologist and the potential data user.

I learned early on that the integration of qualitative and quantitative methods is a research strategy that produces data especially amenable to dissemination when one assumes a policymaking or training role. Descriptive statistics, statistical tests, and generalizations drawn from survey treatments are important to policymakers who must rationalize programs to taxpaying constituencies. Case studies and contextual materials derived from qualitative methods flesh out and make concrete the generalizations drawn from the survey data, give insight into contrary findings, and make clear that the data is grounded in research with real people and their problems, not a view from the "ivory tower." Further, close contact with key informants who work with the population under scrutiny, either in formal and informal capacities, strengthens one's ties to the community infrastructure and make later dissemination of findings easier.

At the end of my first research effort, I returned to the research sites to share my findings with various groups, organizations, and individuals who had helped me and had demonstrated an interest in the research. This is an essential first step in getting one's research used because it establishes the researcher as a person knowledgeable in subjects pertinent to community activities and needs and also underscores the researcher's ongoing interest in the community. Most important, community-based workers who often have the greatest need for the kind of information produced by one's research do not have ready access to the scholarly journals in which research findings are usually published. They are very much more likely than academics to rely on verbal presentations given at their workplace or organizational meetings.

During my work on the state-funded alcohol use project, I had the good fortune to make a number of excellent, long-standing contacts and friends at the state agency. Though this was more than ten years ago, I still keep them informed about the alcohol research I'm doing and about research done by colleagues that I think may be of special interest to them. They call me now and again with requests for information and ask me to serve in an advisory capacity on projects and panels. Maintenance of reciprocal and ongoing communication with the funders of one's previous research is therefore another strategy for keeping one's data "alive" and of creating interest in and potential use of current findings.

I have also learned that it's important to keep in touch with prior research colleagues. The public health professor with whom I worked on the state alcohol contract also has an intensely applied perspective; he recommends me often to speak to service providers or to give technical assistance based on my research. I do the same for him. Additionally several of my research projects have involved collaboration with clinical or social psychologists. My work with them has not only allowed me to broaden my theoretical and methodological perspectives, but has put me in touch with their associations and professional contacts. Consequently, I regularly present my findings to clinicians and mental health professionals.

Overall, then, the cumulative result of having done much research in a limited geographical region and on a number of health-related issues relative to a specific ethnic group is that (1) the body of information I have to draw on in consultant or advisory capacity is in-depth, interrelated and broad-based; (2) my network of contacts is extensive, ranging across several disciplines and through several fields within the public health sector; (3) I am in touch with the culture and language of the persons most likely to use my data in their decisionmaking; and (4) I've learned how service-related policy is made and have seized on a number of opportunities to participate in its making.

Policymaking Roles for Anthropologists

For the researcher interested in actively affecting the policy process, it is important, first of all, to recognize that policymaking in the human services is a dynamic process which involves (at the very least) the interaction of several sectors: (1) the administrators in charge of allocating funds and overall planning of services; (2) persons who actually provide the services, and often, (3) the service users themselves. Each of these categories of participants to the policymaking process exists at the local, county, state, and national levels. Further, information and funding passes among and across these groups and levels of organization. Funds filter down from federal to state to county to city through decision making at each level. Fact finding and information input are necessary and sought after at each level as well. There are opportunities for the researcher to contribute findings and perspectives to each of these sectors and levels though the means of entry and access differ. Entry into local level policymaking entities often precedes movement into groups with a wider geopolitical sphere of influence. To see how this is so, let's take a look at how each sector (i.e., administrative planners and funders, service providers, and user groups) is constituted and what kind of role the researcher can play in the policymaking process at each level.

Roles in Funding and Planning: Much policy is made by the pocketbook, so bodies that determine how funds are allocated and who is to perform what services or research, when, and where are frequently the most critical actors in the policymaking process. Who are they? They include local, state, and national agency administrators, boards of directors, standing and special commissions, ad hoc oversight groups, and review panels. For the applied researcher, serving on such boards or with such groups is often an eye-opening object lesson in the fiscal, legal, political, and staffing realities of service provision. Policy-related decisions made by bodies of this kind determine service and research priorities, the type and location of services, the categories of staff that will be in service, and the degree to which a given service arena articulates with the broader array of human services.

How does a researcher initially become involved in these processes? Usually by being asked to *volunteer* time or being hired as a consultant. Frequently, for example, there exist opportunities to serve on the boards of directors of local non-profit service agencies. My research among Latino families at a day care center, for example, led to my being asked to serve on the board of directors. I was able to work with the director, the client families, and other community members in maintaining an agency policy which was sensitive to cultural differences prevalent in the client population. On this board I became well acquainted with persons involved with other non-profit service agencies in the region. Most of the people I worked with in my capacity as board member had never encountered an anthropologist, but they found my concrete knowledge of the community and its particular needs extremely helpful in the design of programs and articulation of needs to higher level decision-makers. For example, I went with the director and two other board members to a meeting with one of the county supervisors to make our case for revenue sharing funds. I included a small amount of my data on Mexican American families in my presentation. We got the money, but what is perhaps more interesting to me is that, when this same supervisor was up for re-election, he asked me to meet with him to give him a more in-depth briefing on the Latino community and its needs!

Local level involvement often leads to working with policymaking bodies with a wider purview. My own first associations next led to my being asked to serve on other agency boards and on regional commissions. County level commissions and advisory boards are involved in defining and describing regional needs and making recommendations and requests for the allocation of funds (always in short supply and competitively sought) to create or modify programs to answer those needs. An anthropologist can provide data which affect those recommendations, both in terms of program structure and cost of implementation. The researcher's intimate knowledge of a region, a specific service arena, and population composition are useful here, as are budgeting skills learned in research design and development. Information about how needs in a particular service area are perceived by a target population or knowledge of service utilization patterns prevalent in a target group are other kinds of information that can impact on policy made at this level.

In the medium-sized California city in which much of my research has been conducted, for example, there exist several neighborhoods densely populated by Mexican Americans. Some of these neighborhoods are dense enough to be termed *barrios*; others, while heavily Latino, are not. Though most of the areas overlap geographically to some extent, the neighborhoods vary distinctly in terms of the class, generation, and age of their Mexican American populations. A number of my fellow board members on an agency governing body, concerned about maximizing use of services by Mexican Americans, were unaware of the diversity in the city's ethnic population and unaware that this diversity was expressed in family structure and resource and information levels, with these factors in turn affecting service utilization patterns. I called attention to data resulting from two of my studies which suggested that proximity of services was important to the immigrant segment of the Latino population but much less important to later-generation persons, whatever their income level. I also pointed out those densely Latino neighborhoods where immigrants rather than later-generation persons lived. Making these factors clear was useful in a decision concerning placement of a service branch. I cannot say whether citing my research findings was *the* factor that swung the decision. However, the fact that there had been research, that there actually were concrete data that were meaningful in terms of the decision to be made was appreciatively and carefully considered. An important point to underscore here is that research findings presented in such situations are not necessarily going to be the linchpin of the decisionmaking process--at least most of the time. They will be weighed in with all the other factors that persons participating in the policymaking process feel are important. But one is there to see that they do get presented and considered, and one can personally make a case for their importance!

As a researcher's work extends and expands into several areas in the human services (and one's lists of publications, research reports and general visibility grows), other opportunities arise. In my own case, working on the state sponsored alcohol research led to a wide variety of new opportunities to work with policymakers in the alcoholism field. This has included sitting on review panels which determine which programs or services or research gets funded. In review work of this type, one's skills in designing, structuring, and timing large research projects are invaluable in judging the overall workability of proposed programs. Additionally, knowledge of a field or target group allows one to assess the feasibility or salience of a particular research or intervention strategy.

Confidentiality considerations preclude my discussing specific proposals, panels, and situations where the information I've brought to bear on decision making of this kind has been influential. I can say that my research among Latinos has, for example, disclosed a number of obstacles that need to be understood and overcome in doing successful survey research or effective service-related outreach among segments of this population. Further, my findings have also shown real gaps in service delivery and techniques for addressing specific needs of this group. These data have been helpful to the review panels I've worked on in identifying proposed demonstration or research projects that show a realistic grasp of research or service needs and feasible implementation strategies.

In addition to this kind of "bottom line" policymaking, there are opportunities to work with local, state, and national agencies in the business of planning and prioritizing general, long-term directions in a human service area. For example, I have worked this last year with the California Office of Alcohol and Drug Programs on a statewide committee which made recommendations for the structuring of new programs to be funded under the block grant set-aside for women's alcohol programs. My own knowledge of Latino women and their particular needs with respect to alcohol-related issues allowed me to advocate program definitions and approaches which showed responsiveness to those needs. I used data from several research projects to support my arguments. This year, too, I was given the opportunity to serve in an advisory capacity for the Women's Action Alliance, a group that is mounting a nationwide demonstration project in the area of women's alcoholism prevention. They expect to place a demonstration program in the Southwest and will be needing information about programs, people, and demographics in order to determine the appropriate locale and strategies for their programs. I will draw on my research findings and experiences to help fill this information need.

It is important to understand that policymaking groups such as those I've listed vary greatly in terms of the backgrounds, expertise, prejudices, and information levels of the persons composing them. Generally speaking, the broader the geopolitical level and the larger the amount of funds to be allocated, the greater will be the amount of expert knowledge on the part of the constituent individuals. Local level nonprofit agency boards may be made up of civic leaders, businessmen, and persons from other local nonprofits. These persons usually have great good will and considerable community influence but frequently know remarkably little (at least in their initial involvement) about the agency mission, activities, and users of the services they are charged with overseeing. Conversely, state and federal agency boards and panels most often are made up of individuals who are deliberately sought because of demonstrated expertise (service or research) in a given area. Here, too, the "experts" will vary as to the sub-area of expertise, e.g., treatment, prevention, epidemiology, demographics, and economics. The anthropologist has to be able to accurately assess the level of expertise of co-policymakers and decide how best to present data in the context of others' areas of expertise and information.

The important point to be made here is that whenever a researcher sits on one of these policymaking or planning bodies, he or she becomes one of the "wes" who are making decisions, not one of the "theys" who submit information in the form of reports, petitions, or presentations to be considered in the decisionmaking process. In such a capacity, tendering one's research findings as the basis for decision-making is an excellent way to get the research used, but it requires delicacy in the doing. It takes one's skills of listening and timing and piecemealing out pertinent data in a give and take with other individuals who have different kinds of information to bear on the issues at hand. Initially it may involve, for example, seizing on a lawyer's sketchy but accurate comments on, say, the sociocultural characteristics of a client population, sharpening and contextualizing them with data from one's ethnographic observations, then summarizing and synthesizing the two perspectives. Only after a period of low key "teaching" others just what kinds of information you have and how it may be relevant, do you hear the question, "What does your research show about this?" from fellow policymakers.

Influencing the Policymaking of Service Providers: Service-providing professionals and paraprofessionals, are, unlike most administrators, boards and advisory panels, "in the trenches," as they are apt to put it. They are in direct contact with the people they help and in direct confrontation with situations they are attempting to modify. Whereas it might be assumed that service providers are simply engaged in carrying out the directives of the administrators, the true situation is not that simple. The character and delivery of human services is consistently affected by the providers' interpretations of higher level policymakers' directives and by their own information bases and mind sets. Moreover, it is the service providers who supply a great deal of the information upon which higher level bodies act. What are some of the opportunities the researcher has to affect the information base and perceptions of hands-on providers? I have found that involving myself in in-service training and certification programs is one of the best.

As with membership on planning and funding bodies, initiation into training activities often starts at the local level. In my case, for example, as part of the dissemination aspect of my research projects, I often volunteer to conduct information-sharing activities with agencies or associations that provide subject samples or mediate access to informants. They are often hard pressed to find speakers and trainers who can present useful information for staff training.

Sometimes the information I present is as simple as providing a detailed description of the sociodemographic, cultural, and structural characteristics of a special population. Training also frequently involves presenting new information on behaviors, cultural norms, and environmental factors that reduce or increase the risk status of individuals in a target population on a particular health indicator of interest to the service agency. The rich, naturalistic detail generated by anthropological research fleshes out and makes meaningful many of the contexts in which problem-related behavior is embedded. These contexts have to be considered for meaningful interventions to take place. For example, in human services directed to Latinos, recommendations are often made that the familistic nature of the group dictates that the "extended family" be involved in treatment. Usually, the nature of that involvement is not specified nor is the concept of extended family operationalized in any way. Following a study of the way in which alcohol use was integrated into the lives of Mexican American and Anglo couples, I was able to discuss with counselors and clinicians the kinds of class and cultural variations in drinking settings, contexts, and relationships obtaining across groups. Further, I was able to describe variations in extended family structure, identifying kinds of kinship coalitions and relationships that operated to constrain or promote certain types of intervention activities. This kind of information falls on very grateful ears among persons frustrated by the statistical abstractions provided by epidemiological surveys and the often inadequately interpreted data resulting from experimental research designs typical of the other behavioral sciences.

I do not, of course, present my ethnographic data in terms of generalizations or statements about whole cultural groups. On the contrary, an important thrust of my research has been to uncover intra-cultural variations on a number of norms, behaviors, and relationships. Additionally, my data, acquired in naturalistic settings, allow me to use what I call a "case study within cultural context" approach. In this way I exemplify cultural themes, norms, and symbols in case studies which show concrete examples of the effects of culture on specific behaviors.

One of the most successful uses of this approach in a training setting has been a series of vignettes, mini-ethnographies through which the multiple and interrelated ways acculturation impacts on drinking practices are illustrated. Having visited many drinking settings that are associated with specific groups (i.e., immigrant, later-generation Latinos, Anglos, and Latinos of differing class status), I can be very vivid and very specific in bringing to light the complexity of the multiple factors which produce differences in drinking behavior. Service providers report that it is this type of information that alerts them to significant differences within the diverse client population and allows them to structure separate groups and interventions that reflect this variation.

Other types of training opportunities are offered by adult education programs and, especially, by university extension programs for professionals and para-professionals. These programs usually are organized around certification or credits for continuing education. They draw persons from a wide variety of helping agencies. My two-day workshop on alcohol use in the Mexican American population, conducted through several University of California extension and certification programs, for example, is attended by highway patrolmen, probation officers, corporate personnel officers, employee assistance program counselors, nurses, doctors, alcohol and drug counselors, judges, and a scattering of graduate and undergraduate students. They are hungry for useable and concrete information. Most of them, with the exception of students and doctors, do not read scholarly journals. That notwithstanding, they have a plethora of on-the-ground experiences against which they can and do measure the soundness and useability of the information I provide--important to consider when I am designing new policy-related research. The feedback they give me, too, is valuable particularly because they come from so many different backgrounds, each with a different vantage on the subject at hand. Participants in these classes and workshops provide new research ideas and openings into a variety of networks. Contact with service providers keeps me oriented to what *has* to be one of the most important objectives of applied research: the generation of data that are useable in the design of specific strategies to ameliorate problems and answer human needs.

The anthropological perspective in general is useful to service providers, so while I try to get people to consider and use data my research has generated, I also attempt to get them to adopt an anthropological perspective in determining what kinds of data are useful in analyzing a problem area and its solution. Clinicians and other practitioners, for example, will often look for understanding and answers at the individual level, ignoring cultural aspects. In part this is because they are not accustomed to analyzing cultural elements. They may recognize the impact of cultural norms and values on individual behavior, but the effects of culture may seem so vague and unmeasurable that they cannot perceive a way of dealing with them in any concrete way. As a case in point, alcohol abuse is most often viewed by the service-providing community as a problem residing in individuals. One service provider dismissed the concept of social or cultural factors in the etiology of alcoholism with the statement, "All alcoholics drink through their mouths." Anthropological data have shown, however, that what is seen as abusive drinking or even what behaviors comprise drunken comportment vary widely across cultures (MacAndrew and Edgerton 1969). And, our best epidemiological information indicates that ethnicity is an excellent predictor of levels of alcohol use and alcohol-related problems. Quantity and frequency of alcohol use are strongly influenced by culturally based values and cognitions about alcohol: where it should be consumed, when, by whom, and how much. I was and am still surprised by how new that idea is to many people in the alcohol services. Once grasped, however, it becomes a powerful tool for viewing alcohol problems in a broader ecological perspective and allows for innovative approaches which incorporate modifying person/environment relations rather than relying solely on strategies which concentrate on "fixing" individuals.

Another important way to get one's research findings before people who can use it in their service strategies is to give papers at conferences they attend. Presentations at such conferences widens one's network of contacts and often result in invitations to participate on the decisionmaking bodies described earlier. The American Public Health Association, the National Council of International Health, the Coalition of Hispanic Health and Human Services Organizations, and the U.S.-Mexico Border Health Association hold annual or semi-annual national conferences that provide useful forums for applied research findings. Regional conferences, such as the annual California Alcohol Conference or the Southwest Conference on Alcohol are examples of regional, special interest conferences that have been useful for me to attend. Attendance or presentation at such conferences makes one visible to the people who are potential users of anthropological data. One rarely meets these folks at anthropological conferences.

Anthropological Input to the Users of Services: The active and organized participation in policymaking of persons to whom services are directed is a relatively new but growing movement that offers another arena in which the anthropologist can share data and perspectives that influence the character and implementation of services. Some special interest groups are organized around very specific health needs, such as those of head-injured children, natural childbirth participants, or substance abusers. In my treatment-oriented alcoholism research, for example, I have found the influence of Alcoholics Anonymous to be felt in every aspect of treatment and service delivery from philosophy and perceptions of etiology to treatment modality. Research among first-time parents introduced me to parent groups advocating (and getting) particular birthing techniques and organization of hospital services. Other interest and advocacy groups are organized around the needs of specific ethnic, racial or status groups, such as Latinos, Blacks, or refugees. If research within one of these groups is long term and there are reciprocal and mutually supportive relations between the anthropologist and the group, she or he may, in fact, join with them in defining a need to policymakers or service providers.

For example, since I have been involved extensively in community-based research among Latinos and have often focused on the way in which services are or are not utilized by members of the group, I am familiar with the need for culturally relevant service modalities and culturally relevant delivery of services. Most advocacy groups are acutely aware of the lack of such services, but sometimes have difficulty defining what a culturally appropriate approach might be in a given service context. While delivery of services in the language of clients is of major importance, cultural relevance is a concept far broader than just language consonance. Adequate formulations of relevant approaches have to integrate uniquely cultural elements or circumstances into a particular service delivery situation.

Upon several occasions, I have been asked by Latino groups to use my combined knowledge of a service area and Latino culture to give them technical assistance in making such formulations. A specific instance of this kind of request was when I was called on by a group advocating for Latino substance abuse prevention services to consult with them in the preparation of a document which would show how and why prevention programs oriented to Latinos needed to be different from those targeted to the larger society. I had recently reviewed Latino prevention programs (those few available) and the new, community based public health approach to alcohol problem prevention adopted by the state (Gilbert and Cervantes 1987). I was able to discuss with them the problems involved in implementing the new approach with Latino communities and offer some cautionary advice which they included in their document.

Summary

As I have experienced it, the formulation and ultimate structuring of human services is the end result of a dynamic and ongoing dialogue between service-needing interest groups, service providers, and the funders and planners. In the interest of ensuring that one's findings are considered and used in this process, an applied social scientist will find it strategic to interact with all three sectors of the human service community. This is the best way that I know of to develop an emic perspective on institutionalized services. This perspective, in turn, informs and facilitates the research one undertakes by sharpening one's sense of the kinds of research direction and methodology that produce data that are truly needed. Most important, such interaction leads to opportunities for the researcher to enact policy-affecting roles and by so doing personally to ensure that research findings are considered as a basis for action.

Several other strategies follow from and support this general recommendation for active participation in the service community. All have proven useful to me in ensuring application of my findings. And all depend to a large extent on the initiative and assertiveness of the researcher.

It is difficult to conceptualize how an anthropologist might begin to enact roles other than researcher until one understands the structure of the service community, knows some of the major players and how they fit into the overall picture and the way that policy is made at different levels of service provision. Some of this information is learned as one conducts research, but one must also make a special effort to fill in the information gaps that one's research doesn't provide. This first important step allows one to assess which kinds of data might best suit the needs of planners in various positions in the service providing community. As noted, it is helpful to have both quantitative and qualitative findings to communicate.

Opportunities to assume non-research roles result also from maintaining a visible willingness to participate. This involves staying in touch and maintaining reciprocal information exchange with prior sponsors of one's research and former colleagues. Willingness to volunteer (at least initially) one's time on boards, commissions, and advisory bodies is an additional way to build visibility and contribute one's data and perspectives to policymaking. Returning to research sites to recap findings is yet another good technique for getting data used, as is speaking at conferences attended by public service policymakers and implementers. The human services are replete with opportunities to assume training roles, such as in-service training, certification courses, and professional workshops. Initially, one has to seek out these opportunities to do training and be responsive to the special information needs that are required.

As noted, several communications strategies are helpful in the dissemination of research findings in policymaking arenas. The most important of these is to determine first who is most likely to make practical use of specific findings generated through research and then, whenever possible, presenting these *selected* findings to potential users in interactive settings. Communicating one's data in the language and contexts of service planners and providers is especially important. Being willing to "piecemeal" out data as appropriate opportunities unfold is also part of this process. Further, maintaining a willingness to listen to and integrate the data of others with one's own is important when participating on policymaking bodies composed of persons with different backgrounds and perspectives. Non-didactic "teaching" techniques (synthesizing, summarizing, restating) for acquainting co-participants about one's findings and their implications are important.

In sum, all of us who put so much of our lives into problem-oriented research have great concern about whether or not our findings will actually to be used to make human services more effective--whether the data we've generated will sit unused in a report somewhere or be applied. We know, too, that publication of research findings in a disciplinary or practitioner journal is usually not enough, because many planners and providers of services who logically should be reading these publications just aren't. Involving oneself personally in policymaking through the strategies described above is one way of seeing that one's research has impact on human services. Equally important, it is a very specific and accessible means of enlarging the role of anthropology in public affairs.

6

A Utilization Study Using Network Analysis: Maternal and Infant Health Policy Change in Washington, D.C.

Margaret S. Boone

Anthropologists need to plan for eventual utilization from the onset of a project and need to recognize the importance of communicating research results to all types of experts as well as the public.

> Citizen criticism of attempts to apply science to human problems or ecological problems is of the greatest importance. . . . But . . . it must be remembered that everyone--scientist, humanist, artist, technologist, politician--is lay to the specialty of each other citizen. The dichotomy of scientist and citizen is misleading. What is needed are social mechanisms through which the issues embedded in the reports of scientific commissions of inquiry . . . may be organized so that they are intelligible to the lay public who can then participate. . . .
>
> (Margaret Mead, in hearings held March 1, 1976, by the Special Subcommittee on the National Science Foundation, for the Senate Committee on Labor and Public Welfare).

The purpose of this chapter is to illustrate how anthropologists can choose, research, and practice anthropology around a public policy issue as an expert policy participant. Practicing anthropology requires an understanding of the importance of communicating research results to all types of experts and to the public. Anthropologists need to plan their projects from the onset so they will yield results that are geared toward specific types of audiences. In this way, they will increase the use of their findings by many different people in government, academia, and service delivery who are interested in research results related to important policy issues. Anthropologists should also record--from the very beginning of their work--the information needed to reach different target groups. They should plan for the evaluation of their work, including utilization studies. Planning projects for specific audiences and for evaluation requires several deliberate strategies: keeping the utility of the project in mind, documenting all public and private activities with policy participants, and routine research record-keeping. Communication of research results to policy groups requires persistent, hard work because different kinds of audiences need different kinds of data.

Measuring the impact of scientific research and demonstrating its use are difficult steps in utilization studies in almost all fields (Leviton and Boruch 1983; Patton 1978; Suchman 1967; Weiss 1977). Proof of the practical use of anthropological research is a creative challenge at the very least. Government interventions based on anthropological findings are especially difficult to trace. The following discussion concerns the impact of my research on the understanding of the infant mortality problem in Washington, D.C. The utilization of results by different audiences is explored using concepts from network analysis (see Table 6.1), which allowed examination of a diffuse process within and among many sectors of society.

At Issue: Health and Society

Black infant mortality in the United States is a public health problem whose sources are social and cultural. The rate of Black infant death is the highest of any racial or ethnic minority in the nation, and it is consistently highest in Washington, D.C. Black infant mortality in America's largest cities is a demographic phenomenon which can be traced along many lines to the health status and health behavior of disadvantaged Black women. However, the lines of causation are not always clear, so it is very difficult to choose the best policy and program changes. Awareness of the problem of infant mortality is essential for the general public, as well as for inner-city Black women at high risk of a poor pregnancy outcome and the people who work to help them.

Infant mortality is related to some of the gravest problems of our time: Poverty grows worse among single-parent Black households, teenage pregnancy challenges our health care delivery systems and our national values, and substance abuse is epidemic. Many different kinds of social, psychological, political, and economic characteristics find expression in an infant mortality rate. Poverty, the absence of prenatal care, substance abuse, and lifestyle can all affect the health of mothers and children, and this makes infant mortality rate one of the most consistent, sensitive indicators for quality-of-life. It broadly measures a society's commitment to the welfare of its citizens or a group of them.

Legislative Background for the Infant Mortality Project

An Introduction to the Clients

The research on infant mortality in Washington, D.C., and the public service activities to increase awareness of the social and cultural origins of the problem among physicians, politicians, and disadvantaged women themselves, can all be traced back to the funding for the Science for Citizens (SFC) program at the National Science Foundation in 1976.[1] The successor to this pilot program funded my infant mortality research in 1979-80 as a Public Service Science Residency. The grant provided for a year's residency at the only public hospital in Washington, D.C., where I conducted a study on the social and cultural factors related to the high infant death rate among inner-city Blacks.[2] The NSF program was the original "client" for research and outreach on infant mortality.

The legislative history of the funding program provides a rationale for many of the public service activities which accompanied the infant mortality research. It also helps to explain why the documentation of these activities was more complete than for many anthropological research projects. The documentation, in turn, provides a starting point for an assessment of the utilization of research results. The main avenues for dispersal of information on research results are given in Table 6.2 (at the end of this chapter), which is extensive, but *by no means complete*. Monitoring of the project in this manner was an integral part of the Public Service Science Residency.

The goals of the original plan for the Science for Citizens program were to improve public understanding of policy issues involving science and technology, and to support the participation of scientists in public, community, and citizen group activities aimed at the resolution of public issues with scientific and technical aspects. The SFC program provided grants to scientists and to academic and other nonprofit organizations to conduct limited applied research on science and public policy issues and the programs growing out of these concerns.[3] Margaret Mead testified on the need for increased public understanding of the scientific aspects of public policy issues in 1976. She pointed out that the understanding of science is an essential basis for citizen participation (see her quote at the beginning of this chapter). The rationale behind the NSF program, which Mead helped to clarify, explains in part why efforts were made to disperse widely the results of the research on the infant mortality problem in Washington, D.C. Both Figure 6.1 and Table 6.2 (pages 103-105) illustrate the levels (nation, city, hospital), the sectors (medical care, academia, social services, the general public, etc.), and the communication forms (newspaper articles, academic papers, radio and T.V. broadcasts, etc.) which were used to increase public understanding of Black infant mortality in Washington, D.C., during the year of NSF support (1979-80) and for some years thereafter.

The Science for Citizens program was never without controversy because of its support of projects which involved *both* science and public policy issues.[4] The SFC program encouraged activities which brought together different types of individuals or dispersed information to participants on different sides of a public policy issue. The program required that grant recipients make special efforts to involve participants on all sides of a particular policy issue.[5] This requirement led to my original efforts to become publicly involved with the infant mortality issue, instead of simply as a researcher.

Research Methods and Utilization Strategies

An Introduction to the Beneficiaries

The beneficiaries of the research and the public service activities were at several different levels. The ultimate beneficiaries were and continue to be the disadvantaged, inner-city Black women at high health risk. There are also beneficiaries at other levels of government and society. Some are the people whose job it is to help these women, for example, the national legislators who pass laws to fund health care programs; the city health commission which organizes the delivery of services; the local hospital which serves as "family doctor" for so many inner-city residents; and independent facilities and groups which attempt in many ways to compensate for the poverty and social alienation which exacerbate the normal burdens of pregnancy in the inner city.

I used a variety of research methods to uncover the social and cultural characteristics of inner-city Black women who are at high risk of having a poor pregnancy outcome. The methods are classified broadly along two dimensions: quantitative versus qualitative, and comparative versus ethnographic.

I also used a broad selection of outreach techniques to disperse the results of the research. The "events" and "media" columns in Table 6.2 list the basic forms of outreach, and the "sector" column describes the types of audiences. As Mead states in her testimony at the beginning of this chapter, research results must be re-interpreted for both lay persons and scientists in formats which are appropriate for their functions and expertise. The following discussion joins my search for appropriate research methodologies with some explanation of the choices I made concerning the communication media I used to reach specific audiences.

An anthropologist's relative success in re-interpreting research results depends on the choice of the right format for the right audience at the right time, which in turn can influence the degree of utilization of research results. To some extent, fortuitous events and contextual factors also play an important role in the utilization of scientific research. Unplanned and uncontrollable factors can change the way that government uses research, for example, the popularity of an issue at a particular time, especially if a well-known person is supporting a particular cause; the status of the national and the local economy; the political party in power; and the interests of people who work in the news media.

Quantitative, Comparative Methods for Physicians, Epidemiologists, Legislators, and the Newspapers

The basic design for quantitative research on the social characteristics involved in poor pregnancy outcome was a case/control study,[6] using data taken from medical records and other hospital and city health records. I carefully selected two matched samples of women who delivered at an inner-city hospital. One sample had successful deliveries (normal-weight infants) and one had unsuccessful deliveries (very low-birthweight infants). I compared the samples statistically along social and health dimensions using t-tests and chi-squares. This strategy produced a reporting format familiar to physicians and epidemiologists.

The choice of design was not made lightly. Social science research on public health topics must take into account the kind of methods familiar to medical scientists, if the results are to be useful and convincing. Physicians will not re-learn social science for the convenience of anthropologists. However, they are open to discussion of sociological variables if, at the same time, they see and hear research results in a familiar format and linked to standard variables like birthweight, prenatal care, and pregnancy history. If physicians are to be convinced of the importance of social and cultural factors in health processes, and as a result provide help to inner-city women with these social factors in mind, then they must be won over with familiarity. This is what happened in Washington, D.C., as a result of my project and the work of others. For example, when I presented detailed results at a Public Health Commission Forum or at the Washington, D.C., Medical Society, the results I presented first were familiar and expected--such as the importance of prenatal care and usefulness of pregnancy history in predicting outcome. Only when a familiar context was firmly set, did I then lead the presentation or discussion toward less familiar and more controversial and troublesome issues like multiple drug abuse, ineffective contraception, alcoholism among older women, and more subtle factors such as women's inability to obtain social support from expected sources and their depression throughout pregnancy.

The results of the case/control study showed that women with very low-birthweight infants had significantly higher rates of smoking, alcoholism, previous infant deaths and abortions, and a lower rate of prenatal care than women with normal-weight infants (Boone 1982, 1985a). Results also included some surprises. Some factors that distinguish most American women with poor pregnancy outcomes were expected to separate these two samples of inner-city women, but did not; for example, single marital status, lower education, and drug abuse (it was high in both samples). The quantitative comparison of samples also allowed the simple documentation of rates for some social characteristics among inner-city Black women. For example, 75 percent of the women in all samples were unmarried at the time of delivery, and about the same proportion listed a female relative as the person "to contact in case of an emergency" on a hospital intake form. The consistency of these characteristics in all samples suggests that they reflect the nature of the inner-city community in a general way and do not separate women with different pregnancy outcomes.

Fortunately, these results could be given in a fairly straightforward manner in testimony before the House District Committee (Table 6.2, May 1980; at the end of this chapter), which was then reported in the *Washington Post* in a non-technical manner the next day. In fact, when details were given in the *Post* and other newspapers, they were not always reported as comparative results but simply as rates of occurrence for the negative form of the characteristic. This type of reporting should not dismay scientists who are accustomed to a more rigorous reporting format, as long as results can be traced back to technical references.

Fortunately, the results of the infant mortality project have never been misrepresented to the best of my knowledge.

Qualitative, Comparative Methods for Social Scientists, Social Workers, and Listeners of a Radio Talk Show

An epidemiological case/control study has a great deal in common with comparative research in ethnology. In both, some characteristics are held constant while others are systematically changed. Then a comparison is made between cases to explore which characteristics might be causative and which are not. In the infant mortality project both the case/control study and qualitative comparisons relied on documentation of facts from medical records, that is, on a "medical record review." The comparative quality of both approaches makes them more than a "medical audit," which often simply records facts about a particular type of diagnostic category and does not consider comparative cases.[7] The quantitative case/control study in the infant mortality project was an analysis of characteristics which could be coded and analyzed statistically. The qualitative, comparative analysis focused on characteristics which could not be easily quantified, coded, and tested statistically.

When qualitative results were strongly supported by quantitative, and vice versa, they produced compelling portraits of lifestyle among reproductive, inner-city Black women. Qualitative analysis of medical record data showed that women with very low-birthweight infants had poorer social relationships with family, friends, and hospital staff; suffered more from psychological distress during hospitalization; and had records with emergency room reports documenting violent events during pregnancy and on previous admissions. The health of women with very low-birthweight infants tended to be poor. Their records had many notes about both severe and minor health problems--from crippling arthritis to anemia to chronic constipation and cervicitis--while records of women with normal weight infants had very few.

Qualitative, comparative results were most interesting to colleagues in the social sciences and to service providers who worked to help disadvantaged Black women. I made several informal presentations at meetings of experts concerned with the city's high infant mortality rate at the city health commission, at the Washington, D.C., Medical Society, and in public speeches. The social workers in the city health commissioner's office were particularly interested in the documentation of social characteristics and the demonstration of their relationship to poor pregnancy outcome. Results gave them some "ammunition." Social workers were also gratified to see some of the emphasis shift away from medical care--as important as that is for pregnant women--to the problems they confronted every day. Both social workers and physicians were interested to see the documentation of a strong relationship between prenatal care and pregnancy outcome on one hand, and the more qualitative aspects of inner-city lifestyle on the other.

Finally, results from qualitative, comparative methods were useful in a radio talk on which I appeared six years after the original project, along with a physician and a representative from the Children's Defense Fund (Table 6.2, July 1985). The other experts gave substantially different kinds of information--historical, demographic, and medical--but little of a sociological nature. Together we provided a balanced presentation on the topic of infant mortality and teen pregnancy to callers who were listening to the radio talk show. My appearance on this program was one of a seemingly endless series of public service activities in which I participated in the years following the original project. I took some hand in arranging these activities during the fellowship year, although I eventually stopped seeking out these opportunities. When I was sought out by others, I began asking for an honorarium--although I would usually participate without one if my schedule allowed. Anthropologists involved in public policy issues as experts should know that they can provide valuable information, and should require payment when and where it is possible from an appropriate sponsoring institution.

Qualitative, Ethnographic Methods for Anthropologists and Policy Participants of All Types

Interviews with inner-city women who had suffered infant deaths rounded out research on infant mortality at the public hospital. In long interviews, eight women detailed their pregnancy and contraceptive histories, social relationships, and psychological adjustments before and after the infant death. A specially designed Attitudes and Beliefs Section allowed me to explore their culturally-based health and reproductive behavior, relationships with men, their families, and friends.[8] I then combined results of these interviews with case material from medical records to produce a type of documentation which was very realistic and disturbing for most readers.

Journal publications on the infant mortality research first analyze characteristics such as ineffective contraception or alcohol abuse separately, and then draw together the separate elements in examples of socio-medical histories of individual women. The composite quality of this type of documentation renders it ethnographic in nature, and thus endows it with a realistic quality characteristic of all ethnography. The following three histories are examples of qualitative, lifestyle material which has been useful to all types of policy participants. The histories clearly illustrate the long-term nature of disadvantaged health status, and that solutions to the infant mortality problem among urban Blacks must address many disadvantages at the same time.[9]

Case #1: A. was a 33-year-old heroin addict who was hospitalized for an allergic reaction and an anxiety attack. After she was hospitalized she delivered a 2-lb 12-oz female by cesarean section at about 28 weeks. The infant was jaundiced and sent to the intensive care nursery. The infant lived. A. had fallen twice during pregnancy, and continued using drugs and alcohol occasionally. It was her seventh pregnancy, and was preceded by one normal weight delivery, one low-birthweight delivery, and four abortions. She was employed and received prenatal care during pregnancy.

Case #2: B. was a 27-year-old widowed alcoholic who delivered a 1-lb 10-oz stillborn male at 26 weeks gestation. This was B.'s seventh pregnancy and was preceded by two low-birthweight deliveries and four abortions. She was pregnant again by the time of the medical record review and had another abortion seven months following her previous delivery. A year prior to the delivery in question, B. had been kicked in the right flank and shoved down the stairs by her husband. Her chart contained numerous emergency room reports.

Case #3: C. was using foam before her first pregnancy at 17 years but she became pregnant and had an abortion. She used foam once more and became pregnant once more and had another abortion. She and her partner then used condoms and she became pregnant again but miscarried. She used no contraception after the miscarriage and became pregnant again. This resulted in the neonatal death in question. She then began taking contraceptive pills but became pregnant and had another abortion; took pills again, and had yet another abortion.

Quantitative, Ethnographic Methods for Policymakers, Health Specialists, and the Public

A follow-up survey three years after the original project was sponsored by the U.S. Census Bureau to explore the extent of census undercount, and reasons for it, in the same samples of inner-city women.[10] The survey focused on the women and their family members in 1980, so it allowed me to explore a new, expanded data base which included social characteristics such as residential stability and household composition. Some of the information collected for the follow-up study was useful in an eventual re-analysis of Washington, D.C.'s Black infant mortality problem in its inner-city neighborhoods.

Cluster analysis and factor analysis are "data reduction methods" which I used in the re-analysis to describe two aspects of inner-city health and lifestyle. The first of these methods uncovered the underlying dimensions called "factors," which give rise to variation in the separate, measured characteristics; the second of these methods analyzed clusters or groups of similar women according to all variables used. Factor analysis and cluster analysis both use mathematical formulas and a computer to derive these essentially descriptive results. The interpretation of clusters and factors requires the same kind of intuition, reasoning, and model-building found in ethnography and ethnology. The combination of the two methods allows the development of different profiles of reproductive, inner-city Black women.

The results from the data reduction techniques form the foundation for a book-length study of the "profiles" of women who contribute most to the infant mortality problem of Washington, D.C. It was written for a broad, national audience of health specialists and policymakers, but it is also accessible for an informed general public (Boone 1989). Anthropologists who are writing on public issues for various kinds of professional and lay audiences should consider the differences between this longer work and published journal articles. In the book, an attempt was made to keep jargon to a minimum, to clarify and simplify the style, and to reduce passive voice. Policy-related comments introduce and conclude the book, and research results are presented in between. The translation of research results into a readable format for a very broad audience is a challenge for any scientist, but one well worth pursuing.

Project Impacts:
The Utilization of Infant Mortality Research

To determine whether a research project has achieved a practical impact depends on the definition and measurement of "impact." I have previously noted that:

> Measuring the results of an individual's or a group's involvement in a health policy issue is extremely difficult because it requires assessment of public sentiment and political trends whose origins are complex. It is easier to trace bureaucratic efforts, such as a decision to change a regulation or fund a program. To a degree, the impact of my participation in the infant-mortality debate in Washington, D.C., can be determined by asking: Do public health policy makers show any interest in research results? Were congressional testimony and scientific papers picked up by the national and local press? Have any research results sparked public debate and strong reaction? Do privately funded policy reviews quote and publish the results? Do health planning agencies request detailed information for their use in policy recommendations? Is the definition of the problem, as gauged by newspaper coverage and private contacts, changing from a strictly medical model?. . . The answer to all . . . is yes (Boone 1985b:120).

Important changes have taken place since 1979, when the Mayor's Blue Ribbon Committee on Infant Mortality sponsored a city-wide medical audit by the local Professional Standards Review Organization, conducted its review of the infant mortality issue, and when I began my own separate, NSF-funded study at the public hospital. Many individuals worked in many capacities that year to understand the reasons for Washington's high infant mortality rate and to develop solutions. Some program changes have been implemented. Hospitals obtained better equipment for their neonatal intensive-care nurseries, staffs have been upgraded, transport systems between hospitals have been attempted, and public awareness campaigns were begun.

One of the most important changes is a broad policy shift--so broad that it must be called an "attitude change." There has been an intangible, but noticeable shift toward an understanding of inner-city reproductive health as a problem whose causes are partly social and cultural, and whose solutions may also be. This change in problem-perception is difficult to define and measure. In 1979, the predominant belief among major policy-makers was that the only reasonable programs *had* to be medical, because the socio-economic origins of poor Black health were so fundamental and so pervasive that no program with a reasonable price-tag could possibly do any good. At the time of this writing, in 1988, it appears to many policy participants that medicine has accomplished about all that it can. So leaders are turning in other directions. They sponsor programs and support service-delivery research in which there is a consistent, if meandering, drift toward finding and instituting interventions which attack the core of Washington's persistent, inter-generational Black underclass and its effects on reproductive health. It is the social sources of Black infant mortality which remain so stubborn.[11]

The infant mortality rate in Washington, D.C., has fallen at about the same tempo as in other large American cities, so it remains the highest in the nation. However, the rate of neonatal deaths (those in the first 28 days after birth) declined dramatically between 1980 and 1983. This decline suggests that efforts to provide better newborn care may indeed be working. In those same years, two other rates did *not* decline, but remained steady and high: the rate of fetal deaths and the rate of low-birthweight deliveries (under 2500 g.). These types of poor pregnancy outcome are less affected by medical intervention and more reflective of maternal lifestyle. Since 1979, medical care programs have improved, but efforts to affect lifestyle have not had much impact. In Washington, D.C., there has been a delayed and very gradual increase in understanding among many service providers who championed improvements in medical care that programs aimed at changing lifestyle factors are also critically important in the infant mortality picture for Washington, D.C. This understanding came at the same time as a realization that neonatal intensive care could not reduce the infant mortality rate by itself.

It was the social component in the infant mortality problem which the NSF-funded study analyzed and tried to introduce as an important element in the perception of Washington, D.C.'s Black health picture. The extent to which this component of the infant mortality research was utilized by others is measured in two different ways. The first involves an assessment of the extent to which relevant groups of people had access to the information generated by this project. The second measure of impact involved assessing the extent to which changes have occurred, since the time of the study, in both attitudes and activities, toward a more sociocultural model of the infant mortality problem.

Assessment of Access Using Network Analysis

Network analysis was used to determine the nature and extent to which people at various levels (nation, city, hospital), and in different sectors (medical care, social services, the legislature, general public, academia, etc.) had access to information concerning research findings from the project. An assumption underlying this analysis is that a sector's or group's access to project results would increase the likelihood of change in policy, program, or attitude concerning the importance of social and cultural factors in the health status of inner-city Black women.

Figure 6.1 organizes these various sectors and levels of impact. Examples of groups which had access to project results appear in this figure as circled numbers, and are listed to the right of the figure. Table 6.2 presents a detailed log of most activities related to the dissemination of information about the project, as well as the forms of communication used (newspaper articles, academic papers, radio broadcasts, etc.) Table 6.1, on pages 104-105, presents the network analysis, using concepts that are explained below. However, this table does not analyze all of the sectors and groups, but instead gives a partial analysis for sectors of greatest impact, and for some groups within these sectors.[12]

The network characteristics analyzed in Table 6.1 are: duration (length of time with access to project results); range (the number of individuals who had access); frequency (contacts per time); reachability from me and the project (the number of links through which the information had to travel); intensity (my own personal and professional level of involvement in the sector or group); multiplexity (whether my involvement was very multi-purpose or only single-purpose); density (whether the people in the sector all knew each other, or not); and normative constraint (the degree to which I was guided by the rules and perspectives of the individuals in the sector--which is usually strongly related to multiplexity).[13]

The following utilization assessments use the network concepts given in Table 6.1. Several other network concepts are introduced in the course of the discussion, especially the notion of "centrality" of contacts, the idea that networks can be "latent" and "reactivated," and that networks can "intersect."

Government/City Level. Example: City Health Commission: The duration of my direct involvement with the city public health commissioner's office was limited to 1979-80. During that time the number of contacts was fairly low (range), but the central importance of the contacts was critical. The frequency of contact with the

commissioners (there were two during these years), several key staff, a representative from the Centers for Disease Control whose office was located there, and others who came for various meetings, made my impact important for a short time. One of the social workers on the staff became particularly supportive of results produced by the NSF-funded study. There was little need during those two years to contact top staff through aides and other staff; access was easy if not direct. After those two years contact diminished, although influence remained important through some staff.

Several factors worked both for and against a continued high level of contact. I went on to other professional work rather than staying in maternal and child health, so the intensity and multiplexity (multistrandedness) of contacts waned. However, the networks themselves remained intact, and their density, high. Some players changed, but the networks stayed in place. The issue of infant mortality gave way to yet another, closely related issue: inner-city teenage pregnancy. Many of the same individuals were still active. As a result, my name and work remained within easy reach of people who worked in maternal and child health. At the public events which continue to focus on inner-city Black health in Washington, I have on occasion been surprised when someone "new" is introduced and matter-of-factly comments, "Oh yes, you did some of the early work on infant mortality. I've read your reports." The person, persona, and work are indeed separable, and can be followed separately in a utilization study.

Other factors worked against continued influence. Because of the nature of my training and the research itself, results were published first in academic journals. This took several years to accomplish. There was no immediate public report and no press release. Anthropologists interested in public policy work should take heed: Research results must be broadcast openly, loudly, and quickly. If I could go back and re-make any decision, it would be to enlist the help of the public affairs office at either the hospital where I worked, or at one of the two universities with which I affiliated. Barring those contacts, I would hire a public relations expert. However, there was one advantage to the long time-line for publication. The eventual publication of results and the mailing of copies to city officials worked to re-activate networks that had not collapsed. It was relatively easy to link back up, and continues to be.

To summarize, the access of the city health commission to research results was high but short-lived. Influence then remained latent through semi-permanent networks which could be re-activated with relative ease.

Figure 6.1 Impact Sectors and Levels for the Infant Mortality Project

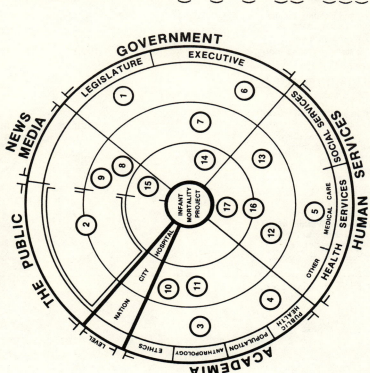

Examples of Impact Groups *

(1) District Committee,
    U.S. House of Representatives
(2) *Washington Post* newspaper
(3) Society for Applied Anthropology
(4) American Public Health Association
(5) National Academy of Sciences,
    Institute of Medicine
(6) U.S. Public Health Service
(7) Commissioner of Public Health,
    District of Columbia
(8) WHUR radio
(9) WJLA-TV
(10) Kennedy Institute,
     Georgetown University
     Classes,
(11) George Washington University
(12) Mayor's Blue Ribbon Committee
     on Infant Mortality
(13) Improved Pregnancy Outcome Project
(14) Ambulatory Care Committee,
     D.C. General Hospital
(15) Public Affairs Office
(16) Infant Mortality Forum
(17) Medical Director's Office

* Groups are marked (**) in Table 6.2

TABLE 6.1

NETWORK ANALYSIS FOR SECTORS OF GREATEST IMPACT IN FIGURE 6.1

SECTOR/LEVEL Groups/Media (from Figure 6.1)	NETWORK CHARACTERISTICS *		
	DURATION (years)	RANGE (hi/lo)	FREQ (hi/lo)
GOVERNMENT/CITY			
City Government/Washington, D.C. Group: D.C. Office of the Health Commissioner. Media: meetings, oral presentations, published reports.	2	low	medium
THE PUBLIC/CITY			
Listening and Reading Public/ Washington Metro Area. Media: *Washington Post*, radio talk show, TV news spots	7	very high	low
ACADEMIA: INTERNATIONAL AND NATIONAL			
Groups: In health,social science. [Know Me] Media: papers at meetings, publication, correspondence. [Know My Work]	8 7	high high	medium low
HEALTH AND SOCIAL SERVICES/CITY			
Health Services/Washington, D.C. Group: Better Babies Project (private, non-private). Media: meetings and reports.	5	low	low

* Definitions given in the text.

REACHABILITY FROM PROJECT (# of links)	NETWORK CHARACTERISTICS *			
	INTENSITY (hi/lo)	MULTIPLEXITY (hi/lo)	DENSITY (hi/lo)	NORMATIVE CONSTRAINT (hi/lo)
1-2	medium to low	low	high	medium
1 - many (increasing)	medium	low	low	low
1	high	medium	high	high
1	low	low	low	low
1	medium	low	high	medium

* Definitions given in the text.

The Public/City Level: The duration of my public contacts has been relatively long, although they began one year later than the project itself because it took almost a year to obtain any research results. The first public contact was at the 1980 congressional hearing where I testified, and then coverage of the testimony in the press. The headline (May, 1980) for coverage of my testimony in the *Washington Post* read: "Alcoholism, Premature Births Linked in Study at D.C. General." After that, I gave public speeches to different audiences in the seven years following the project. This included a speech on alcoholism and pregnancy at one of the city's Drug Abuse Campaign Kick-Offs, which many officials and media newspeople attended.

During the early 1980s a warning about alcoholism appeared in a public service announcement encouraging Washington women to get prenatal care. In 1986, a new public awareness campaign began in which alcoholism, drugs, smoking, social support, and prenatal care--all factors investigated in the project--are featured from time to time. I cannot directly connect my research, testimony, publications, and speeches to these public announcements--but I cannot rule out some influence. Public awareness based on scientific research can build gradually over a long period of time. Anthropologists who are involved in public policy work should not always expect to be able to trace the linkages between research and public knowledge directly--although they should by all means try, and toward this end, document their activities well. They can, however, determine reasonable network linkages for the distribution of research knowledge--both direct and indirect. In the case of the NSF-funded project, those avenues exist and are documented partly in Table 6.2.

In network terms, the duration of my contacts with the public has been long; the range of contacts, very high; and the frequency, low. The number of links between me and the public is only one when I speak, but this number can be high when other people serve as intermediate links. The number of links probably increases through time, because of the increasing number of people who know about my research indirectly. The multiplexity and density of my contacts with the public are necessarily very low, and their normative constraint on me, also low.[14] To summarize, the access of the public was long-lived, and therefore high and has gradually increased over the years through indirect linkages.

Academia/International and National Levels: Academic colleagues have two major routes for access to my work, and the route determines the nature and extent of the access. One route is through a relatively large number of academic colleagues in professional societies. They know of the infant mortality project because they know me. The other route is strictly through published papers. Individuals have written to me from all over the world for copies of papers and the attitudes and beliefs section of my interview schedule. An important route for knowledge of my first published report (which detailed the quantitative results) was through a listing in the *Population Index.*

The density, frequency, intensity, and even the multiplexity and normative constraint of the networks of the first type are relatively high. The density, frequency, intensity, and multiplexity of the second type are low. For both routes, reachability is only one link, although I am beginning to hear of students who know of my work through their professors, or colleagues who hear through other colleagues. The reachability (number of links from the source) probably increases over time, although it probably remains one or two links through published citations and references to published papers.

To summarize, the access of academia was high, and increased with time. Eventually this effect will wane as new studies are completed, unless a major work on the project becomes firmly embedded in the literature.

Health and Social Services/City Level. Example: Better Babies Project: Two years after the activities of 1979-80, a private, non-profit research and service delivery program began in Washington, D.C., under the auspices of the Greater Washington Research Center, and with the help of funding from a wide range of sources. My contact with the program began before its inception, when its founder contacted me with questions about the reports I published on the infant mortality project. Contacts of various types followed the initial meeting and information exchange continues today--as the program obtains further funding, wider public and media support, and now a sophisticated evaluation capacity with the help of the National Institutes of Health.

In network terms, the contact with the Better Babies Project has been fairly long-term, low in range because I know few of the participants directly except its manager, low in reachability because of my direct access to its management, low but steady in frequency of contact, medium in intensity, high in density, and medium in normative constraint on me because it represents that segment of the maternal and infant health network in Washington, D.C., with which I still maintain contact.

To summarize, the access of the Better Babies Project to the results of the infant mortality project has been high from the beginning, and continues at a moderate level to this writing.

Assessment of Changes in Inclinations and Attitudes

Expert interviews are an excellent mechanism to determine the extent of change in broad policies, attitudes, and activities. The following assessments were made by an independent observer who has been active in Washington, D.C., government and health. Assessments were made of people, organizations, and sectors which are, in some cases, more specific than the major areas of impact reviewed above. The observer helped by giving independent assessments of the inclinations of groups and sectors toward social explanations of the infant mortality problem when the project began, and how inclinations changed from 1979 to 1986. Knowledge of a group's (or sector's) existing inclination, combined with knowledge of the nature and extent of its access to research results, went far in explaining a group's change (or failure to change). The observer's knowledge of policy participants was wider, deeper, and longer-lasting than mine.

Physicians: There were indications that physicians in Washington had been forced to examine social factors since the activities in 1979-80. Two factors played a role in this change. First, the PSRO (Professional Standards Review Organization) had conducted its own medical audit, which made a detailed review of medical care by physicians at different hospitals--that is, it asked questions which had not been asked before. A second factor was the composition of the Blue Ribbon Committee on Infant Mortality, which was professionally integrated, and consisted of both physicians and other types of service providers like dieticians and social workers. The composition of the Committee underscored the interrelationships between medical care and "social care" in pregnancy outcome.

Physicians had been forced, "almost by default," to acknowledge the importance of social support and other social factors, because medical care was improving and infant mortality was not dropping proportionally. Something else had to be going on. Ironically, the pressure for an immediate public health response forced a view toward social factors, because medicine could not solve the problem quickly and all by itself.

The Mayor: Mayor Marion Barry was initially inclined toward the inclusion of social factors in any understanding of infant mortality, and if his position has shifted, he has become even more inclined in that direction since 1979-80. The Mayor has shifted toward a position which encourages greater individual responsibility for health behavior. The Mayor has continued in fairly strong leadership and brokerage roles vis-à-vis health issues in Washington, D.C.

The News Media: There has been no substantial change among people who work for the printed media. The independent observer felt that, since they reported the news, they "went where the money was." On the other hand, the free, subsidized "public affairs broadcasting" has done a good job, and continues to be inclined toward inclusion of social factors in health explanations.

The Public: Service providers for inner-city women are beginning to hear more volunteered comments from their patients about the need to quit smoking, cut down on drinking, and eat well. Lifestyle appears to have become part of the health consciousness of many disadvantaged women who now become pregnant in Washington, D.C. (although substantial problems remain for teens). A change in attitude of this type should rely on a large-scale survey, or at minimum, on a survey of service providers. However, it does not, and public awareness remains one of the most difficult aspects of change to assess.

Washington, D.C., Health and Social Services: There are major problems in funding for social and health services. With block grants, it is difficult to compete with other programs and keep a high profile on maternal and child health services. However, city health-care staffs have been upgraded and equipment for newborn care has improved. There are problems in implementing changes among social workers "on the front line" in clinics and hospitals. While they are in one of the best positions to lead in an acknowledgment of social factors, they have not done so. Both the observer and I traced this to an unsupported sense of professionalism and intense "burn-out."

Conclusions

Who Has Changed the Most?

Physicians active in public health and in private hospitals who serve substantial numbers of inner-city patients have changed the most. They have had access to socio-medical research results, and have had good, logical reasons to begin focusing on them. Networks among these physicians are necessarily dense, and since 1979-80 have probably intersected to a greater extent with the networks of other kinds of service providers. The extent to which they have directly used results of the NSF project are not measurable. However, I continue to maintain contact with physicians active in maternal and child health; I have been asked to extend my research to other hospitals by physicians; and I continue to participate in public events with physicians who are concerned with the city's infant mortality rate.

The Role of Leadership

The concept of network easily incorporates the notion of centrality, but not the notion of leadership. The major reason for the continued effect of the NSF-funded project is that several key individuals--all in different positions and professions--have continued to use my research and rely upon it. Once their leadership role is acknowledged, then network concepts become useful in understanding the real and potential avenues for dissemination of project results. In using network analysis to understand utilization of policy-related research, the entry-point of information and leadership roles of entry-point individuals are both important in understanding impact.

The Role of Time

Network analysis is a synchronic methodology and has not heretofore incorporated the notion of change to any great degree. Morphological and interactional network dimensions appear "frozen in time," and public-policy work must consider both long- and short-range change. However, it has been relatively easy to adapt network concepts to a discussion of research utilization and to use them to describe change. The operationalization of network concepts is not a difficult task, as

Figure 6.1, Table 6.1, and Table 6.2 together demonstrate. If assessments of inclination and change could be quantified or systematically ranked, and the units of change accurately specified, then an even more rigorous assessment would be possible.

Recommendations

Recommendations for other anthropologists who want to increase the impact of their work and demonstrate its utilization include practical but sometimes difficult steps. Anthropologists need to plan for eventual utilization from the onset of a project and need to recognize the importance of communicating research results to all types of experts as well as to the public. This requires the recognition that different audiences need different kinds of data presented in a variety of formats. It may also require that varying research strategies be used to generate these diverse types of data. For example, I created a "Log," which included my most important research documents, but also letters, memos, public announcements, even telephone messages. I kept all these materials together in two large notebooks, separate from strictly research files. I also kept my spiral-bound appointment books so I could go back and trace my contacts and activities. Table 6.2 illustrates one way in which this type of information can be organized for future evaluation.

It is also useful to develop skills in forming and maintaining high-level contacts. The telephone can be an important tool for achieving this. I first learned telephone technique as a staffer for the Select Committee on Population of the U.S. House of Representatives. In my work I contacted individuals for information and assistance whom I had only read about. It was intimidating at first, and required making fine distinctions as to relative rank and prestige, appropriate references, and when I should keep information strictly confidential. Telephone contacts work even better when followed up with appropriate mailed notes, letters, and reports. Information sharing and use almost always works on a *quid pro quid* basis.

Finally, utilization of research results can be improved with some judicious consideration of one's own motivations. Many researchers are content to sit and write academic reports and hope, perhaps, that someday their so-called "pure research" will be used. However, this rarely happens. The best way to increase the potential for utilization of anthropological research is to ensure personally that the results are available, accessible, understandable, and appropriate to the audiences that one wishes to reach.

Notes

1.   National Science Foundation Authorization Act, 1977, October 11, 1976. The Science for Citizens Program is covered in 90 Stat. 2054-2055.

2.   The infant mortality project was supported by Grant No. OSS-7917826. The views expressed in this chapter are those of the author, and do not necessarily reflect those of NSF.

3.   H.R. 4723, Sec. 3, 94th Congress, August 9, 1975. See also 42 USC 1864. The introduction of this legislation was the result of broad concerns in the mid-1970s about the participation of American citizens in government decisions based on complex scientific knowledge and sophisticated technologies. Some of the concern developed out of an increased awareness of environmental hazards and technologies. Citizen awareness and participation are, of course, just as important in the area of public health.

4.   Report No. 94-88, to accompany S. 3202, National Science Foundation Authorization Act, 1977, submitted by Edward Kennedy, for the Senate Committee on Labor and Public Works, May 14, 1976, page 29.

5.   Report No. 94-88, page 29. The Boasberg Report--prepared by an independent consulting firm--found that NSF lacked experience in the area of citizen participation, and that as a result there might be conflicts between the Foundation and the "functional agency in whose administrative proceedings the groups will be participating."

6.   A case/control study statistically compares "cases" (usually of a disease, condition, or other health factor) with equivalent "controls" (which have an absence of the disease, condition or factor) with the purpose of determining correlative (and hypothetically causal) factors.

7.   The comparative design of the NSF-funded study was chosen in part to compensate for the lack of a comparative design in the medical audit of infants who died, conducted in 1979-80 by the National Capital Medical Foundation, the local Professional Standards Review Organization.

8. A limited number of samples of the Attitudes and Beliefs Section of Yes/No response items are available from the author at the Dept. of Pathology, George Washington School of Medicine and Health Sciences, Washington, D.C., 20037.

9. Details of individual case histories are modified and rearranged to ensure the anonymity of women, and no case describes any single, real individual. Letters bear no relation to the names of women.

10. This survey was the "Inner-City Hospital Feasibility Study," sponsored by the U.S. Census Bureau, 1983-84. The discussion here is the author's own and does not necessarily reflect the views of the Census Bureau.

11. The persistent, long-term quality of Washington, D.C.'s social and health care problems are dealt with by Maxwell (1985).

12. This methodology is a modification of an exercise I developed for my Urban Anthropology students at Georgetown University, in which they diagrammed and evaluated their own social networks.

13. Most of these network dimensions are modified from Barnes (1972), Mitchell (1969), and Hannerz (1980).

14. "Normative constraint" was a concept we used in the above class exercise (note 12), following material presented in the urban anthropology text by Hannerz (1980).

TABLE 6.2 DOCUMENTING AN APPLIED ANTHROPOLOGY PROJECT:
CHRONOLOGICAL LOG OF OUTREACH EVENTS FOR THE INFANT MORTALITY PROJECT

EVENT	SECTOR	LEVEL	MEDIA	DATE
Coverage of D.C.'s infant mortality problem by B. D. Colen, *Washington Post.*	General Public	City	Newspaper article Telephone conversation	2-9-79 week after
Development of project proposal with Medical Director (**), D.C. General Hospital.	Medical Care	Hospital	Telephone conversation Meeting	February 1979
National Science Foundation awards, Public Service Science Residency Program.	General Public	Nation	News release	June 1979
Coverage of NSF award in *Practicing Anthropology; Medical Anthropology Newsletter,* others.	Academic and Applied Anthropology	Nation	Newsletter articles	Summer, Fall, 1979
Introduction to hospital's Chief Medical Officers under the Medical Director (**).	Medical Care	Hospital	Meeting	10-10-79
Liaison with PHS (**) Task Force on Health in D.C. (its chief and his representative).	U.S. Public Health Service	Nation	Conversations, letters, meetings	6-79 thru 12-80

(**) **Examples of Impact Groups in Figure 6.1**

EVENT	SECTOR	LEVEL	MEDIA	DATE
Meetings of the Data Subcommittee of the Mayor's Blue Ribbon Committee on Infant Mortality (**).	Health Care	City	Group discussion, oral presentations	6-79 thru 7-80
Membership with Hospital's Internal Review Board; and its Ambulatory Care Committee (**).	Health Research	Hospital	Group deliberation	9-79 thru 10-84
Reports on progress of the project to news reporters covering the city health beat.	News Media	City	Telephone conversations	1-80 thru 5-80
Brown-bag lunch, Center for Population Research, Kennedy Institute, Georgetown University (**).	Academia (population)	University	Oral presentation of preliminary results	2-8-80
Public hearing on infant mortality, Mayor's Blue Ribbon Committee on Infant Mortality (**).	Health Care	City	Informal attendance and conversations	2-14-80
Meeting of all D.C. hospital representatives to discuss PSRO's medical audit of infant deaths.	Medical Care	City	Formal attendance, informal conversations	3-10-80
Research session, Society for Applied Anthropology (**) meeting, Denver, Colorado.	Academia (anthropology)	Nation	Oral presentation of professional paper	3-80

EVENT	SECTOR	LEVEL	MEDIA	DATE
Evaluation of maternity-infant high risk index for JCAH review; copy to city health.	Medical Care Public Health	Hospital City	Written evaluation report	4-6-80
Coverage in the Quarterly Report of the Kennedy Institute, Georgetown University.	Academia (ethics)	Nation	Article on project	Spring 1980
Hearing, District Committee of the U.S. House of Representatives (**); Congressional Record.	Legislature General Public	Nation	Oral and written testimony at hearing	5-7-80
News coverage of hearing in the *Washington Post* (**).	General Public	City Nation	Newspaper article	5-8-80
News coverage of the hearing in a Channel 9 Newsnote (local CBS).	General Public	City	Television news	5-8-80
News coverage of the hearing on Channel 4 local news (local NBC).	General Public	City	Television news	5-8-80
News coverage of the hearing on WHUR (**), Howard University Radio.	General Public (esp. Black)	City	Radio news	5-8-80

EVENT	SECTOR	LEVEL	MEDIA	DATE
News coverage of hearing by *The Hill Rag.*	Neighborhood General Public	City	Newspaper article	5-8-80
Public service announcement of hospital forum sent by hospital Office of Public Affairs (**).	Broadcast Media	City	News release	before 5-8-80
Infant Mortality Forum (**), D.C. General Hospital.	Health Care Social Services	Hospital City	Oral presentation	5-8-80
Presentation to Mayor of Blue Ribbon Committee's (**) final report; reception.	General Public	City	Formal attendance, informal conversations	6-19-80
Teaching, Medical Anthropology.	Students	University	Class lectures	1980 to 1984
Evaluation panel, Improved Pregnancy Outcome Project, D.C. (**), (with federal funding).	Health Care Social Services	City Nation	Group discussion	7-7-80
Meeting on current research, at Public Health Commissioner's office (**).	Health Care	City	Oral presentation of research results	7-80

EVENT	SECTOR	LEVEL	MEDIA	DATE
District of Columbia's Infant Mortality Special Initiative, group formation.	Health Care Social Services	City	Formal attendance, group discussion	8-12-80
Liaison with epidemiological investigator from the Centers for Disease Control, Atlanta, GA.	Public Health	City Nation	Discussions, research consultations	8-80 thru 1981
American Public Health Association (**) meeting, Detroit, Michigan.	Public Health	Nation	Oral presentation of professional paper	10-80
D.C.'s Improved Pregnancy Outcome Project (**) in-service training.	Social Services	City	Workshop for counselors of addicted women	11-12-80
Washingtoniana Collection, D.C. Public Library	General Public	City	Written reports sent	11-20-80
American Anthropological Association: "Role Development of the Hospital Anthropologist."	Academia (anthropology)	Nation	Roundtable discussion with anthropologists	12-4-80
Coverage of APHA paper by medical press.	Medical Care	Nation	Newspaper article for family practitioners	1-1-81

EVENT	SECTOR	LEVEL	MEDIA	DATE
Coverage of APHA paper by medical press.	Medical Care	Nation	Newspaper article for obstetricians	1-1-81
Screening of TV special on infant mortality, WJLA-TV (**) news studios; reception.	Media Health Care	City	Formal attendance, informal conversations	4-81
WJLA-TV (**), Channel 7, evening news (local ABC).	General Public	City	TV interview	7-81
Liaison with D.C.'s State Health Planning Agency, Drug and Alcohol Program.	Health Planning	City	Written reports, informal discussions	9-81
Alcohol and Drug Abuse Prevention Campaign Kick-Off for the District of Columbia.	Health Care Social Services	City	Public speech for service providers	4-12-82
Publication of project results in *Human Organization*.	Academia (social science)	Nation	Professional paper in journal	Fall 1982
Liaison with the Greater Washington Research Center and its Better Babies Project.	Non-profit Research	City	Discussions, consultations	9-82 to present

EVENT	SECTOR	LEVEL	MEDIA	DATE
Meeting of Mayor's Advisory Board on Maternal and Infant Health, D.C. Government.	Medical Care Health Care	City	Speech for physicians, other service providers	12-6-82
Praxis Award, Honorable Mention; Washington Association of Professional Anthropologists.	Academia General Public	Nation	Meeting News release	12-82 1-28-83
Forum, Prevention Network for the Promotion of Mental Health, St. Elizabeth's Hospital.	Health Care Social Services	City	Speech for physicians, other service providers	5-12-83
Demographic research on Black undercount in inner city, U.S. Census Bureau.	Census-Taking	Nation	Follow-up research and outreach	7-83 to 7-84
Televised discussion by city health officials on Channel 9 (local CBS).	General Public	City	Reference to study on local TV health forum	6-84
Publication of project results in *Social Science and Medicine*.	Academia (social science; medicine)	Nation	Professional paper in journal	1985

EVENT	SECTOR	LEVEL	MEDIA	DATE
Interview and questions, Diane Reems Show, WAMU radio.	General Public	City	Call-in talk show, radio broadcast	7-25-85
National Academy of Sciences (**), Institute of Medicine panel on outreach for prenatal care.	Medical Care	Nation	Informal discussions	6-19-86

7

The Politics of Planning and Implementing a Statewide Health Service: Medical Rehabilitation in West Virginia

Judith Greenwood

Continuous involvement [of the researcher] with successive stages of planning and implementation contributes to keeping [this] process moving forward.

This case study describes a needs assessment for medical rehabilitation services in West Virginia and the process by which a statewide program of services was planned and implemented. Medical rehabilitation, often a part of vocational rehabilitation, is the medical management of physical disability using all methods of diagnosis and treatment and a number of other procedures and services to bring disabled individuals to their maximum attainable functional level (Gullickson and Light 1968). Thus, it deals not only with the working population, but also with children and the elderly. As described in the next section, the needs assessment in West Virginia was mandated, but not specially funded. The research, therefore, except for one individual case study, was based on secondary data.

Rehabilitation, medical or vocational, is essentially a progressive western world and middle-class concept: a disabled human body can be repaired, can be made to function better, and can often be fitted for economic productivity. Thus, not surprisingly, the stimulus for the needs assessment came from progressive medical providers who had some experience and training in rehabilitation and who in their practices perceived a need for a set of services virtually absent in the state and a need for a locale and equipment necessary to provide the services.

Similar progressive provider/middle-class intervention has been observed during the initial planning of other types of innovative health services, for example the early planning of neighborhood health clinics (*Cf.* May, Durham, and New 1980). The pattern for such intervention appears to begin with a small number of people connected with the bureaucracy who act first on an *ad hoc* basis, then move to use the strength of bureaucratic processes for change and innovation. These processes are set into motion without the aid of consumer groups to be affected by such services and even without their direct input. Thus, the project described in this case study, from needs assessment through planning to implementation, evolved through organizational and institutional politics rather than through pressure group politics.

The needs assessment was conducted without any strategic plan for using the findings other than reporting them to the state Governor's office and legislative bodies. Utilization methods were developed on an *ad hoc* basis and thus very much reflected the personalities and interpersonal relationships of those involved. I advance the argument, given the success of the utilization methods in this case, that there is a strength to such an *ad hoc* approach and that there are certain general strategies that can guide using research findings in such a manner. These strategies (discussed in the "Project Impacts" section) include holding conferences to enlist key political support, involving "conflicts of interest" in negotiated planning, and having a structure for collaboration and negotiation.

Research Methods and Context: Needs Assessment

The client group for the research was the West Virginia State Medical Association. The Association in 1977 adopted a resolution to ". . . undertake with the help of allied groups to document the need for a Physical Medical Rehabilitation Center for the State . . ." When the resolution was adopted, the only physical, or medical, rehabilitation beds available in the State were 55 beds through the Division of Vocational Rehabilitation and, thus, were limited to the requirements of the federal-state program. Essentially, vocational potential had to be proven before an individual's admittance, thus limiting use and delaying expedient use in terms of medical need.

Two key people were involved in this project from the outset. One of these was Dr. Robert Ghiz, an orthopedic surgeon in Charleston, West Virginia, and a native West Virginian, who recognized the value of medical rehabilitation in improving function for persons with physical disabilities. Dr. Ghiz was then chairperson of the Association's Subcommittee on Vocational Rehabilitation of the Economic Committee. The other person was Mr. Charles Lewis, the Executive Secretary and representative for the Medical Association in state government, especially during the legislative sessions.

The resolution was drafted by Ghiz and Lewis, in consultation with others, at the Association's annual meeting in August of 1977. It provided a mandate by calling for an examination of the need for medical rehabilitation services statewide. This gave the structural footing for a needs assessment and for dissemination of its results. More importantly, it provided a solid political basis for translating findings into concrete plans for implementing services. The rest of this section will deal with the historical context for the needs assessment, along with methods and research findings. The rest of the chapter will focus on how these findings were used, i.e., on the politics and process of planning and implementing statewide rehabilitation services.

The State Medical Association did not have immediate financial resources for special projects or studies such as the one proposed in its resolution to document need for a Physical Rehabilitation Center. Thus the clause ". . . with the help of allied groups . . ." became a key clause, and led to the involvement of the Department of Community Medicine of West Virginian University Medical Center. The chairperson, Dr. R. John C. Pearson, had personally been involved with a medical rehabilitation center as an attending physician and with planning community-based rehabilitation services. At Mr. Lewis' request, he supplied preliminary data on the incidence and prevalence of certain disability conditions that would benefit from rehabilitation intervention and some estimated caseloads for West Virginia. A year passed without any further action.

In September 1978, I joined the Department of Community Medicine as Research Associate and was given the opportunity by Dr. Pearson to choose among four different areas of investigation: primary care, women's health, gerontological health needs, and medical rehabilitation. While I had done research in primary care, and I had done a great deal in women's health through volunteer work, I decided to work on the assessment of the "need for a Physical Medical Rehabilitation Center" mandated by the State Medical Association.

The beneficiaries of the needs assessment for a comprehensive medical rehabilitation facility and program in West Virginia were, obviously enough, disabled persons. The outstanding question, however, was what disabled persons and how many. As noted earlier, the Division of Vocational Rehabilitation (DVR) was statutorily responsible for providing medical and vocational services for disabled persons deemed to have "vocational potential." That agency, however, was hampered both by its budget allotment and by federal priorities for service. It could not meet all the needs of persons with vocational potential and, at the time of the study, this limitation was particularly true in the area of medical, or physical, rehabilitation. The efficient medical rehabilitation of clients was impeded by a limited number of in-patient beds (55 in a rural industrial state with 1.8 million population in 1978) and staff budgeting levels that resulted in unfilled positions and high turnover in basic care positions such as orderlies and nursing assistants.

The outstanding questions regarding beneficiaries were "what disabled persons and how many would benefit from medical rehabilitation?" Whether DVR could meet its statutory responsibility or not, was not the issue in terms of defining medical rehabilitation need. The problem became one of discriminating real medical need from service aggrandizement in the name of need. Returning to the definition of medical rehabilitation in the introduction, the goal is to bring a disabled individual to increased functional capacity. If increased functional capacity cannot be achieved, then a constellation of medical rehabilitation services provided to a disabled person would be aggrandizement. Many disabled persons may need certain long-term support services for maintenance of function, but these should not be classed as medical rehabilitation. Service providers and service institutions, however, may want to aggrandize services for income or image. In other terms, the issue was a conservative versus a liberal estimation of new services needed.[1]

The chosen method of study to a large extent determined a conservative approach. Because the State Medical Association's resolution designated that "need for a Physical Rehabilitation Center" be established, only in-patient services were considered. Secondly, because there were no funds earmarked for the study, no population surveys were conducted. Data were primarily gathered from the extant epidemiological literature on disabling conditions regarding incidence and prevalence, morbidity, and mortality. Only select disabling conditions known to need in-patient rehabilitation services were considered. The study was further limited to basically adult needs as the needs for children was determined to require a separate study, even though several of the disabling conditions for which bed need estimates were made contained a small portion of individuals under age 16 (e.g., spinal cord injury).

Data also were collected from a sample of rehabilitation hospitals around the country. This information was compiled to estimate demand for medical rehabilitation in contrast to need. A careful differentiation was made between need and demand. Need was defined as the maximum inpatient services for given disabling conditions. Demand was calculated using occupancy rates and the population of the reported catchment areas of the hospitals surveyed.

To better establish characteristics of the disabled population in West Virginia, the state agencies that provided services or benefits to disabled residents were tapped for information. While disability definitions and categories varied from agency to agency, the information obtained on types of disabled persons served and levels of severity of disability bolstered the need and demand findings.

After all data were collected and analyzed, the beneficiaries of needed in-patient medical rehabilitation services basically fell into five categories of disabling conditions: spinal cord injury, brain damage (stroke and head injury), rheumatoid disease, orthopedic conditions including above and below the knee amputations and multiple fractures, and myocardial infarction. The conservative estimate was that about 1,200 disabled state residents of the state's then 1.8 million population needed services. Based on average lengths of stay observed in medical rehabilitation centers in other states, the recommendation was made for 127 new medical rehabilitation beds with demand estimated to support between 84 and 94 beds at that time for the specified disabling conditions. The findings and recommendations were made in a 209 page planning report comprised of seven chapters, ten appendixes, and 33 exhibits or tables (Greenwood and Pearson 1978) that could easily have gathered dust were it not for a follow-up political strategy designed to accomplish implementation.

Utilization Methods:
Planning and Implementation of Research Findings

The one preconceived strategy for utilizing the study's findings was in the State Medical Association's resolution: "That once such documentation is developed, it be presented to appropriate agencies and committees in the Executive and Legislative Branches of State Government . . ." The method of presentation, however, was not planned in advance, but evolved from questions I put to myself upon looking at the newly bound 209 page planning report: "What do we do with it? What committee or agency will do anything soon with this?" My answer was to have a day-long conference to which decision-makers would be invited.

Presentation of Research Findings: The Conference

The conference on "Medical Rehabilitation Needs in West Virginia: What Direction?" took place on Saturday, December 8, 1978. The following objectives were set:

1. To examine need for medical rehabilitation services in West Virginia.

2. To present alternative models for meeting medical rehabilitation needs.

3. To discuss ways of meeting medical rehabilitation needs in West Virginia.

4. To approach a tentative consensus regarding problem definition and directions for problem resolution.

Faculty for presentations and panel discussion included a local rehabilitation nurse, a state medical school dean, the medical director of the state Division of Medical Rehabilitation, a professor of neurology, two local orthopedic surgeons including Dr. Ghiz, the medical director of a physical medicine program in Kentucky, a professor from a physical medicine and rehabilitation residency training program in Ohio, a specialist for the physically disabled from North Carolina, Dr. Pearson, and myself. Also a father and his quadriplegic daughter who had been rehabilitated in the Kentucky program presented their case as illustrative of problems encountered with no close-to-home rehabilitation services.

While the conference was well attended by 88 participants, the use of state political leaders within the program itself was a decisive factor in its effectiveness. The Governor's executive assistant, the state chairman of the Republican party whose wife happened to be a paraplegic, and the Democratic president of the state senate each moderated a part of the program.

At the end of the day in his summation of the conference, the medical school dean noted that while the findings for medical rehabilitation service needs were not definitive, there was consensus that there was need and that the state should move to address that need. With that, the dean asked the president of the state senate if some legislative funding could be obtained. His response was both positive and cautionary: yes, but probably no more than $100,000.

In the following legislative session a few months later, a $50,000 rider to another bill provided funding in the State Department of Health's budget for assisting interested hospitals in planning medical rehabilitation services. Research findings were beginning to be put into use.

The Ad Hoc Steering Committee and Local Planning

The *ad hoc* steering committee, comprised of representatives from three state agencies (Department of Health, Workers' Compensation, and Vocational Rehabilitation), two state medical schools, the State Medical Association, and the State Hospital Association, was formed to advise and to monitor the local planning process. The committee functioned under the auspices of the Department of Health and was chaired by the Director of Health, Dr. George Pickett. The *ad hoc* committee did not have to be broadly representative of state agencies and organizations nor of the population in general, and it was not: each of the eight original members had a personal and professional commitment to medical rehabilitation--and four had a potential conflict of interest.

The lack of any need for broad representation lies in the fact that there was no resolution or mandate for the committee. Dr. Pickett and I discussed which agencies should be involved, and his request for participation was the only power behind committee member appointment; there did not even have to be a committee other than by his discretion in allocating funds. The conflict of interest for some committee members would come in the process of allocating funds as they represented entities that would be obvious candidates for developing a medical rehabilitation center.

In the meantime, I had resigned from my university position as research associate to accept a position with the Department of Health, directing a National Institute of Mental Health (NIMH) grant to the department. While I remained centrally involved in the rehabilitation services planning effort, time now had to be worked in as it was not part of my NIMH responsibilities. Primarily I prepared the agenda and wrote up minutes for the *ad hoc* steering committee meetings.

The first action of the committee was to request proposals for planning and implementing medical rehabilitation from all licensed hospitals in the state. It was Dr. Pickett's argument that *all* hospitals had to be contacted so there could be no claim of discrimination although only few hospitals could conceivably have the resources to begin to consider a medical rehabilitation program. In September, 1979, a follow-up half day meeting was sponsored by the Department of Health for the representatives from those dozen or so hospitals interested in developing competitive planning proposals. As noted earlier, the State Medical Association's resolution called for a "Physical Rehabilitation Center for the State." During the steering committee's first deliberations on allocating the planning funds, this original concept began changing. Debate centered on the development of one or two "high tech" or tertiary medical rehabilitation facilities/programs vis-à-vis developing general community hospital medical rehabilitation programs. This issue fueled the development of a conceptual basis for a state-wide service plan which became verbalized in the minutes of the April, 1980, committee meeting as "third tier" (tertiary) and "second tier" (community) hospital-based rehabilitation services.

The steering committee members were divided on which should come first, with the slight majority favoring an initial third tier program development. There were six proposals before the steering committee, each competing for $50,000: two from state medical schools, with representative members on the steering committee; one from the state's largest community and teaching hospital with which Dr. Ghiz, a key committee member, was associated; and three from community hospitals. Three contracts were awarded: one to each medical school and one to the major community and teaching hospital. It was acknowledged that by dividing up the legislated appropriation, only very preliminary implementation, or "phase one" planning could be undertaken. But the conflicts of interest on the steering committee were viewed in a positive way, as competition that would produce the information as to which entity could best actually implement medical rehabilitation services. Then, provided funds were available, a new contract for phase two, the development of detailed plans, would be negotiated.

The division of opinion among committee members regarding third tier and second tier services, nevertheless, created the rationale for Dr. Pickett and Mr. Lewis to approach the Senate president requesting a second legislative appropriation of $50,000 to be used to award a planning contract to the one active community hospital that had, by the consensus of all committee members, submitted the best proposal. Again, the Senate President was successful in obtaining an appropriation. The explicit intention of this contract award from the Department of Health's budget was two-pronged: the hospital, in planning for its own second tier rehabilitation program was also to provide a feasibility model for other community hospitals interested in this level of rehabilitation services. With the letting of the contract, the hospital administrator was then included on the steering committee.

For nearly a year there was no further significant state-level activity in medical rehabilitation services planning. The steering committee met only once to review and approve unanimously the second tier, or community hospital-based rehabilitation model. The report submitted to the committee concluded that:

> If the tertiary center is to come close to the model projected in the Greenwood-Pearson study, it would be unrealistic for most of the local physical rehabilitation planning groups to view their projects as the prototype state physical rehabilitation tertiary center. Neither the epidemiological data nor our own studies justify the requirement for more than one or at most two centers of this kind in the state. Rather, the compelling need is for accessible community-based rehabilitation units which are close to home, which can help patients improve daily living functions and can link them immediately to local providing agencies (Newman 1981).

While the second tier model was shown to be feasible in operation, capital financing for implementation was uncertain. In addition, the three earlier contractees--the two medical schools and the state's largest community and teaching hospital--had, to date, submitted only progress reports. And progress was slow. Then, a series of events provided needed momentum to the planning process.

Critical Events

In January, 1982, Dr. Pickett resigned his post and in doing so turned over the responsibilities of chairing the rehabilitation services steering committee to me. I retained that post even after the new Director of Health was named and became a member of the committee. Later that summer, I moved from the Department of Health to the state Workers' Compensation Fund as Director of Research and Development and had the latitude to become more involved with rehabilitation issues.

In spring of the same year, because of the personal interest of the chairman of the Department of Orthopedics, one of the medical schools undertook efforts to develop a Certificate of Need (CON) for a medical rehabilitation program. (U.S. Public Law 93-641 requires that all major new health services and equipment be approved by the CON arm of a State Health Planning and Development Agency). The consultant hired by the University Hospital to develop the CON application was unable to find a capital financing agent (the state-funded hospital did not have investment capital), and eventually redirected her efforts to produce a planning document for a third tier rehabilitation program (West Virginia University 1982).

During this same period, a competing community hospital in the same town as the medical school's University Hospital submitted a CON application for a 45 bed medical rehabilitation service. This hospital had not been part of the *ad hoc* planning process, and the application showed a lack of understanding not only of the systems planning process that had been going on, but, more importantly, of medical rehabilitation facility and equipment needs. However, if otherwise in compliance with CON requirements and regulations, the application's conceptual flaws would not be substantive because there were no legal CON guidelines for medical rehabilitation. The steering committee members and representatives of the institutions that had received planning contracts, along with others concerned about the integrity of a systems planning process, became active in opposing what was considered to be a poor CON application. This competing community hospital eventually withdrew its CON application because of general public relations problems it was having regarding this and other matters.

From Ad Hoc to Formal Planning

The preceding events underscored the need for explicit CON guidelines for judging applications for medical rehabilitation services. The only statutory requirement for CON applications was that they be consistent with the State Health Plan. As a result, there was a shift in the steering committee's role. In the fall of 1982, discussions centered on developing a Medical Rehabilitation Chapter for the State Health Plan, which would provide the legal basis for any future Certificate of Need decisions. Accordingly the CON review and decision-making process would need to consider each application not as an isolated case, but within the framework of a planned statewide medical rehabilitation system. The burden would be on the applicant to submit an application totally consistent with the plan.

The Division of Health Planning in the Department of Health and its constituent group of appointed consumers and providers throughout the state, known as the State Health Coordinating Council, were apprised of the desirability of an authoritative document, and the *ad hoc* steering committee was adopted as the official task force to complete the chapter, although routinely a task force is appointed. The State Health Coordinating Council and its planning arm, the Plan Development Committee, were now in control of medical rehabilitation services planning and the *ad hoc* committee was no longer *ad hoc*, but an entity responsible to a statutory authority.

The process of developing the chapter involved my assuming the role of lead writer (with special dispensation from my boss for this interagency effort) and digesting the trilogy of state medical rehabilitation planning documents: the original needs assessment, the subsequent plans for a model second tier program, and the plan for a third tier program that would address both service, referral, and health professions education in rehabilitation. The need arguments and the concepts and processes necessary to establish a tiered rehabilitation services system were recast into goals, objectives, and actions. Because of my primary care background, I emphasized community-based service linkages and primary care as the first tier of a medical rehabilitation system, an emphasis reiterated throughout the chapter.

Committee members and interested others reviewed a sequence of written chapter drafts. A final draft was publicly reviewed between May and September of 1983 with general expressions of support and little negative reaction to this statewide plan for a new type of health services delivery. The second and third tier distribution of beds and services was, however, still at issue. This was resolved in the last formal meeting of the Plan Development Committee in September 1983. A ceiling of 184 medical rehabilitation beds (8.6 beds per 100,000 population derived from the New Jersey Health Plan) was set through 1986 and until monitoring of rehabilitation services would show need for more. A minimum of 6.8 beds (per 100,000 population) to be developed by 1986 was also set based on the conservative epidemiological estimate from the 1978 need assessment. A range of bed need was deemed best to guide cost-effective development and to ensure that real need would be met.

Interest in rehabilitation was stimulated not only by this official statewide plan, but also by the new federal third-party reimbursement structure of Diagnostic Related Groups (DRGs), which exempted medical rehabilitation services from this new structure. With DRGs in place for acute medical care services, hospitals are reimbursed a set amount for a given diagnosis and related diagnoses by Medicare, the federal health care program. These reimbursement ceilings bring with them shorter hospital stays. Since rehabilitation services are exempt from the DRG scheme, hospitals can transfer a patient once acute care is no longer reimbursable to a rehabilitation program which will be reimbursed by Medicare as long as such a program is in place and there is rehabilitation need. Physical restorative services needed for functional improvement, that would have occurred in an extended acute care phase before the DRG reimbursement system, can now be provided as medical rehabilitation services. However, this situation also provides the potential for fiscal abuse.

In any event, during the summer of 1983, a small arena of competition had developed, since five CON applicants were preparing proposals for the development, implementation, and management of medical rehabilitation programs in West Virginia. Three of these applications dealt with second tier services and were submitted by out-of-state entrepreneurial health care consultants with development capital. The consultants in developing their applications had affiliated themselves with one of the state medical schools, the community hospital that had developed the second tier model study, and another community hospital. Two applications were being developed for third tier programs, one by the other medical school in collaboration with the hospital that had submitted the earlier controversial CON application and the second by the large community teaching hospital. The applicants or their affiliates were strategically located geographically so that the issue would be allocation of beds between the tiers given well documented applications.

The second tier/third tier issue erupted at a meeting which all applicants and the committee members attended in August, 1983. A new official agency had become part of the process: the State Health Care Cost Review Authority. The Authority had statutory responsibility for monitoring fees charged by hospitals, and applicants feared that the Authority would be overly harsh in applying its oversight responsibility to new medical rehabilitation services. The chairperson of the Authority decided to hold a meeting to offer assurance that the Authority recognized the need for medical rehabilitation and would cooperate as far as reasonable with coming new programs and facilities. The issue hotly discussed at the meeting, however, was not cost and reimbursement of services, but allocation of the 186 beds between the two service tiers.

The controversy continued through the fall. The Director of Health submitted the Medical Rehabilitation Chapter to the governor of West Virginia for his approval with a letter suggesting that he approve the plan and require the Department of Health to develop a standard for allocating second and third tier beds. In January, 1984, the governor signed a letter of approval which directed that a bed allocation standard be developed. However, as the health care consultants to the hospitals submitted CON proposals for free-standing medical rehabilitation facilities, amendments were made to the State Medical Rehabilitation Plan to increase the number of beds so that each facility would be built for 40 beds, or for economy of scale rather than according to the epidemiological standards in the State Plan. The amendments, in effect, increased the number of second tier beds making the allocation policy unnecessary.

Project Impacts

This case history demonstrates a mostly successful systems planning effort for improving medical services to disabled individuals. Through a widening circle of interest and participation, medical rehabilitation became part of the official health care agenda in West Virginia. This would seem appropriate: West Virginia has the highest percentage of work-disabled citizens in the nation, according to Social Security Administration statistics (1979), and is one of the three or four most disabled states according to National Health Interview statistics (1980). Epidemiologically, the high rate of disability is not surprising: there are higher than average rates of elderly in the population, of congenital and genetic anomalies, and of industrial injuries, given the heavy industries of coal mining, glass manufacturing, timbering, and metal work in the state. West Virginia is a rural industrial state, and the non-farm rural population showed the highest rate of disability among rural and urban populations in the United States in 1980 (United States Dept. of Health and Human Services n.d.). The rural context of disability, with scant rehabilitation resources, is largely passive (Omohundro et al. 1983). In rural Appalachia, men and women accept disability in large part as an inevitable, enduring fate (Horton 1983).

Given the social and economic conditions in the state, the documented disability, and the assessed rehabilitation need, the process of planning and implementing a medical rehabilitation services system is indeed cultural intervention for cultural change toward an accepted middle class norm of rehabilitation. The widening circle of interest and participation in the planning process brought in physicians, state officials, hospital administrators, appointed citizen consumers, consultants, and lastly health enterprise entrepreneurs. In essence, it was top-down planning that originated from a perceived service gap and service need among key medical personnel and proceeded with other strategically positioned persons and entities participating.

Continuity

While the project called for increasing involvement of others, four persons sustained the continuity of the effort: Dr. Ghiz, Mr. Lewis, Dr. Pearson, and myself. I was most closely identified with the project, having co-authored the need assessment, then assuming the chairmanship of the *ad hoc* committee after Dr. Pickett's departure from the state, and finally writing the official State Plan for Medical Rehabilitation. But in no sense was I perceived to own the project; a clear strength of the project from the outset was the centrality of collaboration. While collaboration is evident beginning with co-authorship of the needs assessment, in terms of project impact it really began with the December, 1978 conference on research findings.

The Conference

After the original need assessment had been completed, there was a printed bound document of 209 pages. The notion of a conference to broadcast the findings was a way to bring the document into the political arena beyond simply distributing it "to appropriate agencies and committees in the Executive and Legislative branches of State Government" as called for in the Medical Association's resolution. Conferences, however, can have the same fate as document readership: attended, or read, only by those who are convinced beforehand and ignored by those key individuals who are not invested and who must be persuaded. The conference was a success to the project because the president of the Senate, one of the three political leaders selected to moderate segments of the day-long conference, identified with the need and had the power to appropriate limited funds. Thus state legislative sanction for the medical rehabilitation planning effort was obtained. While the Senate president was key, certainly having the governor's office represented aided the credibility of medical rehabilitation as a statewide need. Inviting political leaders not only to attend a conference, but involving them in the program as moderators guaranteed their audience and gave the key issue of the conference increased recognition.

Conflicts of Interest

During the actual program planning period from 1979 until the approval of the chapter on Medical Rehabilitation as part of the State Health Plan by the governor's office on January, 1984, the dynamic was what was referred to as conflicts of interest in the Introduction. While conflict of interest is usually considered a negative force in services planning and implementation, "conflicts of interest" can work positively when the tensions between and among them are similarly goal oriented. The *ad hoc* steering committee represented conflicts of interest in that the four entities receiving planning contracts were represented by members of the committee. As planning became formalized, representation from the state Commission on Aging and the State's osteopathic medical school was added. Conflict at the outset between members favoring a single center oriented toward high technology and those favoring a community hospital approach to rehabilitation of more common disabilities was resolved by funding initial planning of the former and using the merit of the community hospital concept to obtain legislative funding for a feasibility study.

The second occasion of conflict was external to the committee and occurred when the community hospital that had not been part of the planning process submitted a CON application. With that submission, the *ad hoc* planning process confronted a legal challenge. The conflict resulted in formalizing the planning process, thus giving it legal status with the resultant chapter for the State Health Plan. For the conflicts of interest on the committee, the challenge of coming up with the Medical Rehabilitation State Health Plan acted as a superordinate goal (Sherif et al. 1961) furthering negotiation of interests. Through the process of debating successive drafts of the Plan, the tiered system of medical rehabilitation programs and facilities was thoroughly developed.

The third occasion of conflict was in the final stage of the formal planning process and was both internal to the committee and external to it. The entrepreneurial interests affiliated with organizations represented by some of the committee members argued for a more liberal estimate of rehabilitation need in the state, based on more current epidemiological information. This conflict over need became expressed as allocation of numbers of beds to the two service tiers. It was not resolved in the State Plan or through the planning process, but after the State Plan had been approved. As noted above, amendments to the Plan divided beds among successful applicants, partly based on standards set forth in the State Plan, but also according to economies of scale for building and maintenance. Final approval was for 80 third tier beds and 150 second tier beds, or 230 beds total, nearly two times as many as the original conservative estimate and 44 more than approved in the State Plan before the amendments to it.

Collaboration and Negotiation

Productive use of the 1978 needs assessment findings over a five year planning period essentially resided in both collaboration and a level of conflict that, for the most part, could be resolved through negotiation of various interests. Both processes were *ad hoc*. As I advanced in the Introduction, there is a strength to such an unplanned process as participants do feel they can contribute to and influence the process. Conflicts of interest can be negotiated through a structure for collaboration that is not controlled by a special interest. In chairing the committee as co-author of the epidemiologically-based need assessment and as representative of an agency that would use, not provide, rehabilitation services, I was neutral to the conflicts as was the Director of Health whose agency had no other role than receiving and disbursing the limited funds for planning.

Even a neutral structure for collaboration and negotiation, however, did not allow for total resolution of conflict. Ensuring that each of the entities that proposed medical rehabilitation services would get a share of the service was at the heart of resolving the conflicts of interest represented on and through the committee. While an epidemiological approach to bed need did not necessarily have to be given up for this to happen, it kept getting weakened, first by an increase in beds according to an availability standard, then by the State's support of entrepreneurial interest in economies of scale for building and maintenance through amendments to the plan. The original conservative estimate of need, however, stimulated and then maintained the negotiation of different interests in providing services through most of the planning process and resulted in the tiered system. It preserved a realistic focus, especially during the preparation of CON applications, constraining parochial and entrepreneurial interests and keeping the program planning in check.

A little more than eight years following the conference and nine years following the first research, two planned medical rehabilitation programs in the state opened: a 40 bed third tier program in the large community teaching hospital in the central part of the state and a 40 bed second tier program in the southern part of the state. Two other 40 bed free-standing facilities, one located with one of the state's medical schools, were under construction. Approval had been granted for construction of a second 40 bed third tier free-standing facility at the other medical school in the northern part of the state and for opening a small 12 bed community hospital program in the eastern part of the State. Eighteen beds were located at a community hospital in the northern part of the state that had opened the small program the year that the planning process had started. CON approval had not been necessary for the bed conversion. This program was brought into the final planning process when statewide bed allocations were being made.

Summary

As stated at the beginning of the last section, West Virginia has the highest rate of work disability in the United States. How much of this disability is amenable to rehabilitation is unknown. It is known that much rural disability is related to social and economic factors as well as to physical or mental impairments. As noted earlier, there is cultural acceptance in the state for being disabled. Thus an educative, heuristic process will need to be undertaken in order to provide a supportive infrastructure for rehabilitative care. Local family physicians, their disabled patients, and human service community programs will need to become tied into a larger referral program. Leaving home and county is not easy for a typical West Virginian, thus the practical importance of a tiered service system in which the closest-to-home services can be accessed with regard to the assortment of services needed. Only the most complex and severe cases should need extended stays at a major center with follow-up and after care closer to home.

Getting an entirely new set of services established systematically throughout the state depended on the following factors:

- A service gap or absence of services

- Medical leadership responsive to need

- Using a conference to disseminate research findings and develop consensus

- A highly communicative *ad hoc* planning committee that brought together conflicting interests and points of view

- A researcher as neutral moderator and organizer of committee meetings

- Legislative appropriation of limited funds

- Moving from an *ad hoc* planning process to a formal process having legal authority

- The serendipitous arrival of a federal Medicare reimbursement scheme for acute care that increased administrative interest in medical rehabilitation

- The continuous involvement of the researchers through the entire planning and implementation planning process

While many of these factors were circumstantial, five can be replicable or generalized to other situations.

First, the use of a conference as a way of presenting research findings to a varied audience, members of which must become active participants in planning and implementation, creates an immediate open forum for debate and consensus building.

Second, key political leaders can effectively be used to moderate a conference in order to secure their attention and to give an issue increased credibility and importance. The trick, of course, is to secure their participation in the midst of busy schedules. On the other hand, conferences provide exposure, the *sine qua non* of political leadership. Personal acquaintance, of course, provides advantage in securing a key leader's participation, as does a leader's own interest in the issue at hand. The president of the Senate who became key to further funding for planning, however, participated simply on the basis of request.

Third, a structure for collaboration and negotiation in which the researcher serves as a neutral mediator and organizer can help resolve conflicts of interest and keep research findings in the forefront. The basic neutrality of an objective perspective on planning focuses debate and facilitates the negotiation of conflicts and differences. The point already discussed about the conservative epidemiologically-based need estimate that guided planning and stimulated negotiation represents such a neutral perspective.

A fourth factor in the utilization of the rehabilitation need research findings was my own continuous involvement with successive stages of planning and implementation. While it is not always possible for the researcher or research team to maintain continuous involvement, if it can be done, it definitely contributes to keeping a planning and implementation process moving forward.

The fifth general factor has been referred to earlier as "conflicts of interest" and an *ad hoc* approach to negotiation of conflict. This was the central creative dynamic to this project. The strength in this approach is that weak, inappropriate, or politically unsuitable planning assumptions can be given up for the negotiation of problem solutions. For example, the assumption of a single medical rehabilitation center was early found unsuitable as a concept that could hold together the interests necessary for actually getting services implemented. Giving it up did not damage or halt the project. As planning developed, the concept of tiered services with a central referral facility supported by decentralized facilities for the bulk of service provision was found politically palatable and more in harmony with bringing services to a population not highly mobile or educated.

A final comment on using research findings, then, is the need to continue to evaluate their utility for solving the problem that originally promoted the research. If one or more of the second tier programs becomes more extended care than rehabilitation, use of the research findings on rehabilitation need would have resulted in something other than intended. There is no guarantee that even apparently successful use of findings actually remains successful in terms of meeting a defined agenda. On the other hand, facilities and programs change and adapt as needs change, so once in existence they may be used to meet other needs.

Notes

1. The problem of a liberal needs assessment approach and service aggrandizement is demonstrated, for example, in Solem et al. (1979) and the critique of this report by Greenwood (1981).

8

Lessons from a Community Study of Oral Rehydration Therapy in Haiti

Jeannine Coreil

The utilization methods which enhanced the practical relevance of our study included involving officials in the proposal planning and instrument development [and] providing rapid feedback of preliminary results to key administrators before fieldwork was completed.

With the emergence of primary health care as the focus of developing nation health policy over the past decade, anthropologists have found new niches for their research in the field of international health. Most recently, the expansion of "child survival" programs through the support of UNICEF, WHO, USAID and private voluntary organizations has created a market for social science methodology applied to health planning and evaluation. In particular, the large scale promotion of oral rehydration therapy (ORT) for childhood diarrhea through social marketing and community intervention has generated a need for medical anthropological expertise.

Oral rehydration consists of giving small drinks at regular intervals of a simple solution of sugar and salt to accelerate intestinal water absorption and replace electrolytes, thereby preventing life-threatening dehydration. Although first developed for clinical use, particularly in the treatment of cholera, ORT is currently promoted as a home-based intervention to maintain hydration during diarrheal episodes. The World Health Organization (WHO) advocates use of a standard, premeasured package of oral rehydration salts (ORS) containing anhydrous glucose, sodium chloride, potassium chloride, and either sodium bicarbonate or trisodium citrate dihydrate. A cheaper alternative for early home use or when packets are not available are homemade solutions of table sugar and salt (SSS) or the more recently developed food-based solutions (WHO 1986). The homemade solutions can adequately correct for diarrheal fluid losses but do not reverse hypokalemia, and correct acidosis slowly. The relative advantages of ORS and SSS from the standpoint of acceptability, ease of instruction, accuracy of preparation and therapeutic efficacy have and continue to be discussed.

Although the distinctive contribution of anthropology in applied diarrheal diseases research remains ethnomedical and qualitative, in practice anthropologists are combining traditional ethnographic techniques with survey and other quantitative methods to address complex problems (Coreil and Mull 1988). Promoters of ORT have recognized the importance of cultural compatibility to program success. Therefore, anthropologists who can provide a rapid ethnographic assessment of popular beliefs and practices, and who are also capable of integrating cultural insight with survey design and operational measurement, can provide a well-balanced social science component to a project.

In the study described in this chapter, we investigated acceptance of ORT in a Haitian community. We wanted to find out which mothers were using the treatment and why, and to what extent traditional healers had incorporated ORT in their activities. A third objective was to describe how ORT fit into traditional practices for home management of diarrhea. We chose to focus on a single community health program to allow for interpretation of findings in ethnographic context.

The research was conducted in the summer of 1984, one year after the start of a multi-sectorial national campaign to educate the public about oral rehydration for diarrhea. The campaign relied on mass media, social marketing, public education, patient instruction in clinics, and community outreach using trained health workers. There were other studies being done around that time, including a national sample survey funded by the Pan American Health Organization (PAHO), as was our project. The large number of evaluation studies reflected the variety of different agencies involved in the loosely coordinated diarrhea control program. By the time we reported our results, public health officials were inundated with data about ORT.

From the start of the well-publicized campaign in 1983, management was fragmented among government bureaucratic divisions and international organizations. It was difficult to discern whether everyone or no one was in charge. This complicated the planning and utilization of the research. To worsen matters, beginning in 1984 and steadily accelerating through 1985, political unrest in Haiti stifled all public health activities and devastated the ORT program. By the time Jean-Claude Duvalier fled the country in February 1986, the momentum and direction of the program had virtually dissolved.

About this time on the international health scene, a renewed interest in the control of communicable diseases through immunizations arose.

Regional and national campaigns to control selected diseases shifted attention and resources away from diarrhea to preventable childhood diseases. In Haiti this shift was on a limited scale because of the political turmoil; nevertheless it was yet another factor in the decline of the ORT program.

These external developments constrained the utilization of our findings, despite careful planning to foster practical application and a generally favorable endorsement of the study recommendations. Awareness that even the best laid plans for knowledge utilization can be thwarted by uncontrollable events serves to caution us to be prepared for extenuating circumstances at the same time that it reminds us that we are only partly responsible for the practical utility of our research.

Research Methods and Context

The project was supported through PAHO's Diarrheal Diseases Control (CDD) Operational Research Program. Funding came directly through the regional office in Washington, D.C., and the client group included both the regional CDD administrators and the PAHO country office in Port-au-Prince. The principal consumers of the research were intended to be Ministry of Health officials in charge of the national diarrheal diseases control program. Other potential consumers included Haiti's UNICEF office, the USAID mission and private agencies, as well as the staff of the community health program, the district health office and the regional department within the Ministry of Health with jurisdiction over the study area. The beneficiaries of the ORT program and, ultimately, this research were infants and children at risk for diarrheal dehydration, through the actions of their caretakers.

The study was carried out in an area served by the community health program based in Montrouis, a coastal town located 80 km north of Port-au-Prince. There were approximately 15,000 people enrolled in the program, including 3,300 families, about half with children under five years old. Preventive maternal-child health (MCH) services are organized through 14 geographic sectors, each having an elected community health worker *(collaborateur volontaire)*. The program is administered by the St. Paul Clinic, which is affiliated with St. Paul Episcopal Church. We collected data during July-September, 1984.

The town of Montrouis has a population of 5,500. It has several schools, churches and stores, but no electricity or piped water. More than half the townspeople subsist through farming, as do almost all the rural families. This is a very poor area even by Haitian standards. The semi-arid climate and eroded, rocky soil are only marginally suited for growing the various grains, fruits, roots and vegetables that are the mainstay of household economy and diet. The densely populated rural villages are situated in the mountains, many without vehicular access. Only one small medical dispensary is found within the rural zones studied. In the town, however, several state and private clinics are operated and there are two hospitals and a few pharmacies in St. Marc, a short drive away.

Like medical facilities, establishments where Serum Oral packets are sold are concentrated in the town. These places include grocery stores, clinics, pharmacies, and the homes of community health workers and a few traditional healers. In the rural areas health workers' homes are the main sales posts for ORS. In this program, however, the use of homemade SSS had been promoted equally heavily as the packaged mix by the health workers in both the urban and rural sectors. In contrast, most other ORT activities in Haiti endorsed ORS as the preferred therapy with SSS presented as an alternative when the former is unavailable.

Despite the argument in recent policy discussions that ORT represents a "selective," quick-fix technologic intervention, as opposed to the more "comprehensive" primary health care (Rifkin and Walt 1986, Unger and Killingsworth 1986), in Haiti as elsewhere (*cf.* Kendall 1988) the teaching of oral rehydration to mothers is integrated with other MCH activities. Community health programs are organized around the concept of periodic rally posts for mothers and children, where trained health workers provide prenatal care, immunizations, vitamin A, growth monitoring, nutrition education, family planning, and ORT instruction. Each health worker is assigned roughly 200 families, about half of which have preschool children or childbearing women eligible for participation.

The overall design of the study can be described as a community survey and ethnography. We interviewed 320 mothers and caretakers of preschool children, selected randomly from registered households served by the Montrouis community health program, about their knowledge and use of ORT. A convenience sample of 37 healers were also questioned about their understanding and practice of rehydration therapy for diarrhea in children. In addition we conducted in-depth interviews with 22 informants about ethnomedical beliefs and home management of diarrhea. Through participant observation and interviews we got to know the social, political, and economic organization of the community.

Utilization Methods

Projects which are commissioned by a client group usually have a utilization strategy that is largely built into the study design (although this does not prevent many reports from merely gathering dust on administrators' shelves). With independently initiated projects, however, the researcher must take deliberate steps to ensure that the results have practical utility, and, as we shall see, even these efforts may not be enough. In our case, the funding program required a certain degree of utilization planning from the beginning, plus we were committed to turning out a policy relevant product. Under the guidelines of PAHO's Diarrheal Diseases Control Collaborative Research Program, projects must be approved by the country's CDD program manager and the local PAHO country office. Also, either the principal investigator or co-investigator must be a native professional residing in the country and currently working on projects related to diarrhea control.

I learned of the CDD Collaborative Research Program through an announcement in the Medical Anthropology Newsletter. The application procedure required submission of a brief prospectus outlining the research design and identifying the host country collaborator. In planning the study I sought to build upon previous ORT research in Haiti, and this entailed obtaining copies of unpublished reports and official documents. For a collaborator I invited a Haitian physician who served at the time on a three-member committee for evaluation of national CDD activities. He held the position of nutrition advisor with Management Sciences for Health in Haiti, a private consulting firm contracted by the USAID mission to provide technical assistance in public health programs to the Haitian Ministry of Health. The other committee members included an epidemiologist from the Department of Public Health and Population (DSPP) and a PAHO staff person responsible for maternal and child health. I sent the prospectus to the PAHO Washington, D.C., office and the co-investigator for comment. PAHO sent it to the country office in Port-au-Prince, and the co-investigator presented it to the CDD evaluation committee.

The feedback from the CDD committee was very positive and helpful. It included suggestions for minor changes in study design and a recommendation to do the project in a different site than I had proposed. The committee thought Montrouis would be a better setting for several reasons: (1) there was a focused community health program, including ORT education, that began about the same time as the national ORT campaign, making it a good area to assess one-year impact; (2) at that time the program was one of very few in Haiti to have completed a household census of all families served, thus providing a population sampling frame; (3) the program was well organized and the staff committed to its goals; and (4) the community health workers had from the beginning placed equal emphasis on teaching the home recipe for rehydrating solution (SSS) as well as the packaged method, allowing us to assess differential acceptance of the two techniques.

The committee's suggestions were communicated to me through my collaborator and through PAHO by way of the country office in their review of the prospectus. All of the suggestions were incorporated into the final proposal. When the study was approved for funding by the PAHO/CDD steering committee, it was with the stipulation that I work closely with the Ministry of Health and particularly the CDD program manager. The review committee wanted to make sure the study responded to the needs of the national CDD program and not merely to the scientific interests of an academic researcher.

Figuring out which officials to work with was not an obvious task. Unlike many countries which have adopted diarrhea control programs, Haiti had no designated CDD manager. From the start the campaign had multiple leadership and funding, including UNICEF, WHO/PAHO, USAID, various PVOs (private voluntary organizations), the Haitian pharmaceutical firm producing ORS packets for the country, as well as several divisions within the DSPP. Most notable among the latter were the Division of Family Hygiene and Nutrition, and the Division of Health Education, both of which viewed ORT promotion as its responsibility. To complicate matters, the first lady of the country, Mme. Michelle B. Duvalier figured prominently in the media campaign, and the first shipment of packets donated by UNICEF were stamped as "a gift from the first lady to the children of Haiti." A PAHO/CDD staff member from Washington, upon return from a trip to Haiti, summed up the situation aptly when he told me it was "hard to tell who was in charge of diarrhea control in Haiti."

During the first week after my arrival in Haiti to do the study, I met with as many of the key officials as possible, and made a brief visit to the study site to meet with the local staff and make living arrangements. I was impressed with the organization of the community health program and appreciative of the support for the project expressed by the program administrator and her staff. Among the government officials visited, the Director General of the DSPP was generally recognized as the national CDD program manager. He expressed interest in the traditional healer component of the study, an aspect which no one had yet looked into. He raised the question of generalizability of the findings from one community for the entire country. We presented our rationale for an in-depth study which would have implications for national policy. The Director General advised us to also meet with the regional and district health officials for the Montrouis area.

The assistant director of the Western Health Region was enthusiastic about the study but not in favor of the project site. He questioned the value of data collected from a program that was atypical in its emphasis of the home preparation method. He advised us to discuss other possible site locations with the district health director. The latter official spent several hours with us revising the survey instrument to include questions of interest to the district. Regarding site selection, he expressed some preference for doing the study in a state- supported program, but he had no objection to doing it in Montrouis and thought the results would be useful. We decided to go ahead with the Montrouis site because of the strengths previously mentioned in the CDD committee's recommendation. Also, another PAHO study funded the same year planned to draw a national survey sample and would complement our community findings with ORT use data representative of the country as a whole.

Overall we found a high rate of knowledge and use of ORT, considering that the national and local programs had been in existence only one year (Coreil 1985). No serious social or cultural barriers to acceptance of ORT were found, mothers reported positive evaluations of the therapy, and children were said to drink the solution well. The main challenges of the program included dissemination of information and supplies to rural areas, and education of caretakers in aspects of ORT preparation and administration. Despite the fact that SSS was emphasized in this community, the majority of users had prepared their solutions from ORS packets. A high rate of misinformation about home preparation techniques was found.

Knowledge and use of ORT was found to be highest among respondents living in the more urban areas, those who were literate and had a better economic position, and those in which a family member had recently used modern medical services. Respondents who initiated therapy early (as is recommended) had higher levels of literacy and material wealth, and incorrectly believed that ORT "cured" diarrhea rather than simply replaced water loss. Finally, respondents who chose the preferred method of preparation, commercial packets, tended to be more urban, have greater wealth, be in conjugal partnership, suscribe to the "hydration" model of ORT effect, and delay initiation of therapy for three or four days after onset of the episode.

A large number of traditional remedies for diarrhea were identified. Most of these consisted of herbal teas called *rafrechi* (literally "refreshment") because they are given to cool the body. Diarrhea is classified as a "hot" illness in the folk medical system, therefore appropriate treatment calls for restoring the body's humoral balance with a cooling remedy. A large number of mothers and traditional healers identified ORT as a *rafrechi*, and a significant proportion of respondents had added guava leaves, the most common herbal diarrhea medicinal, to their hydrating solutions. Although traditional healers treated a fair number of cases of diarrhea in children, they were less informed about ORT than mothers. Midwives and injectionists had significantly greater knowledge and use of ORT than herbalists and shamans. All healers interviewed expressed interest in collaborating with health officials in the control of diarrhea.

We recommended that the following actions be taken to improve the ORT program. The top priority should be expansion of efforts to reach the rural population. Suggestions for possible strategies to achieve this were made. We advocated integrating the popular notion of *rafrechi* in promotional messages about ORT, and suggested investigating the acceptability of guava flavoring for ORS as well as the empirical therapeutic value of guava and other herbal remedies. Because of constraints of cost and supply we recommended promotion of the home recipe as well as the packaged method, but stressed the need for individualized instruction to minimize errors in preparation. Several problem areas were identified regarding understanding and use of ORT that needed special emphasis to correct faulty knowledge and behavior. Finally, we argued for the utilization of certain types of traditional healers in the promotion of ORT.

Our utilization objectives for the study were threefold: (1) to collect data and make recommendations with practical utility for program evaluation; (2) to communicate this information as quickly as possible; (3) to disseminate the results directly to all relevant parties. I will describe specific actions taken to achieve each of these objectives in the remainder of this section.

The steps we took to ensure that the study findings would have practical utility began in the early planning stages, as already described. The collaborative nature of the funding program, and the project approval procedure required that the study objectives have broad policy relevance. At the level of specific data, we solicited input from numerous individuals on design of the survey questionnaire and phrasing of individual items. The instrument went through six revisions after we arrived in Haiti. The most detailed revision took place in response to a review from the director and the health workers of the Montrouis community health program.

With regard to timely communication of results, I think our study was particularly successful in achieving this goal. Too often academic researchers depart from the field with their data, then spend months analyzing the results and preparing the project report. By the time clients finally receive the document, key decision-making events already may have passed. In our case, we began compilation of selected data even before the household and healer surveys were completed. Two field assistants began hand tabulating responses to key questionnaire items about halfway through the surveys. When three-quarters of the sample were completed, I typed up the results in a five-page preliminary report and distributed it to program officials before the final month of fieldwork had begun. This rapid feedback was extremely important in achieving utilization. Program planners were in the process of preparing the one-year interim evaluation and revision of priorities. Having the preliminary results of our study available at that time allowed feedback at a critical period.

Although the final report of the study was not due until July of 1985, nine months after fieldwork was complete, we made every effort to do as much of the data analysis as possible in time for the six-month progress report submitted in January. The progress report summarized all of the descriptive data analyses, including numerous tables, but had no interpretation of findings or recommendations. This report was also sent to several administrators.

The final report included the results of the multivariate analyses and a chapter devoted to study implications and recommendations. It had 69 pages of text, 36 tables, and appendices. We decided to use unspent funds to have the report translated into French in order to facilitate communication with non-English speaking clients. PAHO approved our request for this use of funds and a two-month project extension to allow for translation and typing of the French version. Multiple copies of both language reports were duplicated and bound. The final report was mailed to clients in September.

By the time program administrators received the final report, however, a critical period had already passed. Later I learned that in July an evaluation seminar had been held for representatives of the various agencies involved in diarrhea control. The findings of a number of studies, including those from my preliminary reports, were reviewed. By September, new reports had little practical value and the receipt of my final report was not even acknowledged for several months.

Our actions to achieve direct communication of findings to key individuals included making the report available in French, mailing copies to all persons we thought might use the results, and highlighting the major points in personal visits before leaving Haiti. For example, I set up appointments with the directors of the PAHO office, Management Sciences for Health, the USAID Public Health Division and the DSPP to present, highlight and discuss the preliminary report during the final week before departure. These personal interviews added weight to the impact of the findings. They also gave me the occasion to ask people for suggestions of areas in which to do more in-depth analyses.

Despite the positive steps we took to maximize utilization, a number of external circumstances hindered application of the study findings. The more important of these hindrances were the fragmentation of program management, the large number of contemporaneous ORT studies "competing" for attention, and the disruptive political situation in Haiti. I have already described the multisectorial composition of the CDD program and the absence of a designated authority for setting priorities and standards for the nation. Thus, no matter how important any study findings were there was was no one responsible for acting on perceived needs and endorsed recommendations. To make matters worse, most of the key administrators were replaced between the time our study began and the final report was written. Thus even our strategy for direct communication with all relevant clients was thwarted by the replacement of these individuals with people I had never met and who had little knowledge of the study. By the end of the study or shortly thereafter, the Director General of the DSPP had resigned and taken a post in Africa, the MCH staff person in the PAHO office had taken a new job in Washington, D,C., the USAID public health officer had been reassigned to another country, the director of Management Sciences for Health had relocated, and my co-investigator had taken a position with UNICEF. In short, most of the people I had worked with were either no longer in Haiti or busy with new responsibilities.

In applied research we usually think of a particular study as providing unique information on a problem. In our situation, there were several other ORT studies conducted about the same time, and they all addressed related questions such as extent of ORT use, acceptability, barriers, and evaluation of alternative promotion strategies (Desse 1984; Allman, Lerebours, and Rohde 1985; Rosenfield, Allman, and Allman 1985; Cayemittes and Ward 1985; Ministere de la Sante Publique et de la Population 1985). The various studies were duplicative in some respects, and provided contradictory findings on certain topics. One client expressed exasperation over the stack of reports he had received, unable at that point to sift through the lot and identify clear directives. Another described the situation as "evaluation overkill." Thus our study provided a set of recommendations that was one among many, and none of which had a clear agenda for implementation.

Probably the single most important obstacle to utilization was the mounting political unrest in Haiti that culminated in the overthrow of the decades-long Duvalier regime in February, 1986. Sporadic anti-Duvalier activities have taken place over the past several years, but events became noticably heated in 1984 with the occurrence of food riots in the north. Over the next year, a build up of tension was marked by anti-government protests, public demonstrations, more food riots, outspoken crticism by the Catholic Church, and increasingly violent reprisals from the Duvalier government in a desperate move to crack down on the rebellion. In August 1985 the government openly condemned the Church and denounced its inflammatory teachings. The final blow came on November 28 when three youths were killed in Gonaives, setting off wide-spread rioting and demands for the overthrow of Duvalier. Weeks later, unable to withstand domestic opposition and international pressure to resign, particularly from the United States, Jean-Claude Duvalier and his family fled the country. An appointed provisional government held power until the election of a new president in January 1988.

Needless to say, these political developments have had profound effects on all aspects of Haitian life, including public health programs. With diffuse management to begin with, and hampered by turnover in key administrators within the first two years, the CDD program hardly had a chance to get off the ground. What momentum it had at the beginning steadily declined until by summer of 1985 it was more or less at a standstill. All media activities had been discontinued and no new initiatives or directions were visable. The evaluation committee was defunct. The CDD program had clearly reached a crisis of leadership.

Faced with this dilemma, the Haitian public health community responded by shifting attention away from diarrhea to diseases preventable through immunization. This response was partly elicited by developments on the international health scene in which childhood immunizations became the focus of new programs and funding. The WHO's Expanded Program on Immunization (EPI), got a shot in the arm with the announcement in May 1985 of a new campaign to eliminate polio from the Americas by 1990. The drive is intended to serve as a vehicle for advancing the broader goal of universal immunization against the six major childhood diseases: measles, diptheria, tetanus, whooping cough, tuberculosis and poliomyelitis. USAID and other bilateral agencies have also adopted childhood immunization as a new priority. Thus by 1985, all new energy in the Haitian public health scene was going into immunization programs, and the stack of ORT reports remained largely unused.

Project Impacts

For a year after submission of my final report, my knowledge of the study impacts was limited to a few telephone conversations and letters. The study was praised for timely submission of reports and for the thoroughness of data analysis. The final report, however, added little to the impact of the earlier preliminary and progress reports. It was described as "anti-climatic" because officials were already using the "Coreil findings" a year earlier. Also, I was told that if there was any criticism of the study, it was that the final report was too detailed. I knew that administrators did not have time to read lengthy documents, but I assumed interested persons could skip to the final chapter for the summary and recommendations. Apparently, though, the sheer size of the report tended to discourage closer attention. I was surprised a year later to discover that my five-page preliminary report based on incomplete data was still being circulated by people who had access to the later reports.

In October 1986 I returned to Haiti for another project and had the opportunity to interview program administrators about the study impacts. The general opinion was that nothing had happened with the CDD program at all, much less observing concrete influence on policy and immplementation from a specific study. The large number of other studies done around the same time were mentioned as a limiting factor in that clients were inundated with findings and often faced with conflicting results. Also, in some areas similar recommendations were made by more than one researcher, so that subsequent actions were difficult to attribute to any one study. For example, several reports emphasized the need for greater rural outreach and one-on-one instruction, as ours did, and this priority was endorsed by program leaders.

Probably the most important impact of our study was to stimulate further research into beliefs about ORT and the potential role of traditional healers as promoters of ORT. In particular, our recommendation that ORT be identified as a *rafrechi* was investigated through a focus group study of mothers' attitudes and values regarding diarrhea treatment (Arthur 1986). This study confirmed our findings and supported our recommendations for the potential utility of social marketing messages using the traditional concept of *rafrechi*. The study also probed about use of traditional healers, but it concluded that contrary to our position, this was not a viable strategy. Other aspects of popular beliefs that we had discussed, including concepts of cure versus hydration, were also explored and confirmed in the focus group study.

Based on this follow-up research, certain new directions and emphases have been advocated by program officials, but still there is no leadership or resources to put the directives in action. The Director General of the DSPP was replaced again after the provisional government took over, and a new manager was appointed to direct CDD and EPI activities for the country. In October 1986, first steps were taken to reformulate the CDD evaluation committee. But the challenge of regaining momentum for the program was staggering. Furthermore, in the aftermath of anti-Duvalierism, there was public suspicion about the ORT program, originally identified with the first lady. For instance, one rumor had it that ORT was a Duvalier plot to sterilize Haitian peasant children!

In retrospect, I think the study was moderately successful in achieving practical use, given the external constraints discussed above. Its strongest points were the rapid communication of findings and the cultural insights which stimulated further research and endorsement of strategies based on ethnomedical concepts. Yet even though our timing of feedback on preliminary findings was good, we missed a critical event around the time of the final report because I was not aware of the planned seminar. Had I been, I could have speeded up preparation of the English report and submitted it before the French version was ready. The lesson here is that it is the researcher's responsibility to keep informed of important decision-making events in order to plan for optimal timing of feedback.

With regard to the content of the report, I learned that a full-scale, comprehensive analysis is not always appreciated, and a lengthly report may turn off clients who might be otherwise interested. As a general rule I would advise researchers to find out in advance what the client's expectations are regarding extensiveness of the report, possibly using other reports from similar projects as a guide.

While the ethnomedical findings of the study were used more than the survey results, the qualitative data were actually only a minor component of the overall study, something included more to provide context and allow interpretation of numerical data. Recognizing the value of this traditional anthropological information, were I to do the study over again, I would devote considerably more time and resources to qualitative data collection. Had there not been several other evaluation studies relying primarily on survey data, our own survey findings may have been more useful. This leads me to another issue, that of identifying what the informational needs of clients are in order to avoid duplication and maximize relevance of one's research.

Had I known so many ORT studies would be done around the same time, I may not have submitted a proposal in the first place. Our study was not developed in response to identified client needs but in response to the academic interests of an applied anthropologist. The basic problem here is, to what extent can unsolicited research projects find practical use? Although we had a funding source, this organization was not a client in the usual sense of a bureaucratic entity responsible for program management and policy development. While this chapter has focused mainly on utilization in Haiti, perhaps the more important "client" for the findings is a broader public health audience reachable through publication of scholarly articles, as we have tried to do (Coreil and Genece 1988, Coreil 1988). On the other hand, had there been a more clearly defined management group for the CDD program, client needs might have been more easily identified, and the utility of the study enhanced. Nevertheless, even if the client group and perceived needs had been well defined the unforseen political turmoil and resultant stagnation of public health programs would still have prevented significant application of the study findings.

Summary

The utilization methods which enhanced the practical relevance of our study included:

1. Involving program officials in the proposal planning and instrument development phases of the project;

2. Providing rapid feedback of preliminary results to key administrators before fieldwork was completed, in the form of a brief summary presented in personal visits; and

3. Translating the final report into French and distributing copies directly to individuals who had been involved in the study.

The limitations on utilization of the study findings were to some extent preventable, but largely beyond the control of the research team. The preventable aspects consisted of my failure to coordinate submission of the final report with important program evaluation meetings, partly as a result of preparing too lengthy a document and the delay of its submission until the French translation was complete. The factors beyond our control included the fragmentation of program management, the excess number of evaluation studies related to ORT, and the turbulent political situation in Haiti which paralyzed public health programs for some time afterwards.

In the final analysis it seems the most important lesson of our case is the recognition that we have limited control over the ultimate utilization of research. Even the best laid plans for practical relevance may be thwarted by external events not anticipated or beyond the researcher's control. Furthermore, there may exist only a limited need for the study in the first place, and therefore limited use is all that can be expected. Utilization goals must be based on a realistic assessment of need and tempered by awareness of the possibility that expectations may be compromised through no fault of the researcher.

9

Utilizing Indigenous Healers in National Health Delivery Systems: The Ghanaian Experiment

Dennis M. Warren

Involving all categories of healers and health workers meant that numerous influential individuals participated in and were knowledgeable about the design of the project, [which] resulted in higher levels of motivation and commitment.

Since the mid-1970s an increasing number of donor agencies such as USAID have begun to require social impact analyses in the project design and evaluation stages of development projects. Many agencies encourage client participation in project design decision-making. There is also a trend toward balancing the product orientation of many donors, which emphasizes easily measurable objectives such as the construction of feeder roads and crop storage depots, with what is termed a process orientation to development (Morss and Gow 1985). The process orientation emphasizes the need to strengthen both indigenous human resources and organizations involved in development so their efforts can be effectively sustained after donor resources end.

My development activities over the past decade have focused on identifying mechanisms to facilitate human resource development and participation in the development process. I have argued that a set of methodologies known in anthropology as ethnoscience is one of the mechanisms which agencies should become aware of and utilize. Ethnoscience provides us with techniques to accurately record indigenous knowledge and decision-making systems. A knowledge of these systems can assist us to understand better how a local community defines and classifies phenomena such as diseases or soil types, and how these classification systems provide a basis for decisions regarding health therapy or cropping systems. By formally recording these systems, we can compare and contrast them with western systems, thereby facilitating communications and understanding between change agents and members of local client groups.

Improved understanding can also enhance the possibilities for participation by client groups in problem identification, development planning, and decision-making. Ethnoscience as a set of methodologies is important in development, and the products of the research based on ethnoscience are invaluable to change agents. Frequently, the indigenous knowledge systems are found to be complex and surprisingly sophisticated. Since indigenous knowledge, decision-making, and organizational systems are often overlooked, ignored, and sometimes even maligned by outsiders, the products of such research can have an important impact on changing such negative attitudes.

This case study will focus on my efforts to understand and formally record the disease classification and health delivery system of the Techiman-Bono, an Akan ethnic group of central Ghana, and then to ensure that the research results were used in development. My interest in the research topic was first stimulated during 1964-66 when I served as the first Peace Corps Volunteer at Techiman Secondary School where I taught biology and chemistry. Because of the Peace Corps experience I decided to change my academic career, entered a doctoral program in anthropology and linguistics, and returned to Techiman to conduct the research for my doctoral dissertation on the Techiman-Bono health system during 1969-71. The results of this research proved to my satisfaction the potential of ethnoscience in understanding indigenous knowledge systems, especially when combined with other ethnographic and sociological survey methodologies.

After completing the doctoral degree, considerable effort was made to package the results of the research. It was anticipated that effective information dissemination could lead to attitude and behavioral change on the part of policy-makers, planners and other bureaucrats, which in turn would influence development policy and programs. If international and national development agencies could be made aware of ethnoscience and its potential for improving our understanding of indigenous knowledge, then perhaps it could be added as a standard component to project design efforts. If health ministries could be exposed to the Techiman-Bono data on indigenous health delivery systems, perhaps indigenous healers would be regarded as a valuable and overlooked human resource who could be better reflected in national health care policy and planning, and utilized in health delivery programs. This chapter will outline my activities and assess the effectiveness of my efforts to introduce ethnoscience as a methodology to development agencies and to influence the role of indigenous healers in national health delivery systems.

Research Methods and Context

My research has involved an understanding of indigenous health decision-making within a context where multiple therapeutic options were available, including a wide variety of categories of indigenous health practitioners, spiritualist healing churches, hospitals, an array of Ministry of Health services, and pharmacies. Ghana's changing medical scene is complex and reflected in part by the role played by indigenous healers in Ghanaian health delivery systems, a role which has shifted dramatically over the past century. Until the imposition of British colonial control, indigenous healers were the only health practitioners in what was then the Gold Coast.

Although frequently maligned by Westerners and westernized Ghanaians, we now know that the indigenous healers were organized, and that they supported preventive and promotive as well as curative health measures at the community, household, and individual levels during both the pre-colonial and colonial eras (Maier 1979; Wilks 1974).

In 1878, the British colonial government established a public sector health service based on Western allopathic principles and organizational systems. Indigenous healers were not mentioned in the legislative instrument and hence lacked official recognition. The colonial government set about to eliminate indigenous medical practices, sometimes with the active assistance of certain missionary groups. Negatively stigmatized by the state and some churches, indigenous healers lost prestige and in areas of high colonial presence they were forced to practice in secret.

Despite the legal separation of the Western and indigenous Ghanaian health delivery system, and the official disregard and occasional persecution of the latter, political and economic constraints prevented the extensive spread of Western health facilities and services beyond the major urban areas where the largest populations of expatriates resided. Moreover, the majority of the local citizens who had access to both systems regarded them as being complementary, not necessarily contradictory, and freely patronized both. In the more remote areas of the colony the indigenous healers usually remained the sole source of health care available to rural populations.

In 1964, several years after Ghanaian independence in 1957, I arrived as the first Peace Corps science teacher at the new secondary school in Techiman, a community in the Brong-Ahafo Region of Ghana. Historically, Techiman was important as the second capital of the earliest centralized Akan state which was founded within the first half of the fifteenth century. Because of its strategic geographical location in the ecological transition zone between the rainforest and the savannah, it has become the largest agricultural market town in Ghana (Warren 1981a). Although conquered in 1722 and ruled by the Asante until the Asante themselves were conquered in 1896 by the British, the Techiman-Bono have remained conscious and proud of their heritage.

As a biologist I was very interested in local flora and fauna and soon had become friendly with a number of indigenous herbalists who took me along when they visited the forest to collect plant materials. In 1965, I was formally adopted by the chief of Tanoboase, the head of the royal clan for Techiman Traditional State and also the custodian of the oldest and most important shrine for the Akan people of southern Ghana. Being incorporated into this extended family thrust me more deeply into the local culture and I was privy to ceremonies and rituals which are still closed to outsiders. I resolved to return to graduate school and obtain training in linguistics and anthropology so I could better understand what had become a second culture for me.

From 1969-1971, I conducted doctoral dissertation research in Techiman Traditional State, the traditional administrative unit which now coincides with Techiman District, one of 68 local administrative units within Ghana. The capital of both the traditional state and the district, Techiman is a township which is divided into two distinct parts. Techiman Town is the section populated primarily by Bono, and Techiman Zongo is the part populated mainly by non-Bono ethnic groups.

The primary objective of the research was to delineate the relationships between the Techiman-Bono ethnomedical and religious systems. Perhaps because of my earlier training in biology, I became very interested in ethnoscience as a set of techniques which could allow me to understand the ways in which the Techiman-Bono defined and classified diseases and based therapeutic decisions upon this knowledge. The dissertation research, which was applied in orientation, combined ethnoscience with standard ethnographic and survey methodologies (Warren 1974b). More specifically, it included health-oriented interviews with members of 660 households of Techiman Township, oral histories for all 92 towns and villages and for 394 healing shrines in Techiman Traditional State, as well as analysis of in-patient and out-patient records at the Holy Family Hospital, founded in Techiman in 1954 by the Medical Mission Sisters.

During both the Peace Corps experience and my doctoral fieldwork, I was very conscious of many negative attitudes regarding indigenous healers. Some expatriate doctors referred to indigenous medicines as "native poisons," and sometimes patients brought to a hospital with evidence of having taken indigenous remedies would be sent home without treatment. Even westernized Ghanaians expressed embarrassment and misgivings about the indigenous healers. The Ghanaian head of the Department of Medicine and Therapeutics at the University of Ghana Medical School stated, for example, that "indigenous or traditional medicine . . . is fundamentally based on primitive theories which over the years have been condoned by ignorance, sanctioned by superstition, and sustained by belief in magic and witchcraft. Under such circumstances even the rational use of effective therapy was frequently ascribed to supernatural guidance or intervention" (Dodu 1975: 5). Many of these negative attitudes were based on the writings of nineteenth century social scientists such as Spencer (1877), who generated the concepts of the "primitive" or "savage" and of the "primitive mind" (see a synopsis of the influence of these ideas up to the present in Warren 1979 and 1982b).

Ethnoscience allowed me to understand the Techiman-Bono disease and therapeutic system from the indigenous perspective and to formally record it without bias. That the system was complex and in many ways sophisticated was evident. That many of the earlier writings were inaccurate and biased was equally clear. For example, some researchers had reported that illnesses were primarily of supernatural origin (Field 1960; Rattray 1927), whereas my field and archival research demonstrated that, in fact, the majority of disease names and disease cases were based on concepts of natural causation (Warren 1976a). It became clear to me that indigenous healers could play a vital role in the national health delivery system if they were recognized as an important human resource by both development donor agencies and the Ghanaian Ministry of Health. I have applied my efforts to this problem for the past fifteen years.

My client groups became those organizations comprising the health delivery community at the international, national, and local levels. This included donor agencies such as USAID which I hoped to convince of the usefulness of ethnoscience in efforts to base development on indigenous systems which already exist in communities. It also included mission groups and government units working in health delivery in Ghana.

Several events facilitated my efforts in the Ghanaian context. After independence, Kwame Nkrumah, the first president of Ghana, took steps to organize indigenous healers into a unified national association. The Ghana Psychic and Traditional Healers Association was inaugurated in 1969 and was expanded in 1973 to include priest and priestess healers (Twumasi and Warren 1986). A second important event occurred in 1971 when Ghana passed the Local Government Act. This legislation allowed for decentralization of the government's development functions from the central government to the 68 district councils. These councils were given the right to collect a wide variety of revenues and retain them to cover part of the financial burden needed to implement locally designed development plans (Warren and Issachar 1983; Warren and Blunt 1984). A third event took place in 1974 when the Centre for Scientific Research into Plant Medicine was organized at Mampong in the Akuapim District under the leadership of Dr. Oku Ampofo, a renowned physician and artist who also was known for his skills in herbalism. Fourthly, about 1975, USAID contributed towards the strengthening of a National Health Planning Unit within the Ministry of Health.

Finally, during 1977-79 I had the opportunity to work on the USAID-funded Economic and Rural Development Management (ERDM) Project designed to provide management and development planning training to all 68 district councils and all nine regional councils in Ghana. The project was expected to facilitate the implementation of the 1971 Local Government Act and decentralized development planning and budgeting. Residing in Kumasi, I worked with two regional teams of Ghanaian trainer/consultants which provided district council training in the 18 districts of Brong-Ahafo and Ashanti Regions. The Ghanaian trainer/consultant teams and I worked with every government ministry and department as well as expatriate groups involved in development in the various districts. The project is described in detail elsewhere (Warren 1985). How the doctoral research information from Techiman became utilized at the policy and project level will be described in the next section.

Knowledge Utilization Methods

The strategies for ensuring utilization of my research knowledge focused on ethnoscience as a useful set of methodologies and procedures on the one hand and indigenous healers as a valuable national human resource on the other. Although the two issues are entwined, the audiences for the two have sometimes been distinct. I will first focus on efforts to disseminate information and influence policies about ethnoscience as a methodology, and then turn to the issue of indigenous healers and the specific outcomes within the Ghanaian context.

Use of Ethnoscience within Development Activities

In 1973 the House of Representatives Foreign Affairs Committee introduced amendments to the 1961 Foreign Assistance Act requiring development assistance strategies which would increase local participation in development efforts funded by the United States government (Owens and Shaw 1974, Mickelwait et al. 1979). This legislation became known as the New Directions for USAID and it has had important implications for the role of anthropology and other social sciences in development activities. With the assistance of Glynn Cochrane and other anthropologists, USAID organized the Development Studies Program which included anthropological training for USAID personnel (Cochrane 1971, 1977, 1979). The guidelines for social soundness analysis for project design were developed (USAID 1978), and permanent senior anthropology positions were established at USAID's headquarters in Washington, D.C., as well as at its regional centers in Abidjan and Nairobi. At the same time, the World Bank began to change its policy emphases to stress the involvement of local people in the entire planning and decision-making process (World Bank 1975).

In 1974 I had prepared a proposal for an applied anthropological component for an Iowa State University project proposal submitted to USAID which was designed to increase the production of cereals and legumes in Ghana. Incorporated into the proposal were ethnoscientific approaches and components. As this proposal circulated through USAID in Washington, it reached the office of Edward Hirabayashi who was, at that time, the human resource officer for the Africa Bureau. The issues raised in the proposal were of interest to him, so he travelled to Ames to discuss them. As as result, a weekly seminar was organized involving twenty social and technical scientists from the campus interested in pursuing the implications of the proposal.

One result of this seminar was "A Communication Model for Active Indigenous Involvement in Rural Development and Non-formal Education" which was presented to USAID/Washington by Warren and two colleagues in May 1974, and later, during the summer of 1975, by Warren at a workshop on Communication for Group Transformation in Development at the East-West Center (Warren 1976c). This model provided mechanisms for improved communication and collaboration between indigenous client populations and development agencies.

This model was further developed and presented by Hirabayashi, Warren and Owen in August 1974 at a special session of the Fourteenth World Conference of the Society for International Development held in Abidjan. Aiming at the development practitioner audience, we deliberately divided the model into dimensions which were labelled by acronyms, a procedure very common in development agency bureaucracies. This was a strategy to present new material in a format and language familiar to our clientele group. Having a USAID official as senior author and co-presenter provided more credibility with this non-academic audience. The Indigenous Network Communication (INC) Model for Human Resources Development involved five dimensions. The Ethnoscience (ES) Dimension was expected "to develop ethnoscientific taxonomies of indigenous systems of knowledge; to obtain a local viewpoint in order to tap the local, indigenous genius; and to understand and to utilize local decision-making bodies and processes" (Hirabayashi et al. 1976:65).

The Problem-Oriented Trans-Organizational (POTO) Dimension was designed to facilitate the utilization of the ES Dimension data effectively by facilitating collaborative, interorganizational or multi-sectoral approaches focusing on priority problems identified by the local clientele group. The POTO Dimension was also expected "to assist in the expansion of capacities of individuals and groups to act effectively on their own behalf--while still functioning with civic responsibility; as needs are identified, to locate and make available rural development technical assistance which will be incorporated into relevant ethnoscientific taxonomies and local decision-making processes; to facilitate a process whereby a system of local participation can be incorporated into planning processes for development of an area" (Hirabayashi et al. 1976: 65).

A follow-up seminar on the Indigenous Network Communication model was presented at USAID/Washington by Gerald Klonglan and Warren in December 1975. I was also asked to present the ethnoscience methodology at the West Africa Conference on Natural Resources Management in Arid Regions held at the University of Arizona in 1976. This was co-sponsored with USAID funding by the University of Arizona and Ghana's Council for Scientific and Industrial Research. Several Ghanaians were interested in the INC model and assisted in developing it further (Warren 1976b).

Gerald Klonglan, professor of sociology at Iowa State University, was invited by USAID to conduct one of the Agency's first social soundness analyses. This was done during March and April 1976 for the Economic and Rural Development Management (ERDM) Project proposed for Ghana. Klonglan included ethnoscientific methodologies to better understand and present indigenous concepts of development, participation, coordination, planning and social change. From September 1977 through August 1979, I served as a regional coordinator and helped to administer and implement the ERDM Project in the 18 districts and two regional administrations of the Ashanti and Brong-Ahafo Regions. The ERDM Project provided an opportunity to repackage my research information from Techiman with data compiled by the National Health Planning Unit in Accra. One of the problems we sought to resolve through the training workshops was the fact that many of the government officials were expected to work in unfamiliar districts where they lacked a working knowledge of the local culture and language. This frequently resulted in insensitivities towards local people. Working with three-person Ghanaian trainer/consultancy teams in each region, we prepared and conducted training seminars and workshops on management and development planning for all regional and district heads of government departments and elected district council members. The workshops included a wide variety of topics on cross-cultural and cross-disciplinary approaches to team building, communications skills, management and planning techniques, and problem-solving and decision-making capabilities.

Using ethnoscientific methodologies, teams of District Council workshop participants were asked to develop inter-ethnic and intra-ethnic classifications used by the local populations to define and classify members of Ghanaian society. Other exercises focused on the formal recording of indigenous knowledge systems. These had a positive impact on changing attitudes held by those Ghanaians who looked upon some ethnic groups as being "simple" and relatively "primitive" people. One exercise used Western material which portrayed Ghanaian indigenous healers in very negative ways. By comparing this material with the highly complex disease taxonomy of the Techiman-Bono, Ghanaian officials began to realize that indigenous healers may have been wrongly portrayed as primitive and ineffective.

Incorporating these anthropological concepts and methodologies into the District Council training workshops proved to be popular and useful to the participants. Multi-ethnic communications were visibly improved in the training teams during the course of the three-week workshops. Attitudes towards the local cultures--including the indigenous healers--were modified, as district officials began to rethink the role of these healers in rural health delivery. This utilization strategy of involving all of the elected councillors and all heads of government departments requires sensitive packaging of the concepts into culturally appropriate simulation exercises. It was essential to work with my Ghanaian trainer/consultants in order to develop these exercises. The collaborative presentation of this material in the workshops by both Warren (as an "outside" expert) and his Ghanaian counterparts (as "inside" experts) proved to be an important strategy for establishing credibility for the topic by the governmental officials and the local citizens. Using the simulation exercises in the workshop context provided a non-threatening environment in which participants would identify sensitive local problems and design locally-appropriate solutions.

Utilizing Indigenous Healers in Health Care Systems

One of the major problems facing the 68 districts in Ghana was the universal expectation by local populations that the central government would eventually provide all of the necessary resources to improve government services and basic infrastructure. During the ERDM workshops data were presented which indicated graphically that these expectations were unrealistic, given the continued decline of economic resources coupled with population growth. National Health Planning Unit data indicated that 85% of the Ministry of Health budget supported tertiary and secondary health facilities in the large urban centers, leaving only 15% to cover all types of health services for the 46,000 small towns and villages in rural Ghana where 75% of the population resides. Moreover, 82% of the physicians in the public service worked in the principal urban areas and were reluctant to live in what they considered rural and remote areas of Ghana.

Despite the fact that Ghana has thousands of indigenous healers of various categories, the Ministry of Health personnel had been trained to regard these healers as a nuisance and embarrassment to scientific medicine rather than a potential ally and resource for improving rural health delivery services. Combining the national budgetary and economic data with the Techiman ethnomedical research data had a positive impact on the attitudes of workshop participants, who began to view indigenous healers as valuable resources.

Spending two years on the ERDM Project in central Ghana where I was already well-known helped to facilitate the acceptance of my research data by government officials and medical mission personnel. In addition, during my doctoral dissertation fieldwork, I had established relationships with medical mission personnel and they were already familiar with my work. As the policy emphasis of the Medical Mission

Sisters and the Government of Ghana moved more towards primary (preventive and promotive) health activities to balance the curative focus of Holy Family Hospital, a project to provide opportunities for indigenous healers to improve their skills in primary health care seemed appealing. Most of the mission personnel were already on friendly terms with many of the indigenous healers. Moreover, the hospital had cordial links with the Ministry of Health at the district, regional and national levels, as well as with the Rural Health Training Centre in nearby Kintampo.

The Primary Health Training for Indigenous Healers (PRHETIH) Program was initiated in Techiman District after numerous discussions and negotiations with the various indigenous healers, the District Council, the Ghana Psychic and Traditional Healers Association, the Ministry of Health officials in Techiman, Sunyani (the regional capital), and Accra, the Centre for Scientific Research into Plant Medicine, the Rural Health Training Centre in Kintampo, and the Catholic Bishop in Sunyani and his Diocese staff. The Peace Corps provided a series of outstanding volunteers who served as field coordinators along with the regional secretary of the Ghana Psychic and Traditional Healers Association. Dr. Oku Ampofo accepted a series of indigenous healers from Techiman on internships at his Centre where they were trained in improved methodologies for preparing and preserving herbal materials so they could return to Techiman as part of the PRHETIH training team.

The program was formally inaugurated in June 1979 and reported on national radio and television. More than sixty indigenous and western healers attended the inaugural meeting. A 14-week training program was designed in cooperation with the indigenous healers themselves. This strategy fostered participation of the primary clientele group--the indigenous healers--in the planning process and proved to be an important factor in the motivation of healers to take part in the program. Training sessions were run by the field coordinators, Holy Family Hospital staff, Ministry of Health personnel, and the indigenous healers trained by Dr. Ampofo. During the 1979-83 period more than 120 indigenous healers successfully completed the training programs offered. Although a hiatus occurred during 1983-85 with the untimely death of the regional secretary of the Psychic and Traditional Healers Association, and rapid turnover of hospital and Peace Corps personnel, the program expects to offer more training programs for those healers who were unable to take part in the first sessions. Meetings were held in Techiman in March 1988 involving both the indigenous healers and the Holy Family Hospital staff to discuss these plans. A second cycle of training is also being considered for previously-trained healers who have taken part in the first cycle of training and who have expressed interest in additional topics. The early history of the program is described elsewhere (Warren et al. 1982) and in the film, *Bono Medicines*.

Several important strategies were found to be useful in the initial stages of organizing PRHETIH. Inter-organizational effectiveness and participation were enhanced by both vertical and horizontal flows of information through bureaucratic channels. Key persons were informed and involved at the local, regional and national levels. The project was very low cost. Training was provided by trained indigenous healers, Peace Corps volunteers, and existing health service staff. A "project mentality" which fostered territoriality was avoided. Health workers and indigenous healers from other parts of Ghana were encouraged to visit this unique experiment. This led to a positive multiplier effect when similar initiatives began later in both Berekum and Dormaa Districts. Publicity was most helpful. The project was packaged differently for academic and for popular audiences. The film, *Bono Medicines*, was shown on Ghanaian national television and in the local community, and it has been used widely in the academic and donor agency communities. Credibility was provided by involvement of important and well-known Ghanaians such as Robert Bannerman from WHO/Geneva and Kofi Asare Opoku from the University of Ghana. Both the publications on PRHETIH and the film, *Bono Medicines*, have led to considerable interest in the experiment by persons outside of Ghana. Dr. Edward Green, for example, has initiated USAID programs in both Swaziland and Nigeria along similar lines (Warren and Green 1988).

The PRHETIH experience indicates the necessity of taking the time and effort to discuss and negotiate such a development intervention with a wide variety of local people and government officials. Involving all categories of healers and health workers meant that numerous influential individuals participated in and were knowledgeable about the design of the project. This participation in decision-making resulted in higher levels of motivation and commitment. The fact that the experiment had been adopted in other districts is a sign of a positive multiplier effect. The Dormaa District program has built upon the Techiman experience by basing their training on the principle of dialogue between the indigenous and allopathic healers. Even though the Techiman approach was more one-sided, a strong peer relationship emerged between healers and health workers involved in the PRHETIH project.

Project Impacts

The Techiman research data have been utilized in a wide variety of ways. Information on ethnoscience as a methodology and data on the role of indigenous healers in national health delivery systems have been very widely disseminated and have resulted in better understanding of these issues by numerous policy makers and planners who have incorporated the recommendations into policy reformulations. As an intervention strategy at the grassroots level, the PRHETIH Program has had a dramatic impact in Techiman District, which will very likely have international ramifications. In this section I would like to cover the ways in which information on ethnoscience has been disseminated and has had influence on policy, and then turn to the ways that the Techiman ethnomedical material was disseminated, utilized, and influenced policy.

Use of Ethnoscience within Development Activities

The use of the term "indigenous knowledge" is now commonplace in development donor and practitioner circles where its value is no longer questioned. Internationally-influential social scientists are helping to push the arguments favoring indigenous knowledge. One of the most eloquent has been Robert Chambers, whose latest book (1983), with a full chapter on the topic, has been reprinted numerous times since its publication. Paul Richards has been asked to introduce some of his arguments related to indigenous knowledge to the Office of Technology Assessment in the United States Congress (see Richards 1985, 1986a, 1986b; Roling 1985). In 1980, I co-edited *Indigenous Knowledge Systems and Development* with David Brokensha and Oswald Werner, which has been reprinted several times. A large number of applied-oriented research projects based on indigenous knowledge has been completed in the past decade. Dr. Brokensha and I are in the process of compiling a follow-up volume which will document the impact of utilizing indigenous knowledge systems in a wide variety of development projects.

A training manual on the methodologies for formally recording indigenous knowledge and decision-making systems, for understanding indigenous organizational structures, and identifying indigenous innovations is being prepared by Paul Richards, myself, and Lin Compton. We are aiming at the world's network of extension training institutes and already have strong support from those which have been contacted about the manual. We are also developing guidelines for organizing National Indigenous Knowledge Resource Centers which would provide the means for systematically storing indigenous knowledge which has been formally recorded so it can be used by any interested persons. Werner and Schoepfle have completed their two volume work outlining the methodologies for ethnoscience and this is bound to have a very positive impact on the academic community (Werner and Schoepfle 1987a, 1987b).

In order to achieve a wider and more systematic impact on both the academic and the development practitioner communities, The Center for Indigenous Knowledge for Agriculture and Rural Development (CIKARD) was established at Iowa State University in 1987. I direct this Center with an internationally-recognized and development-oriented external advisory board. The Center is designed to provide a global clearing house service by accessing, storing, and disseminating information on all activities involving indigenous knowledge and decision-making systems in development. A number of proposals to conduct further research on indigenous agricultural knowledge systems, with an emphasis initially on determining gender, class, and ethnic differences in these systems, has been submitted to granting agencies and international donor agencies. Several European donor agencies are currently considering the possibility of funding efforts to establish a national model for the introduction of training in indigenous knowledge systems through the extension training institutes. If successful in the first African nation, the expectation is that Africans from that country would be involved in providing training to establish similar systems in other countries.

The notion of indigenous knowledge has begun to permeate the agricultural sector as well, in part due to the influence of Farming Systems Research programs. In 1984 I was asked to present material on indigenous agricultural knowledge at an international workshop in Lusaka sponsored by CIMMYT (International Maize and Wheat Research Center) and at an international seminar on the Role of Rural Organizations in the Process of Development held in Dschang, Cameroon (Warren 1984a and 1984b). While serving as team leader and senior social policy analyst for the USAID-funded Zambia Agricultural Training, Planning and Institutional Development Project (ZATPID) in Zambia during 1982-1985, I had the opportunity to expose a wide variety of expatriate development workers and Zambian officials to the potential power of formalizing indigenous agricultural knowledge systems. These ideas and team exercises used in national agricultural planning workshops were well received. A special workshop was held on methodologies for recording indigenous agricultural knowledge and decision-making systems for all of the Adaptive Research and Planning Teams (Farming Systems Teams) stationed in each of the nine provinces of Zambia. A summary of the changing attitudes towards indigenous agricultural knowledge at the national level as well as with the international agricultural research centers is available elsewhere (Warren 1989).

Another mechanism used to influence academics as well as international development practitioners in terms of indigenous knowledge has been through the Development Advisory Team (DAT) Training Workshops which I began at Iowa State University in 1981. Offered about twice a year, these intensive one-week workshops focus on cross-cultural and cross-disciplinary team-building, communications, management, and planning. Much of the training material has been adapted from the ERDM training workshops held in Ghana. Materials on ethnoscience, indigenous knowledge, and indigenous healers are covered in detail in these workshops. The thirteenth workshop was completed in January 1989, bringing the total number of development-oriented participants from Iowa State University, more than forty other universities, USAID, the World Bank, and IMF to nearly 550 (Warren 1981b). Participants have included individuals with considerable international experience who have never had a formal opportunity to be exposed to many of these anthropological concepts and approaches. Sixty different academic disciplines have been represented. Graduate students who complete a DAT workshop may further pursue these approaches through a graduate seminar devoted to the investigation of mechanisms which can promote cross-cultural communication in international agriculture and rural development projects.

Ethnoscience methodologies need not be applied only to health and agriculture. During the ERDM workshops in Ghana, we emphasized the techniques for understanding local attitudes and behavioral patterns regarding local revenue. Based on the improved knowledge of local attitudes, new participatory approaches to revenue collection and utilization for development projects were initiated. In Techiman District this resulted in a 422% improvement in local revenue collection within two fiscal years (see Warren and Issachar 1983).

Utilizing Indigenous Healers in the Health Care Systems

Interest in the Techiman research data on indigenous healers has been extensive. A number of articles have been widely used by academics and health development practitioners (Warren 1974a, 1975,

1978b, 1982a). Several of the earlier articles were incorporated into a co-edited reader, *African Therapeutic Systems* (Ademuwagun et al. 1979), which has been reprinted several times. These publications have led to considerable interest in the idea of utilizing indigenous health practitioners in national health delivery systems. I was asked to present these ideas to the Conference on Cultural Transformations in Africa co-sponsored in 1978 by the Social Science Research Council and the American Council of Learned Societies (Warren 1978a). Barbara Pillsbury, a senior anthropologist with USAID at the time, wrote eloquently on indigenous health practitioners (Pillsbury 1979). At the national level in Ghana, the National Health Planning Unit recommended that indigenous healers be utilized in the national health delivery system (National Health Planning Unit 1979). Dr. Hilla Limann, then president of Ghana, stated in 1979 that "Traditional medicine continues to play an important role in the delivery of health care to the majority of our rural folk. My government will therefore encourage modernization of our traditional medical practices" (Limann 1979: 9).

The PRHETIH Program has attracted both local and international attention. In 1981 a number of us presented the program at a special session of the Society for Applied Anthropology meetings in Edinburgh. Dr. Una Maclean organized the Session on Utilization of Indigenous Healers in National Health Delivery Systems which was organized into two panels, one on international and national policy, the other on policy implementation patterns. Most of the papers were published in a special issue of *Social Science and Medicine*.

In 1983, Patrick Twumasi and I presented material on the professionalization of traditional medicine in Ghana and Zambia at the international conference on the Professionalisation of African Medicine sponsored by the International African Institute and held in Gaborone (Twumasi and Warren 1983). In December 1986, I was given the opportunity to update the Program at the Conference on Changing Concepts of Illness and Health in Ghana sponsored by the Tamale Institute of Cross Cultural Studies and held in Tamale, Ghana, as well as at the Conference on African Medicine in the Modern World held at the University of Edinburgh (Warren 1986a, 1986b). Dr. Edward Green was at the conference in Edinburgh and presented the USAID-funded project carried out in Swaziland and based in part on the PRHETIH experience. Warren and Green presented updated material at the symposium on Ethnomedical Systems in Sub-Saharan Africa at the University of Leiden in 1988.

Some of the most exciting impacts of PRHETIH have been in Ghana at the local level. The new initiatives based on the PRHETIH

Program experience in Dormaa District and Berekum District of Ghana's Brong-Ahafo Region have important implications. The Dormaa Presbyterian Primary Health Care Programme began the Dormaa Healers' Project in April 1985 with three year funding provided by the West Germans. The objectives of the Project are to encourage dialogue and cooperation among indigenous healers and between Western and indigenous healers; to facilitate mutual understanding and respect among healers; and to improve the skills of the indigenous healers. It has a Ghanaian field coordinator seconded from the Ministry of Education who was trained at the Center for Scientific Research into Plant Medicine. His counterpart is a Dutch anthropologist with considerable experience in Ghana. During 1986, 45 indigenous healers in Dormaa District took part in training sessions. Dormaa has added valuable improvements over the Techiman experience by putting both indigenous healers and community health workers through the same training programs. Moreover, training topics are discussed from both the indigenous and the allopathic perspectives. Topics dealing with disease diagnosis, causation and treatment provide a forum for the exchange of views from the two sides allowing for discussion and improved understanding of both systems. Training sessions are organized around six major blocks of topics: the hygienic preparation and storage of herbal material; nutrition and nutritional diseases; diagnosis and treatment of the diseases prevalent in Dormaa; pregnancy; disease prevention; and environmental sanitation.

Twelve indigenous healers in Berekum District, being aware of the Techiman and Dormaa programs, visited the medical mission personnel at Berekum's Holy Family Hospital in 1986 and requested a similar opportunity. The healers are currently in the process of establishing a district healers' organization under the auspices of the Ghana Psychic and Traditional Healers Association and will develop a list of topics which they would like to pursue in training sessions in order to improve their health delivery skills. Hospital and Ministry of Health personnel will then provide the training on the subjects desired. This approach is based on the principle of helping people achieve their own expressed needs (Sekyere 1986).

In Techiman District, numerous indigenous and Western health practitioners have now worked together in the different training sessions. This has resulted in dramatically improved cooperation and coordination between the indigenous healers and the Ministry of Health and hospital personnel. There are now numerous mutual referrals of patients between the two systems of health delivery. Holy Family Hospital refers most simple fractures and psychiatric cases directly to a number of trusted indigenous healers; the indigenous healers refer those cases which they feel are beyond their knowledge and capabilities to the hospital. Some indigenous healing practices have been learned by the Western practitioners and introduced as standard practice at the hospital. The technique used by local traditional birth attendants for dealing with retained placenta, for example, is superior to the Western technique and is now used at Holy Family Hospital. During a national strike by nurses and midwives, Holy Family Hospital brought traditional birth attendants who had gone through TBA training workshops to stand in for the strikers.

Indigenous healers have found oral rehydration technique far superior to some of the local methods for dealing with diarrhea problems. It has now become standard procedure not only among the healers who have taken part in the training sessions, but the technique has been taught by these healers to numerous other local practitioners. The multiplier effect has been extensive. Other techniques adopted and diffused widely include the use of sponge baths for infant malarial cases, and use of appropriate foods for nutritional diseases. The role of indigenous healers in environmental health has developed rapidly with close interaction between them and the District Council. This has led to improved latrines and water sanitation. It is very apparent that the primary health care skills of the indigenous healers have improved greatly. A follow-up survey of the first groups of healers who went through the initial training sessions indicated a 60% retention rate of material presented.

Perhaps the most important impact of PRHETIH in conjunction with other health delivery efforts is a dramatic decline in the outpatient load carried by Holy Family Hospital. For the past twenty years this hospital has functioned with one to three physicians and ten to fifteen nurses and midwives. The inpatient load over the past twenty years has been maintained at the capacity of the wards. The outpatient records reveal steady increases in the number of outpatient visits from 40,000 in 1965, 74,000 in 1971 (comprising 24,310 different individuals), 106,000 in 1978, and 120,000 in 1980. This was followed by a drop to 77,000 in 1984 and 65,000 in 1985. During this two decades the population has been increasing by at least 3% per annum. In the past decade 10 health centers and 24 community clinics have been established in Techiman District. All of these operate on the allopathic model. In the first six months of 1985, patient visits to the community clinics numbered 10,528, which could account for at least 20,000 outpatients per year who no longer need to take their cases to the Hospital (Holy Family Hospital 1985). While the development of the community clinics has accounted for some of the decline in outpatient numbers between 1980 and 1985, it does not account for all of it. From informal surveys I made during visits to Techiman in July and December, 1986, it was apparent that the case load of the indigenous healers who have participated in PRHETIH had increased considerably. These healers are most readily accessible to the rural populations as they continue to practice out of their homes and shrine rooms. A formal study is definitely warranted on this issue in order to obtain precise figures.

A drop of 55,000 outpatient visits for Holy Family Hospital over a five year period has enormous implications for health policy and planning. On the practical side the decline has an impact on improved quality of care which can take place in the hospital. The cost of PRHETIH Program training sessions is relatively low. If such training results in indigenous healers handling more of the health cases in an effective manner, then the PRHETIH approach is very cost-effective. As the financial burden of maintaining existing health delivery systems increases for many of the Ministries of Health in the developing nations, indigenous healers may be seen as important allies in the national health delivery system.

Besides the cost-effectiveness of improving and utilizing the skills of indigenous healers in national health delivery systems, the PRHETIH Program has shown that a thorough knowledge of indigenous disease classification and decision-making strategies can provide the basis for viable communication and cooperation between indigenous and Western health delivery practitioners.

Summary

This case study indicates the lengthy time line necessary for dealing with fundamental attitude and value changes. In this case the attitudes of Western health practitioners towards indigenous healers were frequently negative and based on biased material. Using ethnoscience, I was able to present material which was less biased and led to the possibility of a collaborative approach to improving the skills in primary health care for indigenous healers. The case study also indicates the necessity for taking the time to negotiate with all possible interested institutions and their personnel prior to initiating a major intervention which treads on sensitive turf. Working with the Ministry of Health, the Catholic Diocese, the District Council, Holy Family Hospital, and the Rural Health Training Centre was very time-consuming, but these negotiations made it possible to begin the PRHETIH Program with a common understanding which provided the initial basis for success.

It is also necessary to take the time and effort to package research materials so they are accessible to different clientele groups. The Techiman research data have been developed in forms for use by academic audiences, for development agency practitioners, and as exercises for training sessions for local officials and citizens. Attention must be given to both the form and the content of the package. For government and donor agency consumption, one must avoid academic jargon and present succinct and systematic arguments. One should stress that the use of ethnoscience is an additional component which will facilitate current development efforts and make them more effective. A positive approach is critical. Collaboration with local people is important in order to translate academic concepts into culturally-appropriate simulation exercises which can present controversial and sensitive topics in a non-threatening manner. One can use economic benefit/cost ratios to lend credence to the argument of utilizing indigenous healers. National cultural pride can be an important force if one can show that the negative attitudes toward indigenous healers are products of colonialism and nineteenth century social science. It is possible to enhance local participation through improved understanding and communications between the change agents and the clientele groups.

The final point for this type of intervention is the critical need to maintain a positive attitude and approach to the problem. No one responds well to negative approaches. By combining the Techiman data with those made available through the National Health Planning Unit, government officials could see a real economic benefit which might accrue their institutions through working with indigenous healers. This may have influenced their initial attitudes more than the actual field data from Techiman. Once PRHETIH began, however, it was very apparent that such a collaborative approach could be viable and future interventions in other districts have been far easier. Both the National Catholic Secretariat and the Ministry of Health have new emphases on primary health care. As of 1984, 34 of Ghana's 68 districts have established primary health care programs.

One must also be persistent when attempting to influence the policies of international or national institutions. Personnel are always in a state of flux, and one must expect to have to repeat arguments as new persons replace others in a bureaucratic setting. This should not be discouraging, as it is a fact of bureaucratic life. All of these activities lead us to understand that both people and their institutions can be responsive to change programs providing they are given the time and opportunity to see the relevance of the changes.

10

Incorporating Nutrition into Agricultural Research: A Case Study from Southern Honduras

Kathleen M. DeWalt and Billie R. DeWalt

It is important to learn the language of the "culture" in which you are operating. In this case the culture is that of the agency and/or the other investigators with whom one is working.

During the 1970s there were major shifts in policies among some of the leading international agencies concerned with economic development. The World Bank, for example, began a transition to serving "basic needs" and the U.S. Congress passed the New Directions Mandate to re-orient foreign assistance toward greater concern with equity and serving the poorest of the poor (see Foreign Assistance Act 1979; Hoben 1980:356).

Among the results of these new directions are two that directly relate to the theme of this paper. First, there has been a greater effort to develop agricultural research and development projects to *directly* address the food consumption and nutritional problems of the rural poor (FAO 1982; Pinstrup-Andersen 1981; USAID 1982a, 1982b, 1984a, 1984b; Swaminathan 1984). Second, new niches have developed for anthropologists in assisting in the design, monitoring and evaluation of development efforts (see Rhoades 1985; Tripp 1982, 1984; B. DeWalt 1985, 1988). These two trends have neatly coincided with our long term interest in projecting and evaluating the nutritional effects of agricultural research and development (see B. DeWalt 1979; K. DeWalt 1981).

This paper will report on our work to inform the development of technology within the context of the International Sorghum and Millet Project (INTSORMIL) in southern Honduras. Our goal was to show what forms of new and/or improved technology would be most appropriate for helping resource-poor farmers. We thought this could most effectively be done if improving the nutrition of these farm families were explicitly incorporated as a goal of the agricultural research and development process.

INTSORMIL is one of several Collaborative Research Support Projects (CRSPs) funded through the U.S. Agency for International Development (USAID) in the late 1970s and early 1980s. The CRSPs were set up as a mechanism to harness the expertise of U.S. researchers to address food related problems of crucial importance in Third World countries. They were also designed to promote the collaboration of US university scientists and Third World scientists in these research efforts. The primary research goal is to address problems that might have a positive effect on the economic well-being and health of poor populations within developing countries. Because sorghum and millet are grains used by some of the poorest people in drought-prone areas of the world, a CRSP was established to do research on these crops.

INTSORMIL's mandate is to increase the production and consumption of sorghum and millet world-wide. To achieve these goals it has focused on basic science and the development of intermediate level technology. Like the other CRSPs, INTSORMIL's research is expected to be collaborative in nature. These collaborators are expected to take the lead role in translating the basic research into applications suitable for use in their own country or region. INTSORMIL scientists have been collaborating on specific projects with a number of investigators in 10 host countries. Of the more than 50 U.S. scientists involved the greatest number are agrobiological scientists. Plant breeders dominate the INTSORMIL project, along with plant physiologists, entomologists, plant pathologists, and agronomists. There is also a food utilization group that includes cereal chemists and biochemists. Until 1986 about 12% of project funds went to socioeconomic scientists, including economists, rural sociologists and anthropologists. The majority of funds were devoted to carry out farming systems and food consumption research. Budget cuts by INTSORMIL in 1986 effectively eliminated social science participation from the CRSP; the agrobiological scientists deemed the social sciences as the most expendable portion of the project.

During the period of 1981 to 1983 anthropologists from the University of Kentucky carried out farming and nutritional systems work in southern Honduras. Our work was concurrent with the beginnings of biological agricultural research efforts and substantially directed the research of these scientists.

Research Context and the Client Group

Honduras occupies an area of approximately 43,277 square miles and is the second largest of the Central American republics. Population in 1978 was 3.4 million people, with an average population density of 78.6 persons per square mile. Although this is lower than other Central American republics, only about 5% of the total land available is cultivated (Durham 1979) because of the rugged topography. The economy of Honduras is predominantly agricultural, accounting for 33% of the gross domestic product, 75% of exports and employing 68.6% of the labor force. The industrial sector is very small and the GNP of only $ 700 per capita in 1984 (World Bank 1986) is the second lowest in the Western Hemisphere.

National surveys of nutritional status carried out by the Nutrition Institute for Central America and Panama (INCAP) in 1966 (INCAP 1969) and the National Planning Council of Honduras (CONSUPLANE) estimated that in 1979 over 70% of children suffered from undernutrition (SAPLAN 1981). When average diets were compared for 1966 and 1979, the overall availability of energy, iron and Vitamins A and C in the Honduran diet had declined slightly. Food balance data from the nation as a whole indicate trends seen in other Third World countries experiencing declines in nutritional well-being. The country uses much of its cropland to produce commodities like cattle, bananas, coffee and tropical fruits for export (B. DeWalt 1983). In recent years, imports of basic staples like maize, rice, and beans have been necessary. The southern part of the country, along with parts of El Salvador and Nicaragua, is also one of the few regions of the Western Hemisphere in which grain sorghum is incorporated into diets as a human food.

The status of Honduras as a food deficit country, the concentration of basic grain production in the hands of small farmers, the use of sorghum as a human food, and the interest of the Honduran Ministry of Agriculture in improving sorghum production contributed to the selection of southern Honduras as a site for INTSORMIL research activities. In 1980, B. DeWalt and several other INTSORMIL investigators negotiated collaborative agreements with the Ministry of Natural Resources (MRN) of the Government of Honduras (GOH) and the Honduran National Institute of History and Anthropology (IHAH).

As our anthropological research began, it was clear that the principal clients of our work were the other researchers involved in the INTSORMIL project, though we were later able to broaden the applicability of our research. Initial clients were the biological agricultural scientists from INTSORMIL and Honduras who began work on increasing the production and consumption of sorghum. The principal individuals who have been involved in this work are a plant breeder from Texas A & M University and a plant breeder from the Ministry of Natural Resources of the Government of Honduras. This research in southern Honduras began in 1981 and is still being continued. Entomologists, plant pathologists, food quality specialists, and others have done research in the region on a more intermittent basis.

The agrobiological scientists involved in the project are all deeply committed to improving the welfare of resource-poor farmers. Most of the U.S. scientists, however, have been unwilling to spend very much time in Honduras. Their time in the country is spent in the capital city and on experiment stations; rarely do they encounter the farmers who their research is supposed to benefit. We have worked primarily with the two plant breeders, spending time with them at the experiment stations to understand what it is that agricultural researchers do, and having them spend time with us talking with farmers to identify their problems. Along with the two breeders we have then tried to communicate farmers' problems to the other agrobiological scientists who work in Honduras for much shorter periods of time.

As the work in Honduras proceeded, it became part of a wider coordinated research effort in Central America and the Caribbean. Two researchers from the International Crops Research Institute for the Semi-Arid Tropics (ICRISAT), based at the International Maize and Wheat Improvement Center (CIMMYT) in Mexico, created the Consortium of Latin American Sorghum Investigators (CLAIS). This group is composed of sorghum researchers from all of the Central American countries and several Caribbean nations. They have annual meetings to interchange results and to coordinate their research programs and experiments. We and other researchers from the University of Kentucky have participated in several of these meetings. To date, our work has been the only social science included as part of this effort. Unfortunately CLAIS has never been able to obtain major funding to support its efforts, so that research and meetings always seem to be based on resources scraped together from a variety of sources.

We feel that the ultimate beneficiaries of our research are the rural poor of the Pacific Coast of Central America. As we will show, poor farmers are those most likely to grow sorghum and poor families are most likely to include sorghum as a significant portion of their diet.

Research Design, Methods and Findings

The methodology that we developed to include nutritional goals into agricultural research combined farming systems research (see Shaner et al. 1982; B. DeWalt 1985) with a study of and understanding of the *nutritional system* (K. DeWalt 1981, 1983a, 1983b, 1984; DeWalt and DeWalt n.d.; Frankenberger 1985). By nutritional system, we mean those aspects of social, economic, cultural and ritual life impinging on the process of food getting, preparation, and consumption (see Richards 1932; K. DeWalt 1983:11). As we have outlined it (K. DeWalt and B. DeWalt n.d.), this approach requires that four areas be addressed in agricultural research programs that have improvement of nutritional problems as a goal. These include:

1. *targeting* agricultural programs to those at greatest nutritional risk;

2. *understanding* the relationships between crop production, crop utilization, and food consumption in order to predict the impact of new agricultural technology on food consumption and nutrition;

3. *recommending* ways in which agricultural research and development programs may be used to improve the nutritional situation of those most at risk; and

4. *monitoring and evaluating* programs on the basis of their impact on food consumption and nutritional status.

Southern Honduras is the poorest region of the country and, as noted above, is an area in which sorghum was grown and used for direct human consumption. In addition, this area is plagued by climatic conditions that make the drought tolerant sorghum an important crop for small farmers. INTSORMIL research efforts were thus concentrated in Southern Honduras. Our research focused on three agrarian reform communities located on the coastal plains and on six communities located in two ecological zones in the highlands. University of Kentucky researchers were in the field for significant parts of the years between 1981 and 1984. Our fieldwork combined ethnographic, qualitative research with the use of survey instruments to yield quantitative data on the variables of interest.

Ethnographic research was used to determine and document the various pathways by which food enters the household. We were interested in household agricultural production (including field crops, gardening, fruit trees, and small animal production), identifying the numbers and kinds of markets and shops and the food prices in them, looking at informal networks for marketing and sharing food within communities, cataloging the wild food resources and their use, and determining the availability of nutritionally relevant programs such as food-for-work projects and child feeding centers. The ethnographic phase also included the mapping of communities and informal interviews concerning food use. Informal interviews focused on food preparation techniques, desired characteristics of foods (especially sorghum and maize varieties), appropriateness of alternative foods for community members, allocation of household and agricultural tasks among household members, and common health problems in the communities.

Surveys were carried out with random samples of households in the study communities. These were used to collect quantitative data on household and "backyard" food production, other economic resources, and a basic census and determination of household characteristics. Data relating to the nutritional system were collected through recall interviews focusing on all foods entering the household during the week previous to the interview and sources of these foods. A twenty-four hour recall of household meals was conducted as well. The interview also included questions of more general use of alternative grains (maize and sorghum) over the period of a year, the "typical" ways in which key foods such as sorghum and maize were used, and methods of preparation. A twenty four hour recall of the activities of the male and female household heads was conducted in some communities. Finally, all children under 60 months of age were weighed and measured to determine their nutritional status.

We felt that the quantitative and qualitative information collected would be important for the clients of our research. Some of the data would convey the overall social and economic situation in the communities--the land and economic resources people have available, the way in which sorghum fit within their cropping and nutritional systems, the organization of labor within the communities, and so on. Other information related more directly to the traits that an "ideal" sorghum variety would have--what aspects of plant growth were important to farmers (e.g., height, stalk characteristics, properties as fodder), what aspects of grain quality were important in food preparation (e.g., milling properties, color, taste, consistency), and what aspects were important for marketing (e.g., storability, ease of processing, size of seed).   These could be directly addressed by the research of the agrobiological scientists. The most important findings of our research were the following.

Basic grain production in the region must increasingly compete with other commodities.   Southern Honduras is a region in which land is continually being converted from annual crop production to permanent pasture for cattle (see B. DeWalt 1983, 1986).   Small farmers are induced to participate in the deforestation of extensive areas so that pasture can be sown. As less and less land becomes available for the production of grain crops, especially for tenant farmers and sharecroppers, fallowing cycles for hillside lands are becoming shorter (see Durham 1979; Boyer 1983).   Soil fertility is declining and soil erosion is becoming an ever-greater threat to the long-term survival of the ecological system (see B. DeWalt and Alexander 1983; Stonich 1986). Yields of the basic grains cultivated by farmers in the region are declining.   In 1982, for example, the average yield of sorghum per hectare was only 540 kilograms; the comparable figure for maize was 550 kilograms, and for beans 270 kilograms.

Our research in nine communities in the region identified a number of production and storage constraints for the food crops grown in the region. The most important of these related to the erratic rainfall patterns and the declining productivity (and erosion) of the soil. Others included (in approximate order of importance): post-harvest losses to granary weevils, losses in the field due to birds, plant disease, and insect damage (see B. DeWalt and K. DeWalt 1982). These are all problems being addressed by INTSORMIL agricultural scientists. However, in our view, just as important as the recommendations arising out of the farming systems research were the constraints and recommendations identified by the nutrition systems research.

Although sorghum was not reported in dietary surveys carried out by INCAP in 1966, and widespread use of sorghum was denied by staff of the National Planning Council in Tegucigalpa, we found that sorghum accounted for approximately 37% of the grains consumed as food in the study communities.   Sorghum is used as a substitute for maize in a number products including the staple food, *tortillas*, as well as gruels and porridges (*atole*), and hard biscuits (*rosqillas* and *rosquettes*).   Other minor uses of sorghum include the preparation of a beverage by mixing ground, toasted sorghum with water and sugar for use as a soft drink, the occasional use of roasted sorghum as a coffee substitute, and popped sorghum, which is mixed with sugar syrup or honey to make popped sorghum balls. While maize is strongly preferred for many of these products, sorghum is acceptable, and is used by most families at some time of the year (K. DeWalt 1985a, 1985b).

Some families reported using sorghum as the tortilla grain for up to nine months of the year. Others were proud to report that they were forced to use sorghum only a few weeks per year. Sorghum use was greater in the highlands, especially among tenant farmers, sharecroppers and those with less access to land. During drought years, (such as 1982 and 1983) when the maize crop is lost, sorghum use for human food increased in both the highland and lowland areas.

Our anthropometric surveys found that about 60% of children under 60 months of age are below 95% of standard height for age suggesting some degree of undernutrition. In some communities in the lowlands up to 95% of children showed some degree of growth failure. The amount of *acute* malnutrition, represented by weight for height below 90% of standard, also varied among communities, but was much lower, usually less than 15% of children. The children of tenant farmers and households headed by single women were at greater nutritional risk than the children of landowners as measured both by analyses of diets and of nutritional status. Analyses of diets showed that the limiting nutrient in inadequate diets was energy. While a large percentage of families, up to 50% in some communities, failed to meet their calculated requirement for energy, almost all exceeded their requirement for protein, even when the lower protein quality of grain based diets was taken into consideration.

We concluded that increased sorghum production would be likely to differentially benefit the poorest of the poor because it is consumed by the neediest individuals in the population and by the entire population during times of economic stress. Increasing the production and consumption of sorghum in farming families could help to address the energy deficit faced by the children of these households. In other words, in terms of the goals for which the CRSPs were established, southern Honduras is an excellent choice for a concentration of some of INTSORMIL's efforts. Agrobiological research can make an important difference in improving the lot of resource-poor families.

Utilization of Research Results

The results presented above identified a number of key factors in the linkages between agricultural production and nutritional status in Southern Honduras. How then did our research directly influence the agricultural research and development efforts?

Several detailed reports of our research on agricultural production and food consumption are available (B. DeWalt and K. DeWalt 1982, 1985; B. DeWalt 1983; B. DeWalt and Alexander 1983; B. DeWalt and Duda 1985; Thompson et al. 1985; Stonich 1986; K. DeWalt and B. DeWalt n.d.). These have been distributed widely among INTSORMIL scientists. Our impression, however, is that except for those individuals who have spent long periods of time in southern Honduras the reports have not been utilized. Much more important has been information communicated in papers that we have presented and in informal discussions.

INTSORMIL has provided a framework within which interdisciplinary information can be exchanged. Principal investigators meet almost annually to present the results of their research; at several of these meetings, an External Evaluation Panel has been present to make suggestions for reorienting research. INTSORMIL has collaborated with the ICRISAT program in Mexico to hold annual meetings devoted to aspects of sorghum research in Latin America; during 1984, for example, the meeting focused on sorghum in farming systems (see Paul and DeWalt 1985). CLAIS meetings have also provided a forum for exchanging information.

One of the important communication techniques that we learned early in the project was to adapt our style of presentation to conform with that common in the agrobiological sciences. These researchers make substantial use of slides. The first slide or two typically list the objectives of the research, a few tables are shown to present the data collected, and finally the results are listed. Presentations are kept short and to the point. We also attempted to tailor our presentations to the interests of the other agrobiological researchers--that is, to identify constraints to production that could be addressed by their research. Items of interest for anthropological theory held little relevance for the other scientists and were quickly excised from our presentations.

The frequency with which meetings were held to interchange information was a positive feature of the project. Not only did we learn how to tailor our presentation style, but we also learned a great deal from the other scientists. We learned which pests were most harmful, how to identify plant diseases, the kinds of soil problems that might exist, and some of the wide variability that exists in sorghum cultivars. It was important to us to learn the language of the other scientists to facilitate communication, and it also helped us to improve our field research because we were more attuned to the problems and potential constraints in sorghum production systems.

The long-term nature of the project also meant that there were many opportunities for more informal contacts to be made and we believe that these have been the most effective means of communication. Travelling with agrobiological scientists visiting experiment stations, having them accompany us on visits to villages, participating in workshops, and talking at meetings provided ample opportunities for communication of information. As in many other settings, getting to know other people and having them learn to respect and trust you as an individual means a lot. The "good old boy" system is especially important among agrobiological scientists. The informal networks of communication we established have probably been more effective vehicles for getting our work incorporated than all of the reports we have written.

One of the biggest difficulties presented by the project had to do with the priorities of the different scientists involved. The agrobiological scientists were very explicit in saying that their first obligation was to the farmers of the states in which their universities were located. They noted that their Colleges of Agriculture and State Experiment Stations were established to benefit local farmers, not those in foreign countries. Thus, for almost all of the other scientists in INTSORMIL, foreign research was something that they did as a supplement to their normal activities. They might spend two or three weeks travelling to various parts of the world to do some consulting or help set up experiments, but long-term research was not in the cards for most of them. Any benefit of their research programs for developing countries was likely to come only as a by-product of their main research to address the needs of local farmers. Several noted to us that they even had some qualms about helping farmers in other countries because they were, in effect, competing with the U.S. farmers--the main interest group the agrobiological scientists had to satisfy.

We did not face these same kinds of dilemmas. Our research interests had always been outside of the United States, and we were spending substantial amounts of time in field research in countries like Honduras. While we felt that we could communicate effectively and well with the two plant breeders actually in Honduras, we often felt frustrated in trying to persuade other agrobiological scientists to devote more attention to the needs of Honduran farmers.

Thus, the INTSORMIL program had a unique structure compared with other agricultural research and development organizations. It was focused on basic research on a single commodity and carried out primarily by scientists based in the United States. INTSORMIL could not possibly address all of the problems and constraints that we identified in our work. So in the pages that follow, we will focus on the information generated that had the most direct implications for research by the agrobiological scientists in INTSORMIL.

Seasonal Patterns of Food Use and Nutritional Status

Southern Honduras has two growing seasons imbedded in the rainy season which extends from May through November. The first, the *primaria*, begins with planting maize and sorghum in early May and ends with a maize harvest in July, during the *canicula*, a (usually) short dry period that falls in the middle of the rainy season. Maize will not survive the canicula, but the more drought tolerant sorghum will. Sorghum is photoperiodic and will not flower until fall. It stays in the field until December or January, when it is harvested. The second planting season, the *postrera*, begins in late July, at the end of the *canicula*. A second planting of maize may be made and both grain and forage sorghum may be planted at this time.

The leanest time of the year falls in June, just before the first maize crop is harvested. This is the time of year that most families report using sorghum, either from their own production from the year before, or purchased sorghum. Many families purchase sorghum at this time because it is cheaper than maize. Problems of scarcity are largely economic in nature. The poor cannot afford to purchase grain at precisely the time they need it most. However, the situation is exacerbated by the storage problems for both sorghum and maize. Sorghum is quite susceptible to insect damage during storage using traditional methods.

The several kinds of higher-yielding sorghum introduced in the region prior to the INTSORMIL project have much poorer storage properties than many of the existing varieties. For this reason, the introduced varieties have been sold as a cash crop immediately after harvest to eliminate the risk of storage loss for the producer. This means that households cannot store the grain for their own consumption and they must sell their harvest when prices are at their lowest.

Thus, improvement in the storage properties, or improved means of storage, would allow households to retain more sorghum for home consumption and also to smooth out the flow of income from sales of sorghum over a longer period of time. We identified this as a prime area for research and have tried to interest INTSORMIL entomologists in working on low cost improvements in sorghum storage. We have not had much success primarily because those entomologists in the program have had little experience with grain storage problems. In the United

States, grain storage is more of a problem for grain buyers and shippers rather than for farmers. Consequently, few university-based entomologists have developed much expertise in storage problems, especially for small-scale storage needs like those in Honduras. Those entomologists associated with INTSORMIL have focused much more attention on insect pests for plants in the field than on storability of grain.

Through our work and their own observations the breeders working in southern Honduras have recognized the need to include better storage properties as a part of their breeding programs. They realize that storage is one of the most important constraints faced by the farmers. The breeders are addressing this, and several other aspects of grain quality, through an emphasis on maintaining a breeding program that involves using traditional varieties as well as adapting and incorporating exotic germ plasm from the worldwide collections.

Grain Quality Characteristics and Food Utilization

The food consumption surveys identified a number of products produced from sorghum and the grain qualities important for them. In addition, the surveys addressed several issues surrounding the nutritional qualities of sorghum as a human food.

Nutritional issues: Past research by INTSORMIL and other scientists have identified three questions surrounding the nutritional effects of sorghum in human diets. The first concerns the desirability of breeding sorghum for higher quality protein, that is, for higher lysine content. Earlier analysis of world nutritional needs had focused on the importance of several essential amino acids as limiting the protein quality of grain-based diets. However, more recent research (WHO/FAO 1973) argues that energy, not protein or amino acids, is the limiting nutrient in most diets. Data cited above produced by our food consumption studies demonstrated that this was the case for southern Honduras. While many families failed to meet energy requirements almost all met protein requirements. Our data buttressed the findings of researchers in other areas of the world and helped justify the INTSORMIL Technical Committee's decision to discourage directing resources to breeding for protein quality.

The second issue has to do with the digestibility of sorghum protein. Research with small children had shown that protein digestibility for sorghum prepared by grinding and boiling was very poor, resulting in worsening the nutritional status of children (McClean et al. 1981). Some nutrition researchers have even questioned the advisability of promoting a grain with such poor nutritional quality. However, INTSORMIL and other research on sorghum preparation techniques suggested that in traditional settings sorghum is usually subjected to more elaborate preparation techniques than were used in the feeding studies cited above. For example, in Southern Honduras most sorghum based dishes are prepared from sorghum that has undergone heating in an alkaline medium using either lime or ashes (nixtamalization). It is known that this process improves the nutritional quality of maize but the effect on sorghum is less clear.

In our reports, papers presented at various meetings (K. DeWalt 1983b, 1985a) and informal conversations we strongly advised testing products prepared using traditional processes for nutritional quality. INTSORMIL food utilization specialists have been testing some traditional sorghum products for protein digestibility with preliminary results suggesting that these techniques do in fact improve digestibility. For example, Serna-Saldivar et al. (1985) have demonstrated that protein digestibility of pearled sorghum subjected to cooking in a lime solution is equivalent or better than that of similarly prepared maize in young pigs.

Finally, research with guinea pigs (Klopfenstein et al. 1981, 1983) suggests that sorghum based diets increase the requirement of ascorbic acid. Earlier studies (INCAP 1969, SAPLAN 1979) suggested that diets in Southern Honduras were already deficient in ascorbic acid. The University of Kentucky research team, however, documented a wider use of ascorbic acid containing wild fruits than had been previously reported previously, suggesting sufficient availability of ascorbic acid through most of the year in the diet. These results suggest that increased sorghum consumption is unlikely to cause problems in terms of ascorbic acid.

Acceptability: One important aspect of our research was designed to investigate whether there were any cultural obstacles to increased utilization of sorghum in human diets. Our results indicate that there are not any important obstacles and that improvement of sorghum production and consumption can be a means of improving the nutritional status of people in southern Honduras.

Sorghum has probably been a part of diets in Southern Honduras for about 100 years. The *criollo* (i.e., land race) grains used have been selected for their appropriateness as food as well as for their agronomic qualities. A wide variety of products are made from sorghum. Many of these are sorghum equivalents of foods also prepared from maize. Maize is clearly preferred for all of these products. Grain quality characteristics important for sorghum acceptability are those that make the resulting products most like products made from maize. The most important of these are a light color, lighter density and bland flavor. Quick cooking time is also important as a means of saving fuel, although all sorghum varieties cook more quickly than maize.

Researchers from Mississippi State University, INCAP, and the Ministry of Natural Resources have collaborated with sorghum breeders to test sorghum varieties for cooking properties and acceptability. These properties are incorporated into the breeding programs carried out.

A second area of acceptability of sorghum that was investigated had to do with a different "quality" of sorghum. In the indigenous food classification system found in Central America, in which foods (as well as illnesses and medicines) are classified as having an essential quality that can range from hot to cold, sorghum is considered to be "cooler" in essential quality than is maize, which is considered neutral. Although not all people still continue to follow the traditional hot/cold classification system of foods, some people reported that nursing women should not eat sorghum tortillas because the excess coolness could cause the nursing child to become ill. Several nursing women were found to be preparing sorghum tortillas for their families and maize tortillas for themselves. Although not considered by local people to be appropriate for nursing mothers, foods prepared from sorghum are considered appropriate for children, and children consume all the products made.

Household Labor and the Role of Women

Another important aspect of our work was to determine what effect increased sorghum production might have on the allocation of household labor--especially that concerning women. Many development projects have been carried out with little regard for how they might affect labor demands put on women or the status of women.

Women are only infrequently involved in agricultural labor in the subsistence agriculture found in the highlands. Women work in the fields during times of heavy labor demand, such as harvest, but they do not provide the bulk of agricultural labor. However, women are involved in food preparation and marketing, and small animal production in order to generate income (see Fordham et al. 1985). Our data indicate that breeding activities directed towards an improvement in yield of traditional varieties probably will not alter labor demands for highland women.

However, in the lowlands women do generate income through wage labor in commercial agriculture. The reliance of women and landless workers on wage labor suggests that any "improvements" that reduce labor requirements for agricultural production, such as development of a hybrid feed grain sorghum that would be harvested by machine, could be devastating for both men and women in the lowlands. In addition, more female headed households were found in the lowlands as compared with the highlands. Although INTSORMIL and extension programs in Honduras are unlikely to be able to substantially affect the degree of mechanization among larger farmers, we have continually advocated that the largest portion of breeding efforts should be focused on sorghum for the highland cultivators rather than for the lowlands. The plant breeders in Honduras have recognized this and are devoting most of their efforts to improving sorghum cultivars for the highlands.

Income and Expenditure Patterns

Despite increases in production Honduras imports sorghum. Surplus production as a result of improved yields would find a ready market. At the same time, problems in storage noted above result in the need to sell grains, including sorghum, soon after harvest at low prices and buy them back later at higher prices. Improvements in storage and storability are a key to improving the flow of income and subsistence grains from sorghum production for small farmers.

The other areas of importance for small farmers have to do with the balance between the cost of production and the value of the crop produced. Resource poor farmers in Southern Honduras are frequently sharecroppers or tenant farmers for whom it makes no sense to invest in permanent improvements on their land and who cannot afford costly inputs. Furthermore the land they cultivate is, for the most part, located on the steep hillsides of the highland areas. Agricultural technology, then, must be cheap, appropriate, and easily accessible to improve income.

Our position has been that research efforts should focus on improving existing systems of cultivation, rather than developing an expensive technological package. An important element of this is to focus on development of an improved *variety* of sorghum. Improved varieties are populations of seeds that reproduce themselves in farmers' fields and that can be passed from farmer to farmer. Hybrids are plants derived from crossing at least two in-bred lines of sorghum. The resulting "crosses" can only be planted for one year; after that, the succeeding generations of plants revert back to the characteristics of the populations of the parent lines. A "traditional" breeding program among the majority of U.S. scientists would focus on creating hybrids that would mature rapidly and be high-yielding.

Hybrids have to be produced and distributed by someone--either a private company or a government agency. No private seed company has yet seen southern Honduras as a large enough market to set up operations to produce and distribute sorghum. The government infrastructure is still relatively undeveloped and it is unlikely that it would be able to be effective and efficient in the sorghum seed business. In addition, hybrid seeds must be purchased each year by farmers. The logistics of production and distribution and the expense to farmers indicated to us that INTSORMIL breeding efforts should, in large part, be directed toward improvement of existing traditional varieties that have desirable characteristics for resource poor farmers.

Despite repeated criticism from other INTSORMIL scientists who favor the development of hybrids, the major effort in the breeding program in Honduras does not have this focus. Instead the emphasis is on varieties rather than hybrids. This is so that improved varieties can be diffused rapidly from farmer to farmer rather than relying on the creation of an infrastructure to produce and distribute hybrids. The improved varieties are being developed to fit into existing cropping systems. This means that early-maturation is not a goal; in fact, the sorghum varieties being developed are primarily oriented toward being planted in May and harvested in December. High yields are important in the breeding program but *stability of yield* in the variable climate of southern Honduras is given equal emphasis. As we have mentioned earlier, the food quality and storability characteristics are also emphasized. High-yielding sorghum that does not store well will be sold on the market as animal feed, as will sorghum that does not meet the preparation and palatability requirements of the population. Improved nutrition has become a goal for the plant breeders.

As the INTSORMIL breeders have developed new varieties, we have assisted them by distributing small packets of seed so that farmers could try these out on their own land. The expectation was that, if the seeds were successful, they would be increased by the farmers and spread throughout the population. Farmers have been very interested in receiving new seeds and, despite some problems with the early improved varieties, have incorporated them into their own experimental "breeding programs."

The Potential Effects of Changes in
Sorghum Prices on Nutrition

The consumption survey demonstrated that the poor (tenant farmers) used sorghum as a subsistence grain more often than landholders, and that farmers in the lowlands used sorghum during lean times of the year or in lean years. Although this was not studied directly, this suggests that the price elasticity of demand for sorghum is higher among those at greatest nutritional risk. Decreases in price as a result of increases in production are likely to differentially affect the nutritional status of the poor as compared with those less poor. From this point of view, any improvement in the availability of food quality sorghum in Southern Honduras is likely to have a positive impact on the nutritional status of the landless and resource poor farmers as a result of price effects. The choice of sorghum as a commodity for research in Southern Honduras directly addressed this need.

This finding is one that essentially has been used to justify the INTSORMIL work in southern Honduras. USAID administrators and other agrobiological scientists often assume that sorghum in the New World is only used as an animal feed and that therefore research efforts should not be invested in food quality sorghum. As we have shown, however, sorghum is consumed and is differentially eaten by the poor. Thus, work on this commodity is *targeting* research efforts to the most needy parts of the population.

Problems in the Utilization of the Research

Although our work has achieved substantial success, it has not been without its frustrations. The organization of the CRSP is such that each investigator operates independently with his or her own budget. There is some attempt to coordinate efforts through designation of "lead institutions" for specific countries and appointing country coordinators who have the responsibility for coordinating activities within their assigned countries or regions. In part, the sorghum breeder stationed in Honduras coordinated the visits of consulting scientists, including the University of Kentucky nutrition and farming systems researchers. His house and office have served as "headquarters" for much of the research. This arrangement allowed us to directly exchange information and observations. We were able to accompany INTSORMIL scientists to their experimental plots and when they were conducting their research.

We were able to take them to the villages in which we were studying and to get them to directly observe farmers' problems.

On the whole however, collaboration and coordination within INTSORMIL are haphazard. Information is exchanged through technical reports, consultation in the field during research periods and through annual investigators' meetings. However, this arrangement does not represent the most efficient manner in which to transfer information important to the planning and implementation of agricultural research priorities. Most researchers within INTSORMIL must pay more attention to their disciplinary concerns and their domestic constituency (i.e., the people served by their College of Agriculture). Consequently they have little interest in or reward for developing a strong research commitment and understanding of any developing country. The result is that there is not much coordination of research efforts. The articulation of our nutrition systems research with the agricultural research has been no tighter or looser than the articulation of other research components.

We do believe that the work of INTSORMIL in Honduras demonstrates a methodology for generating the kinds of data important in planning agricultural research priorities and directions. The information generated has had a significant impact on INTSORMIL breeding research in Honduras and on the research priorities of some of the agrobiological scientists. Unfortunately, as in many other projects dominated by agrobiological scientists, social science research was not seen as having as high a priority as other research within INTSORMIL. Through the life of INTSORMIL, social science projects were reduced in number and scope and eventually eliminated in 1986.

One result is that the planned monitoring and evaluation of the impact of INTSORMIL sponsored research in Honduras will not be carried out. Though several new varieties of sorghum have been released since 1984, it is unclear whether these have met with acceptance among farmers and their families, whether their productivity is better than traditional varieties, and whether they have had any effect on the nutritional status of farm families.

Continued attention to food consumption and nutrition research was also hampered by our inability to recruit appropriate Honduran counterparts to continue the research. Several U.S. students were trained in methods for conducting food consumption and nutrition research within a farming systems framework but no Honduran students could be identified for such training. Honduras suffers from a shortage of trained personnel, especially in the social sciences and nutrition even at the lowest levels of training.

Thus, it is impossible to say what the longer-term results of our research have been. Although we know that we have affected the work of those INTSORMIL scientists who have been involved in the work in Honduras, and through them we have affected the work of the Consortium of Latin American Sorghum Investigators working in other Central American and Caribbean countries, we do not know whether the ultimate and most important client group has been reached--small farmers and their families.

Conclusions

Anthropologists and other social scientists working in complex organizations like INTSORMIL should be aware of the possibilities and the problems that exist in getting their research utilized. Being cognizant of these at the outset can help in formulating strategies for improving communication and therefore knowledge utilization. There are several general lessons that we have learned.

First, it is important to learn the language of the "culture" in which you are operating. In this case, the culture is that of the agency and/or the other investigators with whom one is working. It was necessary for us to learn something about plant breeding, entomology, agronomy, and the other biological science disciplines concerned with sorghum production and consumption. This helped us in several ways. One is that we were able to better tailor our research to identify problems faced by farmers that could be addressed by the scientists within INTSORMIL. Another is that we were able to "translate" our anthropological findings into language understandable to these scientists. This even extended to adapting our data presentation styles to better fit with that of the agrobiological sciences.

Second, it is important to be able to work, whenever possible, with a data base that is shared with the other scientists. That is, whenever we could show other scientists the problems that existed in villages or in farmers' fields, we felt that we were more effective in communicating our information. Research reports, publications, and presentations are poor substitutes for first-hand experience. This is one of the strengths of the farming systems research approach that stresses rapid rural reconnaissance carried out by multidisciplinary teams (DeWalt 1985; Rhoades 1985). These teams learn a lot from farmers and from each other, and they also come to a greater shared understanding of the problems faced by the people they are trying to serve. The breeders in Honduras came to share our understandings and to appreciate the relevance of our data because they visited the communities we were studying. We had less success with other INTSORMIL scientists who did not also have this first-hand contact.

While it may not be possible for anthropologists to structure things so that the other scientists or policy makers with whom they work can actually visit the clients of the research, they should attempt to present information in such a way that it more closely simulates this experience. While scientifically collected data and presentation of statistical information is important for credibility, qualitative anecdotal information about real people with real problems may in the long run have more of an impact. In retrospect, we might have had more success if we had presented more data of that sort.

A related point that is important to emphasize is that *informal* presentation and discussion of results is probably a more effective means of communicating information than formal presentations. This means that it is important to attend meetings, even those in which a formal paper will not be given, and to take as active a role as possible in the governance of the organization. We probably accomplished more in communicating our results when we were attending technical committee meetings relating to how the CRSP was to distribute its funds and how it was to organize its research efforts than when we made formal presentations. The opportunity for informal interaction with the biological scientists at these meetings allowed us to communicate information directly rather than depending on them to read our technical reports or stay tuned in to our paper presentations at principal investigator meetings.

Third, data that supports the preconceptions or interests of others is much more likely to be acted upon and be utilized than information that requires a substantial redirection of efforts. For example, although storage is a significant constraint for southern Honduran farmers, it did not fit within the interests of anyone in INTSORMIL and was essentially ignored. On the other hand, our recommendation that sorghum varieties prepared in the traditional way be tested for nutritional content, was something that was within the expertise and interest of INTSORMIL and INCAP scientists. Our information was used to help justify the effort.

There are occasions when your information can tip the scales one way or the other when there is disagreement among other scientists or policy makers. An example is the case of high lysine sorghum. A few scientists within INTSORMIL have had this as a research interest. Other researchers, however, have not considered it a topic worth pursuing. Our data indicating that energy was more of a constraint than protein helped to justify not putting INTSORMIL research dollars into work on high lysine sorghum.

We are not arguing, of course, that controversial or "negative" information should not be presented. It is just that one should be aware that research results are used and abused in contexts that will always include political and personality considerations. Knowledge is never utilized in a value-free way. It is wise to recognize the potential political considerations and the personalities that might be bruised when deciding what information will be presented and how it will be phrased. As a social science researcher, one is often confronted with deciding which battles are important to fight, what the appropriate time is to raise delicate issues, and how to create alliances for specific purposes. Idealistic views about "value-free" scientific research need to quickly be replaced by realistic assessments of the social and political milieu if one is to survive in most applied research settings.

11

Knowledge Utilization Structures, Processes, and Alliances in a Psychiatric Hospital Study

Daniel R. Scheinfeld, Patricia A. Marshall, and David W. Beer

The fulcrum of knowledge utilization is the establishment of an alliance between the researchers, the administrators, and those directly affected by implementation.

For the past four years we have been involved in a study of the emotional reactions of psychiatric nurses and aides to disturbed adolescent patients. The research focused on twenty-four staff members on four locked wards in two private psychiatric hospitals. While we are examining all types of emotional reactions to patients, we are particularly interested in strong negative emotions of anger, hostility, and dislike. We are also interested in emotions such as anxiety or self negation which may serve to isolate the staff member from the patient and can be interpreted by the patient as rejection. The basic applied concern in the study is with staff emotional reactions which imply negative definition of the patient or of self and hence are likely to be counter-therapeutic.

The study was designed as a program in basic research, with implications for applied work, and was funded by the National Institute of Mental Health. While no formal commitment to direct knowledge utilization was written into the grant, our intentions from the project's inception were to provide the two participating hospitals with as much information as they could use to pursue their own motives for improving the treatment process. This understanding was part of our overall contract with the hospitals. The first step in the process of knowledge utilization was our commitment and their expressed interest in data feedback.

The major theoretical proposition guiding our research was that each hospital staff member would have a "Role Identity" (McCall and

Simmons 1966/1978), an idealized picture of him- or herself in his or her position as staff member which is confirmed through the staff member's interactions with patients. The role identity of each staff member would be unique in its precise configuration, but would reflect the overall treatment ideology of the ward or hospital. We hypothesized that when patients act in ways which confirm this idealized self-image, the staff member would feel positively towards the patient. Conversely, when the patient acts in ways that fail to confirm this role identity, the staff member would feel negatively towards the patient. Further, we proposed that staff members would feel positively or negatively towards themselves to the degree that they interpreted their own acts to be confirming or disconfirming of their role identity.

Research Methods and Context

Data Collection Methods

Following some introductory sessions with the ward staffs in July 1984, the study formally began in August, 1984 with a two month general ethnography of each of the four wards. This, and subsequent field work, was done by Scheinfeld and Marshall. During this time we were able to develop relationships with staff members and to recruit six aides or nurses from each of the four wards to participate in the study of emotions. With each of these 24 staff participants we then carried out three cycles of data gathering. Each cycle involved a pre-observation interview conducted a day or two before the observation day, 3 to 4 hours of observation on the ward, during which the ethnographer took extensive notes on the staff member's interactions with patients, and a 6 to 8 hour follow-up interview directly after the observations. This interview had two parts. First, the staff member reflected on emotions experienced during 20 interaction episodes randomly selected from the total set of episodes recorded by the ethnographer. In the second half of the interview, a stratified sub-sample of six episodes was discussed in depth, covering a wider range of issues including whether the staff member felt the emotion they experienced was therapeutically "useful" or "counter-productive." The three data collection cycles yielded a total of 60 interaction episodes discussed with each of the 24 participants in the study.

During the observations, the ethnographers recorded their interpretations of the staff member's affect, based on facial expression, voice tone, body gestures, and content of staff member's statements to the patient. Whenever possible, the ethnographer also asked the staff member for an on-the-spot report of how he or she was feeling or had just felt in the previous interaction. Staff members' reports of their affect and ethnographers' interpretations were recorded on a scale ranging from -5 (the most intense negative feeling) through 0 (neutral feeling) to +5 (the most intense positive feeling). The informants took to this method easily. It felt natural to them to report, "That was a -3, anger" or "that was a +2, self-satisfaction."

The three pre-observation interviews for each staff member covered a wide range of topics relating to interactions with patients, relationships with peers and administrators, and interpretations of ward culture. At the beginning of each pre-observation interview the staff member was asked to indicate their liking or disliking of each patient on the ward, using a -5 to +5 "liking" scale (+5, very strong liking, to -5, very strong disliking of the patient). Towards the end of that interview the staff member was asked to indicate the amount of "investment" he or she had in each patient using a 0-5 scale (0, no investment in the patient, to 5, very strong investment in the patient). Both "liking" and "investment" were terms regularly used by staff members in describing relationships with patients.

During the last third of the data gathering period, interviews were carried out with the unit leaders (head nurses and ward managers). The interviews covered ward treatment culture, ward organization, performance ratings on the staff members participating in the study, views on what constitutes counter-therapeutic emotions in staff, and desires for data feedback from the study.

Utilization Goals, Beneficiaries and Clients

Our primary knowledge utilization goal is to reduce the negative affect experienced by staff towards the adolescent patients in their charge, while also reducing the other kinds of negative affect that serve to isolate staff from patients. Our preliminary analyses show that 21% of the emotions reported by staff are feelings of anger, irritation, annoyance, contempt, disgust and other negative feelings towards patients. The large majority of these are accompanied by impulses to aggress against or avoid the patient. Another 22% are feelings of frustration, disappointment, guilt, discomfort, self disparagement, anxiety, and fear.

Similar findings appear in the analysis of liking/disliking ratings, with 20% of the 1,443 ratings indicating "disliking" of the patient. These feelings of dislike usually are accompanied by desires to distance oneself from the patient and less degree of investment in the patient's progress and well-being.

The ultimate beneficiaries of knowledge utilization efforts will be the patients of these hospitals. But other, more immediate beneficiaries include the staff themselves whose relatively high levels of discomfort and anxiety give rise to anger and hostility towards patients, and to feelings of self condemnation when these emotional reactions occur.

The clients for the knowledge utilization include: (1) the staff participants, the majority of whom have now moved on to other jobs or to advanced education; (2) current staff on the four wards; (3) the administrators of the wards; (4) staff and administrators of other units in these hospitals; and (5) administrators at the hospital level, such as the clinical director, the head of nursing, and heads of staff development. Each group has its own agenda.

Utilization Principles and Strategies

Principles of Knowledge Utilization

Ideally, in applied research, the anthropologist and client or clients collaborate in all phases of the project, beginning with the initial formulation of the problem and ending with the implementation of recommendations (Scheinfeld 1987; J. Schensul 1987a, 1987b). This collaborative process includes:

1. Formulation of the practical problem.
2. Formulation of research questions and hypotheses.
3. Planning of the research design.
4. Planning of methods of data analysis.
5. Data collection.
6. Decisions about analytic priorities.
7. Data analysis and interpretation.
8. Dissemination of research findings.
9. Recommendations for implementation.
10. Implementation of decisions and actions.

The rationale for this kind of collaborative effort is based on a substantial literature, now available within and beyond applied anthropology, which suggests how the research process can be structured to promote knowledge utilization (e.g., Seidman 1983; Hakel et al. 1982; Ingman and Thomas 1975; Rothman 1980; Horstein et al. 1971; del Prado 1973; Dobyns et al. 1971). From this literature, three basic assumptions can be gleaned regarding the conditions under which knowledge is likely to be utilized by clients.

The first assumption concerns user motivation. Knowledge is more likely to be used when the participants are actively involved in seeking answers to their own deeply felt problems. An active role gives them a reflection for their competence and integrity. They are in control; they are working on their own issues and developing their own solutions. The second assumption concerns user understanding and acceptance of the data. When participants collaborate in collecting and analyzing the data, the research findings become more internalized, and hence are more likely to lead to action. A third assumption addresses the reality base of the data. Participants involved in a setting have a richness of knowledge regarding the organization (or community), including the motives and investments of its members. Thus, much of the information required at each stage of the process is readily and more richly at hand if these people are involved in formulating research questions, gathering data and interpreting the findings. This makes the research more hard-hitting and precise, and makes recommendations more realistic.

Based on these underlying assumptions, we propose four basic principles that would seem to be essential for knowledge utilization to occur (Scheinfeld 1987). First, develop ongoing working relationships with people of power and influence in the situation. Second, work collaboratively with an established body for planning and problem solving. If possible, this group should be vertically constituted, representing all relevant echelons of the organization or community. Third, build the research around strongly felt problems and issues of the decision makers, information users, and other participants in the setting. Fourth, involve members of the organization or community in as many phases of the research as possible.

The model of total collaboration outlined in items 1 through 10 above was not possible in this study, because it was designed and funded prior to establishing contracts with the hospitals. Nonetheless, we have tried to realize the four underlying principles to the fullest possible extent. The remainder of this chapter is a description of those efforts and processes followed by a critique of the whole.

In this project we approach knowledge utilization in relation to two different and related universes within the hospitals: the first is the wards where the study was done, the second is the wider hospital. The following discussion of utilization strategies deals separately with each of these universes.

Building a Utilization Alliance with the Administrators of the Wards That Participated in the Study

In our estimation, the fulcrum of knowledge utilization at the ward level is the relationship between the researchers and the people who administer the wards. As in all effective working relationships, trust, respect and good will are essential. However, there also needs to be firm agreement on a set of knowledge use goals which are of sufficiently high priority to the users to motivate them to devote the time, energy and resources required for successful implementation of the study's findings. Our description of the knowledge utilization process, therefore, begins with the creation of that alliance.

In both hospitals our most vital administrative connection was the coordinator of the adolescent wards. This person is situated politically between higher administration and the ward leaders. Both had strong influence with the top administration and the ward management, derived in large part from their being interpersonally and therapeutically skilled. In the case of Hospital A, the influence of the coordinator also was underpinned by the fact that he was paid by the outside agency which supplied the large majority of patient referrals to the two wards in the study.

From the beginning of our contact with the hospitals, each coordinator served as our "speaking partner": a friendly contact within the organization who had the political savvy to advise us in our relations with the various echelons within the institution and the influence to successfully pave the way to those individuals and groups (Schaefer 1983). The researcher's connection with such a person is critically important, not only for successfully accomplishing the research, but also for facilitating utilization of the knowledge produced by a study.

The leadership structure at the ward level differs in the two hospitals. In Hospital A each ward is administered by a head nurse (female) and a ward manager (male). The latter may have either a B.A. or M.A. degree. His key qualification is experience. There is not a clear hierarchical relationship between the head nurse and the ward manager. The relationship tends to be one of co-management within a clear division of labor. In Hospital B the key, ever-present person is the head nurse. Each ward also has a psychiatrist who is the formal head of the unit, but who has relatively little contact with the line staff.

The analysis below will describe how the alliance with the ward leadership developed as the research progressed.

Step 1. The Initial Contract. As mentioned above, the issue of data feedback was part of the very earliest negotiations with the adolescent coordinators and ward leaders of the respective hospitals. We and they were both interested in the knowledge being utilized and that became part of our verbal contract. We were not able to get beyond this generalized understanding at that time. In spite of having access to a highly articulated research proposal none of these individuals were able to answer the general question, "What do you want to learn from this study?" We also were unable to generate enthusiasm in either hospital for the establishment of a committee to guide the study and the utilization of its findings. On both counts it was clear that we would have to be patient. A process needed yet to unfold.

Step 2. The Data Gathering Period (Months 1 through 21). During the data gathering period our relationships with the ward leaders deepened slightly. The two ethnographers became frequent visitors who, being minimally obtrusive, contributed to the wards' self esteem as places worth studying. The positive reports from the study participants contributed to our overall credibility and benign image. Yet, by and large the ward leaders, when asked, were still not able to articulate specific questions or interests that they wanted answered by the study. We felt at times that we were putting people in an awkward position by asking them, "What do you want to learn from the study?" We found it more productive to say, "Something you might be thinking about is what you might want to learn from the study". This created opportunities for further discussion about feedback and also created a space for whatever thoughts they had in the moment to come to the surface.

Step 3. Early Data Analysis Phase: The "Menu" Approach (Months 22-29). Convinced that general questions were not going to be effective in establishing the knowledge utilization interests of the ward administrators, we developed a two page "menu" listing the kinds of data feedback that we envisaged being able to provide. The following is a partial list of the items included:

Item 1: "The total range of emotions, both pleasurable and unpleasant, found among the participating staff members, as well as the intensity and frequency of these emotions."

Item 2: "The contexts in which these emotions arise."

Item 3: "The staff members' interpretations of the patients' actions and/or their own actions in the interaction sequence and how these interpretations contribute to the resulting feeling towards self or patient."

Item 7: "Feelings of liking or disliking of patients and how these feelings contribute to interpretations of patient actions and to the resulting emotions."

Item 11: "The relationship between length of experience in the staff member role and the pattern of emotional responses."

Item 12: "Differential emotional reactions to boys vs. girls."

Item 15: "Analysis of factors that contribute to the intensity of emotions."

The menu approach proved to be far more effective than any previous attempts to engage the ward leaders in focused discussions around knowledge utilization. Copies of the menu were sent to the various ward leaders a week prior to our meetings with them. At both hospitals the menu served as a useful device for eliciting interests and priorities of the ward leaders. We found that in most cases they were able not only to select out high priority items from the list, but that the list itself stimulated hypotheses and new interest areas. We felt for the first time that a substantive alliance around knowledge utilization was in the process of formation.

Step 4. Planning Initial Feedback to Staff at Hospital A: Deepening of the Alliance (Month 30). When the time came that we felt we had analyzed enough data for Hospital A to provide an initial wave of feedback, we requested a meeting of the Adolescent Program Committee to plan the feedback sessions for the staff. The Adolescent Program Committee consists of the Adolescent Program Director, his assistant and the four ward leaders. It is a standing group which meets weekly and is the closest, functionally, to the committee structure which we wanted to create at the beginning of the study. We opened this meeting by presenting the unit heads with a hand-out reporting data on frequency of staff rage reactions, aggressive impulses, staff's interpretations of patient acts contributing to these emotions, and the distribution of these emotional reactions across various interaction contexts. The data showed that certain settings were what we called "hot spots," contexts in which staff were particularly vulnerable to experiencing negative feelings towards patients. The hand-out also gave data on disliking of patients and on staff's relationships with each other.

While this meeting produced lively conversation around various aspects of the data, it was slowed down by difficulties that the committee members had in interpreting the statistical tables which we had earnestly provided in our hand-out. One of the first suggestions of the unit leaders was to get rid of the complex tables in our presentations to the staff and present data in the simplest possible manner.

The group agreed on two primary goals for the two feedback sessions with staff:

• Increase staff awareness of when and why they experienced negative feelings towards patients; e.g., "Focus on the hot spots and hot situations." "I want them to know when they are more likely to experience anger, negative impulses and aggress against the kids . . . to reflect about it . . . This includes thinking about the kind of kids that tend to incite feelings of aggression in staff."

• Promote staff reflection on their relations with each other and how these are connected to their feelings about the patients; e.g., "Some truths about staff-staff relations and how these are related to the emotions experienced with the kids."

In follow-up telephone conversations with those who had been at the meeting, and with two unit leaders who had been absent, we deepened our understanding of these goals and of the unit leaders' implicit theories of staff development accompanying the goals. Most believed, for example, that if staff became more "aware" of the kinds of situations in which they were most vulnerable to anger, they would be less likely to experience the anger, and especially less likely to act on it. This enhanced awareness would provide "a stop gap between acting on impulse and knowing they are in a situation where it can occur."

Providing Initial Feedback to the Ward Staffs at Hospital A (Month 32)

Guided by our meeting with the Adolescent Program Committee, we used a radically revised data handout in our two feedback sessions with the staff. In place of detailed statistical tables, we substituted some simple percentages and rankings.

Our highest priority in these sessions was to develop the motivation in staff to use the data. We wished, as in our relations with the ward leaders, to develop an alliance with the staff which focused on their own motives and interests in relation to the study's findings.

Our primary assumption was that staff would most likely be motivated to learn if we presented the material in a way which helped them to identify with the emotional experience of the study participants and, through that identification and reflection, to increase their awareness of their own emotional reactions to the patients. Furthermore, we assumed that simple reflection on what patients do to cause staff anger was not sufficient. In order to learn from the experience, staff would need to examine the self experience that these interactions with patients engendered in them. In other words, our intention was to stimulate the same kind of reflective process during feedback sessions that we had created with the study participants during the research (*c.f.* Marshall, Scheinfeld and Beer 1987).

The sessions were attended by the available staffs of both wards, several ward leaders, and, in the first session, by the Adolescent Program Director. We began the first session with a role-play of the interview process which we had carried out with participants in the study. Scheinfeld played "the ethnographer" and Marshall played the staff member who was "Annoyed, - 4" over the phony, nongenuine, "canned" feedback that one patient gave to another during a community meeting. The role-play worked well. The Adolescent Program Director observed that it "joined" us with the group.

We then distributed the data handouts, and quickly reviewed some of the contents. The ensuing discussion focused primarily on two topics: Anger reactions to patients, in general, and disliking of patients. At times the discussion moved into staff's explicit reflection on their own self experience while interacting with patients. In particular, staff members spoke about their needs to feel "in control" in order not to feel "threatened," and how a loss of that sense of control leads to hostile feelings towards the patient.

The second session, two days later, continued with the theme of "disliking patients" and moved rather rapidly into an analysis of data contrasting a type of anger reaction which the study participants reported to be "counter-productive" and inappropriate, with a type of anger reaction which they said was legitimate and productive. The first, "counter-productive," type of anger arose primarily in staff-patient interactions in which staff felt the patient was deliberately trying to upset the staff member by being non-responsive to the staff member's actions towards the patient. This type of anger involved impulses to aggress against the patient which were usually expressed in the ensuing response of the staff member to the patient. The legitimate type of anger, by contrast, was felt in response to one patient being abusive or uncaring towards another patient. The impulse was to "confront" the patient rather than to aggress against him/her. This fundamental contrast in the data provided a stimulus for reflection, and, in turn, an opportunity for some of the more experienced personnel to talk about alternatives to experiencing interactions with patients in an anger-inducing manner. For example, one person offered, "When I get into a situation like this, I try to suspend my need for efficacy."

This group process encouraged staff members to reflect on their anger-inducing experiences with patients and then helped them to consider alternative, anger-reducing ways of experiencing interactions with patients. Towards the last third of the session we raised the issue of staff-staff relations and the impact of staff tensions on staff-patient relations. This had been a major feature of the ward leaders' agenda. Data about staff relations was provided on the hand-out but, with one exception, staff had not mentioned it up to this point. The group became involved in the discussion but not with the same intensity as with the other material. This was not surprising since one of the concerns of the ward leaders was that the staff were not sufficiently concerned about their relationships with each other. After the session we critiqued the process with the two ward leaders who had been present.

In general, the feedback sessions produced a fairly impressive ferment among the staff. However, the long term impact from this kind of encounter is limited at best. The process can only be valuable if it leads to the building of an alliance with ward leadership and staff in which they actively seek to implement the findings of the study. Accounts of and plans for that building of further alliances will be presented later in this chapter. At this point, in order to follow the chronological unfolding of the process, we turn to a discussion of alliance building in the wider hospital.

Building an Alliance with the Wider Hospital (Months 36-50)

Our initial structural connection with the wider hospital in both institutions has been the "Research Committee." The following will be a description of how that relationship at Hospital A progressed through a sequence of structures and processes that is about to result in knowledge utilization on a hospital-wide basis.

The Research Committee at Hospital A is composed of the major clinical administrators of the institution: The Clinical Director, Head Nurse, Head Social Worker, Director of Training, and Adolescent Program Director. It also includes representatives from other denizens in the hospital; a ward manager from one of the wards outside the study and assistants to the hospital administrator. The committee's primary function is to review the suitability and progress of research done in the hospital. In this capacity the committee has summoned us every six months to give a progress report. At these meetings we always received strong support for the study, but our efforts did not result in significant movement towards a utilization alliance. For example, when the "menu" of feedback possibilities was presented to this committee, they responded with great enthusiasm, but were unable to say which items interested them more than others. Utilization was discussed in only the most general terms.

In the 36th month of the study, we told the Research Committee of our desire to form a knowledge utilization alliance with them, either in their capacity in this committee or in their other capacities. We distributed a three page hand-out summarizing many of the initial findings which point to the clinical significance of the data. Accompanying this hand-out we gave each member of the committee a "Clinical Significance Rating Sheet" which briefly listed fifteen of the dependent variables treated in the three page data hand-out (for example high intensity anger towards patients, low intensity anger towards patients, impulses to aggress against the patient, impulses to avoid the patient, sentiments of dislike towards patients, uncomfortable peer relations among staff, etc.). The instructions on the sheet asked the committee member to rank each item as High, Medium or Low clinical priority and then to rank the high priority items as most important, second most important, etc. Our aim in doing this was to ground the relationship in planning data feedback which would have high salience for the committee's members. The results of these ratings were tallied and reflected back to the committee at the subsequent meeting.

In the course of the discussion however, it became clear that the Research Committee was not the fully appropriate committee with which to engage for purposes of implementing knowledge utilization in the hospital. Two of the committee's members, the Head of Social Work and the Director of Training, invited us to meet with the "Education Committee," of which they are primary members, to further the implementation of the research findings. They felt that the mission of the Education Committee was more directly related to our interest in knowledge sharing.

The Education Committee, like the Research Committee, is a group of about 10 representatives of major leadership positions in the hospital. Roughly one half of the membership is the same across the two committees. Our work with this committee began with an introduction to the study and its preliminary findings. We also asked the members to fill out the "Clinical Significance Rating Sheet" (described above). At the next meeting we discussed their priority ratings. The third meeting focused on their goals for knowledge utilization. However, we realized that progress with this committee would be seriously limited by the large size of the group, their fixed bi-monthly meeting schedule and the brief period (thirty minutes) that they were able to give to the study at each meeting. We requested the formation of a special sub-committee with which we could meet more frequently and in greater depth to plan data feedback to line staffs and other groups in the hospital. This request was readily granted.

The sub-committee was comprised of the Director of Staff Development, the Director of Adjunct Therapy, and a ward manager. A series of meetings with this sub-committee have been extremely fruitful. It is of the right size, composition and flexibility to function as an efficient planning unit. Plans for feedback to the wider hospital are now in place. A major product of our work with the sub-committee has been the development of a useful data feedback construct called the "Clinical Significance Variable" which allows us to combine four aspects of the negative emotion data into a single variable which represents the concerns of a particular unit or hospital. The four aspects of negative emotion which we presented to the sub-committee were: (1) Hostility in the impulse associated with the emotion; (2) Increase in dislike for the patient accompanying the emotion; (3) Intensity of the emotion; and (4) Negative/destructive expression of the emotion to the patient. In our discussions with the sub-committee we discovered that they assigned different degrees of importance to these four aspects of negative emotion. For example, negative/destructive expression of emotion to the patient was given priority over the other three. In response, we asked each of the sub-committee members to rate each of these aspects of negative emotion on a four point scale of "clinical significance" in which a "4" represented the highest degree of significance. "Clinically significant" meant that "If a staff member showed a pattern of this kind of affect in relation to patients, you would be concerned (for the patients' well-being)". The sub-committee's average clinical significance ratings for these four dimensions, from highest to lowest, are represented in the first number column of Table 11.1 below. The ratings of a more inclusive group of sixteen ward and middle hospital level administrators, eight from Hospital A and eight from Hospital B, also is represented in Table 11.1. This latter group includes the three sub-committee members.

TABLE 11.1 Clinical Significance Weightings Assigned to Each of the Dimensions of Negative Emotion on Four Point Scales

	Three Member Subcommittee, Hospital A	Sixteen Administrators Hospital A and B
Expression of the Negative Affect to the Patient	4.00	3.96
Hostility in the Impulse	3.73	3.31
Emergent Negative Sentiments toward the Patient	2.33	2.91
Intensity of the Negative Affect	1.67	2.59

Extension of the Planning Process

The process of giving a significance rating to the four aspects of negative affect has now been extended to the ward leadership in both Hospital A and Hospital B and to a hospital-wide committee including the directors of staff development and quality control in Hospital B. These ratings, and the weightings which they provide, will allow us to construct clinical significance variables which combine all four aspects of negative emotion discussed above and which can be tailored to the priority weightings of any particular hospital audience. The widespread administration of the rating scale has provided an initial step in strengthening dialogue with the leadership of the wards originally involved in the study and in opening dialogue with other wards in the hospitals.

We are now approaching the final and major data feedback efforts in both hospitals. Feedback will be provided to ward staff and to groups of hospital administrators. In each case the feedback process will be guided by a planning group the members of which will help lead the feedback process along with the researchers. At the ward level, these planning groups will be extended to include line staff members who will present data to their peers through role play activities which express many of the findings of the study and which are designed to engage the ward staff at an experiential level. The participation of the planners in the feedback process will, we hope, contribute to a continuity of data utilization beyond our disengagement from the hospitals.

Impacts and Outcome

The observable knowledge utilization impact of the study thus far has been two-fold. The first impact was seen during the course of the data gathering process itself. The comments which we received from many of our twenty-four informants concerning the data gathering process suggests that participation in the study of emotions resulted in a significant form of knowledge utilization by the study participants; namely self-knowledge and an increased capacity for self-reflection in their roles as developmental agents for children. Informants gained a heightened awareness of their own patterns of inner emotional reaction to patients, the ways and frequencies with which they expressed those emotions to the patients, the kinds of interactions that gave rise to those responses, and the interpretations and self-meanings that yielded the emotional results that occurred. In one very dramatic case a staff member reported that having to confront his explicit pattern of rage towards patients caused him to re-evaluate his modes of interacting with patients on the unit.

Several conditions helped foster the success of the interviews as opportunities to gain self knowledge. First was the maintenance of the strictest principles of confidentiality. Virtually every informant, in our estimation, came to accept our commitment that the observations and interviews would be shared with no one outside of the study. It was understood that the findings of the study would be reported as patterns involving the informants as a whole. Illustrative material would be used only with the informant's permission. Secondly, the observations and interviews were non-evaluative. The contract was to collaboratively explore the informant's feeling experiences across a wide spectrum of emotion, ranging from deeply pleasurable feelings to the most intense anger or disgust. The ethnographers were careful to reinforce the informants' attempts at introspection and communication, rather than to evaluate the content of the emotion report itself. Thirdly, partly owing to the above, the informants felt "listened to," an experience for which all of us hunger and of which few receive enough, especially as employees in a high stress environment. The interviews were conducted through a process we came to call "reflective listening" in which the ethnographer embraced the informant's feelings and progressively helped the informant to expand on his or her own meanings in ways which augmented the latter's degree of self understanding (Marshall, Scheinfeld, and Beer 1987). All of this reflects our anthropological tradition, and takes the special form of embracing meanings which lie embedded in another's feeling states.

A second impact occurred during meetings with the Education subcommittee at Hospital A. Members of that group reported that the reflections and differentiations emerging in the priority setting and planning process have led them to re-think their approach to the patterns of negative affect experienced by the staff whom they supervise. Above all, the engagement with these administrators has resulted in enthusiasm about the study and a strong ongoing commitment to a collaborative knowledge utilization process.

Discussion and Conclusion

Our knowledge utilization goal for this study is to bring about a reduction in the experience and destructive expression of negative, counter-therapeutic feelings and sentiments experienced by psychiatric hospital line staff towards patients and themselves. It is a goal in which we have a strong investment, given our personal commitments and our self definitions as applied anthropologists.

In our estimation, the realization of this goal will require a minimum of two complementary approaches. The first is to bring about a change in the consciousness of staff, an evolution in staff's self awareness and modes of construing staff-patient encounters. The second approach is to bring about a change in some of the environmental dynamics that contribute to staff vulnerability to negative affect and which generally inhibit the process of self-reflection.

This type of goal most certainly requires the active and committed participation of staff and administrative personnel for its realization. We would argue that the same could be said of any knowledge utilization effort, and that this is a particularly salient case.

The fulcrum of knowledge utilization is the establishment of an alliance between the researchers, the administrators, and those directly affected by implementation. The strength and success of that alliance depends not only upon general sentiments of trust and good will but also rests on a firmly rooted foundation of agreement concerning the ends of implementation and the means by which it can and should be brought about. Until recently in this study, the mutual definition of ends (use goals) has been insufficiently precise to provide that firm foundation. For example, we are learning that in the eyes of staff and administrators not all forms or aspects of anger or dislike are considered to be significantly counter-therapeutic.

The realization of an effective alliance also requires the development of organizational structures through which researchers, administrators and staff can actively engage in reflection on data, goals and implementation. These structures give continuity and legitimization to the knowledge utilization effort that is vital to its long range success.

We have learned that progress in the overall development of the alliance is vitally dependent upon the ongoing provision of feedback data to the parties involved. It is then that the true relevance of the study and credibility of the researchers becomes firmly grounded.

Our major learning in the area of data communication can be summed up in the principle of "experience near," a term coined by the late psychoanalyst, Heinz Kohut. As applied here, it means that the user's ability to utilize the data will hinge on his or her being able to experience and *taste* the meaning of the data. In virtually every case this cannot be done through quantitative presentations. It must be done through qualitative presentations in which the users can identify with the meanings involved. This is no doubt related to findings elsewhere that qualitative presentations are generally more effective in stimulating knowledge utilization (Van de Vall, Bolas, and Kang 1976). Furthermore, the very process of interaction in these communications ideally will be one in which the ethnographer listens to the users' meanings and encourages them to bring their own experience to bear on the data (*c.f.* Marshall, Scheinfeld, and Beer 1987). In our estimation, quantification has an indispensable role in documenting the numerical significance of a finding. It has an important, but limited, cognitive function in the process of developing user understanding and motivation. Qualitative presentation is essential to help users grasp the significance of the data and, hence, develop the insight and motivation necessary to take action.

In broad summary, our work tells us that the success of knowledge utilization pivots on the development of alliances in which there is a genuine meeting of researcher and users in an experiential understanding of the data. Success equally depends upon whether the data has a high priority significance for the mission of the organization. This paper has attempted to set out some of the structures and processes through which effective alliances can be realized.

12

The Use of Feedback in a Model Project: Guardianship for the Impaired Elderly

Madelyn Anne Iris

Utilization of findings was achieved most effectively through a combination of techniques designed to enhance feedback to all project participants and audiences.

For many years social service agencies have faced a growing need for innovative methods of serving increasing numbers of impaired elderly clients, particularly those with cognitive impairments. Workers are especially concerned with the ethical issues stemming from a client's inability to participate in the decision-making process regarding needed services as well as questions of agency liability when clients cannot give clear and informed consent. To remedy this problem social service providers have looked to their legislatures and the courts for clarification of their roles in decision-making for impaired persons.

In this case study, I describe my role in the development of the Model Project of Guardianship for the Low-Income Elderly and my participation in related activities leading to the development of both legislation on adult protective services in Illinois and a model protective service delivery system.

As principal investigator of an impact evaluation of the model project on guardianship, I had many opportunities to use the evaluation findings in ways which directly contributed to the successful outcome of the Guardianship Project, and to subsequent efforts to define the need for protective services for older adults in Illinois. The evaluation's greatest utility lay in serving as a means of information transfer among project participants, including agency administrators, supervisors, and caseworkers. Members of the evaluation team played a major role in the dissemination of information and findings about guardianship through written reports, the interview format, and the consultative role.

Three types of feedback activities are described: on-going feedback related directly to programmatic issues and ad hoc problem-solving; immediate feedback to participants in the context of open-ended interviews; and written reports documenting changing attitudes about guardianship, issues related to impact, and areas of special interest. My role as a Research Associate at the Metropolitan Chicago Coalition on Aging for the last three years is also described.

Background: Protective Services for the Frail Elderly

There are now approximately 28 million people in the United States over age 65, equal to 11.9% of the U.S. population. By the year 2000 this figure will rise to 13%, or 32 million and by 2030 there will be 65 million older people. In addition to growth in numbers, older people are also living longer. Currently, 2.7 million people are over age 85, and by the year 2,000 there may well be 6.7 million such persons (Neugarten 1982).

The "frail elderly" constitute a particular subgroup of the elderly population. Krauskopf (1983) describes the frail elderly as "economically, physically, and socially" dependent. They are primarily women, 80% are widowed, one-third live alone, and one in three lives in poverty. Those who are frail suffer from chronic, debilitating diseases, and many suffer from mental as well as physical impairments. They, of all the elderly, are at greatest risk for exploitation, abuse, and loss of autonomy.

Various interventions can be used to ensure that the rights, property and persons of the frail elderly remain protected. Such interventions are often labelled "protective services." Examples include home-delivered meals, homemakers, and personal care attendants, provided by a wide-ranging network of privately and publicly supported programs.

Legal protections are often needed as well. In most states these include guardianships, conservatorships, trusteeships, or payeeships. Very often, when the frail elderly are no longer able to make their own decisions and manage their own affairs, guardianships and conservatorships are pursued through the courts. Regan (1972 and 1981) and Horstmann (1975) offer more complete discussions of these protective services, and related issues. In some states advance planning tools such as Durable Powers of Attorney, Living Wills, and Powers of Attorney for Heath Care Decisions can also be implemented.

The focus of this case study is on the use of guardianship as a protective intervention. The Guardianship Project was designed to test the feasibility of using guardianship in this way, with the specific goal of maintaining impaired, elderly people in the community.

The Model Project of Guardianship: Research Context, Design and Methods

Project Description

The Guardianship Project, which began in July, 1982, was a three-year, privately-funded program which brought together representatives from six social service agencies in a unique, collaborative effort designed to provide guardianship services for impaired persons 65 and older who appeared able to remain in the community. The project was administered by The Metropolitan Chicago Coalition on Aging (MCCoA 1985). Project staff at MCCoA consisted of a project director and a research associate.

In the collaborative model, one of the six participating agencies was designated to serve as the guardian for all elderly clients in need of such services, although these individuals continued to receive social services from the original, referring agency. When a family member was appointed as guardian the project provided support, legal consultation and technical assistance to aid the guardian in this role.

The Guardianship Project was unique because of its collaborative nature and because it tested a new provision of the Illinois probate code which allowed agencies as well as individuals to serve as guardians. The Guardianship Project had three components: a service component offering guardianship as well as other protective services; a research component, designed to provide a quantitative analysis of client characteristics, cost of services, and time analysis; and a public policy component, directed at improving social and health care services for the elderly.

Impact Evaluation of the Project

An independent impact evaluation was carried out by a team of three researchers from the Erikson Institute in Chicago, with funding from the Retirement Research Foundation. Conducted simultaneously with the project, the evaluation addressed emerging issues rather than describing specific outcomes.

The evaluation examined several key areas. One major focus was client and worker attitudes toward guardianship, and the evolving service delivery system. A second focus was the impact of the project and guardianship on clients and their families. The research was specifically planned to incorporate the perspective of time, to capture changes in attitudes as well as changes in client status, since it was assumed impact could best be assessed by evaluating change. During the three years of the project, we also explored many issues which appeared to have significant impact on project process, program development and agency and worker functioning. These issues included ethical concerns regarding client consent, difficulties in collaborative service delivery, and the varying perspectives of the medical, psychiatric and legal consultants to the project.

Research Design and Methods

The impact evaluation utilized an ethnographic model of data collection and analysis. The evaluation team, comprised of myself and two colleagues, employed two major methods of data collection: participant observation and open-ended interviews.

Participant Observation: Participant observation activities were carried out at all project meetings. As a member of the evaluation team I attended monthly "practice committee" meetings of supervisory staff from the participating agencies in which cases referred to the project for guardianship services were reviewed and assessed for appropriateness; quarterly "policy committee" meetings of agency executives focusing on policy-related issues; and quarterly meetings of all researchers involved with the project as well as those from other local research centers and agencies. The research committee provided the Guardianship Project staff with technical assistance and advice on the conduct of the project research. Detailed minutes of all these meetings were taken by each evaluation team member, collated, and then compared with the minutes produced by the project researcher. Together, the minutes were analyzed as field notes.

As evaluators, my colleagues and I took a non-participatory role in practice committee and policy committee meetings; we observed proceedings but did not comment or offer information on specific questions. Although this role never changed during practice committee meetings, eventually we were invited to comment on issues raised by agency executives at their quarterly meetings. These issues included a lower than expected rate of client referral and an unequal use of project services across agencies.

Although the strictly observational role was often difficult to maintain, especially when we held a different point of view or perspective on proceedings, our decision not to participate obviated consideration of how such participation might skew the decision-making process on specific cases. In addition, we did not have to deal with the problem of violation of confidentiality.

Open-Ended Interviews: Open-ended interviews were conducted at regular intervals with as many project participants as possible throughout the three years. A relatively structured format was used based on principles of interviewing described by Spradley (1979), Spradley and McCurdy (1972), Werner and Schoepfle (1987a, 1987b), and Tyler (1969). This ensured standardization of focus across interviews and systematized the findings.

The interviews were designed to stimulate an introspective analysis of each participant's experiences in the project and were generally conversational in tone, with comments by the interviewer prompting a cyclical series of responses from the interviewee. Each topic was introduced by the evaluator, who began by asking a general question; for example, "Can you tell me what protective services are?" After the response, the interviewer commented, enhancing the interchange by providing feedback from responses by other participants. This usually stimulated the interviewee to expand her reply. Thus, the interview process was one of building a response from the "inside-out," in which answers to questions spanned several interchanges.

These interviews proved to be a valuable source of data, yielding, through multiple analyses, a set of key concepts which emerged over time. For example, after about one year, we realized that the set of services frequently described as "protective services" was not a well-defined class but rather these services were exactly the same as those provided to other clients who were not part of the Guardianship Project. Thus, we undertook an exploration of the concept "protective service", by building a working definition of the term, and examining its meaning with regard to different sets of clients, different systems of service

"native" definitions proved useful when addressing the issue of protective services and service delivery within the context of the collaborative, multi-disciplinary model used by the Guardianship Project.

Process issues were also examined. One of our objectives was to document the assessment process for protective services and determination of need for guardianship. One important discovery was that the type of process used was partially determined by available resources within an agency, the expertise of the worker, and her knowledge about guardianship. Our findings demonstrated that the assessment process differed from one agency to another, and within agencies as well. Thus, generalizations about assessment standards and practices had to be carefully drawn.

For example, one agency served only elderly clients living within a well-defined geographic area and employed a specialist in protective service casework. This agency referred few cases to the project since the worker was quite adept at working with cognitively impaired clients and could tap a wide variety of resources through her professional contacts and through the agency's network of consultants. In addition, support staff such as homemakers and personal care attendants were employed directly by this agency and were trained and supervised by the social work staff.

In contrast, a large number of cases were referred by one worker at another agency which served a broad spectrum of the population, scattered about throughout the city. Workers at this agency did not specialize in any particular type of case nor did the agency provide access to in-house consultative staff such as physicians, psychiatric nurses, or psychiatrists. Supportive services utilized by the clients were purchased from private providers on an hourly fee-for-service basis.

We conducted open-ended interviews with all the social workers who referred clients to the project; all agency executives; all members of the practice committee, and project consultants. Agency executives and practice committee members were interviewed once every six months. Caseworkers referring clients were interviewed at critical points in the guardianship process, such as at the time of referral, and during the first six weeks following the appointment of a guardian.

Finally, clients for whom guardianship was recommended and who were able to be engage in a face-to-face discussion of their situation were interviewed at least twice; before and after the court hearing. Follow-up interviews were planned for every six months thereafter, but could not always be scheduled. When these clients had families who were willing to be interviewed, the same schedule was followed. Clients referred to the project but who were not recommended for guardianship services were usually interviewed before and after the project review process, if such interviews were deemed appropriate.

Our original plan was to focus the evaluation predominantly on the elderly clients and their families. However, we encountered two major obstacles. First, many of the clients were too cognitively impaired to participate in an interview and others were judged too emotionally unstable. Caseworkers felt such individuals would not be able to deal rationally with their need for protection and would react unfavorably to a discussion focusing on such issues. Thus, only 15 of the 48 clients referred to the project were interviewed.

Second, we also found it difficult to work with families, for few clients had actively involved families. In fact, lack of involvement determined in part whether or not a client would need the legal protection of guardianship and if an agency guardian was needed. When family members were involved with an elderly relative's care, guardianship could often be avoided altogether. Of the 48 clients in the project, fewer than 10 had involved family members. Of these, only five or six chose to serve as guardians.

Through a series of initial interviews with social workers, and through observation at practice committee meetings during the first six months of the project, we determined that impact, as related to change in a client's life and circumstances, was best assessed by examining the ways in which services for the client changed. Thus, the focus of the evaluation shifted to an examination of the impact of the project on agencies and agency workers, vis-á-vis their impaired clients.

Client Group

The evaluation was aimed at several audiences. The funding agency was primarily interested in the results of the study, which were provided through semi-annual reports. As a private, not-for-profit research foundation, however, this agency was not in a position to utilize the findings or implement recommendations through changes in practice or procedures. Other agencies and foundations providing funds directly to the Guardianship Project also received these semi-annual reports.

As evaluators, we also responded to the needs of project staff for information related to project development. Often these needs were immediate, in response to specific problems. Examples of how we contributed to the resolution of such problems are presented below.

In addition, we were responsible to project participants from the six agencies. For example, agency caseworkers, although most involved and knowledgeable about the day-to-day issues related to service provision and protection for the frail elderly, were also the least likely to be involved with project development and had only minimal access to research findings. Many workers had previously participated in research and demonstration projects and verbalized negative feelings about their experiences. They often felt disengaged from the research effort, and exploited by the researchers. Many workers stated that techniques of ethnographic interviewing and the incorporation of feedback into the interview process helped engage them in the research process. This led to feelings of greater commitment to project outcomes.

Although most elderly clients were unable to comprehend the implications of their participation in the project, family members did express an interest in the research. Generally, they were most interested in acquiring knowledge which would help them in their own dealings with their impaired relatives. Thus, their needs were often very specific, and focused on short-term problems and interests. For example, one guardian, herself an older woman, stated that her main problem in being her sister's guardian was the need to find money to repair her ward's home. She hoped that funds for such problems would be provided to guardians as a result of her participation in the research.

Beneficiaries of the Research

In order to describe beneficiaries of the research it is best to take a long-term perspective. Since the completion of the project in 1985 research findings have been disseminated to program planners and policy-makers, both in Illinois and across the country, to use in the development of protective service systems for the elderly, and to enhance understanding of the impact of guardianship on impaired elderly people, their families, and their guardians.

You can also view all older Americans as the ultimate beneficiaries of this research. Although no one individual will benefit, and most likely those elderly persons who participated are no longer living, I do believe the research has contributed to the development of better service systems and more humane approaches to guardianship for elderly persons. For example, project findings are now being used to help shape recommendations for national standards of guardianship practice and reform of the guardianship process (see American Bar Association 1988). It is anticipated that some form of federal legislation regulating guardianship will emerge from these efforts.

Utilization Methods and Process

Utilization of findings was achieved most effectively through a combination of techniques designed to enhance feedback to all project participants and audiences. Because we did not have a direct role in influencing the outcome of the project, or the development of new services, I believe our greatest strength was our ability to provide timely and usable information to program decision-makers. Feedback was provided through three techniques: semi-annual written reports, open-ended interviews, and consultations on specific problems and issues.

Written Reports

Written reports documented evaluation activities and described findings on selected topics. Although the reports were originally intended to inform the funding agency about project progress and to highlight areas of investigation, they quickly evolved into detailed analyses of specific issues, descriptions of process, and changing attitudes. The reports documented changing definitions of guardianship, as well as inter- and intra-agency collaboration around guardianship services. Issues such as confidentiality, the tension between research and practice, and the role of the guardianship agency in a collaborative model were also discussed.

An important characteristic of the reports was that they incorporated and highlighted change over time, in both perceptions and issues. For example, at the beginning of the project many participants described guardianship as a "last resort" which deprived clients of all rights and was generally seen as the first step on the road to institutionalization. Through their own repeated experiences with many different clients, and through the shared experiences of the practice group, workers soon realized that guardianship, in fact, had only a limited effect in bringing about positive change in some specific areas of a client's life. Documenting this attitudinal change, and outlining its implications for use of guardianship as part of a comprehensive protective service program, was an important task in evaluating the impact of the project on agencies and workers.

In retrospect, the written reports appear to have been the least effective method for enhancing utilization of findings by participating agencies. Although the reports were distributed to all agency executives, to provide them with information through a formal channel of communication, we soon realized they were not likely to internalize the findings, disseminate them throughout their agencies, and/or use them as a basis for future program planning.

There were several reasons why this was so. First, agency executives felt the reports were not "timely" enough to meet their informational needs for long-term planning. In addition, once the reports were delivered to the administering agency, the evaluators had no specified role in the dissemination of the reports, or furthering use of the findings. Dissemination and utilization of findings at the agency policy and planning level would have been enhanced had specific roles been incorporated into the research design.

However, over the last three years the evaluation reports have been used repeatedly by policy and planning groups focusing on the need for enhanced guardianship services and an adult protective service system in Illinois. Thus, the research findings seem to have greater usefulness when applied beyond the limited settings of individual agencies.

Open-Ended Interviews

A more effective method for sharing findings with project participants evolved through the use of a unique manipulation of the open-ended interview method. In the early stages of the evaluation a relatively structured interview format was used. However, it became evident that most project participants had a great need for information regarding the project's overall development and the interview setting seemed particularly effective for providing such feedback.

For example, early interviews focused on questions such as client confidentiality, expectations about the impact of guardianship on clients, and the conceptualization of guardianship. By the end of the first two years problems related to confidentiality had been resolved, expectations had turned to experiences, and conceptualizations had been formalized into definitions. Interviews conducted during the last year of the project explored changes within and across agencies, documented the effectiveness and characteristics of the collaborative model and worker roles in such a model, and described how guardianship services are delivered by a not-for-profit agency.

To enhance our discussions we provided feedback on previous findings and current concerns during the course of each interview. Each interviewee was invited to comment and share her perspective and that of her agency. In this way relevant information was made immediately available to all interviewees, including agency directors, supervisory staff, and case workers. This technique increased the timeliness of findings, and enabled us to address issues of greatest concern to all project participants.

Another benefit of such information sharing was the increase in workers' sense of participation since they felt their experiences and ideas were considered important to the development and outcome of the project. This was especially helpful in establishing rapport with agency caseworkers, and in generating more thoughtful and provocative discussions. Incorporating feedback into interviews also guaranteed that information about the project crossed the boundaries of the hierarchical organization within each agency. Since workers were frequently unaware of developments at other participating agencies we soon found ourselves serving as a conduit for information which reached across institutional barriers to interagency communication.

We also served as a major source of feedback on the project to agency administrators who were often unaware of the progress of the project within their own agencies. At several agencies institutional structures kept directors from involvement in the day-to-day operations of the casework services. Caseworkers and agency administrators were often housed in different buildings, or in different geographic locations across the city. Thus, a director's knowledge of specific clients and issues relevant to the guardianship project was limited. During an interview we provided information regarding each agency's participation. Several agency directors commented this process was very stimulating and raised policy and service issues they had not previously considered, giving them a new perspective of the Guardianship Project.

Because we were in contact with all project participants, we able to develop a unique, holistic perspective of events and developments. Project staff sought information about certain problematic issues evolving from the collaborative model, or misunderstandings between family members and agency workers. For example, family members serving as guardians for their elderly relatives frequently reached a "burn-out" stage within one year of being appointed the guardian. To determine how to best aid such individuals, and support them as guardians, we were asked to discuss the efficacy of using family members as guardians for elderly clients of social service agencies. Insights from interviews with the guardians were shared, including specific examples of stress-producing situations and their needs for assistance.

In another example, a conflict over responsibility for nursing home placement and long-term monitoring of clients in sheltered facilities arose between workers from a referring agency and the guardianship agency. This was a new role for caseworkers at community-based social service organizations. However, the guardianship agency now had a legal responsibility to provide care for these clients. Since the clients in question were project clients, this responsibility was judged to be shared, as part of the collaborative model.

In my interviews with the involved staff members I elicited their views of the issue, shared the perspectives of workers from other agencies, and discussed the impact of such questions on the feasibility of a collaborative model of guardianship. In this way each participant was provided with a more generalized view of the problem. This method served to decrease the caseworkers' anxieties and enhanced understanding of the collaborative effort.

Role of Consultant

A third, perhaps most effective way in which evaluation findings were shared with project participants was through consultation. Although two other researchers assisted in the evaluation, as Principal Investigator, and through personal interest, I devoted more time to working with Guardianship Project staff on issues which fell outside the specific purview of the evaluation itself. Through the consultant's role I hoped to increase use of findings by responding to the immediate needs of project participants.

As a consultant I became a more active participant in project affairs. In making the decision to use evaluation findings in this somewhat "proactive" manner I considered the impact this might have on the development of the project, and on the conduct of the evaluation. In the end, I decided that providing input to improve service delivery and enhance outcomes was an appropriate aspect of evaluating a developing program. The ability to respond to the demand for timely information through the role of consultant was a valuable asset of the ethnographic approach, since it enabled me to address major questions regarding the progress of the project and to use my knowledge to help solve problems.

For example, during the first two years of the project the rate of referrals was much lower than had been projected, and continuation funding was threatened. Project staff turned to the evaluation for a possible explanation of this problem. Several approaches were used. First, participants and funders were asked to revise their expectations based on an ethnographic analysis of agency culture. In this analysis, I compared agency philosophies, structures, and methods of operation, using the concept of "agency culture" as a paradigm (see Iris 1984). Differences in these various aspects of agency life were seen to directly affect the number of aged people served, the length of time of service provision, and the customary roles of social workers vis-á-vis their elderly clients. Conclusions from this analysis were presented directly to project staff, as an explanation for differential referral rates among agencies.

Second, the criteria for counting referrals was changed in acknowledgement of the increasing expertise of workers who referred only the most appropriate cases. The Guardianship Project researcher was encouraged to amend her data collection protocol and count all clients considered for referral but judged inappropriate by agency workers, even prior to review by the practice committee. The category "screened out clients" was added to the typology of clients counted. In the interviews with the caseworkers the evaluation team discussed the "screened out" cases with workers, and provided information on the characteristics of such clients and reasons for deferral. This change increased the sample size and brought it closer to the number anticipated in the project proposals. It also provided us with more information regarding the appropriate uses of guardianship as a protective intervention, by describing a set of contrasting cases.

Thus, the evaluation was not implemented as an external measure of outcomes or success, but rather it became an integral part of the project itself. Because the Guardianship Project was perceived as primarily a service delivery program the needs of the researchers had to be balanced against the needs of project participants and their desire to provide services in the most effective and efficient manner possible. Continuous feedback proved to be the most valuable method for meeting these needs.

Constraints on Utilization

Although findings from the evaluation were perceived to be highly informative, participants labored under a set of constraints somewhat unique to the collaborative model, and to voluntary agencies. These constraints hindered, to a certain extent, maximum use of project findings.

For example, the Guardianship Project staff, as employees of MCCoA, were responsible for coordinating project activities, staffing meetings and conducting more quantitatively-based research activities. They were expected to support the activities of MCCoA as a whole, follow the paths set by its organizational structure, and comply with internal operating procedures. MCCoA, in turn, responded to the demands of the foundations and agencies funding the project, the six collaborating agencies, as well as its own Board of Directors.

These multiple responsibilities demanded continual evaluation and adjustment of project procedures and policies. Those policies and procedures specific to the Guardianship Project were negotiated by the project policy committee, described earlier. Each committee member, in turn, acted in accordance with the policies and operating procedures of his own agency.

Because the evaluation was originally designed as an independent impact evaluation, its potential as a tool for program planning for the future was not anticipated. Thus, access to the decision-making boards of the agencies was not negotiated and no members of agency boards were included as interviewees. Since all agency executives responded to the direction provided by the agency Board of Directors, the latter should have been included within the universe of project participants in determining the full scope of project impact. Most certainly, such boards should have been perceived as potential audiences for the findings of the evaluation.

Project Impacts

All ethnographic evaluations contribute in some way to the knowledge base of specific organizations, programs or groups. Whether or not such knowledge is utilized to effect change depends upon participants' perceptions of the reasonableness and reliability of the findings (Rothman 1980; Patton 1978). Scheinfeld suggests that knowledge utilization or application of findings, is most likely to occur, with the greatest benefits, in situations in which (1) the research methodology includes on-going opportunities for feedback to both decision-makers and information-users; (2) findings are relevant to the immediate concerns and issues of participants as they describe them; and (3) the evaluation is integrated into the established decision-making structure of the organization or program (Scheinfeld 1984). Our evaluation of the Guardianship Project met some but not all of these criteria for utilization. Thus, maximal utilization of the findings was not achieved, although certain impacts were clearly noted.

First, through the evaluation process itself, project participants were better able to monitor their own internal changes in attitudes and in practice. Agencies were provided with information describing social work practice within the agency, and the impact of project participation on agency workers. Changes in case management, in assessment, and in client evaluation were incorporated into the evolving system of guardianship services for the impaired elderly.

By providing information to agency executives, particularly that which described the features and demands of a potential service, i.e., guardianship, the evaluation played a role in determining whether or not agencies would choose to direct their resources toward that segment of the elderly population in need of protection.

However, by not accessing the decision-making boards of the agencies, the evaluators remained one step away from playing a direct role in guiding such choices. Instead, information provided through the reports, interviews and consultations was transmitted by other project participants, and in some cases, by agency executives who were not directly involved in the project. Thus, we could not control the interpretation of results, decisions on the significance of certain findings, etc.

While it is appropriate that the audience of any evaluation retain the ability to utilize the results in their own best interests, utilization of findings might have been enhanced if we had played a greater role in this process. However, due to circumstances of funding and because the evaluation was not incorporated into the original project structure, it was difficult to establish more direct links to the policy boards of the agencies once the project began. Thus the potential for multiple uses of the evaluation findings was not met.

Problems of utilization were exacerbated by the use of the collaborative model of service provision and practice. The impaired, elderly clients of the project represented the most minimal fraction of the total clientele by each agency. Thus, although agency workers collaborated on client reviews and guardianship service provision, the agencies remained highly autonomous, even in project-related matters. The result was that participants responded to evaluation findings and recommendations differently, depending on their agency's interest in developing an internal guardianship or protective service component and the agency's concomitant investment and commitment to the project.

The evaluation's greatest impact can be seen by examining the activities of MCCoA since the termination of the project. Since 1985 MCCoA has pursued research and advocacy efforts in the area of protective services, in collaboration with the six original Guardianship Project agencies, plus others, both agencies and individuals. Information and suggestions from the evaluation continue to be used for planning and implementation of this effort.

For example, in 1986 a series of Protective Service Round-Tables were held in Chicago, Illinois. These discussions were designed to stimulate planning and advocacy work in the area of protective services in general, of which guardianship is but one such service. At these meetings agency executives, local planners, state and local policy-makers, judges, attorneys, and staff members from various state agencies shared their interests in the development of a protective service system. They examined various options for such a system, debated ethical issues related to protective intervention, and dealt with political concerns such as the differing and sometimes opposing mandates of the Illinois Department on Aging and the Illinois Department of Mental Health and Developmental Disabilities.

By providing MCCoA with an analysis of these debates, I was able to influence the conceptualization of such a protective service system, incorporating findings from the evaluation of the Guardianship Project as well as new information acquired through my activities as a researcher in the area of elder abuse (Iris 1987, 1988), and my own research on judicial decisionmaking and guardianship for the elderly (Iris 1986b).

Findings from the Guardianship Project and from the evaluation have also been shared with judges of the Probate Court in Cook, Lake, and DuPage Counties in Illinois. These judges preside over guardianship hearings and decide questions of competency and disability. In Cook County, Probate Court judges have met with policy and program planners to discuss issues related to guardianship for the elderly, and, in addition, have participated in follow-up research on judicial decision-making in this area (see Iris 1986b). Their use of the findings, as guides to decision-making, has not been documented, but several changes in practice have been noted (Harrison, personal communication).

Finally, I have continued to work closely with MCCoA and the six agencies of the Guardianship Project, as a Research Associate, to plan for the implementation of a protective service system. My skills as an anthropologist, and especially the unique perspectives of an ethnographic approach to process analysis and descriptions of events, have generated a demand for the kind of information anthropologists are best able to provide. It is clear that such information is perceived to be highly useful, leading to enhanced decision-making and program planning. In addition, I have contributed to several national workshops on guardianship, sponsored by the American Bar Association.

Summary

My activities in the planning and development of a protective service system have now spanned almost five years. Beginning with my role as Principal Investigator of the Impact Evaluation of the Guardianship Project, I have expanded my interest in this area, and increased my involvement through a variety of positions, including program evaluator, policy analyst, researcher, and consultant. In addition to the ethnographic evaluation of the Guardianship Project (Iris 1986a) my work has included research related to elder abuse (Iris 1987) as well as an ethnographic investigation of judicial decision-making (Iris 1986b) and a current study of guardianship proceedings in Cook County. In all these projects I have relied upon the methods and techniques of anthropological inquiry, drawing directly from my training and experience in ethnography. I have addressed the question of how to plan, develop, and implement a protective service system for the elderly at risk.

The ethnographic perspective gives me a unique view of the emerging protective service system in Illinois, as well as many insights into the ethical, legal, and moral issues related to guardianship and protective interventions in general. The techniques of traditional ethnographic research, such as participant observation and open-ended interviewing, have proven to be effective tools for both qualitative evaluation research as well as program planning and policy analysis at the level of practice and implementation. These techniques were adapted to meet the needs of program developers and participants, who wish to learn more about how their programs function, how they impact on the client population, and what sorts of adjustments might be needed to increase efficiency and effectiveness.

The research and evaluation findings I describe here were presented to project participants through an innovative feedback method in which information was provided through three major activities: written reports, open-ended interviews, and consultations on specific problems and issues. Each activity offered information in response to a different set of problems. The open-ended interviews were most effective not only for data-gathering, but also for engaging all participants in the project process, and for ensuring information-sharing across institutional hierarchies and boundaries. Through consultation with project staff, I was able to utilize the findings of the research in a most timely manner, and address my analysis to the specific problems and needs of the information users. Finally, the written reports, although not originally perceived to be as effective in knowledge utilization activities as either consultation or open-ended interviews, have, over time, proven to be of lasting usefulness, not only to original project participants but to those interested in the area of guardianship and protective services generally. Thus, this three-pronged approach has proved most valuable as a means of ensuring utilization of findings and enhancing project and service outcomes by directly addressing the needs of program planners and service providers alike.

13

Using Stakeholders in the Research Process: A Case Study in Human Services

H. Max Drake

As stakeholders shared in the research process, they developed a sense of ownership of the results which often went beyond the use of findings. They often became champions for what they saw as their research.

In a world where complex social problems call for reasoned solutions, social researchers like to contribute research which is objective, responsive, and useful. In spite of this purpose, research often goes unused. One good way to increase use is to understand the needs and agendas of stakeholders. A stakeholder is any individual, group, or organization which perceives that its interests will be affected in some way by the research or its outcomes (Patton 1982:55).[1] A stakeholder may be a client who pays for the research, or a beneficiary, someone other than a client who stands to be affected by it. This chapter[2] reports a variety of ways a research study tried to understand and involve stakeholders in large scale research on services to the mentally ill and mentally retarded.

The study, called the "DI" study, focused on the movement of mentally disabled individuals to community settings in Idaho and Washington (Drake et al. 1978a, 1978b; Johnson et al. 1980). The DI project is instructive because it involved many stakeholders and a complex network of interests. The project staff used stakeholder involvement as a way to cut through this complex network of agendas and politics created by many layers of government and countless public and private agencies. The DI study illustrates the importance of learning the structure of stakeholder interests and behavior. It also provides an example of a successful effort to gain stakeholder cooperation by involving them in the research process.

Research Methods and Context

The purpose of the DI study was to evaluate federal and state efforts to discharge mentally ill and mentally retarded persons from state institutions and to serve them in the community. We set out to determine whether there were any barriers to their receipt of services in the community and to determine the effects of federal and state policy, procedures, and reimbursement. The study was carried out in two phases, each lasting about 18 months and each with a different stakeholder advisory board.

To meet the research objectives a variety of methods was used, forming seven substudies: (1) a review of patient discharge records, (2) a survey of institutional staff, (3) follow-up interviews with a stratified sample of discharged patients, (4) a survey of community service providers, (5) a review of federal and state legislation, policies, and planning, (6) a survey of key decision makers, and (7) a study of the financing of services. Finally, although not a substudy as such, I did an "ethnography" of administrative and service delivery structures stressing the "native" point of view.

Stakeholders in the DI Study

The main clients in the DI study were the regional office of the Department of Health, Education and Welfare (DHEW);[3] the state's Department of Social and Health Services (DSHS); and the Divisions of Mental Health (DMH) and Developmental Disabilities (DDD) in DSHS.[4]

People affected by the research (beneficiaries) fell into two service categories, mental health and developmental disabilities.[5] Some agencies provided services to both populations.[6] The main beneficiaries in the area of mental health were: (1) DMH, (2) DSHS, (3) two consumer advocacy groups, (4) a dozen or so mental health centers, (5) two residential service provider associations representing nursing facility and boarding home operators, (6) county mental health professionals, (7) the state Office of Nursing Home Affairs, (8) the Bureau of Community and Residential Care, (9) two state mental hospitals, (10) several legislators and legislative committees, (11) an association representing hospital social workers, (12) the union representing state hospital workers and (13) a dozen or so private psychiatrists and psychologists.

Beneficiaries in the area of developmental disabilities were: (1) the Developmental Disabilities Planning Council (DDPC), (2) the group home operators association, (3) the state Association of Retarded

Citizens, (4) two residential service provider associations (nursing facility and boarding home operators), (5) five state schools for the mentally retarded, (6) five groups of parents and guardians of individuals served in the state schools, (7) the union representing the state school employees, (8) the state association for the hearing impaired, (9) the state association for the visually impaired, (10) the Governor's Committee for Employment of the Handicapped, (11) the Bureau of Community and Residential Care, (12) several legislators and legislative committees, (13) a university teaching and research center, (14) many sheltered workshops, (15) a host of private programs and practitioners, and (16) a large number of schools, school districts and the state department of education. Many but not all of these interests were represented on an advisory board of the DI study.[7]

Increasing Research Use: How Stakeholders Were Involved

The diversity of stakeholder interests in the DI study is typical of public social programs. The intricacy of stakeholder politics made understanding and influencing stakeholder politics difficult, especially because many of the viewpoints of stakeholders were strongly held and inimical to each other.[8] The variety of interests guaranteed that the recommendations of the DI study, whatever they might be, would be subject to much debate and compromise. Indeed, because of the political power of some of the stakeholders with strongly opposing views, there was no assurance that they would be acted upon at all. If the study were to have any impact at all, we needed some way to harness the energy of stakeholders, to meld the diversity of interests, to open communication, and to foster cooperation from interests with opposing points of view.

How was this all to be done? In the DI study we devised several strategies. First, we identified vital stakeholders other than our clients. Then we identified their needs and power relative to other stakeholders. Finally, we involved them in our study so that they enhanced both the quality of our work and the likelihood that its results would be used. The key strategies used to involve stakeholders were advisory boards and the use of individual consultants.[9] Crucial to our success was a knowledge of who had what stake in our research, their agendas, and the political forces which affected them.

Finding Stakeholders

It was not easy for us to identify which stakeholders to involve in the study, and initially we overlooked some who had active and powerful interests. Early in the study, for example, one very powerful beneficiary and potential ally in the DI study, the Developmental Disabilities Planning Council (DDPC), remained unknown to us until after our advisory board had already been formed. The DDPC was a watchdog organization created in response to federal law and housed within the Division of Developmental Disabilities (DDD), even though it was politically independent of DDD. As a result, the directors of DDD and the DDPC were antagonistic. Because DDD was one of our clients, we did not at first identify the DDPC as a separate entity or a powerful player. Fortunately, constant references to the DDPC by other stakeholders alerted us to its importance. We involved the director as a consultant and arranged for indirect DDPC representation on the advisory board through another board member. This was a case where our client (DDD) had misled us about stakeholder power and interests in order to avoid opposition to their agenda. The experience taught us to systematize the search for board members rather than simply to accept those initially suggested by our clients.

Performing a systematic and fruitful search for stakeholders is not necessarily easy.[10] In our study we knew who our clients were because they supported the research with money, personnel, or time. Beneficiaries were less known to us, though their ability to promote or hinder the use of our research was often just as potent. Finding beneficiaries in the community was often difficult. Surprisingly, finding them in DSHS, the state umbrella social and health services agency within which we worked, was sometimes next to impossible.

We learned to search for stakeholders at several levels in the DSHS bureaucracy. First we looked for offices at the clients' level for programs sharing service recipients, funding, or services (for example, the Office of Nursing Home Affairs, which served large numbers of the elderly mentally disabled). Next we looked for managers, agency heads, legislators, or legislative committees with responsibility for the program under study.[11] At the service delivery level we looked for people who served the same target populations. Finally we sought organizations or individuals who were funded, supported, served, or regulated by our research clients.

Some beneficiaries were well hidden. They kept a low profile or were peripherally involved in the issues, or they were not easily distinguished from the larger organization within which they were embedded. In the DI study, for example, we nearly overlooked the Legislative Budget Committee, a watchdog committee of both branches of the state legislature with a strong political interest in our research. Another time we completely overlooked the Bureau of Community and Residential Care, responsible for monitoring certain aspects of community residences in which the mentally disabled lived.

Eventually we developed more skill in finding these hidden beneficiaries. Using systematic questioning was the key. We constantly asked our stakeholders to tell us who could help or hinder them in achieving their goals and who else might have an interest in the project. Next, while our list of potential board members was taking shape, we asked those listed to look it over and tell us who else ought to be considered. We also asked who could make trouble if not consulted.

This systematic approach proved most useful. The hidden beneficiaries we found through this more systematic effort came from a variety of settings, such as: (1) providers of services, such as education or health, to the target population, (2) local, national or state government offices or organizations whose clients or operations might be affected by our study (e.g., a training and research program at a major university and a county organization of mental health professionals), (3) public or private service providers who might be threatened by changes in the status of their service recipients, (4) lobbying, advocacy, or business entities who feared that their resources would be reduced as a result of the research (e.g., area employers concerned that new standards for care giving employees would cost them more), and (5) related professionals like private psychiatrists and psychologists whose work might be affected by the research. Any of these hidden stakeholders could have derailed the best conceived research unless their interests were taken into account; but in addition our research benefited from their involvement.

Selecting Stakeholders

Our choice of advisory board members for the first phase of the DI study was not as informed as it should have been. We chose only those people recommended by our clients. We gave little thought to how the board should be structured or how different structures might accomplish different ends. As a result the board had too many academics and too few advocates for the mentally disabled. The board had an establishment bias in that several stakeholder groups who routinely opposed DDD and DMH were not represented. Luckily, we were able to remedy this by involving those interests as consultants.

We were more effective in constructing the board for the second phase of our project. First, we tried to locate the powerful stakeholders without regard to our clients' biases. Having located the potent stakeholders we next had to select which ones should be represented on the board. Our clients, of course, were useful in assessing the relative importance of stakeholders because they worked with many of them. The drawback was that the client point of view was limited and their biases might result in a board which did not well represent beneficiary interests. To get around this we used client recommendations only as a starting point. We assiduously sought to list all those who had a stake in the research and to evaluate their level of power. We also made certain to contact and evaluate stakeholders who were on the "outs" with our clients. This led to a second phase advisory board which better represented the variety of stakeholder interests.

It turned out to be easier to locate the important stakeholder constituencies than to select their representatives. Our clients not only suggested which groups should be represented on the board, they often suggested a particular individual to represent that group. But often the recommended individual had little credibility or influence with their particular constituency. Thus, once we had located the main stakeholder interests for board representation, we tried to select the individual to represent those interests on the board. We asked constituencies themselves to identify and nominate their representatives to the advisory board. Asking groups for nominations helped assure that the individuals chosen would be listened to by their constituency while it helped the constituency to become better informed about our study.

Involving Stakeholders

Once stakeholders were selected, we had to make special efforts to involve them in our project and to gain their confidence and support. They had to participate meaningfully in our research, and that is too important a process to be left to chance.[12] We had not only to select people who represented powerful constituencies but we had to figure out how to invite their input but avoid our losing control of the process. In other words, we had to define a role for stakeholders to play and manage their participation so that our work did not become an extension of their agenda. Since their agendas were largely established before we entered the picture, this was a difficult task.

Effective stakeholder participation required both of us to share information and power. Stakeholder needs had to be incorporated in the research program. It also required an open exchange of information between the research staff and the stakeholders. This openness had two distinct advantages. We could help stakeholders more clearly to assess their information needs. This process, in turn, made it easier for us to ask the right questions, do better research, and frame the results more usefully. Finally, as stakeholders shared in the research process, they developed a sense of ownership of the results which often went beyond just the use of findings. They often became champions for what they saw as *their* research.

Forms of Involvement

We found several ways to involve stakeholders: as advisory board members, as consultants, or as members of a "consultant board." Each had its pluses and minuses in regards to the balance of power, stakeholder commitment to the results, and ease of management.

We used stakeholders as consultants on all aspects of our project, using them to ask the right questions, find the best respondents, interpret results, and inform us about the agendas of other stakeholders. We used consultants with both national and local reputations. Sometimes the consultation was formal, sometimes not. It was occasionally paid for but often was volunteered.

Careful use of consultants resulted in a better product and in a higher level of trust. A consultant with a national reputation, trusted by a local constituency, added to local confidence in the research methods. Local consultants provided essential knowledge of data sources and data shortcomings. They provided us with access to informants and information to which we might not otherwise have been privy. Involving local stakeholders as consultants also served to inform them about the study. They, in turn, informed their constituency, thus maintaining good information flow between the research staff and stakeholders.

It was necessary for local consultants to see the possibility of a real payoff for their participation if they were to invest time and effort in our study. Their payoff was that the project would advance their interests or be fair in its assessment of their programs. The consulting role for stakeholders, in addition to encouraging them to invest in our project, gave us access to their expertise in the local political field. Because local consultants were intimately acquainted with the politics surrounding the research, they generally had a good sense of who would support or block our research efforts and who could help increase the level of trust in our study. In using stakeholders as consultants, however, we had to be careful not to rely too much on a particular consultant or to become beholden to any one vested interest. We also needed to carefully frame the consultant's role to manage its visibility.

A disadvantage of the consultant role, in contrast to the advisory board role discussed below, is its low visibility and accountability, making it easy for the stakeholder consultant to disclaim complicity in the outcome. This happened with several superintendents of the state schools who served as consultants to the DI project. Because their input was not public, they were able to claim to their disgruntled constituents, when the report came out, that their viewpoint had been distorted or ignored.[13] Another possible disadvantage of the consultant approach is a half-hearted commitment by the stakeholder who feels the risks of involvement outweigh the benefits. In this case the stakeholder consultant, who is bound to the project only by self interest, sees her or his interest as better served by refusing or avoiding participation.

An advantage of using stakeholders as consultants, though, was that we had more control over their visibility and the way their input was used. An individual consultant's advice is more easily ignored, for example, than is the vote of a whole advisory board.

Stakeholders on Advisory Boards

Both phases of the DI study were guided by advisory boards representing major stakeholders (though the board on the second phase of the study functioned more like the "consultant board" discussed below). We learned a great deal from the two boards. First, an advisory board with virtually total control over the research, like our first board, can be very difficult to work with if it decides to move the study in inappropriate directions. Our first board set the agenda for the research, selected the major research questions, and had the power to accept, reject, or modify the final report and recommendations. It was a demanding job to maintain both stakeholder satisfaction and scientific integrity. While charging an advisory board with oversight of the research increased stakeholder visibility in the research process and made it harder for them to deny partnership in the research outcomes, it simultaneously gave members more say.

A second lesson was that decisions arrived at in open discussions often were a compromise of divergent views. The group process usually moderated extreme positions and dampened the fires of debate. On the other hand, if an extreme view was publicly arrived at, it was not easily changed.

An advantage of an advisory board which represents the major stakeholders is that board meetings allow them to negotiate their interests and modify their positions. Frequent well timed board meetings let the powerful but divergent stakeholders come together and balance their interests. This "advantage" can cut both ways, and the process requires good management to help stakeholders work toward acceptable compromises before their positions became publicly hardened. Such negotiation and compromise took place throughout the DI project. We found that compromises struck after the findings were known, interests threatened, and constituencies angered were harder to make, were less perfect, and were less consistent with our recommendations.

A final benefit of our advisory board structure was that debates, compromises, and decisions were open. This openness often moderated the behavior of otherwise difficult individuals. On the other hand, if the proceedings became too public, some board members were tempted to posture for their supporters.

We had to pay close attention to meeting and seating arrangements, as well as to publicity. The ability to manage group processes effectively turned out to be a critical skill in working with our board. By managing meetings skillfully, by paying close attention to meeting agendas, and by working closely with stakeholders before and after critical board meetings, we were able to meet stakeholder needs and maintain the objectivity and scientific integrity of the study.

By the time we appointed our second board we were more experienced and the board was given somewhat less power. We learned that an advisory board may be granted just the amount of power you wish it to have. The less power they are granted, the easier the process is to control. Without real control over the research process, however, many stakeholders are reluctant to serve on an advisory board. Our experience was that powerful stakeholders may be reluctant to sit on an advisory board unless they have some control over the situation. They fear the appearance of having condoned a process over which they have no real control.

However useful our board was, it was harder to manage than consultation from individuals. Board members tended to be both more independent and more visible. The added visibility allowed them to exert unwelcome public or private leverage on the research process. On the other hand, the visibility lent credibility to our research and encouraged members to champion implementation of the recommendations.

Clearly, working with advisory boards requires a great deal of patience and a wide variety of skills, not all of which are possessed by every research director.[14]   Thus, though a well managed advisory board process has a great potential for getting research used, it should not be undertaken lightly. Much thought must be given to the membership process and logistics. A real commitment must be made to a cooperative effort.

The Consultant Board

For us, the powerful advisory board in the first study phase created difficulties compared to working with consultants, yet it generated stakeholder support for our work. In the second phase of the study we combined the consultant and advisory board approaches and it worked well. We created what I call a board of consultants, a modified advisory group. The consultant board involved the stakeholders, giving us both their expertise and their commitment to the results. At the same time we gained more control over the process.

Unlike the former advisory board, our consultant board met less frequently, was more often informed of actions rather than being asked to approve them, and was asked for guidance rather than for policy. Without directly saying so, we gave the board only the power to recommend, not approve, research decisions. We carried out much of our work with board members on an individual basis, although we did call regular information and action meetings. This approach helped us avoid the problems of managing a powerful stakeholder board. But it had a drawback. It reduced public support for our research and vitiated the ability of our stakeholders to negotiate out their differences. We were able largely to overcome these disadvantages by working intensively with individual stakeholders.

Understanding Stakeholder Needs

Understanding the needs of clients or beneficiaries was hard work. We found it was not enough to ask them to give examples of what they wanted. They were often vague as to exactly how the research would help them solve a problem and were unsure about specific decisions or actions they might take as a result of our study. We had to grasp their view, often unstated and inchoate, of where they were in relation to where they wanted to be.

We tried to do this in several ways. First, we got them to state their needs using concrete examples, for example, giving us an illustration of a desired client service. This specificity helped us design the research to respond to the felt needs and helped us show what the research could tell them in a given situation. To illustrate, both DDD and DMH wanted their clients to get "services appropriate to their needs." We presented them with literally hundreds of hypothetical or actual client cases, each with a different combination of needs. We asked them in each case what services the individual needed. By analyzing their answers we were able to construct a variety of client profiles, each matched with a set of services. Knowing precisely what decisions officials expected to make based on the research helped us clarify their informational needs even further.

A second way we found to focus on our clients' information needs was to sit down with them and draw up a decision tree, a flow chart of alternatives in logical or temporal order. Here is a good example of this method. Both our federal and state clients spoke broadly about people "falling through the cracks" and about "barriers to service" for the deinstitutionalized mentally disabled. Barriers and cracks were their shorthand for a service system that wasn't working as it should. Our clients had only a blurry notion of what these barriers might be or what sort of action might be taken if they were found. That was all to be revealed by the study. No one, it seemed, had ever laid out a template of how the system should work and no one agreed on what the system should do if it did work. Over a period of several years and dozens of decision trees later, we helped transform these overused phrases into concrete statements of system objectives and services. Compelling our clients to think clearly about exactly what the system ought to look like and what kind of people ought to get what services helped all of us to focus on actionable questions.

A third technique we used to help clients focus on what the research could produce was to write up dummy research findings and then share them. For example, during the process of designing our instruments, our federal project officers insisted on including a number of questions in the service provider interview which I felt were inappropriate and would defy analysis. No argument shook their insistence, so I sat down and cross-tabulated their questions with all the possible answers. They finally saw that the questions they asked would not provide the information they wanted. We then sat down together to create more suitable questions.

I got the best results when I faced clients with concrete problem statements, questions, methods, and recommendations at every phase of the project. It enabled me to check whether we had grasped their actual view of things. (It's a bit like sharing your kinship chart with the villagers. When they nod and grin, you know you finally got it right.) I also found it an excellent way to build client investment in our results.

Teasing out the felt needs of the client was not a simple task to be accomplished early, then forgotten. We had to recheck regularly to see whether our "research" view matched the client view. Once, failure to do this was disastrous. After the first phase of the DI study, we submitted a bid for the second phase. We had worked hand in glove with our federal project officers for two years and thought we had a pretty good notion of what they needed. Our proposal missed what they perceived was needed by such a wide mark that they were furious at our insensitivity. We had become so knowledgeable about the details of our study and so comfortable working with the officials that we had failed to see things through their eyes.

One last step was required to fully understand our stakeholders' needs. We had to understand the political context within which stakeholders operated. They existed in an environment consisting of the expectations of their bosses, the legislature, vendors of services, advocates for their clients and citizen lobbies. Any time our clients expressed their needs, it was against a backdrop of political pressures. Yet the stakeholders themselves had only a broad sense of how the research would bear upon their political situation.

Part of the political context within which our stakeholders operated was made up of other stakeholders, each with her or his own goals and each with something to gain or lose from our research. Power to promote one's agenda was perhaps the major principle organizing the relations among stakeholders. Should our efforts diminish the power of one stakeholder or alter the balance of power among them, we could expect resistance.

To grasp our stakeholders' needs, we had to figure out how they thought our study would affect their relations with other stakeholders. This was where our "ethnography" of the actors, their relations to each other, and their analysis of issues was so very useful. It provided us with a view of the playing field "from above," and helped us identify both the power holders and the structure of costs and rewards. These insights were essential to understanding our stakeholders' needs.

To analyze the power relationships among our stakeholders, we listed their interests, power, and position in the system and then catalogued how these might be affected by our work. This helped us map out the powerful players, their interests, and interrelationships. It provided us with an overall sense of who would support or oppose us, on what grounds, and why.

The knowledge gained from this analysis was vital in working with our stakeholders and advisory board. It allowed us to maintain an objective approach to the research and to avoid, for the most part, tendentious demands on the project's resources. For example, at one meeting of the DI advisory board, one interest group wanted data to bolster their point of view. As a result, several members disagreed heatedly over items on a questionnaire. The argument threatened to disrupt the board process, so I suggested that rather than take the whole committee's time over a technical issue that we have a separate working meeting of those concerned. I invited several powerful individuals to the meeting to help solve the problem. They prevailed and, as was my intention, the issue was resolved. The lesson here is that understanding the structure of power among stakeholders allowed me to mobilize resources and keep the board running smoothly.

Some Benefits of Stakeholder Involvement in the DI Study

Routinely stakeholders who don't understand your research or endorse its results attack its methods as flawed. Their belief in research quality often hinges more on their judgment of whether the findings square with their convictions than on the scientific quality of the research. Our stakeholders were prone to support our methods, instruments, samples, and recommendations because they helped formulate them. Because they did participate, they came to possess a good sense of what approaches to the data would yield accurate results. We benefited because they knew where information could be found, how reliable it was, and the flaws or biases built into it. Real stakeholder involvement saved us time in searching for information and provided us better data. Consequently, stakeholders became convinced that our data were reliable and valid. They came to trust the study staff and research objectivity. They came to feel that we gave their point of view an honest and sympathetic hearing. Because of this support, second phase recommendations (some of which augured a sharply diminished role for state hospitals) drew no fire from management, workers, or staff. Not once was the DI study attacked for its research methods, in spite of its recommending substantial changes in the status quo.

Project Impacts

Before I can say whether the DI project had an impact, I need to decide how "impact" is to be measured. How is one to assess the degree to which recommendations are used? How do you know whether change resulted from your recommendations, or from long term plans which were simply confirmed by the research? From the clients' perspective, the research may not have been intended to bring about immediate changes but rather to pinpoint areas for long term attention.

If "use" means that recommendation(s) should have a major effect on specific decisions, then the researcher often will be disappointed. Rarely are decisions of major consequence made on the basis of one piece of evidence on one aspect of the problem. If, on the other hand, "use" is defined to mean some degree of influence on the course of events, then research results are used more often than most researchers realize.[15]

By this more generous standard, the DI research *was* used. Its findings and recommendations had a broad hearing and fit well into the current thrust of system reform. However, the degree of impact directly and solely attributable to the study is hard to assess. The DI study made a total of 38 major recommendations. Recommendations varied from a specific one to amend Section 1861 of the Social Security Act to broad homilies about the need to improve the range of services to the mentally disabled. In addition to the 38 broad recommendations, dozens of specific recommendations were made, some in the written document and many in private briefings or presentations. Recommendations to improve record keeping or document transfers, to speed up payments to providers, to reroute patients or to realign treatment configurations, were implemented quite rapidly given the complexity of the system. These recommendations served all parties well and there was little resistance to their implementation.

Other recommendations, those which implied substantial changes in the service system, moved more slowly through the system and their effects are hard to determine.[16] Many of the broader recommendations in mental health were implemented by both DDD and DMH, as most were planned anyway. The study simply provided the documentation to ask the legislature to fund new programs. Here again, many of the new programs requested already had been proposed and some were already operating in other states. To what extent is our research to be credited for the funding and implementation of the bureau's efforts?

Two years after the DI study was completed a powerful state senator, *not* the one on our advisory board, became interested in the problems of the deinstitutionalized mentally ill. Citing our study as proof of the sad state of affairs, he pushed through a major rewrite of the state's mental health treatment act. The thrust of the act was in the direction recommended by our research, several advocacy groups, and DMH with which the senator worked closely. Who gets credit, the senator, the advocacy group, DMH, or the study? The reaction of the state senator on our advisory board had been mildly negative, since implementation of our findings would require more funding. Clearly the study alone did not bring about the change. On the other hand, it did provide solid and detailed evidence on the extent and nature of the problems so that powerful and dedicated advocates could build toward change.

Change occurs slowly. Most program changes over the years following the study were in a direction consonant with those we recommended. Looking back after nine years I would score impacts of the 38 major recommendations as follows:

Eight changes "pretty much" in line with recommendations;
Nine changes "partially" in line with recommendations;
Five changes "minimally" in line with recommendations;
Two recommendations "unassessable;"
Ten recommendations "not that I know of;"
Four, too vague to assess.

Many changes in federal laws and regulations have been consistent with changes we recommended. Since dozens of studies, conferences, think tank sessions, and lobbying groups urged similar changes, it is impossible to evaluate the impact of the DI project as distinct from the other inputs. I believe that one reason it appeared to have some success locally is that the advisory board members took "their" research back to their constituencies. They took it to their legislators, they cited it in testimony and discussed it in meetings. They did so, I believe, because they perceived that it met their needs, that it was valid, and that it was objective.

As a researcher I might be disappointed that the DI recommendations did not result in immediate, dramatic changes in the lives of the mentally disabled. As a concerned person, though, I am delighted that over the years people's lives in the states studied are better than they might have been without the DI project.

Summary: How to Get Research Used

Involving stakeholders, both clients and beneficiaries, in your research can, if done effectively, help promote research use. Care must be taken to search out all stakeholders and to choose carefully which interests to involve. Attention must be paid to the form which involvement takes, and meetings must be carefully run. Time must be taken to become informed of stakeholder agendas and the power relationships affecting them.

The rules are simple, their execution difficult:

1. Identify all the stakeholders. Use clients and beneficiaries as informants to find others.

2. Take care to understand stakeholders' needs as they see them as well as from an analytic viewpoint.

3. Map out the context within which stakeholders act, paying attention to their power and agendas.

4. Involve stakeholders, both clients and beneficiaries, in all phases of research, from choosing research objectives and methods through the analysis and presentation of findings.

5. Choose carefully whether you involve vested interests as individual consultants or as members of an advisory board. If you use an advisory board, make certain the chair has good group process skills.

6. Do not expect to see all of your recommendations implemented instantly. Allow time for your recommendations to percolate through the system and for negotiations to take place. If you did your work well you will probably have more impact than you will know.

Notes

1.   The researcher should not be a stakeholder in the research other than to ensure research objectivity and quality.

2.   I wish to thank Dr. Ann M. Drake, one of the authors of the first DI study, for her ideas and assistance in writing this chapter.

3.   During the course of the study it became the Department of Health and Human Services.

4.   The political climate and administrative structures of the two states differed sharply so the illustrations are drawn from one state only.

5.   Calling stakeholders beneficiaries does not imply that they will benefit from the research; they may be harmed by it as well. Indeed, in much research which has a government agency as the client, "beneficiaries" may fear harm and oppose the research. Even so, their cooperation is often crucial to implementation of its recommendations.

6.   Notice that both DDD and DMH are listed both as clients and beneficiaries. Each contained a number of subunits whose interests opposed those of other subunits and sometimes the policy of the Division itself. Even though DMH and DDD were clients, they also took policy orders from higher officials in DSHS, often not to their liking.

7.   The federal government through the regional office of the (then) Department of Health, Education and Welfare was, by choice, not represented on the board. The other stakeholders represented were the Divisions of Developmental Disabilities and Mental Health, a state senator, the president of the group home operators association, the director of a major community mental health clinic, the superintendents of a state mental hospital and health clinic, the superintendents of a state mental hospital and a school for the retarded, the director of a university teaching and research program, members of the nursing home and boarding home operator associations, a member of the hospital social workers association, the president of an advocacy organization representing families of the seriously mentally disturbed, a professor specializing in research on the mentally retarded, and a private consultant in mental health. Missing were the president of the state association for retarded citizens, a member of the Developmental Disabilities Planning

Council, a representative from a "friends of the state school" society and the office of the Superintendent of Public Instruction.

8.   The notion that truth (in the form of research findings) will win out or even that the research findings represent truth is not particularly useful in evaluation research. To evaluate is to estimate the worth or value of something. That estimation is set in a field of social values and depends on your point of view. The political and social field in which our study was done was seen from dozens of distinct points of view. The lesson is that findings and recommendations will be evaluated from many points of view, that of the researcher being only one.

9.   Our first experience working with an advisory board had mixed success. The board of the first study was formed quickly from a list of names gathered unsystematically. Some of our board members had much expertise and academic bias, but little influence. There was little representation by powerful stakeholders, especially in the area of developmental disabilities. Some board members were not liked or trusted by others. Our amateurishness in selecting this first board resulted in DDD burying our report. I did not learn all the strategies I suggest below on the DI studies, even though I illustrate my points with that study. It took many years of forming and working on boards before I consciously thought the process through.

10.   A good discussion of the kinds of stakeholders may be found in Rossi and Freeman (1982:310).

11.   Here is a case where the line between clients and beneficiaries is not clear, nor is the distinction particularly useful. Higher management may be either a client or beneficiary, or both simultaneously.

12.   For example, a state senator appointed to our first advisory board was selected on recommendation of our client but she turned out to view the study only as a way to fleece the taxpayer and was hostile throughout the study.

13.   One of the six state school superintendents (both states) served as a member of the advisory board.

14.   Patton has written an absolutely excellent chapter on "Collaborative Evaluation Practice with Groups" in *Practical Evaluation* (Patton 1982:55-98). I highly recommend it.

15. Patton provides some interesting data on how bureaucrats define use (Patton 1978:26-33).

16. For example, the superintendents of two state hospitals and several state schools for the retarded were eventually replaced. To what extent was that an indirect result of the study which detailed numerous problems in their operations? The director of the bureau of developmental disabilities was replaced. To what degree did that change result from the study which had exposed some real problems in the system? The bureau director was under fire before the study was initiated, one hospital superintendent was near retirement, and the other directed an institution in difficulties with the Joint Commission on Accreditation of Hospitals. It would be almost impossible to measure the study's impact on these personnel changes.

14

Policy and Community-Action Research: The Farm Labor Movement in California

W. K. Barger and Ernesto Reza

Applied research calls for being eclectic in our methodology, particularly in selecting those methods that combine depth and breadth and that will produce the most valid results for how they will be used.

Social and behavioral scientists have long shown concern about the "applied" uses of their concepts, methods, and expertise (Angrosino 1976; Chambers 1985; Eddy and Partridge 1978). The most emphasized of applied models has been *policy science*, the study of political decision-making and the provision of expert knowledge in the formulation, implementation, and evaluation of socioeconomic legislation and programs (Bernard 1974; Chambers 1977; Cochrane 1980; Geilhufe 1979; Hinshaw 1980; Kimball 1978; Lasswell 1971; Spicer 1976; Weaver 1985a).

A less common model of applied change is *community action*, using professional expertise to support the goals and efforts of a particular community-based group (Barger and Reza 1985a; Barger and Truong 1978; Schensul 1973, 1974; Schensul and Schensul 1978; J. Schensul 1985). With this approach, the social scientist may provide many of the same functions as with policy science, such as research and expert information, but there are two principles which distinguish this model from others. First, it is the needs and goals of a particular community-based group which are being served, and it is this "target group" which has the initiative in seeking changes. Second, the applied scientist takes a clear value position and an active involvement in change events. A primary value is that democratic self-determination is the most effective and constructive means of change, both for the community group concerned and for the larger society. Community action is not generally perceived as policy research (Schensul 1985), partly due to the different "clients" involved; action research serves community-based groups, rather than government and social agencies. However, it can be argued that community action is most effective when it *is* policy oriented; that is, when applied activities support the policy efforts of a particular social group.

The purpose of this report is to illustrate the policy impacts of community action research in a project in support of the farm labor movement in California and the United Farm Workers of America (UFW). Most people are aware that farmworkers, who are a basic element in the production of food in America, are one of the most socioeconomically deprived groups in the country (Barger 1987; Barger and Haas 1983; Burnaway 1976; Friedland 1969; Harper, Mills, and Farris 1974; Moore 1965; Sosnick 1978; West 1964). A major policy issue concerning farmworkers is their exclusion from the legal rights, protections, and benefits enjoyed by other American workers (Craddock 1979; Goldfarb 1982; Shenkin 1974; U.S. Senate Subcommittee on Migratory Labor 1970). For example, farmworkers are specifically excluded from many key labor laws like the National Labor Relations Act, and where they do have legal protections, standards are often reduced for them, as with child labor laws, or regulations are not enforced, as with regulations concerning dangerous pesticides.

When the various alternatives for improving farmworkers' living and working conditions are considered, only the farm labor movement led by the United Farm Workers (UFW) in California has historically proven to be truly effective (Denny 1979; Friedland and Thomas 1974; Hoffman 1978; Jenkins 1984; Jenkins and Perrow 1977; Levy 1975; London and Anderson 1970; Majka 1981; Majka and Majka 1982; Walsh 1978; Walsh and Craypo 1979). The UFW has been able to develop a strong internal support base among farmworkers, and it has also been able to mobilize considerable external support from church, labor, political, and civic groups, including broad public participation in farmworker-sponsored boycotts. As a result, the UFW movement has achieved greatly improved living and working conditions for farmworkers. Much of this success is a result of the UFW's ability to make substantive changes in public policy. For example, all farmworkers in California are now covered by the state's Agricultural Labor Relations Act.

In recent years, however, the UFW has faced new policy challenges. The UFW charges that Governor Deukmejian of California was heavily supported by agribusiness in election campaigns, and that as a consequence the Governor has blocked the Agricultural Labor Relations Board (ALRB) as an effective agency to regulate farmworker affairs (*Bakersville Californian* 1984; Chavez 1985; *San Francisco Chronicle*

1984a, 1984b, 1984c, 1985; *Los Angeles Times* 1984; and *The Packer* 1984). To counter such political reversals in the hard-won rights of farmworkers, the UFW has called a new citizens' boycott of nonunion California table grapes (*Fresno Bee* 1984; *Sacramento Bee* 1984; *Los Angeles Times* 1984; *Catholic Universe Bulletin* 1984). The rationale of this boycott, as of previous ones, is that the combined social and economic power of millions of Americans who are concerned with justice can counterbalance the political powerlessness of farmworkers.

A major issue in these new events is whether the UFW indeed represents farmworkers. The UFW has recently been criticized as being behind the times, played out, and lacking followers (*Village Voice* 1984; *San Francisco Chronicle* 1984b; *San Jose Mercury News* 1984). If farmworkers themselves do *not* support the UFW, its goals, and its methods, then the union loses its social and moral legitimacy as a force in farm labor affairs. If, on the other hand, it *does* validly represent farmworkers, then it can be justified in seeking to achieve its goals, particularly in a mass appeal to the American public to support its cause by boycotting table grapes.

The action research project considered here involves this issue: how much the UFW validly represents farmworkers. In the quarter of a century that the farm labor movement has been a major social concern, there has never been a representative study of what farmworkers *themselves* think about the movement in general and about the UFW in particular. To investigate this issue, the Department of Anthropology at Indiana University at Indianapolis and the National Farm Worker Ministry cosponsored applied research among California farmworkers in the summer of 1984, in cooperation with the United Farm Workers.

Research Methods and Results: California Farmworkers Endorse the UFW

Our involvement in the community action project was founded in our association with the farm labor movement in the Midwest, represented by the Farm Labor Organizing Committee (FLOC). We had conducted research both on public views regarding farm labor issues and boycotts (Barger and Haas 1983) and on the support of farmworkers themselves for the farm labor movement (Barger and Reza 1984a, 1984b, 1985a, 1987). Due to its close cooperation with FLOC, the UFW learned of these earlier applied research projects. UFW leaders expressed interest in our work and in having similar research conducted among California farmworkers. We had experienced very satisfying relations with FLOC, and were interested in continuing our work with the farm labor movement.

We met with the UFW leaders to identify their concerns. The first question raised was how they wanted to *use* the results of a farmworker survey. We learned more about their long-range goals to achieve active participation by farmworkers in decisions that affect their lives, and to gain permanent working and living rights for farmworkers. In essence, these goals involved larger *policy* issues. We also learned about their more immediate objectives of organizing farmworkers around the new political setbacks, political lobbying for support of the farm labor cause, and appeals to the public for support. These objectives represent activities in the policy *process*.

With these goals in mind, we did preliminary qualitative field work with California farmworkers to identify their concepts and concerns regarding the project issues. We met again with the UFW leaders and specifically raised the question of research standards. We noted that since the results of the survey had very serious implications for the farm labor cause, it was imperative to uphold the highest standards possible to be sure of results and their effective use, even where this may involve extra time and effort in both data collection and analysis. We then began developing the research plan.

At this point, we coordinated with the National Farm Worker Ministry, an ecumenical group with a long history of involvement in the farm labor cause, with whom we had many previous contacts. The NFWM agreed to cosponsor the project, which involved recruiting bilingual volunteers to conduct the survey interviews and logistical support for the project team.

Relationships among the parties involved with the project were also discussed. We donated our time and expertise, though all our expenses would be covered. We were also able to utilize university computer facilities available to faculty for quantitative analysis of the survey data. We specifically agreed that the farm labor goals would take precedence in the research design, data collection, and analysis. This was in keeping with the "community action" nature of our involvement, though we also included some theoretical concerns for our own professional use.

The Applied Research

In July-August 1984, applied research was conducted among California farmworkers, with the primary purpose of documenting how much farmworkers themselves consider the farm labor movement as a viable alternative for improving their living and working conditions (Barger and Reza 1985b). The study was a joint project with the National Farm Worker Ministry and was conducted in cooperation with the United Farm Workers. The project was an example of a community action model of applied change, where our role as professionals was to support democratic self-determination of farmworkers.

The research population was defined as those workers involved in the table grape industry in Kern and Tulare counties of the San Joaquin valley, at the height of the harvest season. This group was chosen because this is where the farm labor issue has its longest history, and these people can thus provide the greatest contrast with Midwestern farmworkers, where the farmworker movement is still in the process of becoming established. Both local seasonal and migrant farmworkers were included in the study. Local workers in the sample were selected by straight random sampling from lists of ranch workers.[1] Migrant workers were selected by stratified random sampling of labor camps, housing units, and sex for family units or occupant bed for singles dormitories. A representative proportion of migrant workers was determined by an evaluation of nonlocal workers on the ranch lists.

Members of the sample who were contacted were explained the general purpose of the survey and their rights, and informed consent was obtained before being interviewed.[2] All interviews were conducted with a standardized, pretested questionnaire, which included about 200 open and closed questions, which had built-in validity checks and which took an average of 58 minutes to administer. The personal interviews were conducted by sixteen volunteers with the National Farm Worker Ministry, all of whom had farmworker backgrounds, were bilingual in Spanish and English, and who were trained with the questionnaire, interview techniques, and observation of behavioral and contextual validation cues for making evaluations on key variables after completion of the interview. After the original interviews, open-ended follow-up interviews were conducted with a subsample of respondents, in order to verify the responses and to acquire a qualitative understanding of response patterns. Completed interviews were coded and then recoded for accuracy by a second coder. The data was then entered into a computer file, and then a printout of this file was checked against the original interviews in order to verify the accuracy of the data.

A total of 195 California farmworkers were interviewed. These included workers from 10 different ranches, 138 (71%) local workers and 57 (29%) migrant workers. Of these, 28% were workers on ranches contracted to the UFW, and 72% were workers on nonunion ranches.

About 86% of the interviews were conducted in Spanish, and 14% in English. The overall response rate was 65%.[3] There is a maximum 95% confidence interval of ± 6.8%; that is, there is a 95% chance that responses will not vary by more than 6.8% (and as little as 0%) for the total research population.

A series of data checks indicated that there was an exceptionally low rate of data errors (0.5%), but even so all errors detected were corrected. Split-half reliability tests, and reliability tests based on time frames and interviewers indicate that all variables used in the analysis were replicable. And a series of tests comparing responses on like items and comparing responses to key questions with interviewers' evaluations demonstrate that the analysis variables could be taken as valid. Calculation of 95% confidence intervals for the key variables indicated that these variables reasonably reflect the study population, and that interpretations and conclusions can be based on empirical data.

We wish to emphasize that we used the highest scientific standards possible in the research, just because the study did focus on a major social issue. This is an ethical as well as a professional position, and we wanted to be absolutely sure of the concepts and methods used in collecting and analyzing the data for two reasons. First, the results of applied work can impact directly on people's lives, and we therefore have a moral obligation to be sure that findings are both accurate and predictive, and that we are very sure of where we are valid and where we are not valid. And second, just because we are committed to our social convictions, we want to be sure our understandings are as accurate and predictive as possible, so we *can* make effective changes. We should add that we are not greatly concerned about charges of bias from those opposed to the cause which we are supporting, since they are not likely to be convinced by any studies which do not support their positions. This is also true of those allied to our cause. But we are concerned that our work and its results must be acceptable to those who are not informed nor aligned to our cause, whom we wish to win over by grounded arguments. This means that our work must meet basic standards of scholarship as evaluated by our professional peers, as this is the basis for the credibility of our findings. We believe most applied scientists would agree that there is no such thing as "bias-free" or "objective" research, since all research involves many subjective judgements from beginning to end. Grounded scientific research is based primarily on the *control* of biases and limitations involved, not their absence. Controls must be exercised in the conceptualization of the issue, in the collection of data, in the analysis of data, and in making grounded interpretations of findings.

We thus went to considerable effort to maintain the highest professional standards possible in the survey, and built in controls for limitations and biases throughout the project. Both qualitative and quantitative methods were used throughout the project to validate data and findings, and to ensure both depth and breadth of findings and interpretations.[4] For example, in planning the research design, we visited the survey area and discussed the project with a number of farmworkers, in order to identify the best method of sampling and to develop questions that reflected their conceptual categories. We also trained the interviewers to recognize and control their own biases, and to develop their empirically grounded judgement. And we conducted follow-up interviews with farmworkers to verify responses and to understand better the meanings of findings. In the data analysis stage, we spent considerable time evaluating the data set itself to identify limitations and problems, before beginning data analysis on the research issues. We also verified every finding and result with a variety of statistical techniques.

In summary, we were eclectic in our methodology. Research methods are tools, and we attempted to carefully evaluate and select those methodological tools which would provide us with the most valid understandings of the applied issues. We believe that the combination of methods and controls we used have considerable strength for the issues being addressed. We are thus confident that the findings are both valid and accurately represent the study population, and we also feel confident that interpretations are empirically grounded. Where we have felt we could not fully support interpretations with solid data, we have tried to qualify them accordingly.

A Mandate for the UFW

The demographic characteristics of California grape workers, as indicated in Table 14.1, include an average of 35 years old, predominately male and Mexican heritage, married with an average of over three children and with just under half owning their own homes, an average of a sixth grade education, and an average annual household income right at the poverty level ($11,782). Their farmwork experience, as indicated in Table 14.2, includes an average of over a decade working in the fields with most tending grapes as well as harvesting them, and working on an average under eight months of the year, and 88 percent generally liking their occupation. It is worth noting that these workers

TABLE 14.1 Demographic Characteristics of California Grape Workers

Average age	35	
Sex:		
Female	37	%
Male	63	%
Ethnic heritage:		
Filipino national	1	%
Central American national	1	%
Mexican national	22	%
Filipino American	1	%
Mexican American	75	%
Anglo American	1	%
Marital status:		
Single	14	%
Widowed, separated, or divorced	9	%
Married	77	%
Average number of people in the household	5.2	
Home ownership:		
Non-rental housing	3	%
Rental housing	52	%
Owns home	45	%
Average education (highest grade completed)	6	
Average total income for household in 1983 (for all members, from all sources)	$11,782	

are aware of being exposed to pesticides on an average of sixteen times a year. The attitudes of grape workers toward their working conditions are indicated in Table 14.3. In general, they believe that they have poorer wages and have more health problems and child labor than other workers. They have moderate dissatisfactions with their jobs, though they are particularly unhappy with the lack of paid vacations. And specific work complaints include bosses pushing workers too much, bosses threatening to lay off workers if they don't work harder, and having to work too hard for what they are paid.

As indicated in Table 14.4, the survey of California farmworkers shows that they overwhelmingly endorse the United Farm Workers, and believe that the UFW offers the best alternative for improving their lives. For example, 91% believe that the UFW is good for farmworkers, and 83% think that the UFW's efforts and activities have improved the lives of farmworkers. While 61% believe that unions have helped farmworkers, only 31% express any such faith in growers and only 39% think that new laws and social programs have actually improved farmworkers' conditions. And 78% said they would vote for the UFW in a union election on the ranch where they work. In contrast to attitudes about the UFW, the workers commonly complained about maltreatment by bosses.

To put the survey results in perspective, when a candidate in national elections wins more than 55% of the votes, he is deemed to have won a "landslide" victory and received a "mandate" from the people. A candidate that wins less than 40% of the vote is seen to be ineffective and in disarray. In these terms, then, the UFW has a landslide mandate from farmworkers in seeking its goals.

It is important to note that endorsement of the UFW is as strong among those farmworkers who are not affiliated with the union as among UFW members. Farmworkers working under UFW contracts, however, experience significantly better living and working conditions than nonunion workers in at least three areas, as indicated in Table 14.5. First, UFW workers express far greater job satisfaction, particularly with job benefits like paid vacations and retirement pensions. Second, union workers report up to three times the access to health care as nonunion workers. And third, UFW workers exhibit significantly greater social stability in such areas as marital status, living in the area where they work, and literacy in English. They are also more politically responsible, in the sense that they vote far more regularly in elections than nonunion workers. It is clear that working under a union contract has had important positive impacts on the living and working conditions of farmworkers. These results reinforce the historical record that the farm labor movement has been the most viable alternative for improving farmworkers' living and working conditions.

Positive attitudes towards the UFW appear to be based on three sets of factors. One is an underlying belief that farmworkers are entitled to basic working rights, such as those enjoyed by other American workers.

TABLE 14.2 Farm Labor Experience of California Grape Workers

Average years have worked on farms or ranches	12.6
Type of farm work:	
Temporarily laid off	9 %
General agricultural labor/harvesting	12 %
Grape tending/pruning/harvesting (only)	71 %
Irrigation	2 %
Agricultural sheds/plants	1 %
Agricultural equipment operator	4 %
Agricultural supervision	1 %
Average months of employment during the past year	7.7
Average times sprayed by pesticides in past year	16
How much like farmwork in general:	
Not at all or not very much	12 %
Some or very much	88 %

A second factor is a negative feeling about farmworkers' conditions, particularly the way they are treated by bosses. And a third factor is a pervasive positive image of the UFW and a belief that improvements in farmworkers' lives are a direct result of the UFW's efforts.

The survey data indicates that one predominant factor influences farmworkers' overwhelming pro-UFW attitudes: a strong belief that any improvements in farmworkers' lives in recent years is primarily due to the UFW's efforts. For example, in comments in open-ended questions and in follow-up interviews, people spoke of the UFW in rational and unemotional terms, such as: "The Union has helped us learn about our rights." "The Union helps people when they need it." And, "Look at it. Things are much better off now than before there was a Union. We have

TABLE 14.3 Farmworkers' View of Working and Living Conditions

Believe Farmworkers Experience Worse Conditions than Others:		
Greater exposure to dangerous pesticides	81	%
Poor housing and sanitation	68	%
More child labor	68	%
Poor wages	61	%
Poor education	60	%
Discrimination and prejudice	57	%
Diseases and health problems	55	%
Dissatisfaction with Job Conditions:		
Paid vacations	53	%
Medical insurance	27	%
Pay rate	21	%
Pace of work	21	%
Treatment by bosses	21	%
Fellow workers	3	%
Specific Work Complaints:		
Have to work too hard for what was paid	52	%
The boss pushes and harasses workers too much	52	%
The boss threatens to lay workers off to make them work harder	52	%
Temporary workers are given better jobs	48	%
The boss cuts out or cuts down work breaks	48	%
The boss favors some workers over others	43	%
The boss makes promises but does not keep them	37	%

better wages, more benefits, and bathrooms in the fields." Such statements were common among both UFW and nonunion workers. The survey thus indicates that most farmworkers see the UFW itself as the primary alternative for achieving better rights and conditions for themselves.[5]

A secondary factor related to pro-UFW views is that farmworkers feel abused by bosses. For example, people spoke negatively of bosses in strong emotional terms, such as: "They do not think we are human beings." "They treat us like slaves." And, "All they are interested in is using us to get money for themselves." These findings indicate that

TABLE 14.4 Views Concerning the Farm Labor Movement

Belief That Farmworkers' Lives Have Been Improved by:		
Farm labor unions	61	%
Laws	39	%
Social programs	39	%
Growers	31	%
Basic Rights to which Believe Farmworkers are Entitled:		
Access to fresh drinking water while working	100	%
Access to restroom and hand washing facilities	100	%
Regular break periods during the working day	100	%
Earnings that average at least the minimum wage rates	98	%
Workers' compensation for work injuries	98	%
First choice of new jobs created when old jobs are eliminated by machines	93	%
Labor organizing and collective bargaining	93	%
Retraining programs when jobs are eliminated by machines	92	%
Views About the United Farm Workers:		
Have heard of the United Farm Workers	91	%
Think the UFW is good for farmworkers	91	%
Think that conditions for farmworkers have improved as a result of UFW's efforts	83	%
Have a positive attitude towards the UFW	75	%
Would vote for the UFW in a union election	78	%
Membership in Labor Unions:		
Union affiliation:		
None	76	%
A non-U.S. labor union	1	%
United Farm Workers	21	%
For those who are not members, are interested in belonging to a farm labor union (47% of the total sample)	59	%

* Figures represent the interviewer's rating of the respondent's attitudes, based on behavioral observation and on the content of the interview responses (n=182).

TABLE 14.5 Conditions of UFW and Nonunion Farmworkers *

	UFW	Nonunion
Satisfaction with Job Benefits:		
Paid sick leave	83%	65%
Paid vacations	59%	41%
Paid holidays	67%	35%
Retirement pension	79%	56%
Legal services	79%	59%
Access to Health Care:		
Average months since have seen doctor	7.9	15.7
Average annual utilization of health care services	3.4	1.3
Demographic and Social Characteristics		
Married	92%	73%
Live in area where work	88%	55%
Family members who can read English	2.8	2.0
Voted in the last state elections	83%	19%
Voted in the last national elections	83%	28%

* All comparisons indicated have a statistically significant difference at the 0.05 level or less.

farmworkers have strong reactions both to the immediate maltreatment they receive from bosses and to the structure of the agricultural system that fosters such maltreatment.[6]

It is worth noting that motivating factors do not include such commonly perceived factors as low wages and lack of benefits. Instead, the farmworkers' views emphasize basic conditions that affect their feelings of dignity and worth. Such feelings reinforce commitments to the UFW as the primary means for addressing such conditions.

Policy Impacts of the California Farmworker Survey

The action research among California farmworkers involved several policy implications. This project, along with our survey of Midwestern farmworkers (Barger and Reza 1984a, 1984b), is the only empirical and representative study of the support base among farmworkers themselves for the farm labor movement. The survey documents that farmworkers overwhelmingly endorse the UFW as the most viable means for achieving basic improvements in their lives. There is a primary rational recognition by both union and nonunion workers that the UFW has already been effective in improving farmworkers' lives. In essence, farmworkers feel their case for better working conditions has been directly represented through the UFW. This faith in the proven record of the UFW is a predominant influence that "pulls" farmworkers towards the UFW. A secondary but essential factor in farmworkers' endorsement is a feeling of being abused by bosses, which "pushes" workers towards the UFW.

Following the study, the UFW leaders were thoroughly briefed on the findings, and over a series of meetings four specific implications have been discussed. The first is that the survey validates the UFW's claims that it represents the will of farmworkers. The UFW leadership and members, of course, were already confident of this, but now they have solid documentation that the UFW's support base among farmworkers is both substantial and widespread. The UFW leaders are better able to understand their position with farmworkers, and have used this understanding in making organizational decisions relevant to the Union's internal constituency. For example, the survey results have been used in campaigns to organize workers, in developing services for members, in lobbying to meet farmworkers' felt needs, and in representing farmworkers' views to other segments of society.

The second implication is that any problems in achieving and maintaining farm labor rights are largely *external* to the farmworker community. Again, the UFW leaders had already believed this, but the study provides support for their allegations that vested political interests are blocking the realization of farmworkers' rights. The UFW has used the survey results in publicity and lobbying efforts to discredit the claims of growers and conservative state government officials that problems are due to lack of farmworker support for the UFW. It is clear that farmworkers have consistently expressed their will to be represented by the UFW. Yet in a democratic society this will of the majority has not consistently resulted in collective bargaining rights, as specified in the California's Agricultural Labor Relations Act, and there are clear indications that hostile political interests have undermined the ALRB.[7]

The third implication of the survey is that efforts to achieve greater justice for farmworkers must also focus in the external arena. Since its internal support base in the farmworker community is so solid, the

UFW's limited resources can be more efficiently focused on mobilizing external support for the farm labor cause to counter vested political interests. Again, the UFW leaders had already felt this, but they can now make decisions in this area with greater confidence. The UFW's primary effort along these lines is the new boycott of table grapes (*Fresno Bee* 1984; *Sacramento Bee* 1984; *Los Angeles Times* 1984, *Catholic Universe Bulletin* 1984). The rationale of this boycott, as of previous ones, is that the combined social and economic power of millions of individual Americans who are concerned with justice can counterbalance the relative political powerlessness of farmworkers. The survey has been cited in the boycott and public education campaigns to document the UFW's social and moral legitimacy (*Bakersfield Californian* 1985; *Los Angeles Times* 1985; *San Joaquin County Record* 1985; *San Jose Mercury News* 1985; *Western Grower and Shipper* 1985).

It should be noted that related research indicates that there is substantial support among the public for the farm labor cause, including 85% of Americans who endorse labor organizing and collective bargaining rights for farmworkers and 57% who endorse farmworker boycotts (Barger 1987; Barger and Haas 1983). There have been many attempts to organize farmworkers in California over the past century, and a critical factor that has enabled the UFW to succeed where previous efforts failed is its ability to mobilize external popular and political support (Jenkins 1984; Jenkins and Perrow 1977; Majka and Majka 1982). With grounded documentation of its legitimacy among its internal constituent group, there is a positive hope that the UFW will continue to organize this external support in its efforts to consolidate farmworkers' hard-won rights.

The fourth implication of the survey findings is that the UFW is clearly a firmly established force where farmworker affairs are concerned. With such an overwhelming support base among its constituents, the UFW is likely to continue to be a major influence in farm labor policy. The UFW clearly has social and moral legitimacy in its efforts to achieve farmworker rights and justice. There is also an intriguing suggestion that such social movements may act as a means of social control for societal institutions which excessively deviate from standard norms shared by the general population (Zald 1978). It does seem clear that the UFW will remain a significant force in farm labor affairs, and is not likely to be deterred by the political opposition of vested interests.

In reviewing the California farmworker survey as a whole, the main uses and impacts of the survey have been related to the internal goals of the United Farm Workers, and to the UFW's efforts to achieve meaningful changes in farmworkers' external societal environment. The primary purpose of the survey was to support the long-term goals of the UFW as a community-based group, and policy impacts have been made *through* this group. Also, it should be noted, this research project was only one in a series of studies in support of the farm labor movement, where we have sought to integrate research activities around the larger issues related to long-term goals.

Utilization Strategies: Principles in Community-Action Research

In reviewing the community-action approach of the California farmworker survey, several principles can be identified which facilitate the effective and meaningful use of applied research:[8]

(1) Self-determination model: The community-action model is essentially based on the principle of self-determination, and there are several reasons why this model enhances the effectiveness of research results. One is that community members are in the best position to determine what is good for their own group, and therefore how research results can best be used. In our case, for example, UFW leaders explained from the beginning how our project could best serve their goals. We were never in the dubious position of deciding what is best for others or what farmworkers "should" do, nor were we in the position of providing information to some external agency that would make such decisions for farmworkers.

A second reason is that when a community group makes the basic decisions for a project they then have a significant investment in utilizing the results. UFW leaders, for example, defined the goals for the research project in terms of their larger concerns about farm labor issues, and so from the beginning they were invested in utilizing research results.

A third reason that action research can enhance the effective use of research results is that it provides community-based groups with new decision-making tools. Such tools and knowledge are normally limited to the more advantaged segments of society, but there is no reason why community leaders cannot make effective use of them, just as political and business leaders do. For example, marketing and political research has been greatly utilized by agribusinesses and state politicians to achieve their goals in farm labor policies, and our involvement in the farmworker survey helped provide the UFW with more grounded information to use in *its* decision-making processes.

It is our position that self-determination is the most effective and constructive means of social change to resolve the problems of community groups, both for the particular group involved and for the society as a whole. The UFW, for example, knows best what rights and conditions are needed by farmworkers, and also what it can give as well as take in order for farmworkers to reach an optimal balance with the larger society. And, most important, the UFW can best pursue such a balance by *direct* negotiation with other segments concerned with farm labor policies; it can best make its own decisions in the give and take of negotiations. In the action model, the applied workers support the community group in this adaptive process, by conducting projects around community goals and using grounded information and their expertise to advise community leaders. We can therefore have an effective impact on public policy *through* the social group being served.

(2) Goal identification: Applied activities are most effective when long-term goals and short-term objectives are made clear.[9] Goal identification is the first and most important step in applied projects, and includes the general and specific goals of the community group being served, and also the objectives of the particular project in helping the achievement of the larger goals. Thus in our first meeting with UFW leaders we focused on their *uses* of the results, and throughout the project we consciously sought clearer understandings of the UFW's goals in the project.

The reason goal identification is so important is that the goals provide the criteria for making all decisions throughout the whole project. For example, at one point in the farmworker survey we realized that we had sufficient information about local workers who spent much of the year at the same ranch on different seasonal tasks, but we had very little information about migrant workers who moved from ranch to ranch harvesting crops. Because comprehensive information was needed about all different workers in order to meet the UFW's needs, we then devised alternate sampling methods to ensure migrant workers were appropriately represented in the results.

We should note that goal-oriented applied activities are also open-ended, in the sense that a particular project can be a single piece in a series of activities to achieve the larger goals. For example, we have been involved in a number of projects in support of the farm labor movement, and each has built on and has been integrated with previous ones (Barger 1987; Barger and Haas 1983; Barger and Reza 1984a, 1984b, 1985a, 1985b, 1987). Thus a goal-oriented approach has led to a more comprehensive and long-term involvement with farmworker issues; and each new activity is enhanced by the breadth and depth of previous activities.

(3) Clarification of roles and relationships: In community-action work, the primary role of the researchers is to support the community group concerned. The main issue in the action model is: "Whose interests are being served?" In our case, we have accepted that the UFW is both "boss" and "client," the one who makes the ultimate decisions concerning what goals are being served. The applied researchers bring professional expertise (knowledge and skills), as well as their personal values to help the community group achieve *its* goals. For academic (and academically trained) professionals, this often conflicts with traditional emphasis on "independence" and "objectivity" in research, and it also calls for an ethical decision of agreement with the community group's goals and means before assuming the position of supporting them.

The roles which the researchers and the community group assume in their relationship with each other is one of the major foundations for successful utilization of research results. The responsibilities and benefits of each party should be identified and negotiated from the beginning, in order to maximize constructive and rewarding relations for both. It is also advisable to be informed and selective about with whom one works, and for both parties to be straightforward and concrete from the beginning about what they can and cannot do.[10]

(4) Holistic project team: One of the strongest ways to ensure the effectiveness of applied work is to build a holistic project team. This includes pooling a variety of knowledge, skills, and experience. Our project, for instance, included a team of academics, farm labor leaders, and farmworkers--people with complementary skills in research, ethnicity, language, community, political, and change skills. The researchers themselves were both interdisciplinary and interethnic in nature, with an anthropologist and an organizational psychologist whose both qualitative and quantitative research skills reinforced and complemented each other. It also included interviewers whose ethnic and social background was that of the research population. But there was another aspect to the team approach. The researchers were in close coordination with the UFW and the National Farm Worker Ministry, and this enhanced a much deeper understanding of the research issues and, in particular, how the research could be effectively utilized. All this added complications to the project, but in the long run contributed to more comprehensive and grounded data and to more in-depth interpretations.

(5) Eclectic methodology: For applied work to be most effective, researchers should be eclectic in their design and methods. The issue is not whether a particular discipline or methodological tradition is appropriate for a project, but rather which methods can best serve the project objectives and the community group's goals. Our methodology combined qualitative and quantitative techniques, which could supplement each other for both breadth and depth in understanding influences in farmworkers' views about the farm labor movement. Quantitative sampling and survey methods ensured that the results are representative of the farmworker population concerned.[11] They also provided us with the means for determining multiple associations, the combined and interactive influences in farmworker attitudes and behavior (including ruling out some factors as influences). Qualitative methods provided us with a better understanding of the emic issues and conceptual categories of the research population, which contributed to the development of a more exact questionnaire. Even more important, they provided us with more grounded understandings for interpreting the meanings of responses and for making more valid interpretations of the survey results.

Research methods are *tools* for valid learning, and all methodological tools need to be carefully evaluated and selected to determine which combination can provide us with the most grounded understandings of the applied issues. In developing research designs for applied projects, then, methodological choices need to be made, and it is necessary to be aware of the strengths and limitations of methods of data collection and analysis. In our case, for example, interview responses inherently involves self-reported views and recall, which may vary in accuracy and truthfulness. To control for this, we built a number of internal checks into the questionnaire. We also included independent evaluations on key and sensitive variables by the interviewers, who were trained in observational techniques. Another limitation was that cross-sectional data does not lend itself well to causal interpretations. But we were able to qualify this problem in three ways. First, the farm labor movement itself represents an event across time, and so allows some assumptions about baseline conditions and behavior in assessing changes. Second, the study built in a history of the respondent's involvement in farm labor issues, which provided some basis for assessing changes over time. And, third, the study also included a comparison of UFW and nonunion workers, and therefore permitted some interpretations about causal effects of unionization. Finally, we have also qualified conclusions where we could not make empirically grounded interpretations.

The basic methodological issue in applied research is the scientific *quality* of the data. Where can we make empirically grounded conclusions? Where not? And how can we control for limitations and biases? In our case, we invested considerable effort in maintaining high qualitative and quantitative controls throughout the whole project. These included a preliminary field investigation to identify effective sampling techniques and to identify appropriate concepts of the research population for developing the questionnaire. We also trained interviewers in validation techniques, and conducted follow-up interviews to build a qualitative understanding of results. And we included quality-control techniques in the data analysis.

Applied research calls for being eclectic in our methodology, particularly in selecting those methods that combine depth and breadth and that will produce the most valid results for how they will be *used*. This partly means we need to be familiar with a wide variety of methods beyond traditional disciplinary boundaries, including methods of data collection such as participant-observation and survey research, and also of qualitative and statistical methods of data analysis.

(6) Maintenance of professional and ethical standards: Both professional and ethical issues are involved throughout applied activities, and they need to be specifically addressed from the beginning. Community action workers have to agree ethically with the community group's goals, and its means for achieving these goals, before assuming the position of supporting them. In our case, we consciously recognized our own social values that led us to become involved in supporting the UFW in achieving its goals. Such a commitment was essential in the effective utilization of research results, because the project was specifically designed with these values and goals in mind.

We would like to make clear, however, that taking value positions does not mean that professional standards are compromised. Some social scientists are uneasy that applied work is somehow less valid or rigorous than "pure" research, and there are cases, of course, where this negative view has been justified. But we argue that holding the highest scientific standards possible in applied activities is an *ethical* as well as a professional responsibility. Since applied work inherently involves social changes and can therefore make direct impacts in people's lives, we need to be very sure of where we are valid in our understandings and also of where we are limited. When pressed, most scientists would agree that there is no such thing as purely "objective" research, because the whole research process from beginning to end is influenced by conceptual, methodological, situational, and personal biases. Valid scientific research is therefore based on the *control* of biases and limitations (rather than their absence), and such controls must be consciously included in the conceptualization of the issue, in the collection of data, in the analysis of data, and in making grounded interpretations of findings.

We argue that it is because of the very value positions involved that the highest scientific standards are needed in applied work, because we have to have valid understandings if our contributions are to be effective and constructive. For example, in the farmworker survey it would have been satisfying to find that all farmworkers were solidly behind the UFW, and it would have been easy to make a lesser effort because we were "sure" this was the case. But in order for the UFW to be truly effective in achieving farm labor reforms, we needed to validly understand the views and motivations of those workers who were unconcerned about the issues, and also of those who were opposed. From the beginning of the project and at each stage, we openly discussed our value biases and consciously made the job tougher in terms of the quality of data and analytical procedures. In training the interviewers, for example, we emphasized that we needed to be absolutely careful not to let our own values influence the respondents' answers, and that it was important to learn what each worker thought; otherwise, we might as well interview ourselves. Because of our very value commitments for effective changes, we had to prove to ourselves what the UFW's actual position with farmworkers was, so we would not rely on something that was not there.

In applied work, we need to maintain the highest scientific standards possible, both as an ethical and as a professional position. A key to this is realizing that grounded scientific research is based more on the *control* of biases and limitations, rather than "objectivity." We also need to consciously build in such controls because our results can have a direct impact in people's lives.[12]

Summary

The survey of California farmworkers represents a community action model of applied research. The survey was the first systematic and empirical study of what farmworkers themselves think about the farm labor movement, even though the UFW movement has been a prominent social issue for almost a quarter of a century. The survey documents that farmworkers overwhelmingly endorse the UFW as the best alternative for improving their lives. These findings are consistent with a previous survey of Midwestern workers (Barger and Reza 1984a, 1984b), indicating that there is widespread support for the farm labor movement among farmworkers across the nation and in a variety of agricultural enterprises. When union workers are compared to nonunion workers, the California survey also indicates that where the farm labor movement is successful there are significant improvements in farmworkers' living and working conditions. The research results are thus consistent with the historical record that the farm labor movement has been the most viable alternative for improving the living and working conditions of farmworkers.

Several principles are evident in the California farmworker survey that can provide guidelines for the effectiveness of applied activities. These include adherence to a self-determination model of applied change; clear identification of long-term community goals and short-term project objectives; clarification of roles and relationships where the applied workers support the goals of the community concerned; use of an eclectic methodology; organizing a holistic project team; and maintenance of scientific and ethical standards. In particular, we would like to emphasize that the California farmworker survey represents a community-action model, where applied workers can contribute to effective policy impacts *through* the community-based group being served.[13]

Notes

This chapter is based on field research among California farmworkers during the summer of 1984, which was supported by the National Farm Worker Ministry and the Liberal Arts PDP program of Indiana University at Indianapolis. We wish to thank the NFWM staff and volunteers who worked with the project for their commitment to the truth and to high standards in the collection, coding, and computer entry of the data. In particular, we wish to dedicate this chapter to the memory of Rev. Fred Eyster, who gave his all for farm labor justice. We also wish to thank Rosio Yaselli for her sense of responsibility, initiative, and hard work in the data analysis. We are particularly grateful to those farmworkers who agreed to be interviewed and to share their views and experiences with us, and to Cesar Chavez, Arturo Rodriguez, David Martinez, and the other UFW staff members whose creative commitment to the human worth of farmworkers originally inspired the applied research project.

1. These lists were originally prepared within the preceding year by growers for workers on their ranches, which varied in size from 50 to 3,000 workers. The lists had been obtained by the United Farm Workers for a variety of purposes, and were obtained in turn by the National Farm Worker Ministry for the purpose of the survey. An evaluation of the biases which this introduced into the study indicates that workers on these ranches were probably more informed about the research issues, though the ranches represented a range from those which had experienced active organizing to those which had not. Being more informed, however, was consistent with the purposes of the study, to investigate those workers where the issue was most present, in comparison with Midwestern farmworkers. Otherwise, in our experience, the workers on the ten ranches included in the study are fairly representative of table grape workers in particular, and probably overlap considerably in their views with other California farmworkers. The method of sampling local workers used was chosen as the most efficient and effective available. The only other alternative was to select possible respondents by a complicated stratified area sampling method in communities where there are a heavy concentration of farmworkers, with the hope that perhaps one in a hundred would fit the definition of the research population.

2. Respondents' rights were built into the introductory statement of the questionnaire, and specifically stated that they had the rights to confidentiality and not to be individually identified, not to answer any question, and to ask any question about the study. When sensitive questions were asked during the interviews, respondents were specifically reminded of their rights.

3. The response rate of those actually contacted and asked for an interview was 95%. But we experienced considerable difficulty with false names, addresses, and Social Security numbers in the lists. Some of these were used by undocumented workers, but, based on the limited evidence of those respondents who volunteered information, we believe that a majority were "ghosts," created by foremen and supervisors and used for fraudulent purposes.

4. Specific qualitative methods used included presurvey participant observation with the research population, pretesting and discussing the draft of the questionnaire with farmworkers, training the interviewers to understand the research issues and to make grounded judgements about the respondent (such as immigration status and attitudes towards the

UFW), daily debriefings with the interviewers, going over each completed questionnaire with the interviewer, conducting follow-up open-ended interviews with a subsample of the respondents, and, after analyzing the data and drawing conclusions, going back to the research area and discussing the results with farmworkers. Quantitative methods included double-coding all responses before data entry, checking data records with all original interviews after data entry, statistically checking the dataset for accuracy, reliability, and internal and independent validity, and to identify the best measures of the research variables. We also took care to ensure all statistical techniques were appropriate for the level of data, and also to test the significance levels and confidence intervals of the results.

5. In open-ended questions and in follow-up interviews we found that "union" means "United Farm Workers" to most farmworkers. Only one respondent raised the Teamsters and one other mentioned a union in Mexico to which he belonged, compared to hundreds of comments on the UFW. Even though "the union of Chavez" (*la union de Chavez*) is a common term for the UFW among California farmworkers, Chavez' name was not used in the survey in order to avoid personalities and to maintain a focus on the main issues.

6. "Bosses" (*patrones*) generally referred to those in more direct contact with workers, such as foremen and labor contractors. But the term was also generalized to include supervisors and growers.

7. The UFW has made two charges along these lines. One is that growers have circumvented the intent of the law by not negotiating in good faith, and in some cases by reorganizing their operations under new names to bypass election results. Appeals to the ALRB of about 36% of these nonnegotiated cases have not produced any results, and even in those cases where growers were found guilty of not negotiating in good faith there has never been enforcement of such decisions. As indicated earlier, the second charge is that the new Deukmejian administration in California is attempting to use the Agricultural Labor Relations Board to support the growers against the farm labor movement, rather than to guarantee farmworkers' rights. Examples of these charges include the appointing an attorney who had represented growers as chair of the ALRB, changing ALRB policy to reduce levied back payments against growers by more than 80%, and giving growers access to confidential ALRB files (*Bakersville Californian* 1984; Chavez 1985; Packer 1984; *San Francisco Chronicle* 1984a, 1984c, 1985).

8. A comprehensive analysis of such principles in another action project has been reviewed elsewhere (Barger and Reza 1985a). The principles presented here are intended to supplement those previously discussed, and are particularly appropriate for action *research*.

9. Goal identification is often one of the most important contributions applied workers can make to a community group with whom they are working. In the farmworker survey, the UFW already had very clear goals, but there are many community groups which do not have their goals clearly developed, and this can greatly hinder the effectiveness of any applied activities.

10. From our perspective, our relationships with the UFW leaders and staff are ideal, in the sense that we work with people of great integrity, who had their own goals and operations clearly developed, and with whom we share basic social values and commitments. But we know of cases where community organizations may have worthy commitments and needs, but who are so disorganized and ineffectual that productive outcomes of cooperative projects are highly unlikely; so working with such groups results mainly in disappointments. Potential problems can also exist on the part of applied workers, of course; and there are some who do not have a clear understanding of their own abilities, resources, and limitations, and so commit themselves where they cannot really deliver. It is therefore advisable for both parties to be straightforward and concrete from the beginning about what they can and cannot do.

11. Because the results closely resemble those of an earlier survey of Midwestern farmworkers, we are also confident in generalizing to most farmworkers in the U.S.

12. We also believe that applied work can make as important theoretical contributions as with "pure" research. This is because the validity of concepts and methods are prospectively tested in the real world. Since applied work inherently involves change, we need to be validly grounded in our understandings if those changes are to be predicted and constructive. The model of sociocultural change used in applied projects (or the lack of clear conceptual understandings of change) poses a serious challenge, for our concept of change will be tested in concrete life situations, for better or for worse. The model which we believe has the greatest predictive validity is a "systems reorganization" concept (Barger 1977, 1982; Barger and Reza 1987). Just as culture is seen as an integrated and functional whole, this model views change as related to a

dynamic system composed of a population and its environment. The emphasis is on the *process* of change as the system reorganizes itself in response to a challenge, in order to achieve a new adaptive balance (Barger 1982, 1977). Our main point here is that in applied change projects there has rarely been an in-depth consideration of the guiding model of change, much less a comprehensive test of these guiding models. Change itself is rather taken for granted in too many cases, and this has serious implications for the outcomes of applied change.

13. Another issue of relevance here is the training of applied workers. Of particular concern is the experience and practical skills of those who train the applied workers, particularly where "applied" may have a hidden meaning of "academic." This issue has been addressed elsewhere (Barger and Reza 1985a; Barger and Sutton 1980), but needs to be considered along with other principles in applied work.

15

The Use and Non-Use of Anthropology: The Diarrheal Disease Control Program in Honduras

Carl Kendall

Anthropologists could do more to amplify their findings by participating in all aspects of research, especially by influencing the design of surveys. It also appears that anthropological research is more acceptable to collaborators when they spend time in the field.

This is a report of the use of ethnographic study findings in the Mass Media and Health Practices Project (MMHP) in Honduras (1980-1983).[1] The MMHP project in Honduras was an undertaking of the Ministry of Public Health and Social Assistance, Honduras, Central America, with technical support from the Academy for Educational Development, Washington, D.C., (AED 1980). It was known in Honduras as the *Proyecto de Comunicacion Masiva Aplicada a la Salud Infantil* (PROCOMSI) and its purpose was to introduce oral rehydration therapy (ORT) and other behaviors related to the treatment and prevention of infant and childhood diarrhea in rural Honduras. An evaluation (Evaluacion PROCOMSI) was conducted concurrently with the project by the Institute for Communication Research and the Food Research Institute of Stanford University and by Applied Communication Technology, Palo Alto, California. The author was Field Director of this evaluation.

Diarrheal diseases are the most common illnesses of children in Honduras and throughout the world. The Diarrheal Diseases Control Program of the World Health Organization estimates that there are 1.6 billion episodes of diarrheal disease in the world (excluding China) in children less than five years of age each year. Diarrheal illnesses account for approximately three million child deaths per year worldwide and greatly impair the growth and development of children who survive.

Diarrheal disease deaths, in part, are brought about through dehydration, or fluid and electrolyte loss. These deaths due to dehydration can now be controlled by administering a special oral rehydration solution, and a massive world-wide program has been undertaken by UNICEF, WHO, AID, and other donors to provide this solution to children. The PROCOMSI project was one of the first to attempt to promote ORT through public health communications.

The target population for the project were the approximately 200,000 rural Hondurans living in Health Region I, adjacent to the capital, Tegucigalpa, and extending east to the border with Nicaragua. The target behaviors included treatment of cases of diarrhea, promotion of breast-feeding for all infants, feeding during diarrheal episodes, and preventive actions that mothers could undertake at home. The treatment behaviors involved the administration of an oral rehydration solution mixed from packets of salts containing the WHO standard mix of sodium, potassium, bicarbonate and glucose. The packets were called Litrosol by the project ("litro" for liter, and "sol" for solution). The packets were manufactured in Honduras by the government and distributed at the clinic and community levels by the Ministry of Health at no cost.

The evaluation was designed principally for the donor community, including AID, WHO, and UNICEF, interested in promoting ORT.[2] The project and the evaluation were designed to test the efficacy of a public health communications project in the promotion of ORT, at a time when both mass communications and ORT were being challenged as successful strategies.

The PROCOMSI intervention used broadcast, print, and interpersonal communication channels to deliver a coordinated set of messages about a fairly narrow set of issues--responses to infant diarrhea. The knowledge and behavioral objectives and the strategies for behavioral change were developed using intensive planning or market research (called the developmental investigation here) that included ethnographic and survey methods conducted by the in-country staff of the Academy for Educational Development, with design assistance by the author. The campaign incorporated elements of social marketing[3] and systematic development of messages using formative evaluation.[4] The approach has been termed development communications (Hornick 1988). The evaluation focused on communications issues such as the effectiveness of mass campaigns to change behavior, or the decay in knowledge about ORT once the campaign ended, but it also identified additional questions in health communications.[5]

The locale for the project, South-Central Honduras, is typical of many parts of Central America. Terrain ranges from rolling hills and valleys to steep hillsides. It is populated primarily by subsistence farmers, although some townships support large-scale commercial agriculture. Half of these subsistence farmers own land, which they plant with corn and beans. Communities are small (seldom larger than 1000 people), and houses are often widely separated from one another. The municipal headquarters (*cabecera municipal*) have some service infrastructure such as occasional electricity, all-weather roads in two of the three cases, bus service, health centers, and a post office telephone connecting the *cabecera* to the capital, but services in the other communities are generally limited to elementary schools.

This paper will discuss the ways the findings from the ethnographic studies were incorporated into this successful ORT promotion project. It will also discuss issues which impeded the use of specific anthropological findings and led to the failure of certain components of the project. Finally, the paper concludes with suggestions to improve the use of anthropology in primary health care programs.

Research Methods and Context

The multiyear intervention and evaluation involved many different components. First, preliminary ethnographic research was conducted by the author, in January, 1980, prior to intervention. The purpose of this research was to conduct a "rapid assessment" of beliefs and practices related to diarrheal disease and to explore the possibilities for success of the upcoming project. The report produced from this research served as background to the developmental investigation, several elements of the intervention design, pilot testing of the evaluation survey instruments, and baseline for an ethnographic evaluation.

Next, a developmental investigation was conducted by the Academy for Educational Development. This research activity involved participant observation, open-ended and close-ended interviewing, and focus group research in a small convenience sample of communities and households. The purpose of the investigation was to explore beliefs and popular vocabulary associated with diarrheal disease, to determine audience media preferences, and perhaps most importantly, to expose the implementors to the living conditions and actual circumstances of the target population. The investigation was conducted solely by on-site staff, none of whom had previous training in anthropology. The author assisted in design and site selection but was not present in-country for the actual research. The research was conducted in July, 1980.

The largest data collection effort was the PROCOMSI Evaluation survey, initiated in February, 1981. The survey included a number of studies with different methodologies, but relied primarily on large-scale survey data from repeated visits to a panel of mothers of small children. The design utilized a panel of 750 families in twenty separate sites visited monthly over a twenty-eight month period. The first sweep, in February 1981, was conducted before the PROCOMSI project began broadcasting and was considered a baseline. The survey used a battery of instruments to measure morbidity and treatment, anthropometry, nutrition and breastfeeding practices, and knowledge of the campaign. The instruments were developed from pilot instruments used in the initial ethnographic study. To control for the influence of repeated measurements on the sample mothers' knowledge and behaviors, comparison groups were also measured in additional communities that received all the elements of the campaign but not of the evaluation. The experimental and control samples were structured to yield quasi-equivalent groups of women of child-rearing age that were representative of the full range of differences found in Honduras.

The PROCOMSI campaign itself began in March, 1981 and terminated in March, 1983. Concurrently, the PROCOMSI Evaluation survey and an ethnographic evaluation was conducted. This ethnographic evaluation began in June, 1981, continued for two years, and was conducted in two adjacent rural villages. The primary site, Nance, was not a site for the PROCOMSI Evaluation survey. Here, in addition to ethnography, with the active collaboration of community members, field workers were trained and baseline survey instruments pretested prior to the initiation of the campaign. The secondary site, Los Dolores, was visited for a two-week period in 1981 and a one-month period in 1982. [6]

Project Results [7]

The evaluation survey was designed to demonstrate the feasibility of using mass media to promote the campaign. To determine this, the evaluation survey needed to demonstrate access, exposure, and changes in behavior due to exposure. Access appeared very high. Radio carried the largest portion of the campaign's messages. On the average, two thirds (67.4%) of the families had a radio that worked on any given day. The survey determined that radio listening peaked in the early morning and at noon, and tapered off fairly abruptly after eight to nine in the evening. Radio spots were timed to reach this audience. An average of 60.0% of mothers listened to the radio on any day.

Interpersonal contacts with health care workers and traditional healers were also measured. In general, families reported about one contact every six months with some type of care worker, with the majority of contacts taking place at fixed facilities. When contacts with traditional sources of care were included, the Ministry's health care workers at both community and fixed facility levels accounted for four out of five contacts (80.5%). Traditional healers accounted for the rest.

Over half of the mothers in the sample (56.8%) could read well by themselves, as determined by a reading test; the household literacy rate was 86.8%, so there was almost always someone in a household who could read print materials.

Exposure to campaign messages was also high. Over the course of an entire day, nearly three-quarters (73.2%) of women who listened to the radio at all during the day reported hearing at least one spot. Even if women who did not listen to the radio were included, coverage was still 43.9% of all women hearing a PROCOMSI spot every day.

Two examples of measurement of learning in major areas are knowledge about Litrosol and knowledge about breastfeeding. Within six months after broadcasts began, half the mothers (49.5%) could name it as the medicine being promoted. By the end of the period, this figure leveled off at about three-fourths of all mothers able to remember the name of the medicine. A composite index of knowledge of the messages of the breastfeeding campaign rose from 9.2% before any significant broadcasting about breastfeeding began to 41.1% at the end of the project.

In identifying health behavior change, the evaluation focused on three major areas; diarrheal disease and the use of oral rehydration therapy, feeding behaviors, and observation of the preparation and administration of Litrosol. Prevalence of diarrhea was high and showed seasonal fluctuations. Point prevalence among children five years or less in age averaged 14.3% in the rainy season and 9.9% in the dry season.

Litrosol use was measured both as a percentage of mothers who had ever tried it and as a percentage of episodes being treated. Within six months of the start of broadcasting, over a third of the mothers (36.7%) said they had tried Litrosol. This percentage rose to 62.4% by the end of the intensive campaign. When calculated as a percentage of episodes occurring in the two weeks prior to the interview (the most reliable reporting period used) the proportion of episodes treated rose from none before the start of the project to a maximum of 35.7%, with an average of roughly 20% of episodes over the final 18 months of the campaign.

Mothers reported that the single most useful source of information for learning about how to mix and administer Litrosol was the packet itself, which came in an envelope printed with instructions. However, interpersonal instruction (from health care workers) and learning from the radio also were significant information sources. Mothers reported correct mixing behaviors in using a liter of water and using the whole packet of salts over 90% of the time. However, they did much less well at behaviors such as throwing away unused liquid after one day (an average of 36% of mothers) and knowing that they should seek help if three days of Litrosol use did not improve the situation (an average of 10%).

Use of other medicines concurrently with Litrosol was common. An average of 43% of Litrosol-treated cases was also reported to be treated with other medicines. About 20% of all episodes were taken to the clinic for treatment. Slightly over ten percent of cases were seen by village health workers. Both these numbers remained stable over time. Reported treatment by *sobadoras* or other traditional healers averaged four percent of episodes but fluctuated more over time.

Feeding behaviors, particularly breastfeeding and feeding during episodes of diarrhea, were also targets of the campaign. Breastfeeding prevalence and duration were high in rural Honduras and appeared to have been increased by the campaign. Early in the intervention, 65% of children under 18 months were reported to be breastfeeding; by the end of the campaign, the number had risen to 81% of children under 18 months. Similarly, reported bottlefeeding of the young children dropped from 64% to 50% over the same time period. Continuation of breastfeeding and bottlefeeding during episodes of diarrhea was at about the same levels (i.e., virtually all mothers who were breastfeeding or bottlefeeding reported that they continued to do so during episodes of diarrhea).

Health status change was the ultimate objective of the campaign effort. Health status was measured with a variety of anthropometric measurements as well as mortality rates. There was evidence that the overall nutritional and growth status declined during the campaign period. The percent of stunting went from 27.8% to 33.4% for boys and from 31.1% to 38.3% for girls. The percent "normal" under the Gomez categories fell from 43.4% to 36.7% for boys and from 40.9% to 33.3% for girls. However, wasting was essentially zero throughout, and there may even have been a slight improvement in arm circumference measures over time. The decline in nutritional or growth status seemed to be a secular trend toward increased growth retardation. It was consistent across sex, age, municipio, and type of village.

Reliable and accurate mortality data could not be provided by the study due to sample size. Efforts were made to expand the study population for the mortality study by adding reports of non-respondent families in the twenty study sites through interviewing village leaders. This was feasible for two of the municipio study sites. In the other urban municipio site, reports of death were collected from the official Death Registers kept in the municipalities. This procedure is subject to numerous flaws: the total population at risk is not available, so that rates cannot be calculated; substantial underreporting exists, and is unlikely to be uniform through the life of the project due to the presence of immigrant populations from Nicaragua in the study area; and finally, cause of death cannot be accurately determined.

Still, an analysis of mortality for children less than five using the cause of death reported by the mother showed marked declines in deaths involving diarrhea in any way. In the two years prior to the campaign, death of children under five involved diarrhea in 39.8% of the cases. In the two years after the start of the campaign, deaths reported to be associated with diarrhea fell to 24.4% of all mortality, a statistically significant drop. Total mortality dropped, although by a slightly smaller amount. Virtually identical reductions in the percentages of cases involving diarrhea before and after the campaign are found when the analysis is restricted to children less than two years and to children less than one year, but the drop in total mortality is smaller. The changes are also consistent when analyzed by time relative to the start of the intervention.

Utilization Methods and Impact

Knowledge of community beliefs and practices was a significant part of the project. Initial ethnographic research was incorporated into the project, local categories for disease were part of campaign messages, and the description of the physical environment of the household developed by anthropology was accepted as valid.

At the same time, especially with regard to developing the intervention strategy and the goals for the campaign, the entire portrait provided by anthropology regarding local perception and treatment of diarrhea, and local concerns about ill health in general, was not really considered. When anthropological evidence clashed with the viewpoint of medical authorities and with evidence collected from other sources, the former was not considered to be of sufficient weight to change the implementation strategy.

One design feature that led to successful incorporation was the presence of the ethnographer during the entire project due to the concurrent design of the evaluation. However, the role of evaluator sometimes made collaboration difficult.

Some of the successful incorporation was undoubtedly due to the fact that both members of the expatriate Academy team were familiar with Honduras, one having completed a communications research project in Honduras and the other having served in the Peace Corps there. The results of the rapid assessment were taken for granted. Several of these ethnographic findings were confirmed in the developmental investigation.

In addition, the Academy staff, as well as Ministry staff, were captivated by the idea of anthropology. One Academy staff member subsequently wrote an article on the utility of qualitative research in designing communication campaigns (Booth and O'Gara 1984). As Booth and O'Gara note: ". . . formative research should begin with unstructured observation to maximize discovery . . . Observation should then be expanded into open-ended, in-depth interviews with key informants . . ." (1984:5). The successful incorporation of ethnography in this communication process has been validated by WHO, which describes the PROCOMSI project as an example of a successful communications project and lists ethnography as an appropriate communication research method in the guidelines for communications published by the World Health Organization's Diarrheal Disease Control Program (WHO 1987).

Before discussing the difficulties in the utilization of anthropology in this project it is important to document its successes. Several key campaign elements utilized insights generated from this ethnographic corpus. These results are documented elsewhere (Booth and O'Gara 1984; Kendall 1983, 1984; O'Gara and Kendall 1985), but several examples are cited here.

Successful Utilization: The Worms Messages

A successful example of use was the incorporation into the promotion campaign of one of the locally attributed causes for diarrheal disease, worms (*lombrices*). Worms are believed to be a cause of diarrhea, but also a symbiote of the gut and are transmitted *in utero* to the fetus. This belief was confirmed by 63.9% of the respondents to the PROCOMSI Evaluation baseline survey.

According to ethnographic informants, these worms are said to develop in a sack or *bolsa* in the gut just below the stomach. During the first year of life the worms are underdeveloped and cannot digest dense compact foods. This fact underlay villagers' explanations for infants' limited diet and the fact that some foods, such as beans, may cause gas and diarrhea. The infants' diet is restricted, and meat and beans, liquid animal milk, and eggs are not regular components of the diet. Should they be begun in the diet, and the "worms" adjust to their presence, they must be continued, or the worms would wander in the body in search of other rich food sources, causing diarrhea and other illnesses such as worm fever. Evidence for wandering is provided by ascaris and pinworms, sometimes visible. If worms are properly and regularly fed, however, this symbiosis is beneficial and necessary for human survival, for if an adult or child should lose his worms, death is certain.

This folk etiology, identified in the ethnographic research, was utilized in the campaign. The implementors broadcast messages advising parents that ORS could be used for worm-produced diarrhea, as well as other kinds of diarrhea. The implementors also developed prevention messages that used this local explanation of diarrhea, talking about food preparation, for example, in terms of what would please or displease worms. Since the implementors conducted rigorous pre-testing of messages, they also received a positive response from their audience. Perhaps most crucially, the Ministry of Health was willing to allow the dissemination of messages about the worms because they believed that worms (i.e., ascaris) were a significant problem even if not a diarrheal disease problem. Here, interestingly enough, the Ministry was willing to use the local gloss of "worms" even if this did not coincide with a medically accurate definition of the problem.

Why were worms acceptable? Tedlock, in a recent paper (1987), discusses "folk etic" disease classifications, such as the hot-cold dichotomy, which researchers tend to impose on informants, to the detriment of accurate data collection, understanding, and the development of an interpretive social science. "Worms" or other ethnographic categories used in the campaign may be other folk etic categories in creation, especially since they become the target of mass media campaigns. One reason the development of such categories is convenient for applied anthropology (*cf.* Scrimshaw and Hurtado 1987) is that health and communication professionals can relate to these folk disease models, especially when the models help order their own experience of these concepts and valorize their own memories of their parents' or grandparents' use. The very consistency presented in these studies confirms that local beliefs are rationally structured and knowable without indepth study.

It is important here, however, to be more explicit about what the ethnographic research demonstrated. "Worms" are part of a lay explanatory model for digestion and disturbances of digestion, including diarrhea, that is wide-spread and requires no special vocation to diagnose or treat. A worm-caused disease (with the exception of "worm fever") requires secular therapy, occasional administration of a vermicide or purgative, and control of diet. Worms as a folk diagnostic category are part of an elaborate home-based folk-medical system of diagnosis and treatment that is substantially different from the cosmopolitan medical system. Although the health professional explanatory model is different, the treatment regimen is surprisingly similar. Understanding exists within the medical community of how this lay explanatory belief may derive from, or is at least consistent with the professional explanatory model.

Worms also appeared in answer to the question "What causes diarrhea?"(Table 15.1, page 297). Because it is treated as a secular cause, and because there was some support from the medical community for the use of this term, informants did not hesitate to use it.

It is also important to understand the way in which this knowledge was used in the campaign. The implementors did not believe that discussing "worm"-caused diarrhea had to have an effect on a particular episode of diarrhea caused by worms to be a successful promotion. Particulars of case histories, the use of worms in explaining diarrheal diseases, the relationship between child growth stages and worm growth stages, the symbolism of mutual digestion, farming and symbiosis, none of these was crucial for the campaign or even worthy of being understood from the implementor's perspective. What the implementors were sure it did do was demonstrate an identity with local beliefs and aid in breaking down the barrier which exists between users of health services and providers. All the staff in Honduras experienced the reaction on the part of campesinos to a mention of "evil eye" (*ojo*) or *empacho* (indigestion) in an appropriate context: "Aha, Doctor, you speak of *empacho*!", followed by a voluble discussion of these diseases. This discourse between the professional and lay healers already existed with regard to worms, and made worms a suitable intervention component. Folk etic categories become ideal for promotion, for they serve as a token of knowledge about the local context.

Successful Utilization: Water Boiling

Another example of the successful incorporation of knowledge generated through ethnography was the decision on the part of the implementors to not promote water boiling as a means of reducing the incidence of diarrhea. In addition to the logistical problems of collection, firewood, and utensils, field notes record the following:

> Water is stored in low fired clay pots often elevated on pronged sticks. A wooden plank or a dipping bowl often partially covers the top. The clay allows evaporation, and cools the stored water, but is difficult to clean. When the pot begins to leak too much water, the outside will be coated with a slurry of mud and water . . .

> Little or no purification of water takes place at home. Visible contamination, such as insects, will be removed from the water. The residents of Los Dolores are attached to the flavor of their water and do not like to alter it by, for example, boiling. Discussing contamination of water, Los Dolores residents note that water is collected from a stream that flows over dirt, or in a well where dirt filters water. "Dirt" doesn't necessarily contaminate water. Contaminated water should also taste bad. Inhabitants of Los Dolores know about water sources in town that make one sick. Water can cause illness and diarrhea for conventional cosmopolitan reasons, but country people believe that water drunk at the wrong time can also produce sickness (Kendall 1985:44).

These findings were incorporated into discussions held by the implementors and the author prior to the selection of campaign intervention foci. Discussions of the feasibility of each potential intervention were constant. The implementors drew on their experience in the developmental investigation, while the anthropologist provided detail about beliefs and practices within the two communities in which the ethnographic evaluation had been initiated. The discussion of water boiling dealt with beliefs about water quality and purity, but also dealt with issues of availability of fuel, cooking pots, the bad taste of boiled water, cost to women in time, etc. This led to the decision to not promote water boiling. The implementors felt the behaviors and practices related to water collection, storage, and use were little susceptible to change with the means available. Also, difficulties with water boiling campaigns are well documented in the applied anthropology literature as far back as Edward Wellin's work in 1953

(1955). In this instance the anthropologist was viewed as providing unique and authoritative information about the physical circumstances and popular water and food beliefs of local life. Consequently, there was little debate about water boiling.

Failures of Utilization

At the same time several recommendations generated by ethnographic research were not utilized in the program. Two of these will be presented as examples: the importance and complexity of the lay model of diarrhea and the recognition of *empacho*.

Oversimplification of the Lay Model of Diarrhea

A case history (#7), drawn from the ethnographic evaluation, can best provide an example of the complexity of treatment decision making and the inadequacy of the evaluation's survey component in capturing this model.

> Marta B. lives in a small house overlooking the valley where the school is. She lives with Ruben A., an old and feeble man that has never lived up to her expectations. They live with their children and grandchildren, a total of 13 people in a house the size of a two-car garage, kept orderly only by Marta's constant intervention. The family is originally from C. and moved here eight years ago. Marta says she left C. because of the shortage of water there. Marta's household is also one of the poorest in Los Dolores, and they are eating tortillas made of sorghum at present.
>
> Marta's three year old grandson, Esteban, has had diarrhea for a week and has it on the day of the interview. The diarrhea, claims Marta, has not been serious, never exceeding three stools a day, nor are the stools, says Marta, especially different from normal. But Esteban has been complaining of stomach pains, and Marta thinks that is due to diarrhea. His appetite is unchanged and he shows no signs of dehydration. She has administered only "bismuto" (a local store-purchased remedy similar to Pepto-Bismol tablets) to Esteban and doesn't plan to do much more unless the diarrhea gets much worse. He had a similar episode two months previously (in June), while he was still using a bottle but she stopped using the bottle during the previous episode and does not plan to reintroduce it.

She herself knows how to massage and in the beginning of June, when Esteban had lost his appetite, she massaged him and purged him with "Pildoras de la vida" (Pills of Life, another Honduran manufactured popular remedy, similar to Carter's Little Liver Pills). She's the only person I know in Los Dolores who uses "Pildoras de la vida." In February of the previous year she claimed to get two packets of Litrosol from the local health promoter which she used then. She has not used Litrosol for any of the related diarrheal episodes Esteban has suffered. She volunteered a number of other remedies for illnesses, such as cloves for worms and salt water baths to cure fever. She was unfamiliar with posters on PROCOMSI but listens to the radio. Her favorite stations are local ones, however, and she doesn't listen that much to Radio Station HRN (where most program messages were broadcast). She was unable to define dehydration, confusing the term with malnutrition. A host of responses are predicated on that observation. She felt that children taking Litrosol during an episode didn't get thin, therefore, that it was a *suero*, or liquid food. She knew how to prepare ORS. She claimed she had heard Dr. Salustiano say that if the child doesn't eat, give him Litrosol (Kendall 1985:83).

This example is important because the campaign strategy depended on two simple messages: (1) for any diarrhea, administer Litrosol; (2) if symptoms of dehydration occur, visit your health clinic. In Marta's case, she did not use Litrosol and she did not know what was meant by "dehydration." She had used the packets, however, even if inappropriately. Finally, Esteban did not suffer especially grave consequences from this. Although Esteban's diarrhea could not be accurately described as chronic diarrhea, he was clearly suffering from a pattern of diarrheal disease that was not particularly relevant to the project's implementation strategy. ORT is aimed at acute watery diarrhea and not these more persistent episodes. Fieldwork had demonstrated a "mixed diarrhea" both in an anthropological and an epidemiological sense. Recommendations based on ethnographic research called for targeting especially those episodes that warranted ORS. Instead PROCOMSI chose to identify a new unknown condition, dehydration, and to promote ORS for all diarrheal episodes.

This issue arose early in the design of the PROCOMSI Project. The preliminary ethnographic research was conducted during the first three months of the project. This research demonstrated the basic outline of a familiar folk medical explanatory model. As discussed above, this model includes a complex discrimination of "diarrhea," and a number of folk etiologies for diarrheal disease such as *empacho* (indigestion), *ojo*, (evil eye), *caida de mollera* (fallen fontanelle), and *lombrices* (worms) (*q.v.* Kendall 1984,1985).

In addition, ethnographic research demonstrated that diarrheal diseases are closely associated with developmental markers such as crawling and first teeth, and under these circumstances can be considered normal. Transient episodes that leave no sequelae may not be considered an episode of disease at all by the mother or caretaker of the child, or may be are attributed to simple physical causes such as excess cold or dirty water. Episodes which last unduly long and which cause severe illness may be attributed to one of the folk etiologies mentioned above.

Also, the ethnographic research confirmed that the household environment was substantially different from the clinical environment in which the case management strategy of treatment of every episode of diarrheal disease with pre-packaged oral rehydration solution had been developed. This differentiation of the household or domestic domain and the public domain has recently become an issue in the development of new public health interventions (*cf.* Leslie 1987, for example).

Anthropology helped the implementors focus on means, but could not force a revision of ends, as Hoben (1982:349 *ff.*) has pointed out. Certainly some of this disregard is due to professional autonomy and the relation of the social sciences to medicine. However, some of this is also due to the perception of ethnography as subjective and unsound science.

Group interviews and traditional surveys, conducted at the same time by the implementation team as part of the developmental investigation, failed to elicit either this pattern of multiple causes of diarrheal disease or a complex model of health seeking behavior. Instead, these other research activities found that a number of etiologies conforming more closely to cosmopolitan theories, such as "dirty water," were reported as causes of diarrhea. For example, Table 15.1 presents the responses to the item from the PROCOMSI Evaluation baseline survey: "What are the main causes of diarrhea?"

These research findings appeared to support the following contentions: that folk explanatory models were important for only a small proportion of the population, that diarrhea was not a highly elaborated folk illness suitable for anthropological treatment, but rather was a well known uncomplicated disease, and that mothers shared, for the most part, the physicians' explanatory model. Here again, as for worms, use of cosmopolitan health vocabulary was taken as evidence for shared explanatory models.

TABLE 15.1   Frequency Distribution of
Responses to: "What are the
main causes of diarrhea?"

Response:	Percentage
Dirty Water	25.1%
Sunken Fontanelle	0.6
Ojo	0.3
Empacho	4.3
Worms	21.0
The Rains	0.7
Amoebas	1.2
Other, combination	45.2

Source: ACT 1985:43.

That this was not the case is supported by responses to other items in that same survey. For example, when asked if "worm movements" in the body caused diarrhea, 87.6% of mothers replied that they did (ACT 1985:43).   Worm movements refers to a popular belief that the way diarrhea is produced is either by shifting the *bolsa* and interrupting the worms in the process of digestion or because the worms become so agitated that they churn the intestinal contents to mush.

However, these discrepancies in responses both within the survey and between the results of the ethnography and close-ended survey responses were not taken as meaningful (*cf.* Foster 1987a).   If the ethnographic finding could not be confirmed through survey research, the finding was ascribed to idiosyncracies of informants. This procedure guaranteed that only folk etic categories could be identified for use in the project.

One consequence of this strategy is demonstrated by the longitudinal evaluation.   After seven months of radio programming, 37.9% or 327 mothers in the PROCOMSI sample could state that dehydration referred to the loss of water that could accompany diarrhea, at the end of two years, 38.5% of mothers could provide an adequate definition. In fact, one can argue that the explanatory model used by mothers was little affected by the campaign.[8]

Does Utilization Failure Really Make a Difference? The Case of "Empacho"

The implementors could argue that these failures of utilization did not have particularly grave consequences. After all, ORS was developed to respond to dehydration, not diarrhea, and local practices are constantly changing in response to new information and medicines. Hondurans readily adopted ORS and appeared to use it successfully. A mixed strategy, utilizing cosmopolitan concepts such as dehydration and select local vocabulary and etiologies, such as *lombrices*, was used to achieve these ends. The PROCOMSI evaluation results suggest that this was clearly a good and successful compromise. However, other folk etiologies were seen as more problematic; one of these, *empacho*, was found to be especially challenging (Kendall 1984).

Empacho is a folk illness, potentially fatal, that causes great pain, loss of appetite, explosive defecation, and other generalized problems, such as subdural swelling. The disease is considered within the local Honduran explanatory model of diarrheal disease to be a practical disease, one caused by food, rather than a disease caused by witchcraft or supernatural intercession. The disease in children is considered to be serious.

Empacho can strike anyone, although it is most frequently found in children older than one year of age and adults. *Empacho* can be caused by eating the wrong foods, or eating at improper times. These actions leave a residue in the gut that must be evacuated. To encourage this evacuation, a masseur or masseuse rubs the body, drawing this residue from the extremities. A purgative is administered to clean the gut and restore normal function. The practical nature of the condition is reinforced by the status of healer. Massaging for *empacho* is not considered to be an especially esoteric craft, but a skill which anyone may learn. Since a purgative (which can greatly worsen dehydration) was involved, and because treatment for *empacho* precluded the use of ORS, the PROCOMSI Project at first attempted to promote Litrosol as an antidote for *empacho* in children. Proposed spots claimed oral rehydration therapy was a mild purgative for *empacho* that would be safe in children. Since strong saline solutions were occasionally given as purgatives to children, a message was given that oral therapy solution contained salts useful for *empacho*.

This plan elicited a wide range of negative responses. From the professional medical community they elicited strong reactions: *empacho* was a folktale that demonstrated the backwardness and ignorance of Honduran peasants. To mention the word *empacho* on the air was to lend credence to this belief. Furthermore, by promoting the use of ORS as a purgative, the use of a purgative was being acknowledged and accepted in the campaign. From others the promotion elicited an uncomfortable suspicion that the program was patronizing and trying to manipulate Honduran peasants with sophisticated mass media techniques. Especially since survey data, as presented in Table 15.1, appeared to suggest minimal association of *empacho* as a cause of diarrhea, there was little resistance to abandoning this campaign.

Here, unlike "worms," the local vocabulary could not be used. But I would like the reader to consider another significance for *empacho*. Much like Rubel's work on the epidemiology of *susto* (Rubel 1960, 1964, 1985), there may be a relationship between severe disease and *empacho*. This term may serve to identify especially serious episodes of diarrhea, episodes which should be targeted by a diarrheal disease program. Since only a very small proportion of diarrheal disease episodes will result in dehydration, only a very small number of cases of diarrhea need to be treated with ORS. Informants' statements are a window on not only a metaphorical system but also on a practical system. To dismiss these local facts as untrue because of their apparent incongruity with current scientific knowledge is not only a presumptuous act, but also one which undermines the idea of anthropology as an interpretive, as opposed to a reductionist, social science (*q.v.* Tedlock 1987).

In fact, the local model of diarrheal disease, which takes into account the child's age, nutritional status, repeated episodes, and other developmental and behavioral markers, is an important key to the nature of the diarrheal disease problem in both a biological and a cultural sense. These folk etiologies are associated with more persistent episodes of diarrhea, and the special concern they manifest in the local explanatory model also identify critical cases from a biomedical point of view, if only because their diagnosis will trigger a strong response from parents or sufferers. This, of course, is not the only reason to study these illnesses from an anthropological perspective. As diarrheal disease control programs begin to discover the importance of nutrition, prolonged diarrhea, the significance of the household as an institution, and women's special role in delivering these services, anthropology's contribution has been vindicated.

Conclusion

The PROCOMSI Project, then, successfully incorporated many findings generated through anthropology. It is an example of the way in which anthropology can be used in public health communications. However, the project fell short of utilizing the full potential of this research. Folk etic categories, or local common knowledge about popular beliefs, were incorporated into the programs in a rather superficial sense when these were considered benign. Special information the anthropologist has from observation about the physical or ecological aspects of rural households were also considered unique and appropriate contributions. However, much information provided by the ethnographic component could not be used, either because it challenged professional autonomy or because the techniques and results were considered especially esoteric. The problem, when it did occur, was not with the implementors and collaborators per se, but with the challenge posed to accepted ideas about the local perception of diarrheal diseases and goals predetermined by health authorities. Since diarrheal disease control programs can only achieve their targets through local perception and treatment of diarrheal disease, such concerns should be paramount. Instead, when these ideas challenge accepted wisdom, they are discarded.

The way results were used demonstrated a willingness to incorporate anthropology in the project to achieve predefined means. On the whole, as Hoben (1982:349 *ff.*) has pointed out, most anthropological contributions to development have focused on means. In public health as well, anthropology is conceived of as a discipline which helps raise "compliance" to a predetermined treatment regimen. Critics would argue that the anthropologist is used, not anthropology.

The following observations regarding the use and non-use of knowledge can be made based on this case study. First, anthropologists need to emphasize that their tools are systematic, appropriate, and scientific and independent of the findings of other disciplines. As Foster (1987a) argues, a structured disciplinary response to this challenge is necessary to convince our colleagues in other fields.

Second, as the example of *empacho* demonstrated, anthropologists could do more to amplify their findings by participating in all aspects of research, especially by influencing the design of surveys, and preparing our colleagues from other disciplines for what they might find. The fact that a belief (e.g., *empacho*) or a behavior (e.g., use of local healers) are reported infrequently in a survey does not mean they do not play a crucial role. Furthermore, research needs to focus not only on verifying the existence of folk etic categories but also on providing colleagues insight into the complex local response to disease that public health programs deal with.

Third, when evidence generated through anthropological research paralleled biomedical research, and could be couched in language acceptable to the biomedical disciplines, there was little difficulty in incorporating anthropological research in program planning. This is one reason why applied anthropologists must have technical training and competence in the area of application. When it deviated, however, and especially when it challenged program goals, argument by analogy failed.

The preceding observations suggest a final point. Programs which adopt a step-wise problem solving approach to determining goals are likely to prove more successful for anthropologists than those which serve pre-defined ends. It also appears that anthropological research is more acceptable to collaborators when they spend time in the field.

Notes

1. The project and the evaluation were funded by the Office of Education and the Office of Health of the Bureau for Science and Technology, United States Agency for International Development, Washington, D.C. (USAID/W), with additional support from the USAID Mission in Honduras and the Ministry of Public Health. MMHP was a seven-year multicountry project administered by the Academy for Educational Development, Washington, D.C., and evaluated by the Institute for Communications Research, Stanford University. MMHP is the precursor for the current HEALTHCOM project sponsored by USAID and administered by the Academy for Educational Development. Honduras was the first country site for the MMHP project.

2. The Ministry of Health had been convinced of the efficacy of ORS in clinical settings during a hospital trial conducted in a pre-project visit, and was willing to accept the results of Evaluation PROCOMSI as a measure of the field intervention's success. In 1982, the progress of the project was independently evaluated by the Ministry and the Pan American Health Organization using standard WHO/CDD format. The results of the evaluation are discussed in Kendall (1988).

3. Social marketing is the application of conventional advertising techniques to the promotion of a social good, either a product or a behavior. The term often elicits a strong reaction, since health care in rural areas of developing countries is almost always the domain of the public sector, and many marketing efforts, whether the promotion of infant formula, cigarettes, bottled beverages or snack foods, are often deleterious to health. This compound term, however, defines a different kind of marketing. The term "social" would appear to describe a paradox for marketeers.

4. Message and print material pre-testing in the target population constituted the largest component of this evaluation. Additionally, convenience samples of mothers would be polled during the campaign. Evaluation PROCOMSI field workers provided another source of information about the community's reaction to the campaign.

5. The Office of Education, USAID, was the originator and designer of the project. Key staff involved in design and selection of contractors were trained in Communications Research, a field which is highly quantitative and which draws heavily from social psychology. This fact played an important role in the development of the project and the utilization of anthropology.

6. Los Dolores was visited by a Guatemalan anthropologist, Lic. Liza Vielman. This site was part of the survey evaluation. Ms. Vielman conducted research concerning beliefs and practices related to diarrheal disease treatment and local response to the presence of field workers.

7. This summary is paraphrased from the Executive Summary of "The Mass Media and Health Practices Evaluation in Honduras: Findings from the First Two Years." Applied Communication Technology, Palo Alto; June 1985.

8. For example, although there was some concordance between the "germ theory of disease" and the local concept of *bichos*, informants in the ethnographic study reported that *bichos*--little small things--can only live in the warmth of the body, and when they are defecated they die. That is why, they continued, feces could be handled and baby bottoms cleaned without concern for diarrheal disease being transmitted.

The semantic difficulties with the term "bichos," or the apparent germ theory of disease discovered in the informant response "dirty water," is an example of "researcher effect" reading into a datum a convenient interpretation. This is not only a problem for non-anthropologists. Short-term "rapid-assessments" also suffer from this difficulty, and may only prove worthwhile if the anthropologists conducting the research are thoroughly familiar with a locale from previous research.

The difficulty of inducing health behavior change through the promotion of cosmopolitan beliefs and the apparent synergism between local and cosmopolitan beliefs have led health educators to call for the incorporation of these beliefs in programs, as was achieved in the PROCOMSI Project. However, this incorporation is not without risk. In Jocotan, Guatemala, Chorti Maya informants reported that *bichos*--tiny little animals that live in dirt--were the spirit companions of barnyard animals. Whereas for Ladino Hondurans *bichos* were animate, biological organisms with physical properties that lent them to use in the PROCOMSI Project, for Chorti informants they were spiritual entities with properties that derived from a very different domain. These anecdotes demonstrate not only the variety of local interpretations of a single term "bicho" which was glossed as "germ" in the PROCOMSI Project, but also the danger of collecting anecdotes and traditional beliefs from here and there, even if they are the product of "ethnographic surveys." Out of context, like an archaeological relic stolen from a site, they lose much of their power to information, and become curiosities, as Tedlock (1987) has demonstrated.

16

Trends in Applied Anthropology and Public Policy: Concluding Remarks

Lucy M. Cohen

How have things gone between the rich and the poor in the 1980s, and how have public policy directives influenced the lives of the people among whom anthropologists in this volume worked?

It appears that private and public behavior are separable in our minds. A possibly apocryphal story relates that President Ronald Reagan left a meeting about the national budget to be photographed for an Easter Seals poster. He was moved by the problem of the crippled child who joined him and said afterward that he would have done anything to help her. "Mr. President," someone remarked, "you have just cut from the budget $350 million for children like her" (Schorr 1986:1).

The case studies in this volume show how anthropologists have made important contributions to policy and to the advancement of knowledge about problems of individuals and communities in diverse cultures. As we approach the year 2000, we should identify processes through which anthropology does, in fact, assist the work of those involved in making policy--the decision makers, as well as citizens and special interest groups. We have come of age in contributing to policy deliberations and with this awakening, we should re-examine the value dimensions and dilemmas that influence our knowledge and the people among whom we choose to work, their problems, and the policies involved.

Richard Titmuss emphasizes that at every stage in the policy process we should be aware that to become involved in social policy is to participate in issues of moral and political values. He states that when we concern ourselves with the knowledge upon which social policy is based, we need to ask "whose social policy." Policy refers to the "principles that govern action directed towards given ends." The concept refers to "action about means as well as ends and it therefore implies change and changing situations" (Titmuss 1974:23-24).[1]

Throughout this volume, references have been made to knowledge utilization in the policy process--the methods and the impacts. Contributors were invited to outline principles underlying the use of anthropology which could lead us toward developing a theory of practice. In offering concluding comments, I would like to suggest that we address the concerns posed by Titmuss which focus on the values and the contexts within which policy deliberations take place. We should ask, "How have things gone between the rich and the poor in the 1980s, and how have public policy directives influenced the lives of the people among whom anthropologists in this volume worked?"

The settings for action were systems of health, mental health and welfare, networks of urban communities, legislative and judicial offices, and rural communities. In most cases, the authors had maintained long-term involvement with the people, the problem area, and the setting. Theirs were not the results of short term visits to unknown foreign communities, to street corners of our inner cities, or to institutions. Most authors were employed by public agencies, non-profit organizations, and international agencies, rather than the for-profit sectors. Within these contexts, their work was frequently conducted in response to legislative and policy mandates within which problems and needs were addressed.

Those who had worked in the United States were concerned to a large extent with populations whose members have been excluded increasingly from major social and medical programs. The programs included among others, mothers with children "at-risk," the long-term physically and mentally disabled, and the frail elderly, who have become known as the "bad risks" of the 1980s in American society. These groups have been the casualties of changing values and social structures. They are the "moneylosers" of the growing, private profit-making services in our nation (Titmuss 1974:42-43).[2]

Abramovitz (1986) points out that since 1981, privatization, "the placing of public tasks in private hands" has been part of a broad strategy to cope with the economic crisis in our midst. Privatization results from the belief that "business and industry can do a better and cheaper job than government, whether in building weapons, running city buses, or delivering social services." This author states further that under the ideology of the Reagan government, "arguments for privatization on the grounds of efficiency have been used to rationalize its efforts to dismantle social programs, to reverse employment gains made by women, minorities and the poor, and to create even greater investment opportunities for private enterprises" (Abramovitz 1986:257-258).

The anthropologists in this volume who had worked in international settings followed an established legacy in American anthropology of applied anthropological work in health and development. The commitment of sponsoring agencies was clear in policy statements concerned with populations and their problems. For example, in 1977 the World Health Organization's governing body resolved that the main target of governments and the Organization should be that by the year 2000 all the people of the world were to attain a level of health to permit them to lead a socially and economically productive life. This has become known as "Health for All by the Year 2000" (Mahler 1988:72). The Alma-Ata Health Conference of 1978, jointly sponsored by WHO and UNICEF further declared that primary health care is crucial for the attainment of health for all by the year 2000. It emphasized that member States individually were to formulate the national strategies to reach that goal and to cooperate in regional and global strategies. Mahler (1988:75) notes, furthermore, that in 1981, the WHO World Health Assembly approved as a goal the immunization by 1990 of all the children in the world against the six major infectious diseases of childhood: diphtheria, pertussis, tetanus, measles, poliomyelitis, and tuberculosis.[3] Thus, work in the evaluation of diarrheal control programs took place within a context in which international, national and local policy objectives shaped the changing scene of program policy and development.

Overall, the research presented in this volume contributed to an understanding of the nature and extent of problems which required policy-relevant deliberations and action. George Weber (1984:216) describes the process of incorporating knowledge in the policy development process as one which includes articulation and understanding of a problem, formulation and implementation of policy, conduct of evaluation studies, and the provision of feedback for policy reformulation. In roles as consultants, researchers and evaluators, the authors contributed to a determination of policy-making goals before and after programs were implemented. This is crucial for as Weber (1984:221) points out, policy formation and reformulation is a "daily, on-going activity" and it is in the domain of various government workers, committees, staff, and constituency groups. It involves offering leadership and promoting compromises and agreements among contending groups.

Moreover, in roles as advocates, a number of the authors demonstrated that applied anthropologists today stand ready to serve not only as contributors to knowledge but as professionals whose critical judgments and commitments lead to an active participation in policy-making itself. Some were members of policy-making boards, commissions and other committees. Others were key advisors to members of legislative and executive branches of local government or as experts for the judiciary. From these vantage points, they have become active participants in the political process which facilitates change.

Stephen and Jean Schensul (1978:133) describe advocacy as "the use of professional skills and information to facilitate representation and participation of a specific group in societal plans and programs which affect them." According to these authors, the advocacy approach requires the practitioner to take a value-explicit position with a group and to facilitate rather than to impose direction and action upon members. The Schensuls emphasized that while most anthropologists lacked the required orientation, there was great need for advocacy. The awakening of social concerns and activism of the 1960s led to the view that advocacy was a politically controversial, professionally daring, and a conceptually divergent practice modality. The Schensuls (1978:162) hoped that as more anthropologists became advocates, it would be increasingly possible to identify the concepts, methods, and experiences underlying such activities.

The cases presented by L. Girdner, M. Iris, M. Poland and P. Giblin, J. Gilbert, and J. Wood show that advocacy has now become an established approach in translating knowledge into policy-relevant terms. These authors were deeply involved with social concerns *within* major systems of welfare, law, and government in order to bring about change.

Linda Girdner's contributions to the body of policies and practices relating to child custody disputes between divorcing and divorced parents took place within the interstices of the judicial and human service institutions. Her knowledge was derived from experiences in research and in practice among the parties involved in mediation and settlement. She has participated in the training of practitioners and in collaborative work with representatives of the courts. Her critical reflections about research and practice have contributed to her understanding of policy-relevant information so that today, she is recognized as a major contributor to a national movement in family policy.

Madelyn Iris' evaluation of a model guardianship project for the elderly had built-in components of service, research, and public policy. Over a period of five years, she worked in research and evaluation roles, as well as in policy anallysis. The beneficiaries of this research were not only the elderly but the social service administrators and workers. Her reports, interviews, and in-service training have provided the basis for the advocacy work to which the sponsoring agencies have now committed themselves on behalf of the frail elderly.

In addressing problems of infant mortality in Detroit, M. Poland and P. Giblin worked as researchers but Poland also served on a city-wide Health Promotion Coalition. Collaboration between university, local, and state agencies resulted in the development of a paraprofessional outreach program. Thus, in addition to providing needed documentation on the problems of infant mortality and morbidity, the authors actively strengthened linkages among various community segments which were needed to set policy in action.

Having spent a decade in research among Mexican Americans, Jean Gilbert emphasized that it is largely through our participation in policy-making roles that we can get data to those most able to use it in the human services. These include, among others, the users themselves, providers, administrators, and policy makers. Her emic perspective of the cultures of human service agencies has enabled her to serve on numerous occasions as a major source of information for needed policy directives among Mexican American populations at local, regional and national levels. Gilbert views applied anthropology as an ongoing process in which problem-oriented research offers a basis for policy and action.

John Wood's advocacy in the offices and halls of Congress on behalf of the Navajos at Big Mountain, Arizona, led him to recommend the need to study those whom we try to influence, as well as client communities. Lewis Anthony Dexter's (1970) study of elites in Congress and Jack Weatherford's (1985) views of the "tribes" on the Hill suggest innovative paths to pursue in such research. As advocates, moreover, anthropologists should be prepared to accept the responsibilities of appointed and elected offices. Indeed, one of the positive outcomes of the knowledge generated by applied anthropological work should be a recognition of our abilities to assume direct positions of influence as well as to influence others.

Although each of these authors has worked with different problems, all shared one characteristic: each stepped in to contribute and participate in advocacy for specific policies, they viewed the issue in its specific context, and identified the basic assumptions which have shaped it. The authors showed that advocacy requires the ability to shift perspectives with respect to action and the amelioration of human problems. It calls for the ability to be close to as well as to engage in "distancing" as they conducted a critical analysis of issues. Thus, anthropologists who draw on advocacy as a model oriented to change are not simply "activists" or "adversaries." They understand, furthermore, that to increase knowledge of social problems does not in and of itself result in greater equity or social justice.

This process of critical analysis was illustrated, in particular, by Judith Greenwood's analysis of needs in planning statewide medical services to the disabled in West Virginia. In her case history, Greenwood described the political processes through which a successful system of planning for the improvement of medical services to disabled individuals took place. West Virginia is the state with the highest percentage of work-disabled citizens in the nation. The model of change she followed was based on organizational and institutional politics rather than pressure group politics. She presented a detailed analysis of the political process involved in long-range planning and valuable documentation on the compromises and agreements made by contending groups. Her emphasis, however, was on the importance of understanding the assumptions upon which the concept of need is based.

Richard Titmuss (1987:43) emphasizes that socially recognized needs, upon which social policy and social services are based, change with time and over the life of societies. Change is dependent on prevailing notions of what constitutes need and service and in what circumstances and to what extent needs should be met. Greenwood points out that the process of needs assessment in West Virginia took place by understanding how medical rehabilitation is defined and how the need for medical rehabilitation services could be established. The issue could not be addressed without understanding contrasting views labelled as "conservative" versus "liberal" estimation of the need for services. Disabled persons who required *long term* support services for maintenance of "functional capacity" were not to be classified as persons eligible for medical rehabilitation. Only selected disabling conditions known to need *in-patient* rehabilitation services were to be considered, namely spinal cord injury, stroke and head injury, rheumatoid disease, orthopedic conditions, and myocardial infarction. Over the years, however, the original concepts changed as different interest groups became involved, and as new statutory requirements for state health planning were implemented.

Not all cases, however, can be addressed through negotiation strategies which lead to consensus within a system. W.K. Barger and Ernesto Reza's community action research on behalf of the United Farm Worker movement in California suggests that participatory action research has become an important model for the work of anthropologists concerned specifically with the reform of public policy.

Anton de Schutter (1981:172-180) states that in participatory research, the goals are not to produce descriptions of the states of marginality, dependency, or other characteristics of oppressed populations. The objective is to obtain conjointly with the marginal groups, the knowledge necessary to identify actions which are needed in order to accomplish the transformations which lead to comprehensive social development. Explanations of social processes which are sought are based on concrete reality and the common sense understandings of those who are assumed to best know this reality, those who are living it.

To engage in this conjoint work, researchers need an awareness of the historic forces which contribute to the conditions being investigated. The movements to unionize farm workers in California have engendered major conflicts between the political forces of agri-business and their allies, and the farm workers. Ernesto Galarza's (1977) historic analysis contributes to an understanding of the background context within which Barger and Reza's research has taken place.

By the early 1950s, corporate farmers had organized the "bracero" system of labor as a deterrent to unionization. This involved contracting Mexican citizens for employment in the United States. Public Law 78 enacted by Congress in 1951 gave this system federal sanction to mobilize what appeared to be inexhaustible manpower from Mexico. The accounts that emerged from the experiences of union organizers in the 1950s and early 1960s revealed that support for corporation agriculture was maintained by interlocking intellectual and political interests, state and federal policies, universities, the rural press, and international diplomacy. Galarza (1977:91) quoted a college administrator who stated that the research and development efforts of a major college of agriculture in California were designed "to serve adequately the agriculture of a highly developed commercial civilization such as characterizes California today," and its maintenance "on the highest profitable basis in the face of surpluses."

Cast against these conflicts, Barger and Reza's findings show that in the 1980s, farm workers continue to support the United Farm Worker movement. Their research has contributed to public education and political mobilization for major reforms in the conditions of these laborers. Few anthropologists have conducted research in this field. The authors have contributed to the beginning of a more equitable distribution of research resources to match the marketing studies which agri-business and state politicians have used to support their partisan views.

Despite the studies which have illuminated policy-oriented advocacy, assessment of needs, and reform-oriented policy, applied anthropologists cannot avoid encounters with the contradictions which have impact on a public understanding of policy. This is evident in

Margaret Boone's case of maternal and infant health policy change in Washington, D.C. Boone reported that over the years since her original infant mortality research in 1979-1980, there has been a shift among policy makers from a broad interest in the social and cultural context within which poor Black women live, to the perspective which emphasizes "life style" factors and individual responsibility for health behavior.

Anthropologists must meet the challenge presented by a model based on individual consciousness of personal failure and which reduces public responsibility for human services. We must understand the ideological forces which support such a program (Titmuss 1974:52-54). As Jeannine Coreil et al. (1985:431) have pointed out, in our present use of the life style concept, the underlying notion is that "personal habits are discrete and independently modifiable, and that individuals can voluntarily choose to alter such behaviors." Consequently, they argue, little if any attention is given to altering the larger society in which individuals participate. Behaviors such as weight control and diet, exercise, and stress management are treated as "isolated elements, divorced from their social context and bereft of the meaning which derives from the larger cultural fabric."

At the same time however, this approach also serves as a low-cost solution proposed by public officials who, in the face of lower funding, are searching for ways to control expenditures in health and human services. It is essential that anthropologists involved in policy-making identify the assumptions which dominate the discussions regarding the health and welfare of poor women and their families. With this understanding anthropologists are then in a position to actively participate in the debate about changing responsibility for medical care.

In mental health settings, anthropologists have also addressed the changing ideologies within institutional and community contexts. Models based on alliances and collaboration offer avenues for influencing policy, as illustrated by the present contributions of D. R. Scheinfeld and his colleagues and by Max Drake. There has been a history of anthropological involvement in clinical settings in order to have impact on the ways of work of designated staff, as described by Marion Pearsall and Sue Kern in their article, "Nursing Services and the Collaborative Process: A Case Study." Pearsall and Kern (1967:243-244) indicated that while collaboration had increased, only rarely did we study collaborative situations as sociocultural systems with careers of their own. Scheinfeld and his colleagues emphasize that it is important for anthropologists to participate in "experience near" approaches through which they can understand negative emotions of those among whom they establish collaborative alliances.

Max Drake's evaluative research on the processes of deinstitutionalization of the mentally ill and disabled in two western states emphasizes the importance of collaboration and involvement with those who have a formal "stake" in the results. His findings, together with those of a number of other authors in this volume, underline the necessity of broadening the network of collaborators in formal organizations in order to insure that a maximum use is made of anthropology. Indeed, participation in the institutions and communities where mental health ideologies are in the processes of transformation opens an avenue for the involvement of anthropologists not only with those in formal positions of power but also with those who are part of the "informal" sector--the powerless and hidden caregivers. Clients, overlooked staff members such as night shift admitting officers, and support personnel, as, for example, the bus drivers who transport persons in time of crises. All are vital in the informal systems of caregiving and power. All have important stakes to play in policy implementation.

Collaboration at the international level has also been a long-standing tradition of American anthropological research. This is well illustrated through the cases here presented by Carl Kendall and K. and B. DeWalt in Honduras, J. Coreil in Haiti, and Dennis Warren in Ghana. These researchers document changing aspects of interorganizational collaboration within which anthropologists have contributed to the implementation of policy. Notwithstanding the differences among representatives of organizations and disciplines, the opportunity for success of policy implementation depends, to some extent, on a clear commitment to the common good as well as on an understanding of the political processes within and among representatives of these organizations.

Carl Kendall's analysis of participation in a multiple intervention and evaluation project of an Oral Rehydration Therapy program project in South Central Honduras contributed to an understanding of the way in which anthropology is used in public health communications. The challenge which remains, nevertheless, is to find new ways to incorporate native models of children's health and illness in the standard paradigms of health promotion and treatment.

The Honduras research undertaken by the DeWalts points to the importance of giving attention to interdisciplinary dynamics within the home-sponsoring institution and their impact on the goals and objectives of a program undertaken in a foreign country. As anthropologists from a major North American Land Grant university, the DeWalts had the advantage of working with agrobiological scientists devoted to agricultural research. This team became part of a Collaborative Research Support Project (CRSP) sponsored by the International Sorghum and Millet Project. Anthropological research findings were expected to contribute to an understanding of linkages between agricultural production and nutritional status and to have impact on resource-poor families. The DeWalts concluded that a major problem which needs to be addressed was the contrasts in assumptions and priorities of the scientists involved. While the anthropologists had a long-term commitment to field research in foreign areas, the agrobiological scientists emphasized that under the mission of their home Land Grant university, their first obligation was to their College of Agriculture and Experiment Station at home which they believed was established to benefit local farmers in a state and not those in foreign countries.

Work on the evaluation of diarrheal control programs in Haiti and in Honduras took place also within a context shaped by local, national and international policy objectives. In the 1980-1985 period, Haiti had a reported life expectancy at birth of 52.7 years, the second lowest of all nations in the Americas, while Honduras had a reported life expectancy of 58.8, the third lowest (*Organizacion Panamericana de la Salud* 1984).

In discussion about utilization of the findings in these programs, Coreil gives us the benefit of her experience by indicating the problems of implementing the findings of research conducted under difficult circumstances. The more important obstacles in the Haitian case were the fragmentation of program management and the disruptive political situation within the country, as well as the large number of contemporaneous Oral Rehydration Therapy studies "competing" for attention, which Coreil described as "evaluation overkill." It was difficult, if not impossible to establish meaningful utilization linkages. Coreil's honest appraisal of these obstacles is important particularly in light of the fact that the problem of agency competition is not unique to the Haitian circumstances.

The problems of competition between donor agencies has results which may not be beneficial to host countries, as George Foster (1987b:1045-1046) indicates. He states that the so-called abundance of foreign aid in some countries is far from being an unmixed blessing. Help to communities is filtered through intermediate clients, e.g., the health ministries and services of the receiving countries. These clients are limited in number in proportion to the members of the community; there may not be a sufficient number to satisfy the demands of all of the international agencies involved. Thus, the problems with collaboration and utilization of findings result not only from conflicts internal to the researcher's home institution or with the nation being served, but also some external difficulties arising from the uncoordinated and competing efforts of multilateral, binational, and private non-governmental organizations.

Dennis Warren's work on the use of indigenous healers in Ghana, which spans a period of 20 years, clearly points to the cumulative nature of the process of translation of anthropology into policy development and implementation. His contributions to ethnoscientific methodology and to an understanding of indigenous knowledge systems demonstrate how it is necessary to work within the realities of the continuous changes of personnel at national and international levels, a reality which he describes as a fact of bureaucratic life.

Warren's research helps to clarify discussion in the field of applied anthropology about the time-effectiveness or time constraints in policy-relevant research. Problem-focused, short term research is a *sine qua non* among anthropologists involved in policy oriented advocacy. Short term assessments are cast within an ideological framework, a plan, and an articulated strategy, but they are conducted with commitment to long-term investment in the transformation of social reality. Warren's work and that of most contributors to this volume offer clear testimony of this commitment.

This volume expands our understanding of applied anthropology and offers many insights into the implications of this knowledge for policy. The articles show that in the 1970s and 1980s anthropology has become firmly established in a variety of work settings.

Given this trend, I would suggest that the careers of applied anthropologists begin to emerge during the period of graduate study, incorporating concepts and problems drawn from both academic and field experience. It therefore behooves us as educators and supervisors of field work, where learning also takes place, to give careful attention to the processes through which applied anthropology becomes the main focus of the student. We need to understand the stages of development as the student moves through the various phases of training culminating in graduation and continuing professional growth.

Although we have concerned ourselves with issues of program development, policy impact, and strategies through which anthropology can be used in action, there is need to pinpoint the ways in which mentors and others who serve as role models contribute to the formation of those who become applied anthropologists. Certainly, the process through which anthropologists incorporate research and action drawing on models of collaboration and advocacy involves a complex set of responsibilities which merits our full attention.

Notes

1. The writer gratefully acknowledges comments from Professor Kathleen Jones, Department of Social Policy and Social Work, University of York, England, on the life and contributions of Richard Titmuss to the development of British social policy and social administration.

2. See also Schorr 1986:79-113.

3. "Declaration of Alma-Ata" in *Primary Health Care*: Report of the International Conference on Primary Health Care, Alma-Ata, U.S.S.R., 6-12, September 1978. Jointly sponsored by the World Health Organization and the United Nations Children Fund. Geneva: World Health Organization, 1978.

Bibliography

Abramovitz, Mimi. 1986. The Privatization of the Welfare State: A Review. *Social Work* 31 (July-August).

ACT. 1985. *The Mass Media and Health Practices Evaluation in Honduras: A Report of the Major Findings.* Palo Alto, CA: Applied Communication Technology.

Adelski, M. Elizabeth. 1983. The Role of Cotton in the Agricultural System of Southern Honduras. *Practicing Anthropology* 5(3):14,18.

Ademuwagun, Z., J.A.A. Ayoade, D.M. Warren, and I. Harrison (eds.). 1979. *African Therapeutic Systems.* Los Angeles: Crossroads Press.

AED. 1980. *Implementation Plan: Honduras.* Academy for Educational Development.

Alcocer, Anthony, and M. Jean Gilbert. 1979. *Drinking Practices and Alcohol-related Problems of Spanish Speaking Persons in Three California Locales.* Sacramento: California Office of Alcohol and Drug Programs.

Alkin, Marvin. 1985. *A Guide for Evaluation Decision Makers.* Beverly Hills, CA: Sage.

Alkin, Marvin, Richard Daillak, and Peter White. 1979. *Using Evaluations.* Beverly Hills, CA: Sage.

Allman, James, Gerald Lerebours, and Jon E. Rohde. 1985. Lessons Learned in Implementing and Evaluating the National ORT Program in Haiti. Paper presented at the American Public Health Association Meetings, November 17-21, Washington, D.C.

American Bar Association. 1988. The Commission on Legal Problems of the Elderly. Recommendation of the National Guardianship Symposium. Wingspread, Racine, Wisconsin.

Angrosino, Michael V. 1976. The Evolution of the New Applied Anthropology. In *Do Applied Anthropologists Apply Anthropology?* Michael V. Angrosino, ed. Athens: University of Georgia Press.

Arthur, Anne. 1986. *De Nouvelles Bases Pour Le Serum Oral. Proposition d'un Plan de Marketing et de Communication Susceptible a Encourager l'Utilisation du Serum Oral en Haiti.* Port-au-Prince: Corbin Advertising Haiti S.A.

Bakersfield Californian. 1984. Stirling Took Ride to Hearing From Grower's Lawyer: Ethical Questions Arise in Wake of ALRB Counsel's Disclosure. *Bakersville Californian* (April 29): A2.

————. 1985. UFW Seen As Best Hope For Farmworkers in Kerne, Tulare. *Bakersfield Californian* (January 20):84.

Ballard, Steven C., and Thomas E. James. 1983. Participatory Research and Utilization in the Technology Assessment Process. *Knowledge* 4(3):409-427.

Barger, W.K. 1977. Culture Change and Psychosocial Adjustment. *American Ethnologist* 4:471-495.

————. 1982. Cultural Adaptation. *Anthropology and Humanism Quarterly* 7(2-3):17-21.

————. 1987. California Public Endorses the United Farm Workers. *La Red* 105:4-6.

Barger, W.K., and Ain Haas. 1983 Public Attitudes Toward Mexican-American Farmworkers in the Midwest. *La Red* 63:2-4.

Barger, W.K., and Ernesto Reza. 1984a. Views of Midwestern Farmworkers Concerning the Farm Labor Movement. *La Red* 78:2-7.

————. 1984b. Midwestern Farmworkers Support the Farm Labor Movement. *Science for the People* 16(5):11-15.

————. 1985a. Processes in Applied Sociocultural Change and the Farmworker Movement in the Midwest. *Human Organization* 44(3):268-283.

————. 1985b. Views of California Farmworkers Regarding the Farm Labor Movement. *La Red* 91:3-5.

————. 1987. Sociocultural Change and Community Action: The Farmworker Movement in the Midwest. In *Collaborative Research and Social Change.* Donald D. Stull and Jean J. Schensul, eds. Boulder: Westview Press.

Barger, W.K., and Susan Sutton. 1980. Personal Abilities in Applied Work and Training Programs in Anthropology. *Practicing Anthropology* 2(3):6-7, 24-25.

Barger, W.K., and Tham Van Truong. 1978. Community Action Work Among the Vietnamese. *Human Organization* 37(1):95-100.

Barnes, J.A. 1972. *Social Networks.* Addison-Wesley Module in Anthropology. No. 26.

Barnett, H.G. 1956. *Anthropology in Administration.* New York: Harper and Row.

Bernard, H. Russell. 1974. Scientists and Policy Makers: An Ethnography of Communication. *Human Organization* 33(3):261-276.

Bernard, H. Russell. (ed.). 1988. *Research Methods in Cultural Anthropology.* Newbury Park, CA: Sage.

Berreman, Gerald D. 1973. The Social Responsibility of the Anthropologist. In *To See Ourselves.* Thomas Weaver, ed. Glenview, IL: Scott Foresman.

Beyer, Janice M., and Harrison M. Trice. 1982. The Utilization Process: A Conceptual Framework and Synthesis of Empirical Findings. *Administrative Science Quarterly* 27:591-622.

Boone, Margaret S. 1982. A Socio-Medical Study of Infant Mortality Among Disadvantaged Blacks. *Human Organization* 41(3):227-236.

————. 1985a. Social and Cultural Factors in the Etiology of Low-Birthweight Among Disadvantaged Blacks. *Social Science and Medicine* 20(10):1001-1011.

————. 1985b. Policy and Praxis: Anthropology and the Domestic Health Policy Arena. In *The Training Manual in Medical Anthropology.* Carole E. Hill, ed. Pp. 111-129. Washington, D.C.: American Anthropological Association Special Publication No. 18.

————. 1989. *Capital Crime: Black Infant Mortality in Washington, D.C.* Newbury Park, CA: Sage.

Booth, Elizabeth Mills, and Chloe O'Gara. 1984. *Percentages or Perspective: A Comparison of Quantitative and Qualitative Research.* Field Notes #12, Mass Media and Health Practices.

Boyer, Jefferson. 1983. *Agrarian Capitalism and Peasant Praxis in Southern Honduras.* Ann Arbor, MI: University Microfilms. Ph.D. dissertation.

Brokensha, David, D.M. Warren, and O. Werner (eds.). 1980. *Indigenous Knowledge Systems and Development.* Lanham, MD: University Press of America.

Bruner, Edward. 1986. Experience and Its Expressions. In *The Anthropology of Experience.* V. Turner and E. Bruner, eds. Pp. 3-30. Urbana, IL: University of Illinois Press.

Bryk, Anthony S. (ed.) 1983. *Stakeholder-Based Evaluation.* San Francisco: Jossey Bass.

Burnaway, Michael. 1976. Functions and Reproduction of Migrant Labor. *American Journal of Sociology* 81:1050-1087.

Burry, James. 1984. *Synthesis of the Evaluation Use Literature. NIE Grant Report.* Los Angeles, CA: UCLA Center for the Study of Evaluation.

Caplan, Nathan. 1976. "Social Research and National Policy: What Gets Used, By Whom, For What Purposes, and With What Effects?" *International Social Science Journal* 28(1):187-94.

————. 1977. A Minimal Set of Conditions Necessary for the Utilization of Social Science Knowledge in Policy Formulation at the National Level. In *Using Social Research in Public Policy Making.* Carol H. Weiss, ed. Pp. 183-198. Lexington, MA: D.C. Heath.

Caplan, Nathan, Andrea Morrison, and Russell J. Stambaugh. 1975. *The Use of Social Science Knowledge in Policy Decisions at the National Level.* Ann Arbor, MI: Institute for Social Research, University of Michigan.

Catholic Universe Bulletin. 1984. Chavez Renews Grape Boycott, Old Alliances. *Catholic Universe Bulletin* (November 9):17.

Cayemittes, Michel, and William Ward. 1985. *Promotion of Oral Rehydration Therapy in Petit Goave.* Final Report, Pricor Project, Port-au-Prince.

Chambers, Erve. 1977. Policy Research at the Local Level. *Human Organization* 36(4):418-421.

————. 1985. *Applied Anthropology: A Practical Guide.* Englewood Cliffs: Prentice-Hall.

Chambers, Erve, and M.G. Trend. 1981. Fieldwork Ethics in Policy-Oriented Research. *American Anthropologist* 83(3):626-628.

Chambers, Robert. 1983. *Rural Development: Putting the Last First.* London: Longman.

Chavez, Cesar. 1985. Deukmejian Has a Bitter Crop for Farm Workers. *Philadelphia Enquirer* (July 10):9A.

Clem, Harry. 1987. Letter of reference written for Linda Girdner, 3/10/87.

Cochrane, Glynn. 1971. *Development Anthropology.* New York: Oxford University Press.

————. 1977. Social Inputs for Project Appraisal. *International Development Review/Focus* 19 (2):9-12.

————. 1979. *The Cultural Appraisal of Development Projects.* New York: Praeger.

————. 1980. Policy Studies and Anthropology. *Current Anthropology* 21(4):445-458, and 21(5):682-684.

Coreil, Jeannine. 1985. *Community Acceptance of Oral Rehydration Therapy in Haiti.* Final Report Project No. 107USA4, Pan American Health Organization, Washington, D.C.

————. 1988. Innovation Among Haitian Healers: The Adoption of Oral Rehydration Therapy. *Human Organization* 47 (1):48-57.

Coreil, Jeannine, and Eddy Genece. 1988. Adoption of Oral Rehydration Therapy Among Haitian Mothers. *Social Science and Medicine* 27 (1):87-96.

Coreil, Jeannine, Jeffrey Levin, and E. Gartly Jaco. 1985. Life Style--An Emergent Concept in the Sociomedical Sciences. *Culture, Medicine and Psychiatry* 9 (4).

Coreil, Jeannine, and Dennis Mull (eds.). 1988. Anthropological Studies of Diarrheal Illness. Special issue of *Social Science and Medicine* 27 (1).

Craddock, Brian R. 1979. *Farmworker Protective Laws.* Austin: Motivation Education and Training, Inc.

Davidson, Judith R. 1987. The Delivery of Rural Reproductive Medicine. In *Anthropological Praxis.* Robert M. Wulff and Shirley J. Fiske, eds. Pp. 262-272. Boulder: Westview Press.

Davis, Howard R., and Susan E. Salasin. 1975. The Utilization of Evaluation. In *Handbook of Evaluation Research.* E. Struening and M. Guttentag, eds. Vol. 1. Pp. 621-666. Beverly Hills, CA: Sage.

Davis, Nancy Y., R.P. McConchie, and D.R. Stevenson. 1987. *Research and Consulting as a Business.* NAPA Bulletin 4. Washington, D.C.: National Association for the Practice of Anthropology.

Dawson, Judith A., and Joseph J. D'Amico. 1985. Involving Program Staff in Evaluation Studies: A Strategy for Increasing Information Use and Enriching the Data Base. *Evaluation Review* 9(2):173-188.

del Prado, O.N. 1973. *Kuyo Chico.* Chicago: University of Chicago Press.

DeLoria, Dennis, and Geraldine Kearse Brookins. 1982. The Evaluation Report: A Weak Link to Policy. In *Learning From Experience: Evaluating Early Childhood Demonstration Programs.* J.R. Travers and R.J. Light, eds. Pp. 254-271. National Academy Press.

Denny, William M. 1979. Participant Citizenship in a Marginal Group: Union Mobilization of California Farmworkers. *American Journal of Political Science* 23:330-337.

de Schutter, Anton. 1981. Investigacion Participativa Una Opcion Metodologica Para la Educacion de Adultos. Patzcuaro Michoacan: CREFAL.

Desse, Ginette. 1984. Utilization du Serum Oral et Impact de la Politique de Communication du Programme National de Lutte Contre la Diarrhee. Unpublished report, Port-au-Prince.

DeWalt, Billie R. 1979. *Modernization in a Mexican Ejido: A Study in Economic Adaptation.* New York: Cambridge University Press.

————. 1983. The Cattle Are Eating the Forest. *Bulletin of the Atomic Scientists* 39:18-23.

————. 1985. Anthropology, Sociology and Farming Systems Research. *Human Organization* 44:106-14.

————. 1986. Economic Assistance in Central America: Development or Impoverishment. *Cultural Survival Quarterly* 10:14-18.

————. 1988. Halfway There: Social Science *in* Agricultural Development and the Social Science *of* Agricultural Development. *Human Organization* 47(4):343-353.

DeWalt, Billie R., and Sara Alexander. 1983. The Dynamics of Cropping Systems in Pespire, Southern Honduras. *Practicing Anthropology* 5(3):11,13.

DeWalt, Billie R., and K.M. DeWalt. 1982. *Socioeconomic Constraints to the Production, Distribution and Consumption of Sorghum in Southern Honduras.* INTSORMIL, Farming Systems Research in Southern Honduras. Report No. 1. University of Kentucky College of Agriculture: Lexington, KY.

————. 1985. El Contexto Socioeconomico para la Investigacion sobre el Sorgo en el Sur de Honduras. In *El Sorgo en Sistemas de Produccion en America Latina.* C. Paul and B.R. DeWalt, eds. Mexico: INTSORMIL/CIMMYT.

DeWalt, Billie R., and Susan Duda. 1985. Farming Systems Research in Southern Honduras. In *Fighting Hunger with Research.* Judy F. Winn, ed. Pp. 184-92. INTSORMIL: University of Nebraska.

DeWalt, K.M. 1981. Diet as Adaptation: The Search for Nutritional Strategies. *Federation Proceedings* 40:2606-2610.

————. 1983a. *Nutritional Strategies and Agricultural Change.* Ann Arbor: UMI Research Press.

————. 1983b. Usos del Sorgo en Honduras: El Caso de Pespire. *Proceedings of the Grain Quality Workshop for Latin American.* INTSORMIL, INIA, ICRISAT.

————. 1984. Nutritional Strategies and Farming Systems Research in Southern Honduras: The International Sorghum and Millet Project (INTSORMIL). In *Animals in the Farming System: Proceedings of the Farming Systems Research Symposium.* C.B. Flora, Manhattan, Kansas: Kansas State University.

————. 1985a. El Lugar de la Investigacion en Sistemas de Cultivos en el Tratamiento de Asuntos del Sorgo como Alimento Humano. In *El Sorgo en Sistemas de Produccion en America Latina.* C. Paul and B.R. DeWalt, eds. Mexico: INTSORMIL / CIMMYT.

————. 1985b. Sorghum Consumption and Diet in Southern Honduras. In *INTSORMIL: Fighting Hunger with Research.* J.F. Winn, ed. Lincoln, Nebraska: The Grain Sorghum/Pearl Millet Collaborative Research Support Program.

DeWalt, K. M., and Billie R. DeWalt. n.d. Nutrition and Agricultural Change in Southern Honduras. *Food and Nutrition Bulletin* (in press).

Dexter, Lewis Anthony. 1970. *Elite and Specialized Interviewing.* Evanston: Northwestern University Press.

Dillman, Don A. 1978. *Mail and Telephone Surveys: The Total Design Method.* New York: John Wiley and Co.

Dobyns, H.F., Paul L. Doughty, and Harold D. Lasswell (eds.). 1971. *Peasants, Power and Applied Social Change: Vicos as a Model.* Beverly Hills: Sage.

Dodu, Silas R.A. 1975. Meeting the Health Needs of Our Developing Countries: Past, Present and Future. *Universitas* (University of Ghana), New Series, 5 (1):3-16.

Drake, H. Max, et al. 1978a. *An Evaluation of the Deinstitutionalization Process in the U.S. Department of Health, Education, and Welfare, Region X. 2nd ed.* Olympia: State of Washington, Department of Social and Health Services, Planning and Research Division.

_____. 1978b. *An Evaluation of the Deinstitutionalization Process in the U.S. Department of Health, Education, and Welfare, Region X. Vol II.* Olympia: State of Washington, Department of Social and Health Services, Planning and Research Division.

Dunn, William N. 1980. The Two-Communities Metaphor and Models of Knowledge Use. *Knowledge* 1:515-36.

_____. 1983. Measuring Knowledge Use. *Knowledge* 5:120-33.

Durham, William. 1979. *Scarcity and Survival in Central America: The Ecological Origins of the Soccer War.* Stanford CA: Stanford University Press.

Eddy, Elizabeth M., and William L. Partridge. 1978. Training in Applied Anthropology. In *Applied Anthropology in America.* Elizabeth M. Eddy and William L. Partridge, eds. New York: Columbia University Press.

Eddy, Elizabeth, and William L. Partridge (eds.). 1987. *Applied Anthropology in America: Past Contributions and Future Directions*, 2nd Edition. New York: Columbia University Press.

FAO. 1982. *Integrating Nutrition into Agricultural and Rural Development Projects: A Manual.* Nutrition in Agriculture No. 1. Rome: Food and Agricultural Organization.

Fay, Brian. 1975. *Social Theory and Political Practice.* London: George Allen and Unwin.

Field, Margaret Joyce. 1960. *Search for Security: An Ethno-Psychiatric Study of Rural Ghana.* London: Faber and Faber.

Fordham, Miriam, Billie R. DeWalt, and Kathleen M. DeWalt. 1985. *The Economic Role of Women in a Honduran Peasant Community.* INTSORMIL, Farming Systems Research in Southern Honduras. Report No. 3. Lexington, KY.: University of Kentucky Experiment Station, 1985.

Foreign Assistance Act. 1979. Legislation on Foreign Relations through 1978: Current Legislation and Related Executive Orders (Vol. 1). Washington, D.C.: United States Senate-House of Representatives Joint Committee.

Foster, George M. 1953. Use of Anthropological Methods and Data in Planning and Operation. *Public Health Reports* 68(9):841-857.

————. 1987a. World Health Organization Behavioral Research: Problems and Prospects. *Social Science and Medicine* 24 (9):709-717.

————. 1987b. Bureaucratic Aspects of International Health Agencies. *Social Science and Medicine.* 25 (9):1039-1048.

Frankenberger, Timothy R. 1985. *Adding a Food Consumption Perspective to Farming Systems Research.* Washington, D.C.: USDA, Nutrition Economics Group, Technical Assistance Division, Office of International Cooperation and Development and USAID, Bureau for Science and Technology, Office of Nutrition.

Fresno Bee. 1984. Chavez Renews Grape Boycott. *Fresno Bee* (July 12):6.

Friedland, William. 1969. Labor Waste in New York: Rural Exploitation and Migrant Workers. *Transaction* 6:48-53.

Friedland, William, and Robert T. Thomas. 1974. Paradoxes of Agricultural Unionism in California. *Society* May-June:54-62.

Galarza, Ernesto. 1977. *Farm Workers and Agri-business in California, 1947-1960.* Notre Dame: University of Notre Dame Press.

Gearing, Frederick O. 1970. *The Face of the Fox.* Chicago: Aldine.

Geilhufe, Nancy L. 1979. Anthropology and Policy Analysis. *Current Anthropology* 20(3):577-579.

Giblin, P.T., M.L. Poland, and J.B. Waller, Jr. 1986. Detroit Maternal and Child Health Initiatives Addressing Infant Mortality, Low Birth Weight and Prenatal Health Seeking. Paper presented at the Annual Meeting of the Michigan State Association of Obstetrics and Gynecology, Gull Lake, MI, May 1986.

Giblin, P.T., M.L. Poland, J.B. Waller, Jr., and J.W. Ager. 1988a. Correlates of Neonatal Morbidity: Maternal Characteristics and Family Resources. *Journal of Genetic Psychology* 149:527-533.

————. 1988b. Correlates of Parenting on a Neonatal Intensive Care Unit: Maternal Characteristics and Family Resources. *Journal of Genetic Psychology* 149:505-514.

Gilbert, M. Jean. 1978. Extended Family Integration Among Second Generation Mexican Americans. In *Hispanics in Cultural Context: New Directions in Research on the Family and Mental Health.* Susan E. Keefe and Manuel Casas, eds. Pp. 24-48. Monograph No. 7, Spanish Speaking Mental Health Research Center, University of California, Los Angeles.

————. 1980. *Los Parientes: Social Structural Factors and Kinship Relations Among Second Generation Mexican Americans in Two Southern California Communities.* Dissertation Abstracts, 42, 11-12, 5172-5173A (University Microfilms No. 82-07, 651).

————. 1985. Mexican Americans in California: Intracultural Variation in Attitudes and Behavior Related to Alcohol. In *The American Experience with Alcohol: Contrasting Cultural Perspectives.* Linda Bennett and Genevieve Ames, eds. Pp. 255-277. New York: Plenum Press.

————. n.d. Alcohol-related practices, problems and norms among Mexican Americans: An overview. In *Epidemiology of Alcohol Use and Abuse Among U.S. Minority Groups.* National Institute on Alcohol (in press).

Gilbert, M. Jean, and Manuel L. Carlos. 1979. *Mexican American Families and Institutional Interface: A Study of Broker Networks.* Final report to the Office of Child Development. Washington, D.C.

Gilbert, M. Jean, and Richard C. Cervantes. 1987. *Mexican Americans and Alcohol.* Monograph No. 11, Spanish Speaking Mental Health Research Center, University of California, Los Angeles.

Girdner, Linda. 1982. Family Mediation in Theoretical and Social Perspectives. Paper presented at the Annual Meeting of the American Association of Marriage and Family Therapy.

————. 1983. Contested Child Custody Cases: An Examination of Custody and Family Law in an American Court. (Doctoral dissertation, The American University, 1981). *Dissertation Abstracts International* 43, 08A.

————. 1985a. Adjudication and Mediation: A Comparison of Custody Decision-making Involving Third Parties. *Journal of Divorce* 8(3/4):33-47.

————. 1985b. Strategies of Conflict: Custody Litigation in the U.S. *Journal of Divorce* 9(1):1-15.

―――. 1986a. Child Custody Determination: Ideological Dimensions of a Social Problem. In *Redefining Social Problems*. E. Seidman and J. Rappaport, eds. Pp. 165-183. New York: Plenum.

―――. 1986b. Family Mediation: Toward a Synthesis. *Mediation Quarterly* 13:21-29.

―――. 1987. A Critique of Family Mediators: Myths, Themes, and Alliances. *Mediation Quarterly* 18:3-8.

―――. 1988. How People Process Disputes. In *Divorce Mediation: Theory and Practice*. J. Folberg and A. Milne, eds. Pp. 45-57. New York: Guilford.

Glaser, Edward M., and S. Taylor. 1973. Factors Influencing the Success of Applied Research. *American Psychologist* 28:140-146.

Glaser, Edward M., Harold H. Abelson, and Kathalee N. Garrison. 1983. *Putting Knowledge to Use: Facilitating the Diffusion of Knowledge and the Implementation of Planned Change*. San Francisco: Jossey-Bass.

Goldfarb, Ronald. 1982. *Migrant Farm Workers: A Caste of Despair*. Ames: Iowa State University.

Goldschmidt, Walter (ed.). 1979. *The Uses of Anthropology*. A special publication of the American Anthropological Association, No. 11, Washington, D.C.

Goldwater, Barry. 1981. Letter dated June 5, 1981.

―――. 1986. Letter dated January 30, 1986.

Green, Edward C. (ed.). 1986. *Practicing Development Anthropology*. Boulder: Westview Press.

Greenwood, J.G. 1981. Community-Based Care Systems for the Functionally Disabled. *Practicing Anthropology* 3(2):49-51.

Greenwood, J.G., and R.J.C. Pearson. 1978. *Medical Rehabilitation Needs in West Virginia*. Morgantown, WV, West Virginia University, Department of Community Medicine.

Gullickson, G., and S. Light. 1968. Definition and Philosophy of Rehabilitation Medicine. In *Rehabilitation and Medicine*. S. Light, ed. Pp. 1-14. Baltimore, MD: Waverly Press.

Hakel, Milton D., Melvin Sorcher, Michael Beer, and Joseph L. Moses. 1982. *Making It Happen: Designing Research With Implementation in Mind*. Beverly Hills: Sage.

Hannerz, Ulf. 1980. *Exploring the City: Inquiries Toward an Urban Anthropology*. New York: Columbia University Press.

Harper, David, Bobby Mills, and Ronald Farris. 1974. Exploitation in Migrant Labor Camps. *British Journal of Sociology* 25:283-295.

Harrison, The Honorable Miriam Ellen. 1986. Personal Communication.

Hinshaw, Robert E. 1980. Anthropology, Administration, and Public Policy. *Annual Review of Anthropology* 9:497-522.

Hirayabashi, Edward, D.M. Warren, and W. Owen, Jr. 1976. That Focus on the 'Other 40%': A Myth of Development. *Third World Review* 2 (1):60-67.

Hoben, Allan. 1980. Agricultural Decision Making in Foreign Assistance. In *Agricultural Decision Making: Anthropological Contributions to Rural Development.* Peggy Barlett, ed. New York: Academic Press.

————. 1982. Anthropologists and Development. *Annual Review of Anthropology* 11: 349-375.

Hoffman, Cecil. 1978. Empowerment Movements and Mental Health: Locus of Control and Commitment to the United Farm Workers. *Journal of Community Psychology* 6(3):216-221.

Holmberg, Allan R. 1955. Participant Intervention in the Field. *Human Organization* 14(1):23-26.

————.1958. The Research and Development Approach to the Study of Change. *Human Organization* 17:12-16.

Holy Family Hospital. 1985. Annual Report. Techiman: Holy Family Hospital.

Hornick, Robert C. 1988. *Development Communication: Information, Agriculture, and Nutrition in the Third World.* Longman: New York.

Hornstein, Harvey A., et al. 1971. *Social Intervention: A Behavioral Science Approach.* New York: Free Press.

Horstman, Peter. 1975. Protective Services for the Elderly: The Limits of Parens Patriae. *Missouri Law Review* 40 (2):215-278.

Horton, C. 1984. Women Have Headaches, Men Have Backaches: Pattern of Illness in an Appalachian Community." *Social Science and Medicine* 19(4):615-622.

Hyland, Stanley, Bridget Ciaramitaro, Charles Williams, and Rosalind Cottrell. 1987. Redesigning Social Service Delivery Policy: The Anthropologist as Mediator. In *Anthropological Praxis.* Robert M. Wulff and Shirley J. Fiske, eds. Pp. 109-117. Boulder: Westview Press.

INCAP. 1969. Evaluacion Nutricional de la Poblacion de Centroamerica y Panama: Honduras. Guatemala City, Guatemala: Institute of Nutrition of Central America and Panama.

Ingman, Stanley R., and Anthony E. Thomas (eds.). 1975. *Topias and Utopias in Health.* The Hague: Mouton.

Iris, Madelyn Anne. 1984. The Culture of Social Service Agencies: The Impact of Collaboration. Paper presented at the Annual Meeting of the American Anthropological Association, Denver, Colorado.

————. 1986a. Impact Evaluation Final Report. Model Project of Guardianship for Low-Income Aged. Chicago: Metropolitan Chicago Coalition on Aging.

————. 1986b. The Use of Limited Guardianship as the Least Restrictive Alternative for the Impaired Elderly: An Ethnographic Examination of the Probate Court and the Decision-Making Process. Final Report. Park Ridge, IL: The Retirement Research Foundation.

————. 1987. Final Report. The Elder Abuse Project. Chicago: The Metropolitan Chicago Coalition on Aging.

————. 1988. Findings From an Elder Abuse Demonstration Project: The Link Between Research and Policy Development. Paper presented at the Annual Meetings of the National Council on the Aging. Washington, D.C.

Jenkins, J. Craig. 1984. *The Politics of Insurgency.* New York: Columbia University Press.

Jenkins, J. Craig, and C. Perrow. 1977. Insurgency of the Powerless: Farmworker Movements (1964-1972). *American Sociological Review* 42:249-268.

Joe, J.R. 1985. *The Effects of Forced Relocation of a Traditional People.* San Francisco: Institute for Scientific Analysis.

Johnson, Gary W., et al. 1980. *An Assessment of the Community Adjustment and Service Needs of Former State Hospital Patients: A Study of Deinstitutionalization.* Olympia: State of Washington, Dept. of Social and Health Services, Analysis and Information Division 03-12.

Jones, Delmos J. 1976. Applied Anthropology and the Application of Anthropological Knowledge. *Human Organization* 35:221-229.

Kendall, C. 1985. *An Ethnographic Evaluation of the Mass Media and Health Practices Project in Honduras, 1980-1983.* Menlo Park: Applied Communications Technology.

————. 1988. The Implementation of a Diarrheal Disease Control Program in Honduras: Is It 'Selective Primary Health Care' or 'Integrated Primary Health Care'? *Social Science and Medicine* 27 (1): 17-23.

Kendall, C., et al. 1983. Anthropology, Communications, and Health: The Mass Media and Health Practices Program in Honduras. *Human Organization* 42:353-360.

————. 1984. Ethnomedicine and Oral Rehydration Therapy: A Case Study of Ethnomedical Investigation and Program Planning. *Social Science and Medicine* 19:253-260.

————. 1985. *The Mass Media and Health Practices Evaluation in Honduras*. Menlo Park: Applied Communications Technology.

Kimball, Solon T. 1978. Anthropology as a Policy Science. In *Applied Anthropology in America*. E. M. Eddy and W. L. Partridge, eds. New York: Columbia University Press.

Kimball, Solon T., and Marion Pearsall. 1954. *The Talladega Story: A Study in Community Process*. University, AL: University of Alabama Press.

Klopfenstein, Carol, Carl Hoseney, and Elizabeth Varriano-Marston. 1983. Effects of Ascorbic Acid in Sorghum-, High Leucine-, and Casein-fed Guinea Pigs. *Nutrition Reports International* 27:121-129.

Klopfenstein, Carol, Elizabeth Varriano-Marston, and Carl Hoseney. 1981. Effects of Ascorbic Acid in Casein vs. Sorghum Grain Diets in Guinea Pigs. *Nutrition Reports International* 24: 1017-1028.

Krauskopf, Joan. 1983. *Advocacy for the Aging*. St. Paul MN: West Publishing Co.

Lasswell, Harold D. 1968. Policy Sciences. *International Encyclopedia of the Social Sciences* 12:181-188. New York: Macmillan.

————. 1971. *A Preview of Policy Sciences*. New York: American Elsevier.

Lasswell, Harold D., and Allan R. Holmberg. 1966. Toward a General Theory of Directed Value Accumulation and Institutional Development. In *Comparative Theories of Social Change*. H.W. Peter, ed. Ann Arbor, MI: Foundation for Research on Human Behavior.

Leslie, Joanne. 1987. *Time Costs and Time Savings to Women of the Child Survival Revolution*. Washington, D.C.: International Center for Research on Women.

Leviton, Laura C., and Robert F. Boruch. 1983. Contributions of Evaluation to Education Programs and Policy. *Evaluation Review* 7(5):563-598.

Leviton, Laura C., and E.F.X. Hughes. 1981. Research on the Utilization of Evaluations: A Review and Synthesis. *Evaluation Review* 5:525-548.

Levy, Jacques. 1975. *Cesar Chavez: Autobiography of La Causa*. New York: W. W. Norton.

Limann, Hilla. 1979. Press Release. 3 December. Accra: *Daily Graphic*.

London, Joan, and Henry Anderson. 1970. *So Shall Ye Reap*. New York: Crowell.

Los Angeles Times. 1984. Chavez Launches a New Global Grape Boycott. *Los Angeles Times* July 21(IV):5.

————. 1985. Study Backs Chavez. *Los Angeles Times* January 16(IV):5.

Lynn, L.E., Jr. 1978. The Question of Relevance. In *Knowledge and Policy: The Uncertain Connection*. L.E. Lynn, ed. Washington, D.C.: National Research Council.

MacAndrew, Craig, and Robert Edgerton. 1969. *Drunken Comportment: A Social Explanation*. New York: Aldine.

Mahler, H. 1988. Present Status of WHO's Initiative, Health for All by the Year 2000. *Annual Review of Public Health* 9. Palo Alto, CA: Annual Reviews, Inc.

Maier, Donna. 1979. Nineteenth Century Asante Medical Practices. *Comparative Studies in Society and History* 21:63-81.

Majchrzak, Ann. 1986. Information Focus and Data Sources: When Will They Lead to Use? *Evaluation Review* 10(2):193-215.

Majka, Linda C. 1981. Labor Militancy Among Farm Workers and the Strategy of Protest: 1900-1979. *Social Problems* 28(5):533-547.

Majka, Linda C., and Theo J. Majka. 1982. *Farm Workers, Agribusiness, and the State*. Philadelphia: Temple University Press.

Maquet, Jacques. 1964. Objectivity in Anthropology. *Current Anthropology* 5:47-55.

Mark, Melvin M., and R. Lance Shotland. 1985. Stakeholder Based Evaluation and Value Judgements. *Evaluation Review* 9(5):605-625.

Marshall, Patricia A., Daniel R. Scheinfeld, and David W. Beer. 1987. Making It Work: Effective Feedback of Ethnographic Findings in a Psychiatric Hospital. Paper presented at the Annual Meetings of the Society for Applied Anthropology, Oaxaca, Mexico.

Mason, Leonard E. 1958. Kili Community in Transition. *South Pacific Commission Quarterly Bulletin* 18:32-35.

Maxwell, J.P. 1985. *No Easy Answers: Persistent Poverty in the Metropolitan Washington Area*. Washington, D.C.: Greater Washington Research Center.

May, J.T., M.L. Durham, and P.K. New. 1980. Professional Control and Innovations: The Neighborhood Health Center Experience. In *Research in the Sociology of Health Care*. J.A. Roth, ed. Greenwich, CT: JAI Press, Inc.

McCall, George J., and J.L. Simmons 1966/1978. *Identities and Interactions*. New York: Free Press.

MCCoA. 1985. Final Reports of the Guardianship Project for the Low-Income Aged. Chicago: Metropolitan Chicago Coalition on Aging.

McElroy, Ann, and Patricia K. Townsend. 1989. *Medical Anthropology in Ecological Perspective*. 2nd Edition. Boulder: Westview Press.

McLean, W.C., et al. 1981. Protein Quality and Digestibility of Sorghum in Preschool Children: Balance Studies and Plasma-free Amino Acids. *Journal of Nutrition* 111:1928-1936.

Mead, Margaret. 1979. Anthropological Contributions to National Policies During and Immediately After World War II. *In* Walter Goldschmidt, ed., *The Uses of Anthropology.* Pp. 145-57. Washington, D.C.: American Anthropological Association.

Messerschmidt, Donald A. (ed.). 1981. *Anthropologists at Home in North America: Methods and Issues in the Study of One's Own Society.* New York: Cambridge University Press.

Mickelwait, Donald R., Charles F. Sweet, and Elliott R. Morss. 1979. *New Directions in Development: A Study of USAID.* Boulder: Westview Press.

Ministere de la Sante Publique et de la Population. 1985. *Enquete Nationale Pronacodiam, PEV, PF.* Port-au-Prince: MSPP.

Mitchell, D.E. 1980. Social Science Impact on Legislative Decision Making: Process and Substance. *Educational Researcher* 9(10):9-12, 17-19.

Mitchell, J. Clyde. 1969. The Concept and Use of Social Networks. In *Social Networks in Urban Situations: Analyses of Personal Relationships in Central African Towns.* J. Clyde Mitchell, ed. Manchester: Manchester University Press.

Montgomery, Edward, and John W. Bennett. 1979. Anthropological Studies of Food and Nutrition: The 1940s and the 1970s. In *The Uses of Anthropology.* Walter Goldschmidt, ed. Washington, D.C.: American Anthropological Association.

Mooney, James. 1896. *The Ghost Dance Religion and the Sioux Outbreak of 1890.* Washington, D.C.: Bureau of American Ethnology.

Moore, Truman E. 1965. *The Slaves We Rent.* New York: Random House.

Morss, Elliott R., and David D. Gow (eds.). 1985. *Implementing Rural Development Projects: Lessons from AID and World Bank Experiences.* Boulder: Westview Press.

Murray, Gerald F. 1987. The Domestication of Wood in Haiti: A Case Study in Applied Evolution. In *Anthropological Praxis.* Robert M. Wulff and Shirley J. Fiske, eds. Pp. 223-240. Boulder: Westview Press.

National Health Planning Unit. 1979. *An Approach to Planning the Delivery of Health Care Services*. Manual No. 1. Accra: Ministry of Health, National Health Planning Unit.

Neugarten, Bernice. 1982. *Age or Need? Public Policies for Older People*. Beverly Hills, CA: Sage.

Newman, E. 1981. *Prototype Plan for Community Hospital-Based Rehabilitation Services for St. Joseph's Hospital of Parkersburg, West Virginia*. Falls Church, VA: Del Price Associates.

O'Gara, Chloe, and Carl Kendall. 1985. Fluids and Powders: Options for Infant Feeding. *Medical Anthropology* 9 (2):107-122.

O'Reilly, Kevin R., and Michael E. Dalmat. 1987. Marketing Program Evaluation: Birth Attendant Training in Kenya. *Practicing Anthropology* 9(1):12-13.

Omohundro, J., M.J. Schneider, J.N. Marr, and B.O. Grannemanu. 1983. *Disability in Rural America: A Four-County Need Assessment*. Fayetteville, AK: Arkansas Rehabilitation Research and Training Center.

Organizacion Panamericana de la Salud. 1984. Salud Maternoinfantil y Atencion Primaria en las Americas Hechos y Tendencias. Publicacion Cientifica No. 461. Washington, D.C.

Owens, Edgar, and Robert Shaw. 1974. *Development Reconsidered*. Lexington, MA: D. C. Heath.

Packer (The). 1984. ALRB Policy Allows General Counsel to Question Levied Specifications. *The Packer* (July 28):6.

Padfield, Harland, and Courtland Smith. 1968. Water and Culture. *Rocky Mountain Social Science Journal* 5(2):23-32.

Parker, Patricia L., and Thomas F. King. 1987. Intercultural Mediation at Truk International Airport. In *Anthropological Praxis*. Robert M. Wulff and Shirley J. Fiske, eds. Pp. 160-173. Boulder: Westview Press.

Partridge, William L. 1987. Toward a Theory of Practice. In *Applied Anthropology in America*. Elizabeth M. Eddy and William L. Partridge, eds. Pp. 211-233. New York: Columbia University Press.

Patton, Michael Quinn. 1978. *Utilization-Focused Evaluation*. Beverly Hills, CA: Sage.

———. 1980. *Qualitative Evaluation Methods*. Beverly Hills, CA: Sage.

———. 1982. *Practical Evaluation*. Beverly Hills, CA: Sage.

———. 1986. *Utilization-Focused Evaluation*. 2nd edition. Beverly Hills, CA: Sage.

Patton, Michael Quinn, et al. 1977. In Search of Impact: An Analysis of the Utilization of Federal Health Evaluation Research. In *Using Social Research In Public Policy.* Carol Weiss, ed. Pp. 141-64. Lexington, MA: D.C. Heath.

Paul, Compton, and Billie R. DeWalt (eds.). 1985. *El Sorgo en Sistemas de Produccion en America Latina.* Mexico: INTSORMIL / ICRISAT / CIMMYT.

Pearsall, Marion, and M. Sue Kern. 1967. Behavioral Science, Nursing Services, and the Collaborative Process: A Case Study. *The Journal of Applied Behavioral Science* 3 (2).

Pelto, Pertti J. 1970. *Anthropological Research.* New York: Harper and Row.

Pelz, Donald C. 1978. Some Expanded Perspectives on the Use of Social Science in Public Policy. In *Major Social Issues: A Multidisciplinary View.* J.M. Yinger and S.J. Cutler, eds. New York: Free Press.

Pillsbury, Barbara K. 1979. *Reaching the Rural Poor: Indigenous Health Practitioners are There Already.* AID Program Evaluation Discussion Paper Series, No. 1. Washington, D. C.: United States Agency for International Development.

Pinstrup-Andersen, Per. 1981. Nutritional Consequences of Agricultural Projects: Conceptual Relationships and Assessment Approaches. *World Bank Staff Working Paper #456.* Washington D.C.: World Bank.

Poland, M.L. 1986a. Factors Associated With Adequate Prenatal Care and Reproductive Outcome. Paper presented at the Annual Meeting of the Society for Applied Anthropology, Reno, NV.

————. 1986b. Infant Mortality: Detroit. Paper presented at the Annual Meeting of the Michigan Public Health Association, Flint, MI.

Poland, M.L., J. Ager, and J. Olson. 1987. Barriers to receiving adequate prenatal care. *American Journal of Obstetrics and Gynecology* 157:297-303.

Poland, M.L., and P.T. Giblin. 1986. Application of Multivariate Studies of Prenatal and Infant Health Care Seeking to Reduce Infant Mortality in Detroit. Paper presented at the Annual Meeting of the Society for Applied Anthropology, Reno, NV.

Powell, John Wesley. 1881. *First Annual Report of the Bureau of American Ethnology.* Washington, D.C.: Government Printing Office.

Preister, Kevin. 1987. Issue-Centered Social Impact Assessment. In *Anthropological Praxis.* Robert M. Wulff and Shirley J. Fiske, eds. Pp. 39-55. Boulder: Westview Press.

Rappaport, Julian. 1981. In Praise of Paradox: A Social Policy of Empowerment over Prevention. *American Journal of Community Psychology* 9(1):1-25.

Rappaport, Roy. 1986. President-elect Calls for Advice on Association Initiative. *Anthropology Newsletter* 27(7):1,15. American Anthropological Association.

Rattray, Robert Sutherland. 1927. *Religion and Art in Ashanti.* Oxford: The Clarendon Press.

Reeves, Edward C., Billie R. DeWalt, and Kathleen DeWalt. 1987. The International Sorghum/Millet Research Project. In *Anthropological Praxis.* Robert M. Wulff and Shirley J. Fiske, eds. Pp. 72-83. Boulder: Westview Press.

Regan, John. 1972. Protective Services for the Elderly: Commitment, Guardianship and Alternatives. *William and Mary Law Review* 13:569-622.

————. 1981. Protecting the Elderly: The New Paternalism. *Hastings Law Journal* 32:1111-1132.

Rhoades, Robert. 1985. *Breaking New Ground.* Centro Internacional de la Papa: Lima, Peru.

Ricci, Isolina. 1980. *Mom's House/Dad's House: Making Shared Custody Work.* New York: MacMillan Publishing Co.

Rich, R.F. 1975. Selective Utilization of Social Science Related Information by Federal Policy Makers. *Inquiry* 239-45.

————. 1977. Uses of Social Science Information by Federal Bureaucrats: Knowledge for Action Versus Knowledge for Understanding. In *Using Social Research in Public Policy Making.* Carol H. Weiss, ed. Lexington, MA: Lexington Books.

Richards, Audrey. 1932. *Hunger and Work in a Savage Tribe.* London: Routledge and Sons.

Richards, Paul. 1985. *Indigenous Agricultural Revolution: Ecology and Food Production in West Africa.* London: Hutchinson.

————. 1986a. *Coping with Hunger: Hazard and Experiment in an African Rice-Farming System.* London: Allen and Unwin.

————. 1986b. *New Models for Low-Resource Agricultural Research and Extension in Sub-Saharan Africa.* Draft Report for the Office of Technology Assessment, U.S. Congress. London: University College.

Rifkin, Susan B., and Gill Walt. 1986. Why Health Improves: Defining the Issues Concerning 'Comprehensive Primary Health Care' and 'Selective Primary Health Care.' *Social Science and Medicine* 23(6):559-566.

Rogers, Everett M. 1983. *Diffusion of Innovations*. 3rd ed. New York: Free Press.

Roling, Niels. 1985. Extension Science: Increasingly Preoccupied with Knowledge Systems. *Sociologia Ruralis* 25:269-290.

Rosaldo, Renato. 1986. Ilongot Hunting as Story and Experience. In *The Anthropology of Experience*. V. Turner and E. Bruner, eds. Pp. 97-138. Urbana: University of Illinois Press.

Rosenfield, Alan, Suzanne Allman, and James Allman. 1985. *Treatment of Childhood Diarrhea in Rural and Urban Haiti: Community Level Knowledge, Acceptance and Use of Oral Rehydration Therapy*. Final Report, Project No. 123HAI4, Pan American Health Organization, Washington, D.C.

Rossi, Peter H., and Howard E. Freeman. 1982. *Evaluation: A Systematic Approach*. Second Edition. Beverly Hills, CA: Sage.

Rothman, Jack. 1974. *Planning and Organizing for Social Change: Action Principles from Social Science Research*. New York: Columbia University Press.

————. 1980. *Using Research in Organizations: A Guide to Successful Application*. Beverly Hills, CA: Sage.

Rubel, A.J. 1960. Concepts of Disease in Mexican-American Culture. *American Anthropologist* 62:795-814.

————. 1964. The Epidemiology of a Folk Illness: Susto in Hispanic America. *Ethnology* 3:268-283.

Rubel, A.J., et al. 1985. *Susto: A Folk Illness*. Berkeley: University of California Press.

Rynkiewich, Michael A., and James P. Spradley. 1976. *Ethics and Anthropology: Dilemmas in Fieldwork*. New York: John Wiley and Sons.

Sacramento Bee. 1984. UFW's Chavez Announces New Grape Boycott. *Sacramento Bee* (July 12):A3.

San Francisco Chronicle. 1984a. New Direction Seen for ALRB. *San Francisco Chronicle* (August 19):6.

————. 1984b. Cesar Chavez's Fall From Grace. *San Francisco Chronicle* (October 21):8.

————. 1984c. State Farm Labor Board Sues Its Attorney in Power Struggle. *San Francisco Chronicle* (November 27):12.

————. 1985. ALRB Official's Ouster Demanded: Church Leaders' Charges. *San Francisco Chronicle* (October 22):8.

San Joaquin County Record. 1985. Most California Farm Workers in Poll Show Support for UFW. *San Joaquin County Record* (January 15):12.

San Jose Mercury News. 1984. Cesar Chavez: Is Anyone Following the Leader? *San Jose Mercury News* (August 19 West Magazine):6-8.

———. 1985. 83% of State's Farm Workers Like UFW, Survey Finds. *San Jose Mercury News* (January 16):1B, 3B.

SAPLAN (Sistema de Analisis y Planificacion de Alimentacion y Nutricion). 1981. *Analisis de la Situacion Nutricional durante el Periodo 1972-1979*. Tegucigalpa, Honduras: Consejo Superior de Planificacion Economico (CONSUPLANE) [mimeo].

Schaefer, Christopher. 1983. Personal Communication.

Schein, Edgar H. 1969. *Process Consultation: Its Role in Organization Development*. Reading, MA: Addison-Wesley.

Scheinfeld, Daniel. 1984. The Problem of Getting Organizational Research Utilized by the Organization Being Researched. Erikson Institute Seminar on Ethnographic Program Evaluation.

———. 1987. A Collaborative Approach to Research Utilization. *Practicing Anthropology* 9(1):4-5.

Schensul, Jean J. 1985. Systems Consistency in Field Research, Dissemination, and Social Change. *American Behavioral Scientist* 29(2):186-204.

———. 1987a. Knowledge Utilization: An Anthropological Perspective. *Practicing Anthropology* 9(1):6-8.

———. 1987b. Urban Comadronas. In *Collaborative Research and Social Policy: Anthropology and Action*. Donald D. Stull and Jean J. Schensul, eds. Boulder: Westview Press.

Schensul, Jean J., and Donald D. Stull. 1987. Introduction. In *Collaborative Research and Social Change*. Donald D. Stull and Jean J. Schensul, eds. Pp. 1-5. Boulder: Westview Press.

Schensul, Stephen L. 1973. Action Research: The Applied Anthropologist in a Community Mental Health Program. In *Anthropology Beyond the University*. Alden Redfield, ed. Athens: University of Georgia Press.

———. 1974. Skills Needed in Action Anthropology: Lessons from El Centro de la Causa. *Human Organization* 33(2):203-208.

———. 1987. Perspectives on Collaborative Research. In *Collaborative Research and Social Change*. Donald D. Stull and Jean J. Schensul, eds. Pp. 211-219. Boulder: Westview Press.

Schensul, Stephen L., and Jean J. Schensul. 1978. Advocacy and Applied Anthropology. In *Social Scientists as Advocates: Views from the Applied Disciplines*. George H. Weber and George J. McCall, eds. Beverly Hills, CA: Sage Publications.

Schorr, Alvin L. 1986. *Common Decency Domestic Policies After Reagan*. New Haven: Yale University Press.

Scrimshaw, Susan C.M., and Elena Hurtado. 1987. *Rapid Assessment Procedures for Nutrition and Primary Health Care: Anthropological Approaches to Improving Program Effectiveness (RAP).* Los Angeles, CA: UCLA Latin American Center Publications.

Seidman, Edward (ed.). 1983. *Handbook of Social Intervention.* Beverly Hills, CA: Sage

Sekyere, Steve. 1986. Uniting Herbal and Western Healing. Accra: *The Ghanaian Mirror.* September 13.

Serna-Saldivar, S.O., et al. 1985. Nutritional Value of Sorghum and Maize Tortillas. *Cereal Foods World* 30(8): 539.

Shadish, William R., Jr. 1984. Lessons from the Implementation of Deinstitutionalization. *American Psychologist* 39(7):725-738.

Shaner, W.W., P.F. Philipp, and W.R. Schmehl. 1982. *Farming Systems Research and Development: Guidelines for Developing Countries.* Boulder: Westview Press.

Shenkin, Budd N. 1974. *Health Care for Migrant Workers: Policies and Politics.* Cambridge, MA: Ballinger.

Sherif, M., O.J. Harvey, B.J. Shite, W.E. Hood, and C.W. Sherif. 1961. *Intergroup Conflict and Cooperation: The Robber's Cave Experiment.* Norman, OK: University of Oklahoma Press.

Siegel, Karolynn, and Peter Tuckel. 1985. The Utilization of Evaluation Research. A Case Analysis. *Evaluation Review* 9(3):307-328.

Skar, Harald O. (ed.). 1985. *Anthropological Contributions to Planned Change and Development.* Goteborg: Acta Universitatis Gothoburgensis.

Social Security Administration. 1979. Notes and Brief Reports. *Social Security Bulletin* 42(5):41-44.

Solem, R.A., M.A. Garrick, and H. Nelson. 1979. *Community-Based Care Systems for the Functionally Disabled: A Project in Independent Living.* Olympia, WA: Washington Department of Social and Health Services.

Sosnick, Stephen H. 1978. *Hired Hands.* Santa Barbara: McNally and Loftin, West.

Spencer, Herbert. 1877. *Principles of Sociology.* Vol. I. New York: D. Appleton and Co.

Spicer, Edward H. 1976. Anthropology and the Policy Process. In *Do Applied Anthropologists Apply Anthropology?* Michael V. Angrosino, ed. Athens: University of Georgia Press.

―――. 1979. Anthropologists and the War Relocation Authority. In *The Uses of Anthropology.* Walter Goldschmidt, ed. Pp. 217-237. Washington, D.C.: American Anthropological Association.

Spillius, James. 1957. Natural Disaster and Political Crisis in a Polynesian Society: An Exploration of Operational Research. *Human Relations* 10(2):113-25.

Spradley, James. 1979. *The Ethnographic Interview.* New York: Holt, Rinehart and Winston.

Spradley, James, and David W. McCurdy. 1972. *The Cultural Experience: Ethnography in Complex Society.* Chicago: Science Research Associates.

Stern, Gwen. 1985. Research, Action, and Social Betterment. *American Behavioral Scientist* 29 (2):229-248.

Stewart, Omer C. 1961. *Kroeber and the Indian Claims Commission Cases.* Kroeber Anthropology Society paper No. 25. Berkeley, CA: Kroeber Anthropology Society.

Stonich, Susan. 1986. *Development and Destruction: Interrelated Ecological, Socioeconomic, and Nutritional Change in Southern Honduras.* University of Kentucky, unpublished Ph.D. dissertation.

Stull, Donald D., and Felix Moos. 1981. A Brief Overview of the Role of Anthropology in Public Policy. *Policy Studies Review* 1:19-27.

Stull, Donald D., and Jean J. Schensul. (eds.). 1987. *Collaborative Research and Social Change: Applied Anthropology in Action.* Boulder: Westview Press.

Suchman, Edward A. 1967. *Evaluative Research: Principles and Practice in Public Service and Social Action Programs.* Baltimore: The John Hopkins University Press.

Swaminathan, M.S. 1984. Nutrition and Agricultural Development: New Frontiers. *Food and Nutrition* 10 (1):33-41.

Tedlock, Barbara. 1987. An Interpretive Solution to the Problem of Humoral Medicine in Latin America. *Social Science and Medicine* 24 (12):1069-1083.

Thompson, Karen S., Kathleen M. DeWalt, and Billie R. DeWalt. 1985. *Household Food Use in Three Rural Communities in Southern Honduras.* INTSORMIL, Farming Systems Research in Southern Honduras, Report No. 2. Lexington, KY.: University of Kentucky Experiment Station.

Thompson, Laura. 1950. Action Research Among American Indians. *Scientific Monthly* 70: 34-40.

————. 1951. Personality and Government. *Ediciones del Instituto Indigenista Interamericano, Mexico. D.F.*

Titmuss, Richard. 1974. *Social Policy: An Introduction.* London: George Allen and Unwin, Ltd.

————. 1987. *The Philosophy of Welfare: Selected Writings of Richard M. Titmuss.* Brian Abel-Smith and Kay Titmuss, eds. London: Allen and Unwin.

Tripp, Robert. 1982. Including Dietary Concerns in On-Farm Research: An Example from Imbabura, Ecuador. El Batan, Mexico: *CIMMYT Working Paper.*

————. 1984. On Farm Research and Applied Nutrition: Some Suggestions for Collaboration between National Institutes of Nutrition and Agricultural Research. *Food and Nutrition Bulletin* 6(3):49-57.

Twumasi, Patrick, and D. M. Warren. 1983. Professionalization of Traditional Medicine in Ghana and Zambia. Paper presented at the Conference on Professionalisation of African Medicine sponsored by the International African Institute, Gaborone.

————. 1986. The Professionalisation of Indigenous Medicine: A Comparative Study of Ghana and Zambia. In *The Professionalisation of African Medicine.* Murray Last and Gordon Chavunduka, eds. Pp. 117-135. London: The International African Institute and Manchester University Press.

Tyler, Stephen. 1969. *Cognitive Anthropology.* New York: Holt, Rinehart and Winston.

Unger, Jean Pierre, and James R. Killingsworth. 1986. Selective Primary Health Care: A Critical Review of Methods and Results. *Social Science and Medicine* 22(10):1001-1013.

United States. Department of Health and Human Services. n.d. National Health Interview Survey. Unpublished Data. Washington, D.C.: U.S. Center for Health Statistics.

United States Senate Subcommittee on Migratory Labor. 1970. *Migrant and Seasonal Farmworker Powerlessness.* Washington, D.C.: U.S. Government Printing Office.

United States Senate. 1983a. Hearing before the Select Committee on Indian Affairs, United States Senate, 96 Cong., 2nd Session, on P. L. 93-531, Report and Plan of the Navajo-Hopi Relocation Commission, May 20, 1981. Washington, D.C.: U.S. Government Printing Office.

————. 1983b. Hearing before the Select Committee on Indian Affairs, United States Senate, 97 Cong., 2nd Session, on S. 1795, An Exchange of Lands Between the Hopi and Navajo Tribes, July 13, 1982. Washington, D.C.: U.S. Government Printing Office.

USAID. 1978. *Social Soundness Analysis.* AID Handbook 3, Appendix 4A, Pp. 1-12. Washington, D.C.: United States Agency for International Development.

————. 1982a. *AID Policy Paper: Nutrition.* Washington, D.C.: United States Agency for International Development.

————. 1982b. *AID Policy Paper: Food and Agricultural Development.* Washington, D.C.: United States Agency for International Development.

————. 1984a. *Nutrition Sector Strategy.* Washington, D.C.: United States Agency for International Development.

————. 1984b. *Africa Bureau: Nutrition Guidelines for Agriculture and Rural Development.* Washington, D.C.: United States Agency for International Development.

van de Vall, Mark, and Cheryl Bolas. 1980. Applied Social Discipline Research or Social Policy Research: The Emergence of a Professional Paradigm in Sociological Research. *The American Sociologist* 15:128-137.

van de Vall, Mark, Cheryl Bolas, and C.D. Kang. 1976. Applied Social Research in Industrial Organizations: An Evaluation of Functions, Theory and Methods. *Journal of Applied Behavioral Science* 12:158-177.

van Willigen, John. 1980. *Anthropology in Use: A Bibliographic Chronology of the Development of Applied Anthropology.* Pleasantville, NY: Redgrave Publishing Co.

————. 1986. *Applied Anthropology: An Introduction.* South Hadley, Massachusetts: Bergin and Garvey Publishers, Inc.

van Willigen, John, and Billie R. DeWalt. 1985. *Training Manual in Policy Ethnography.* A Special Publication of the American Anthropological Association, No. 19, Washington, D.C.

Village Voice. 1984. Cesar Chavez's Fall From Grace. *Village Voice* (August 14):6-8 and (August 19):12.

Wallace, Anthony F.C. 1976. Some Reflections on the Contribution of Anthropologists to Public Policy. In *Anthropology and the Public Interest: Fieldwork and Theory.* Peggy Reeves Sanday, ed. Pp. 3-14. New York: Academic Press.

Waller, J.B., et al. 1986. An Analysis of Births, Infant Morbidity, and Infant Deaths as Outcomes of Prenatal Care Delivered by Inner City Detroit Clinics. Paper presented at the 114th Annual Meeting of The American Public Health Association, Las Vegas, NV.

Walsh, Edward J. 1978. On the Interaction Between a Movement and Its Environment. *American Sociological Review* 43:110-112.

Walsh, Edward J., and Charles Craypo. 1979. Union Oligarchy and the Grass Roots: The Case of the Teamsters' Defeat in Farmwork Organizing. *Sociology and Social Research* 63:269-293.

Warren, Dennis Michael. 1974a. Bono Traditional Healers. *Rural Africana* 26:25-39.

————. 1974b. *Disease, Medicine, and Religion Among the Bono of Ghana: A Study in Culture Change.* Doctoral Dissertation. Bloomington: Indiana University.

————. 1975. The Role of Emic Analyses in Medical Anthropology. *Anthropological Linguistics* 17 (3):117-126.

————. 1976a. *Bibliography and Vocabulary of the Akan (Twi-Fante) Language of Ghana.* Indiana University Publications, Africa Series, Volume 6. Bloomington: Indiana University, Research Center for Language and Semiotic Studies.

————. 1976b. Ethnoscience and Integrated Rural Development. Paper presented at the West Africa Conference on Natural Resources Management in Arid Regions, University of Arizona, Tucson.

————. 1976c. Indigenous Knowledge Systems for Activating Local Decision-Making Groups in Rural Development. In *Communications for Group Transformation in Development.* Godwin Chu, Syed Rahim, and D. Lawrence Kincaid, eds. Pp. 307-329. Communications Monographs No. 2. Honolulu: The East-West Center.

————. 1978a. Indigenous and Western Health Delivery Systems in Africa: Theories and Case Studies of Accommodation and Conflict. Paper presented at the Conference on Cultural Transformations in Africa sponsored by the Joint Committee on African Studies, Social Science Research Council and the American Council of Learned Societies, Elkridge, Maryland.

————. 1978b. The Interpretation of Change in a Ghanaian Ethnomedical Study. *Human Organization* 37 (1):73-77.

————. 1979. Humanistic Approaches to Applied Anthropology. In *Essays in Humanistic Anthropology.* Bruce Grindal and D. M. Warren, eds. Pp. 115-135. Lanham, MD: University Press of America.

————. 1981a. Ethnic Heterogeneity and the Growth of Market Unions and Ethnic Associations in Techiman, Ghana. *Papers in Anthropology*, No. 5. Ames: Iowa State University.

————. 1981b. *The Development Advisory Team (DAT) Training Manual.* Ames: Iowa State University.

————. 1982a. The Techiman-Bono Ethnomedical System. In *African Health and Healing Systems.* P. Stanley Yoder, ed. Pp. 85-105. Los Angeles: Crossroads Press.

———. 1982b. The Western Image of Non-Western Civilization as a Euro-American Cultural Product. Paper presented at the Annual Meeting of the International Society for the Comparative Study of Civilizations, Pittsburgh.

———. 1984a. Cost Effective Methods for Obtaining Indigenous Technical Knowledge. Paper presented at the International Workshop on the Role of Rural Sociology in Farming Systems Research sponsored by CIMMYT, Lusaka.

———. 1984b. The Role of Indigenous Knowledge Systems and Indigenous Organizations in Facilitating a Participatory Approach to Agriculture and Rural Development. Paper presented at the International Seminar on the Role of Rural Organizations in the Process of Development, The University Centre of Dschang, Cameroon.

———. 1985. Anthropology and Rural Development in Ghana. In *Anthropology and Rural Development in West Africa*. Michael Horowitz and Thomas Painter, eds. Pp. 63-91. Boulder: Westview Press.

———. 1986a. The Expanding Role of Indigenous Healers in Ghana's National Health Delivery System. Paper presented at the Conference on African Medicine in the Modern World, University of Edinburgh.

———. 1986b. Ghana's Changing Medical Scene: How Attitudes and Expectations are Affecting the Nature and Quality of Health Care. Paper presented at the Conference on Changing Concepts of Illness and Health in Ghana, sponsored by the Tamale Institute of Cross Cultural Studies, Tamale, Ghana.

———. 1989. Linking Scientific and Indigenous Agricultural Systems. In *The Transformation of International Agricultural Research and Development*. J. Lin Compton, ed. Pp. 153-170. Boulder: Lynn Rienner Publishers.

Warren, D.M., and Peter Blunt. 1984. Decentralization in Ghana: The Impact on Organizational Effectiveness of Management Training among District and Regional-Level Officers. *Journal of Contemporary African Studies* 3 (1/2):35-58.

Warren, D.M., et al. 1982. Ghanaian National Policy Towards Indigenous Healers: The Case of the Primary Health Training for Indigenous Healers (PRHETIH) Program. *Social Science and Medicine* 16 (21):1873-1881.

Warren, D.M., and Edward C. Green. 1988. Linking Biomedical and Indigenous African Health Delivery Systems: An Assessment of Collaborative Efforts During the 1980s. Paper presented at the Symposium on Ethnomedical Systems in Sub-Saharan Africa, African Studies Centre, University of Leiden, The Netherlands.

Warren, D.M., and J. Issachar. 1983. Strategies for Understanding and Changing Local Revenue Policies and Practices in Ghana's Decentralization Program. *World Development* 11 (9):835-844.

Weatherford, Jack McIver. 1985. *Tribes on the Hill.* South Hadley, MA: Bergin and Garvey.

Weaver, Thomas. 1985a. Anthropology as a Policy Science: Part I, A Critique. *Human Organization* 44(2):97-105.

_____. 1985b. Anthropology as a Policy Science: Part II, Development and Training. *Human Organization* 44(3):197-205.

Weber, George H. 1984. Social Science and Social Policy: An Experiential View. In *Social Science and Public Policy: The Roles of Academic Disciplines in Policy Analysis.* George J. Mc Call and George H. Weber, eds. New York: Associated Faculty Press, The Policy Studies Organization Series Publication.

Weber, George H., and George J. McCall (eds.). 1978. *Social Scientists As Advocates: Views from the Applied Disciplines.* Beverly Hills, CA: Sage.

Weiss, Carol H. (ed.). 1977. *Using Social Research in Public Policy Making.* Lexington, MA.: D.C. Heath.

Weiss, Carol H.. 1981. Measuring the Use of Evaluations. In *Utilizing Evaluation.* James A. Ciarlo, ed. Pp. 17-33. Beverly Hills, CA: Sage.

Weiss, Carol H., and Michael Bucuvalas. 1980. Truth Test and Utility Test: Decision Makers' Frame of Reference for Social Science Research. *American Sociological Review* (April): 302-313.

Weiss, J. A., and Carol H. Weiss. 1981. Social Scientists and Decision Makers Look at the Usefulness of Mental Health Research. *American Psychologist* 36:837-847.

Wellin, Edward. 1955. Water Boiling in a Peruvian Town. In *Health, Culture and Community: Case Studies of Public Reactions to Health Programs.* Benjamin D. Paul, ed. Pp. 71-103. New York: Russell Sage Foundation.

Werner, Oswald, and G. Mark Schoepfle. 1987a. *Systematic Fieldwork. Volume I: Foundations of Ethnography and Interviewing.* Beverly Hills, CA: Sage Publications.

_____. 1987b. *Systematic Fieldwork. Volume II: Ethnographic Analysis and Data Management.* Beverly Hills, CA: Sage Publications.

West Virginia University. 1982. Guidelines for the Development of Physical Rehabilitation Services in West Virginia. Morgantown, WV: West Virginia University, School of Medicine.

West, Irma. 1964. Occupational Diseases of Farm Workers. *Archives of Environmental Health* 9(1):92-98.

Western Grower and Shipper. 1985. Growers Should Heed Poll of Farmworkers. *Western Grower and Shipper* 56(4):24.

Whiteford, Linda M. 1987. Staying Out of the Bottom Drawer. *Practicing Anthropology* 9(1): 9-11.

Whiteman, David. 1985. Reaffirming the Importance of Strategic Use. *Knowledge* 6(3): 203-24.

WHO. 1978. *Declaration of Alma-Ata in Primary Health Care: Report of the International Conference on Primary Health Care, Alma-Ata U.S.S.R.*, 6-12, September 1978. Jointly sponsored by the World Health Organization and the United Nations Children Fund. Geneva: World Health Organization.

———.1986. Oral Rehydration Therapy for Treatment of Diarrhea in the Home. WHO/CDD/SER/86.9. Geneva: World Health Organization.

———. 1987. *Communication: A Guide for Managers of National Diarrheal Disease Control Programs*. Geneva: World Health Organization.

WHO/FAO. 1973. *Protein and Energy Requirements*. Geneva: World Health Organization.

Wilks, Ivor. 1974. *Asante in the Nineteenth Century*. New York: Cambridge University Press.

Wood, J.J. 1986. Navajo Relocation from Hopi-Partitioned Lands. Paper presented at the 1st Navajo Studies Conference, Symposium on The History and Effects of Relocation on the Navajo, Albuquerque, New Mexico.

Wood, J.J., and K.M. Stemmler. 1981. *Land and Religion at Big Mountain: The Effects of the Navajo-Hopi Land Dispute on Navajo Well-Being*. Flagstaff: privately printed.

Wood, J.J., and W.M. Vannette. 1979. *A Preliminary Assessment of the Significance of Navajo Sacred Places in the Vicinity of Big Mountain, Arizona*. Flagstaff: Navajo and Hopi Indian Relocation Commission.

Wood, J.J., W.M. Vannette, and M.J. Andrews. 1982. *Sheep is Life: An Assessment of Livestock Reduction in the Former Navajo-Hopi Joint Use Area*. Flagstaff: Northern Arizona University Anthropological Papers No. 1.

World Bank. 1975. *The Assault on World Poverty: Problems of Rural Development, Education, and Health.* Baltimore: The Johns Hopkins University Press.

———. 1986. *World Development Report 1986.* New York: Oxford University Press.

Wulff, Robert M., and Shirley J. Fiske (eds.). 1987. *Anthropological Praxis: Translating Knowledge into Action.* Boulder: Westview Press.

Zald, Mayer N. 1978. On the Social Control of Industries. *Social Forces* 57:79-102.

About the Authors

W.K. Barger

Ken Barger received his Ph.D. in Anthropology from the University of North Carolina in 1974. He is Associate Professor of Anthropology at Indiana University at Indianapolis. His professional interests include sociocultural adaptation, social movements, medical anthropology and public health, applied change, Native Americans, and Mexican Americans. Since 1978, he has been involved with health and education programs for Midwestern farmworkers, and he has worked in community organizing and applied research projects for the Farm Labor Organizing Committee (FLOC), which represents the farm labor movement in the Midwest, and for the United Farm Workers of America (UFW) in California. Applied research has included field surveys of Midwestern and California farmworkers regarding the farm labor movement, and public surveys in Indiana and California regarding the farm labor movement and farmworker boycotts. He has published on social change and the farmworker movement in *American Ethnologist*, *Human Organization*, and *La Red*.

David W. Beer

David W. Beer is Research Associate at the Erikson Institute in Chicago. He received his M.A. in Anthropology from the University of Chicago, where he is completing a dissertation on knowledge and practice of the Yunani system of medicine in Pakistan. Besides traditional medicine in South Asia, his interests include psychiatric hospitals, preschool and early elementary education, child protective services, and interviewing children. His recent publications include "Guidelines for Interviewing Children," in *What Children Can Tell Us*, James Garbarino and Frances Stott, eds. (1989), and "Text and Knowledge in Yunani Medicine," in *Well-Being: Nutrition, Health, and*

Healing in South Asia, Guy Welbon, ed., Department of South Asia Regional Studies, University of Pennsylvania (1989; in press).

Margaret S. Boone

Margaret S. Boone received her Ph.D. in Cultural Anthropology from The Ohio State University in 1977. She is Adjunct Associate Professor with the Department of Pathology, School of Medicine and Health Sciences, The George Washington University. After the two projects described in this volume, she went on to work for the U.S. General Accounting Office, Program Evaluation and Methodology Division. She will publish two books in the near future: *Capital Crime: Black Infant Mortality in America*, and *Computer Applications for Anthropologists*, co-edited with John Wood.

Lucy M. Cohen

Lucy Cohen received her Ph.D. in Anthropology from Catholic University of America in 1966. She is Professor of Anthropology and Chairperson of the Department of Anthropology at Catholic University of America. Her research interests include community health and mental health services, Colombian women in the professions, the health of Latin American immigrants, and the ethnohistory of Chinese in the Americas. Publications include *Culture, Disease and Stress among Latino Immigrants* (1979), *Chinese in the Post-Civil War South: A People Without a History* (1984), and "Controlarse and the Problems of Life among Latino Immigrants," in *Stress and Hispanic Mental Health Relating Research to Service Delivery*, W.A. Vega and M.R. Miranda, eds. (1985).

Jeannine Coreil

Jeannine Coreil received her Ph.D. in Applied Medical Anthropology from the University of Kentucky in 1979. She is Associate Professor in the College of Public Health at the University of South Florida. Recent work focuses on sociocultural factors and child survival, particularly maternal utilization of oral rehydration therapy and immunizations in Haiti, and allocation of family resources for health. Current research aims to promote breastfeeding among low income women in the southeastern United States. A current publication is "Innovation among Haitian Healers: the Adoption of Oral Rehydration Therapy," *Human Organization* 47(1):48-57, 1988.

Billie R. DeWalt

Billie R. DeWalt received his Ph.D. in Anthropology from the University of Connecticut in 1976. He is currently Chair of the Department of Anthropology and Professor in the Departments of Anthropology, Sociology, and in the Patterson School of Diplomacy at the University of Kentucky. His research interests include agricultural anthropology, food policy, and political ecology. Among his publications are *Modernization in a Mexican Ejido: a Study in Economic Adaptation* and *Micro and Macro Levels of Analysis in Anthropology: Issues in Theory and Research*, edited with Pertti J. Pelto. He is one of the co-editors of the series *Food Systems and Agrarian Change*.

Kathleen M. DeWalt

Kathleen M. DeWalt received her Ph.D. from the University of Connecticut in 1979. She is currently Associate Professor of Behavioral Science and Anthropology at the University of Kentucky. She is principal investigator of the Cooperative Agreement on Nutrition in Agriculture with the U.S. Department of Agriculture's Nutrition Economics Group and a co-investigator on a study of young children's acquisition of food and exercise habits related to cardiovascular risk in a rural Kentucky community. Her research interests include nutrition in agriculture, medical anthropology, and the implications of dietary change for human health. Among her publications are *Nutritional Strategies and Agricultural Change in a Mexican Community* and *A Cultural Feast*, written with Carol Bryant, Anita Courtney, and Barbara Markesberry.

H. Max Drake

Max Drake received his Ph.D. in Sociology/Anthropology from the University of North Carolina in 1976. He is Professor and Chair of the Department of Sociology, Anthropology, and Social Work at Southeast Missouri State University, where he is presently evaluating the programs and services of a regional counselling center. He has fifteen years of experience in research and evaluation for county, federal, and state governments, including three years evaluating the Malawi Public Health Program in Malawi, Africa. Publications include: "Being a Bureaucrat: Is It the Same As Being An Anthropologist?" in *Mainstreaming Anthropology: Experiences in Government Employment*, Karen Hanson, ed., NAPA Bulletin #5 (1988), *Directory of Practicing Anthropologists* (with Roger D. Karlish and Ann M. Drake), NAPA Bulletin #1 (1985), and *A Descriptive Study of Persons with Development Disabilities Living in Group Homes, Tenant Support, and Alternative Living* (with Wendy Cox), Division of Information and Personnel, Olympia, WA (1983).

Paul T. Giblin

Paul Giblin received his Ph.D. in Developmental Psychology from The Ohio State University. He is Associate Professor in the Department of Pediatrics at Wayne State University, Director of the Division of Adolescent Medicine at Children's Hospital of Michigan, and Co-Director of the Institute of Maternal and Child Health. His recent projects have addressed barriers to obtaining prenatal care and establishing school-based adolescent health care centers. Recent publications include a review of clinical applications of self-esteem and locus of control to adolescent health, a review of employing indigenous workers in health care programs, and a series of articles on the correlates of semen quality in humans, co-authored by Marilyn L. Poland.

M. Jean Gilbert

Jean Gilbert received her Ph.D. in Anthropology from the University of California at Santa Barbara in 1980. She is currently National Institute on Alcohol Abuse and Alcoholism Scholar in Hispanic Alcohol Studies at the University of California, at Los Angeles. She is senior author of *Mexican Americans and Alcohol*, Monograph 11 of the Spanish Speaking Mental Health Research Center, UCLA (1987). Current activities include editing a proceedings publication resulting from a binational (U.S.-Mexico) Conference on Alcohol-Related Issues which Dr. Gilbert convened and chaired in July, 1987. Dr. Gilbert also has two clinic studies underway among Mexican American clients to assess the relationships between alcohol cognitions, acculturation, and alcohol use patterns.

Linda Girdner

Linda Girdner received her Ph.D. in Anthropology from The American University in 1981 and then took a position at the University of Illinois in Urbana-Champaign. In 1987 she returned to Washington, D.C., to accept the American Anthropological Association Congressional Fellowship. During the fellowship year she worked on judiciary and family issues as a legislative assistant for Rep. Patricia Schroeder and on women, children, and family issues on the research staff of the Democratic Senatorial Campaign Committee. She is presently Director and founder of CONSENSUS, a firm specializing in dispute resolution consulting, in Alexandria, Virginia. She is also on the Board of Directors of the Academy of Family Mediators and Chairperson of the Academy's Legislative and Research Committees. Her most recent article is "Custody Mediation in the United States: Empowerment or Social Control?", published in the *Canadian Journal of Women and the Law* 3(1):134-154, 1989.

Judith Greenwood

Judith Greenwood received her M.P.H. in 1977 and her Ph.D. in Social Sciences and Health Behavior in 1978 from the University of Oklahoma. She is currently Director of Research for the West Virginia Workers' Compensation Fund and Clinical Associate Professor in the Department of Community Medicine of West Virginia University Medical Center. Her current research interests are in occupationally-related disability, disability management, and workplace wellness. Most recently she directed a controlled study of early intervention in back disability among coal miners. Publications include "Work Disability Determination: The Need for an Integrated Approach," *Social Science and Medicine* 19(6), 1984; "Disability Dilemmas and Rehabilitation Tensions," *Social Science and Medicine* 20(12), 1985; and "Job Satisfaction Affects Rates of Occupational Accidents," *Occupational Health and Safety News Digest* 3 (1) 1987.

Madelyn Anne Iris

Madelyn Anne Iris received her Ph.D. in 1981 from Northwestern University. She is a Visiting Scholar at Northwestern University where she teaches courses on aging and public policy and a Research Associate at the Metropolitan Chicago Coalition on Aging where she is completing a study of guardianship in Cook County, Illinois. She is active in the National Association of Practicing Anthropologists, the National Guardianship Association, and serves on the Advisory Board of Innotek (Innovations in Technology) at the National Lekotek Center. In 1987 Dr. Iris received an Honorable Mention for her work on elder abuse in the Praxis Award Competition sponsored by the Washington Association of Professional Anthropologists. Recent publications include "Guardianship and the Elderly: A Multi-Perspective View of the Decisionmaking Process", in the *Gerontologist*, June 1988, and "Strategies for Service Provision: The Use of Legal Interventions in a Systems Approach to Casework," with Susan R. Segal, in *Elder Abuse: Practice and Policy*, R. Filenson and S. Ingman, eds., (1989).

Carl Kendall

Carl Kendall received his Ph.D. in Social Anthropology from the University of Rochester in 1974 and completed post-doctoral training in the Medical Anthropology Training Program at Michigan State University. He is Associate Professor in the Departments of International Health and Health Policy and Management at the School of Hygiene and Public Health, Johns Hopkins University, and Director of the Center for International Community-based Health Research. Dr. Kendall is currently conducting research in Peru on preventing diarrheal disease and research in Mexico and Honduras to develop a new *Aedes aegypti* control program. Other research projects include developing and testing interventions to reduce the transmission of AIDS in street children in Brazil and an evaluation of the Pan American Health Organization's Polio Eradication Project. Publications include "The Implementation of a Diarrheal Disease Control Program in Honduras: Is It 'Selective Primary Health Care' or 'Integrated Primary Health Care'?", *Social Science and Medicine* 27(1):17-23, 1988, and "Ethnomedicine and Oral Rehydration Therapy: A Case Study of Ethnomedical Investigation and Program Planning (with Dennis Foote and Reynaldo Martorell), *Social Science and Medicine*, Vol. 19 (3), Pp. 253-260, 1984.

Patricia A. Marshall

Patricia A. Marshall is Assistant Professor/Assistant Director in the Medical Humanities program at Loyola University Stritch School of Medicine. She received her Ph.D. in Anthropology from the University of Kentucky in 1983. Her teaching and research focus is on the psychosocial, cultural, and ethical dimensions of patient-practitioner communication. She currently is conducting research on patients' fear of AIDS in health settings and symptom management within the context of the family. Publications include "Reducing Emotional Stress Associated with Childhood Illness," *Comprehensive Therapy* 15(1), Pp. 3-7, 1989, and, with James T. Barter, "The Public Psychiatric Hospital," in *Modern Hospital Psychiatry*, J.R. Lion, W.N. Adler, and W.L. Webb, Jr., eds. (1988).

Ann McElroy

Ann McElroy received her Ph.D. in Anthropology from the University of North Carolina at Chapel Hill in 1973. She is Associate Professor of the Department of Anthropology of the State University of New York at Buffalo, Director of the program in Anthropology and Social Epidemiology, and Co-Director of the U.S. Department of Education (FIPSE) supported Research Careers in Anthropology program. She has done research on psychological aspects of modernization in Arctic Canada, on educational change in Iran, on health care for the elderly in West Germany, on health care for farmworkers in California, on communication dynamics in an inner-city pediatrics clinic in Western New York, and most recently on health care in a migrant farmworker clinic in Niagara County, New York. Publications include *Medical Anthropology in Ecological Perspective*, Second Edition, with Patricia K. Townsend (1989) and "Boundaries and Breakdowns: Applying Agar's Concept of Ethnography to Observations in a Pediatric Clinic," with Mary Ann Jezewski, *Human Organization* 45 (3):202-211, 1986.

Marilyn L. Poland

Marilyn Poland received her Ph.D. in Physical Anthropology from Wayne State University. She is Associate Professor of Obstetrics and Gynecology at Wayne State University, Director of the Division of Reproductive Anthropology, and Co-Director of the Institute of Maternal and Child Health. Her recent projects have addressed barriers to obtaining prenatal care and establishing networks of health professionals and human service agencies to reduce infant mortality levels. Recent publications include a co-edited book entitled *New Approaches to Human Reproduction: Social and Ethical Dimensions.*

Ernesto Reza

Ernesto Reza received his Ph.D. in Organizational Psychology from the University of Michigan in 1989. He is currently Assistant Professor of Management at California State University, San Bernadino. His professional interests include organizational theory, organizational development, work and health, the innovating process in organizations, and the Mexican-American worker. His experience with farm labor includes working in the field, working for the Farm Labor Organizing Committee (FLOC), and conducting social research on farmworkers in the Midwest and in California. He has worked as a researcher in a national survey of Mexican-Americans, a national survey on the adoption of new technologies by municipalities, and a national survey on the adoption of automated manufacturing technologies in private organizations. He has published on farmworkers and the farm labor movement in *Human Organization* and *La Red.*

Barbara Rylko-Bauer

Barbara Rylko-Bauer received her Ph.D. in Anthropology from the University of Kentucky in 1985. She is Adjunct Assistant Professor in the Department of Anthropology at Michigan State University, where she also serves on the Editorial Board of the Women in International Development Working Papers Series. Current research concerns health services delivery and public policy, as well as issues relating to childbirth and postpartum care. Publications include "The Development and Use of Freestanding Emergency Centers: A Review of the Literature," *Medical Care Review*, 1988.

Daniel R. Scheinfeld

Daniel R. Scheinfeld is Research Associate at the Erikson Institute in Chicago and an adjunct faculty member in anthropology at Northwestern University. His Ph.D. degree in Anthropology is from the University of Chicago. Currently he is directing two applied projects: the ethnographic study of the emotional reactions of psychiatric line staff reported in this volume, and a study of family and child rearing among Vietnamese refugee families to be utilized by Head Start in their work with Vietnamese children and parents. His applied research interests focus on relationships between caretakers and children in families, schools, and psychiatric settings. His most recent publication in the area of knowledge utilization is "Relationship, Process, and Explanatory Frames," *High Plains Applied Anthropology*, Spring, 1989.

John van Willigen

John van Willigen is Professor of Anthropology and Coordinator of Applied Studies of the Department of Anthropology at the University of Kentucky. A graduate of the University of Arizona, he has served as a development administrator for the Papago Tribe of Arizona and has worked in farming systems research in Kentucky and Indonesia. He has also done research on the social relationships of older people in rural Kentucky. He directs the Applied Anthropology Documentation Project at the University of Kentucky Library and publishes materials from this project regularly in the "Sources" section of *Practicing Anthropology*. He is author of *Applied Anthropology: An Introduction* (1986), *Anthropology in Use: A Bibliographic Chronology of the Development of Applied Anthropology* (1980), *Training Manual in Policy Ethnography*, with Billie R. DeWalt (1985), and *Getting Some Age on Me: The Social Organization of Older People in a Rural American Community* (1989).

Dennis M. Warren

Dennis Michael Warren received his Ph.D. from the University of Indiana in 1974. He is Professor of Anthropology and Chairperson of the Technology and Social Change Program at Iowa State University. He has done research and consultant work in Zambia, Ghana, and other African nations on development anthropology, indigenous healers in health systems, indigenous agricultural knowledge in agricultural planning, and decision making systems for development. He is co-editor of *Indigenous Knowledge Systems and Development* (1980) and *African Therapeutic Systems* (1979). Recent articles are "Anthropology and Rural Development in Ghana," in *Anthropology and Rural Development in West Africa* (1985) and "Ghanaian National Policy Towards Indigenous Healers," *Social Science and Medicine* 16 (21): 1873-1881, 1982.

John J. Wood

John J. Wood received his Ph.D. in Anthropology from the University of Colorado in 1967. He is currently Professor of Anthropology at Northern Arizona University, where he has been teaching since 1966. His applied work with the Navajo began ten years ago with his involvement in a project to assess the impacts of livestock reduction in the former Navajo-Hopi Joint Use Area. More recently, his activities have focused on the relationships among religious beliefs and practices, occupancy and land tenure, and the impacts of relocation on the rural Navajo of the former Navajo-Hopi Joint Use Area. Publications include *Sheep is Life: An Assessment of Livestock Reduction in the Former Navajo-Hopi Joint Use Area, Rural Western Navajo Household Income Strategies*, and *Western Navajo Religious Affiliations*.

Index